CERAMICS STUDIO HANDBOOK

Fred Herbst

2nd Edition

SUNY CORNING COMMUNITY COLLEGE

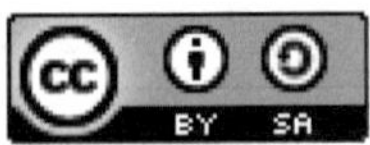

Published by SUNY OER Services
Milne Library
State University of New York at Geneseo
Geneseo, NY 14454

Distributed by State University of New York Press

ISBN: 978-1-64176-061-4

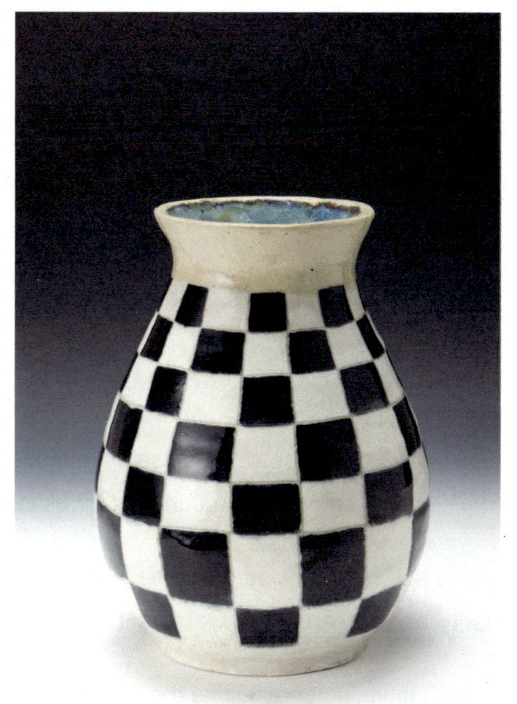

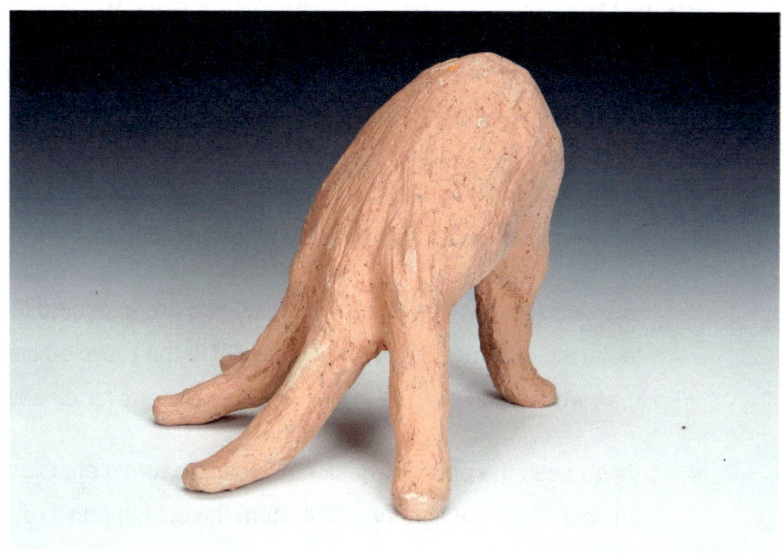

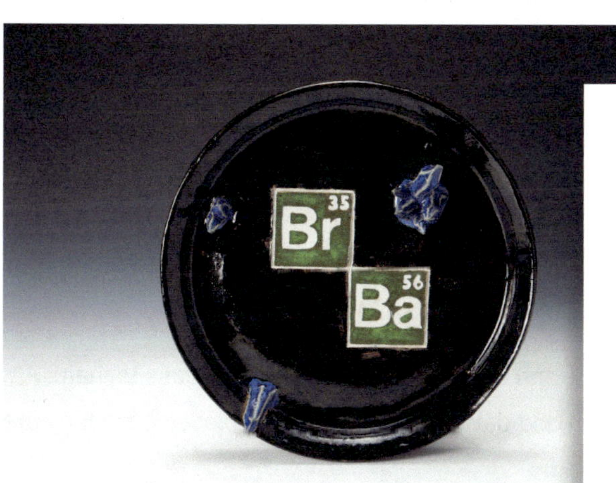

1

STUDIO INTRODUCTION

SUNY-CCC Ceramics Studio Policies and Procedures

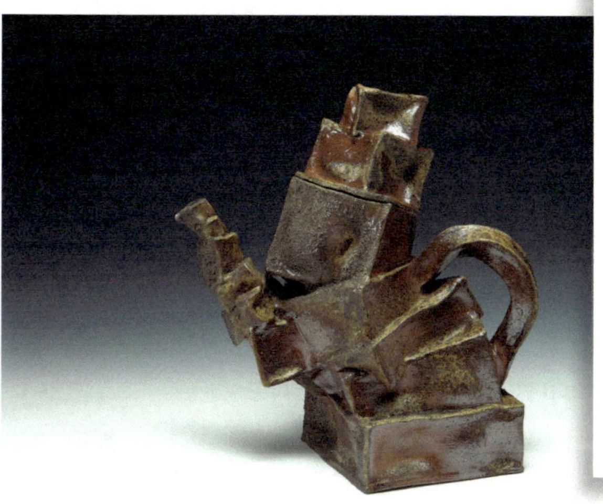

Examples of SUNY-CCC student work from Ceramics 1, Ceramics 2, and Ceramic Sculpture[1]

Please follow these rules during your time in class and during open studio access.

1. Make sure to write your full name on all your tools with marker. If they are left behind, we will try to return them. Any unmarked tools become property of the studio.

2. Bring your tools and studio manual with you each class and / or work session. Lockers are available in the Nursing Building if you would like to leave them on campus.

3. You need to clean up your own mess. You are expected to put your projects away, clean your table space, wheel, tools, etc. All clay scraps need to be put in the recycled clay bin. Any tool or any space you used should be cleaner than when you started. Always use wet sponges for cleaning- dry cleaning creates too much dust for us to breathe.

4. If you used the potters wheel, make sure to turn it off. Clean out the splash pan, wipe down the surface and wipe up any clay from the floor or wall. Return the splash pan to the wheel when you are done cleaning it.

5. Always use the large green prewash bucket in the sink. Do not wash anything directly into the sink. Clay will build up in the trap and plug the drain. We have one sink in the studio- it needs to work for us to have class.

6. Clean off your wareboards and wash used bats carefully before returning them to the shelf.

7. Always use a layer of newspaper between your project and boards or your storage shelf. Throw away newspaper when finished.

8. Cover your projects with plastic between working sessions to make sure they don't dry out. We gladly accept donations of newspaper and plastic bags for the studio.

9. Do not store your projects on turntables, there are only a few and everyone needs to have access to them. Always store your work on a bat, board, or directly on the shelf. Sign and date the bottom of your pieces once they are completed and before they dry out. Unsigned work will not be fired.

10. After glazing has been demonstrated, make sure to check the shelves for your work that has been bisque fired. Glaze the projects and return them to the correct shelf to be glaze fired. Make sure the bottom of every piece is wiped clean of glaze before it goes on the shelf.

11. Always wash any tools / cups / brushes / buckets after glazing.

12. Avoid using cell phones or texting inside the studio. Please step outside to make / answer your call. Electric devices don't like the clay on your hands.

13. Food and drink are allowed in the studio but make sure to wash your hands before eating.

14. Open studio access will be stopped if you don't clean up your mess when working outside of class.

The critique (crit) in studio art

Individual and group evaluations of art works (critiques) are key to learning in the studio art environment. This experience will help you to see where your projects are successful, where they need more work, and also discuss other students' work in the same manner. The critique process should be one of constructive criticism that in the end, helps you make better decisions about your work and become a stronger visual artist. It is not a process used to give everyone a "pat on the back" just for showing up or as a way to put others down. The crit should be about the work that is being discussed separate from the maker. Every object / artwork ever made could be better somehow and the goal of the critique process is to discover how the works could be more effective and interesting.

Effectively presenting your ideas, projects, or objects to a group is a skill that matures with experience and has a great deal of value outside the college art studio. The critique process should help you develop your confidence with talking about your ideas, receiving criticism, and responding appropriately. These are skills that should serve you well in your future career, whatever that may be.

In this studio course, we will be looking at your projects and discussing a number of issues. Some of these aspects include how well your work fits the assigned criteria, how visually dynamic your solutions are, how interesting your concept is, and how well crafted your objects are. Sometimes a piece will be very strong in some of these areas but not in others. For example, a work might have a very exciting idea behind it but it is poorly constructed and is falling apart. Or another might be extremely well crafted but the idea behind the project is weak. The best works always have a balance of idea, visual interest, and careful construction. We will use critiques to help you see where your work is strong and where it needs to continue to improve.

There are a number of questions to ask when **analyzing** an art work in a studio art class.
For example, did the maker use the required materials and techniques skillfully?
Does the piece work as a successfully integrated object or are there parts that don't fit?
Did the artist use the elements and principles of art (see Chp 2 Ceramic Design) in the work effectively?
If the work is meant to be functional, does the piece make you want to pick it up and use it?
Would it comfortably function or would the handle not feel good, the spout drip, or the lid not fit?

There are a number of questions to ask when **interpreting** an art work in a studio art class.
For example, what is your response to the piece?
How does it make you feel, does it make you think of anything from your own experience?
Can you tell what the artist was trying to communicate to the viewer / user?

There are a number of questions to ask when **judging** an art work in a studio art class.
For example, if you think the piece is successful, why do you feel that way?
What are the works strengths and what could be done to make it more successful?
What would the maker want to do over? What would be the next idea in a series of these kinds of pieces?

Critiques should be a valuable experience for all involved. Carefully looking at, thinking about, and discussing the works will help to make everyone a better artist. Remember, everything could be better somehow!

Safety Information

Every art making process has its own safety concerns. In ceramics, the main issues include dust inhalation, metals exposure, and burns from hot kilns.

Over time, excessive exposure to ceramic dusts will cause a lung condition called silicosis (also known as "coal miners lung"). Proper use of dust masks or respirators and good ventilation will minimize this exposure and help to ensure healthy conditions. When clay and glaze dry mixing, always wear a dust mask rated for at least N95 (an industrial rating for filtering particles) or a respirator with dust filtering cartridges. When cleaning up your workspace, always use **wet sponges**, use a HEPA filtered vacuum, and/or wet mop. **DO NOT sweep the floor** as this causes dust to get airborne. **DO NOT brush your clay crumbs onto the floor since they will get crushed into dust that you will breathe later**. AVOID sanding dry clay or bisqueware since that will produce a large amount of dust. AVOID adding dangerous materials to clay that could end up in the dust.

When mixing and using glazes, it is a good idea to wear latex gloves to prevent exposure to the metals used in some glazes. Minerals like copper, chrome, and cobalt are used create color in glaze and slip. In excessive amounts, these minerals can cause health problems. The CCC glazes are designed to not use dangerous materials (like lead, barium, and manganese) but simple habits like wearing gloves will help prevent any other problems.

Kilns used to fire ceramics can reach VERY high temperatures. The woodfired kilns will reach over 2,300 degrees Fahrenheit. The electric kilns inside are commonly firing to between 1,800 and 2,200 degrees Fahrenheit. The outside surface of all these kilns can get very hot and burn you! **NEVER** place anything on top of the electric kilns. **NEVER** stand next to a heating kiln, there are small "spy holes" in the side that can burn you or your clothes. When we are firing the woodkilns, you must NEVER wear fleece, nylon, or other synthetic clothes. These materials will melt very quickly and burn you horribly. During a firing, the best things to wear are jeans, cotton t-shirts or hoodies, denim, and work clothes like Carhartts. In addition, closed toed shoes are always required since it is common to have hot coals on the ground outside the firebox.

Always know where your hands are, what you're breathing, what's protecting your eyes and ears, and were the hot things are. Having an awareness and using logical steps toward safety will ensure a long career in art making.

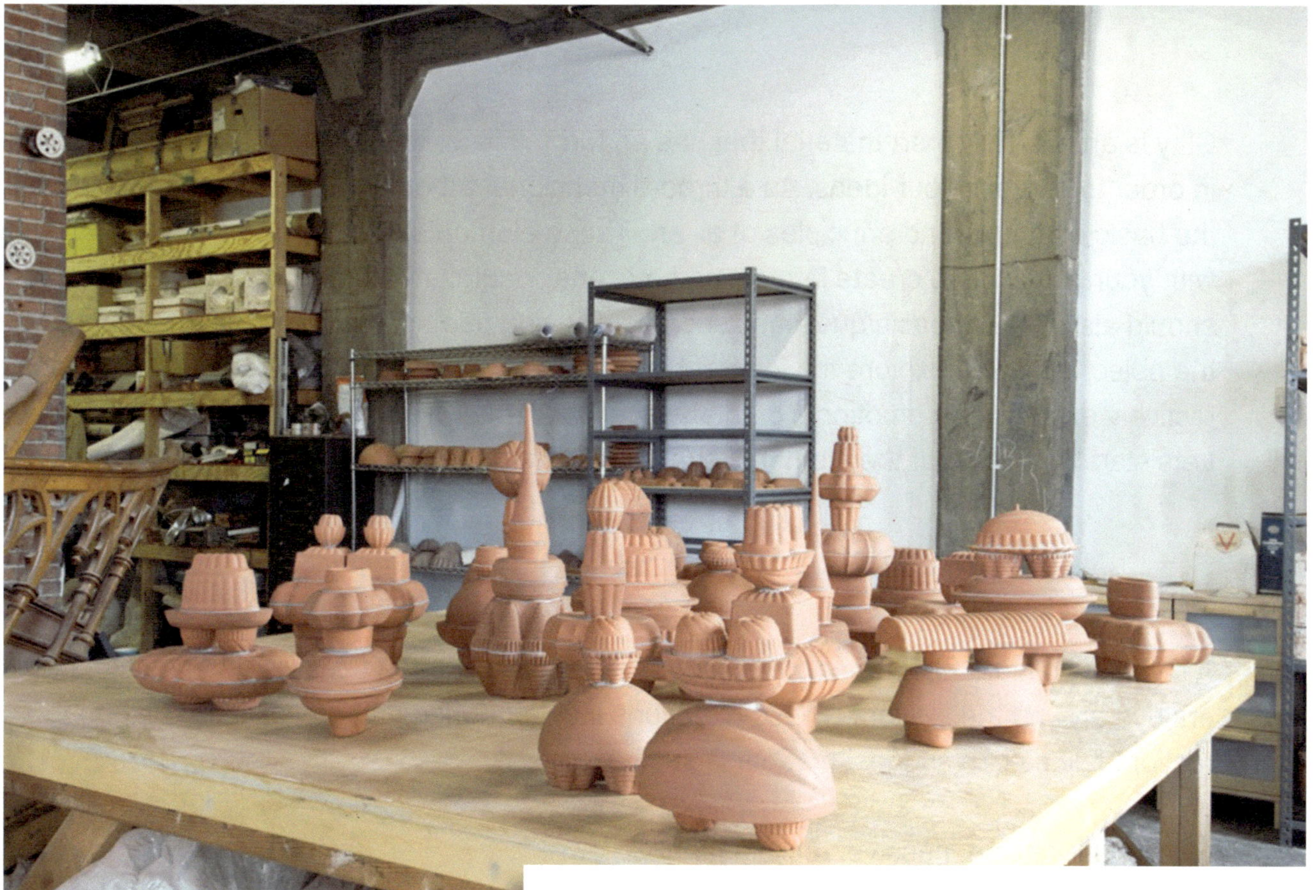

Studio view, Nicholas Kripal[2]

2

CERAMIC DESIGN

Elements and Principles of Art and Design as they apply to ceramics

Clay is an naturally inert material that has no form. It is up to you to control tools and techniques in order to express your ideas. As a three-dimensional art object, your work needs to deal with the basic elements and principles of all art. These elements and principles should work together with your concepts to create interesting functional, sculptural, or hybrid forms. Each work should also answer basic questions such as: Did you use appropriate craftsmanship to create the object? Did you explore the inherent character of the clay in the piece? Does the object effectively express any emotional or intellectual concepts? Is the work visually dynamic? Lets start by looking at the elements shared by all art forms.

Line

A line is a point that has been stretched for a distance. It often controls the direction of the viewers eye around the artwork. These directions include horizontal, vertical, and diagonal. The direction of lines can suggest meanings such as:

Horizontal- resting, passive, reclining forms
Vertical- reaching, growing, stretching forms
Diagonal- moving, active, changing forms

Line also has character that could include the following: straight, curved, wavy, broken, implied (your eye completes the line without it being there), angular, thick, thin. Line can also be used in the surface decoration applied to the shape.

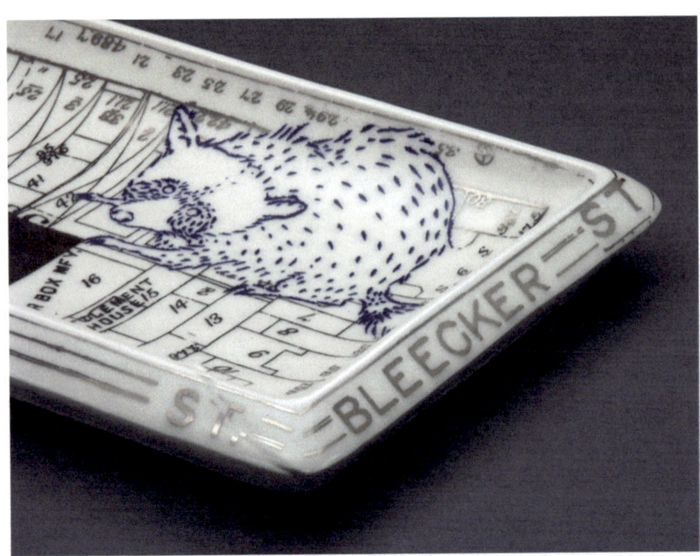

"Racoon Platter" by Ayumi Horie and Andy Brayman, slip cast porcelain[3]

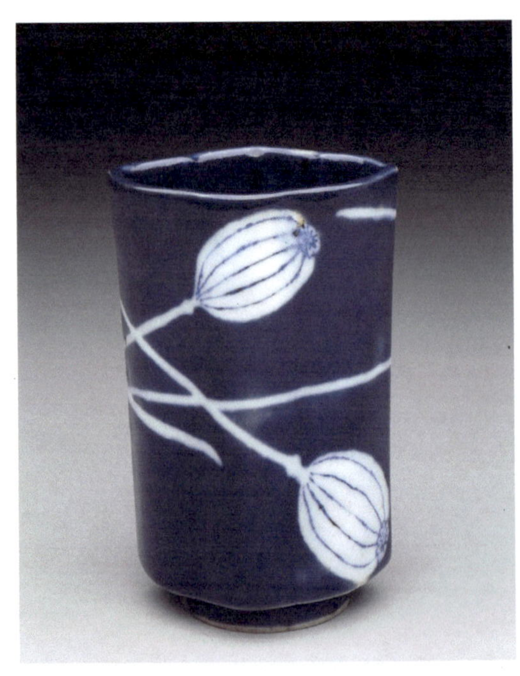

17th century Japanese Nabeshima porcelain cup[4]

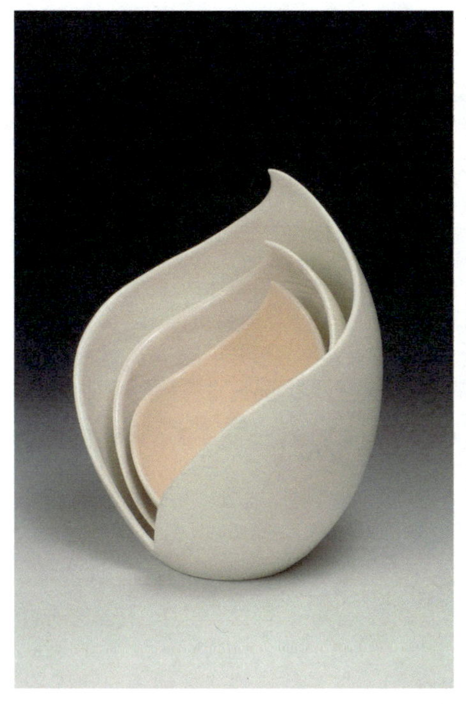

Karen Swyler, "Nest"[3]

Simon Levin, "Cup, Tumbler, and Mug"[5]

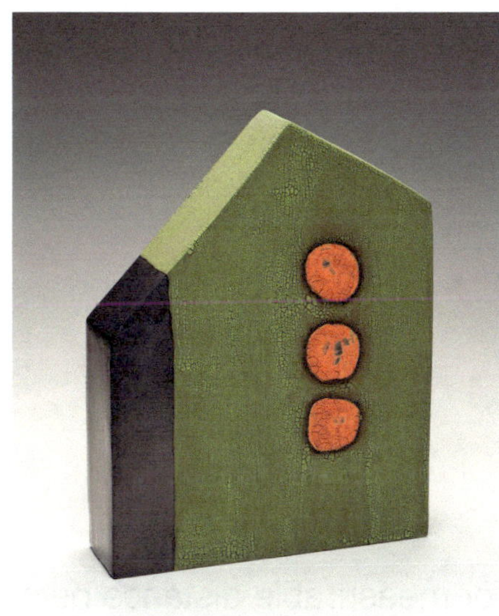

Thomas Orr, "Green Marker with Suns"[2]

Shape

Shape is an area that stands out from the space next to or around it due to a defined or implied boundary.

In ceramics, we are mostly dealing with three dimensional shapes but we may also see two dimensional shapes on the surface of an object. There are a wide variety of shapes possible, each expresses a different idea.

Basic shapes include convex (moving out), concave (moving in), organic (created by nature), geometric (hard edged man-made). A complex shape may include both convex and concave sections or both organic and geometric forms.

Some construction techniques make certain types of shapes easier:

Coil building usually allows for more organic forms
Slab building allows for more geometric shapes
Wheel throwing most often creates round shapes

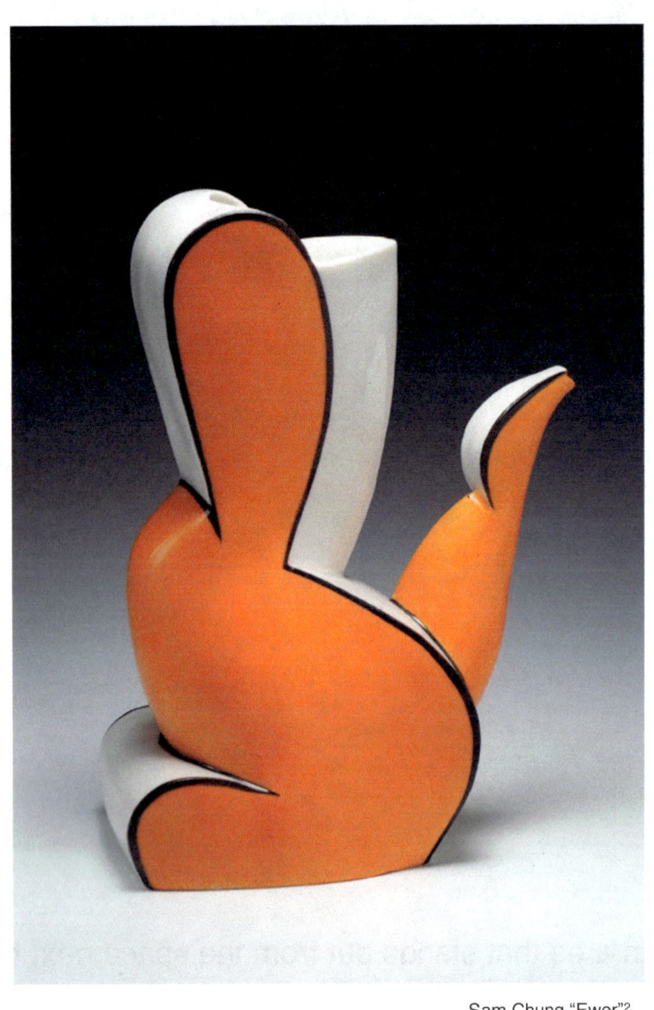

Sam Chung "Ewer"[2]

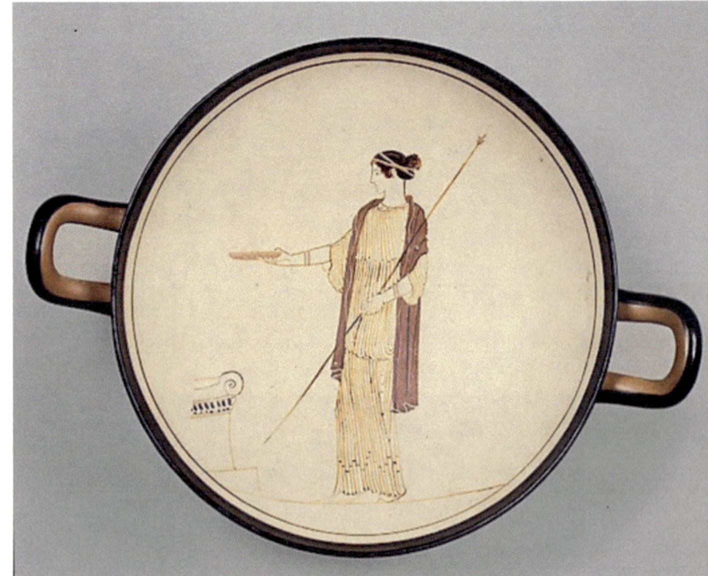

Ancient Greek kylix[4]

Space

Space is technically the interval, or measurable distance between pre-established points or objects.

Positive space is the space that the object and its parts take up. Negative space is the empty space around the object that it influences. Some good examples are the shape of the empty (negative) space inside a cup handle or the space between a spout and the body of a pot.

Closed shapes (no openings) look heavy, open shapes (or those with holes punched through) appear lighter.

Positive and negative space relationships can also occur in surface decoration.

Texture

Texture is the surface character of a material which can be experienced through touch or the illusion of touch. Since many ceramic objects are made to be picked up (cups, bowls..), surface texture is a very critical issue to address. Surface texture can mean anything from glass smooth to gravel rough.

Texture can also be purely visual as in examples where the glaze has a very mottled appearance but actually have a smooth glassy surface. Highly textured surfaces can be very visually dynamic since they cause some glazes to change color on the broken surface.

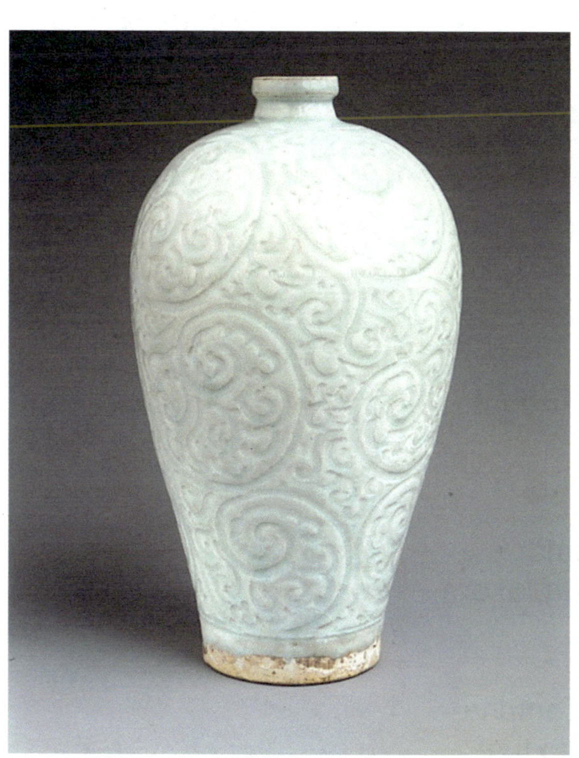

Louis Reilly, "Lidded Jar"[5]

Chinese Song Dynasty bottle[4]

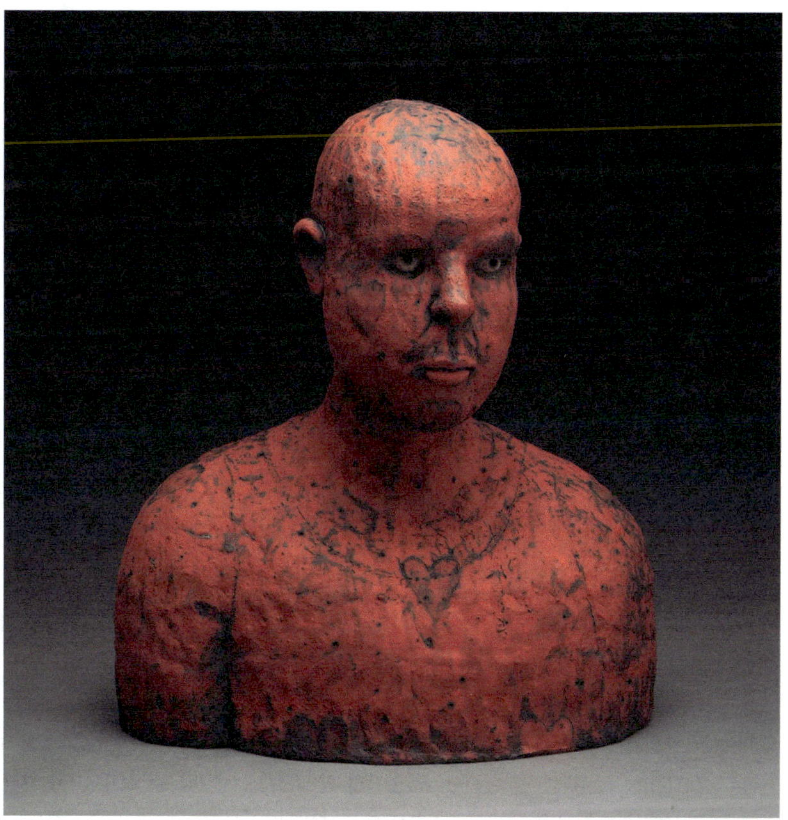

Tom Bartel, "Red Heart Bust"[3]

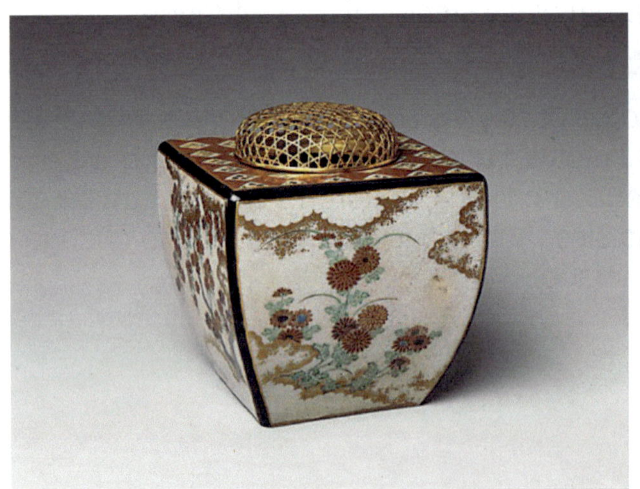

Japanese porcelain incense burner[4]

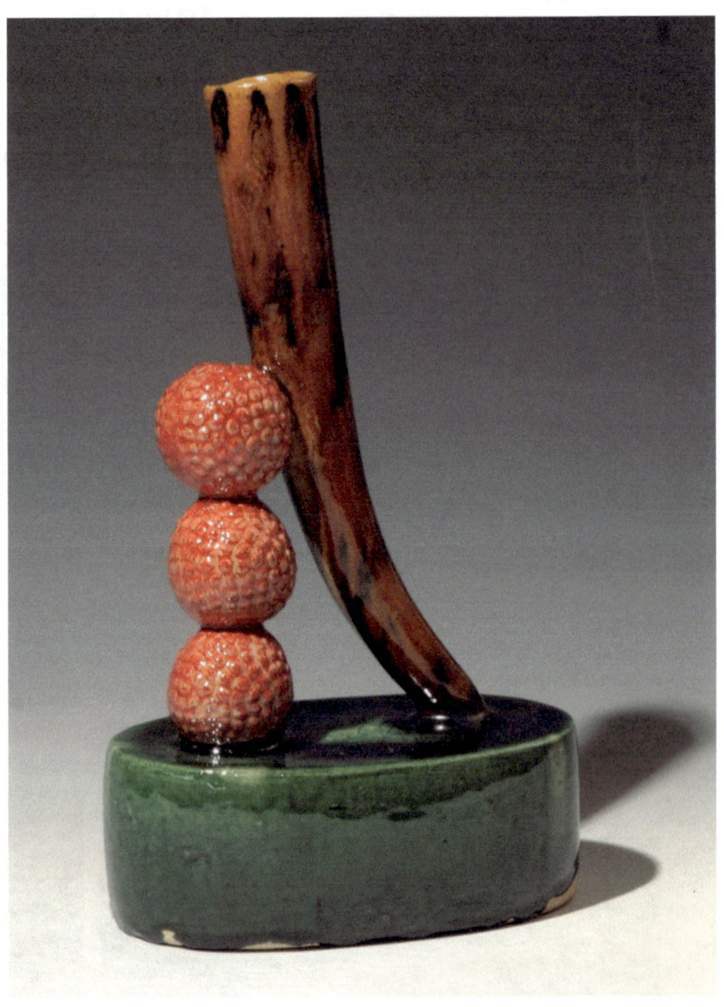

Eva Kwong, "Maroon Horn & 3 Litchis Vase"[3]

Color

Color is the visual response to the wavelengths of light identified as red, green, blue, etc.

Warm colors (red, yellow, orange) seem active and closer to the viewer. Cool colors (blue, green, purple) are more subdued and recede away.

Using one or few colors on a very complex form emphasizes the shape. Using a variety of colors or those that strongly contrast on a simple form makes that object more visually interesting.

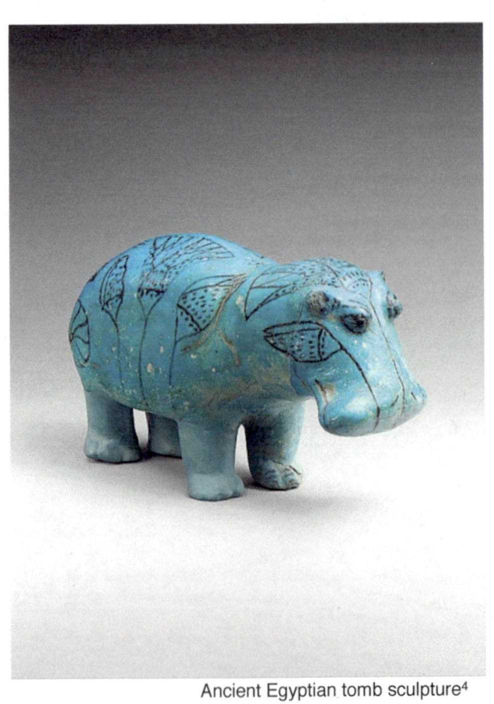

Ancient Egyptian tomb sculpture[4]

Value

Value is the relative degree of light or dark on an object. It can also refer to the shadows or shading created by the effect of light on an object. This explains why ceramic objects often look more dramatic in a gallery as opposed to siting on the shelf in the studio.

Dark glazes can make a piece appear smaller and light glazes can make a small piece appear larger.

Mika Negishi Laidlaw. "All One"[2]

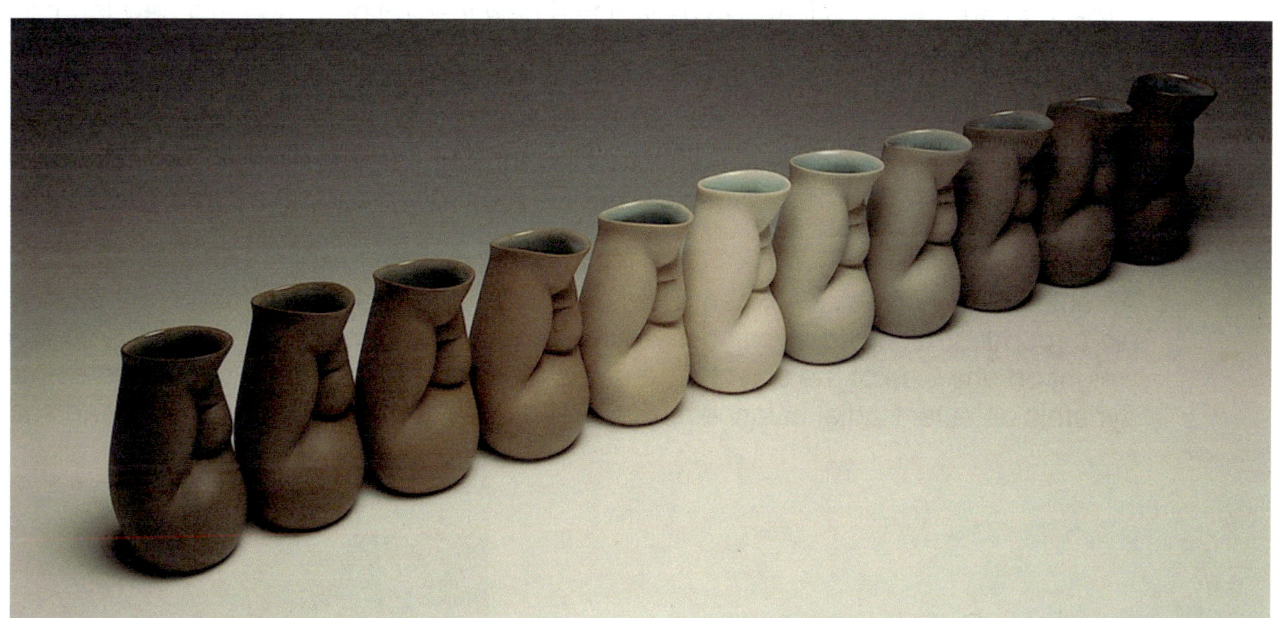

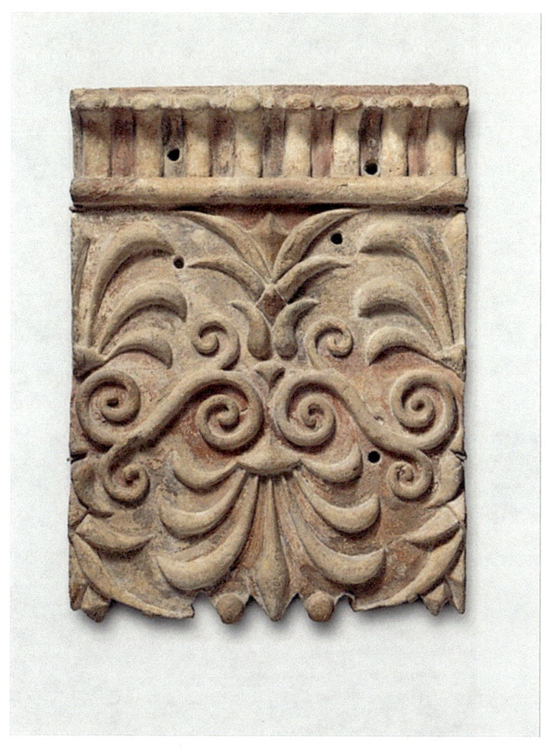

Etruscan Tile[4]

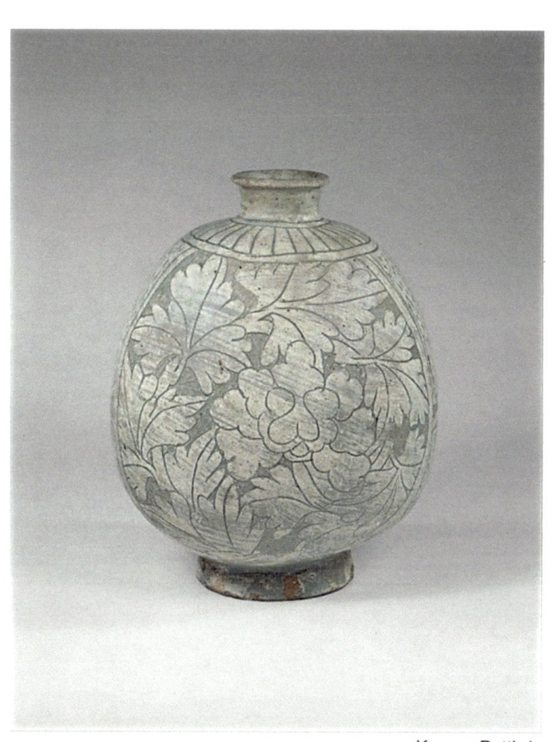

Korean Bottle[4]

Principles of Art

The principles of art are a way of organizing the elements in order to make interesting images or objects. When looking at a work, we often generalize about how the principles are used to create a feeling or overall effect. You may also want to think about the elements of art as the alphabet and the principles are the words that you can create.

As you become a more experienced object maker, the elements and principles of art will become a subconscious part of what you do. You will consider the entire object and make critically informed decisions about what would make it more aesthetically pleasing. Your personal approach to art making will evolve as you find new inspirations and build new technical skills.

Balance

Balance is the sense of equilibrium achieved through implied weight, attention, or attraction within an artwork. The three types of balance most often used are symmetrical, asymmetrical, and radial balance.

An object has symmetry is when it feels like all parts are a mirror image of the others, for example a round, straight sided cylinder. Asymmetry is when there is an uneven amount of visual weight on one side of the object. The use of asymmetrical balance often creates more visually dynamic objects. Radial balance refers to a circular or wheel-like balance in the shape.

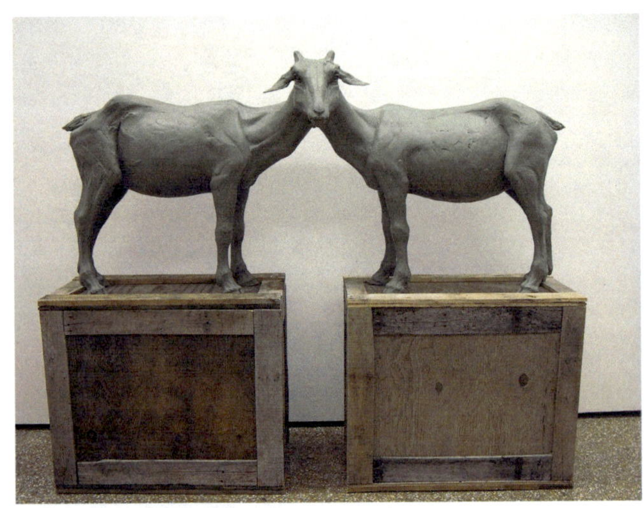

Beth Cavener Stichter, "Inquisitors"[3]

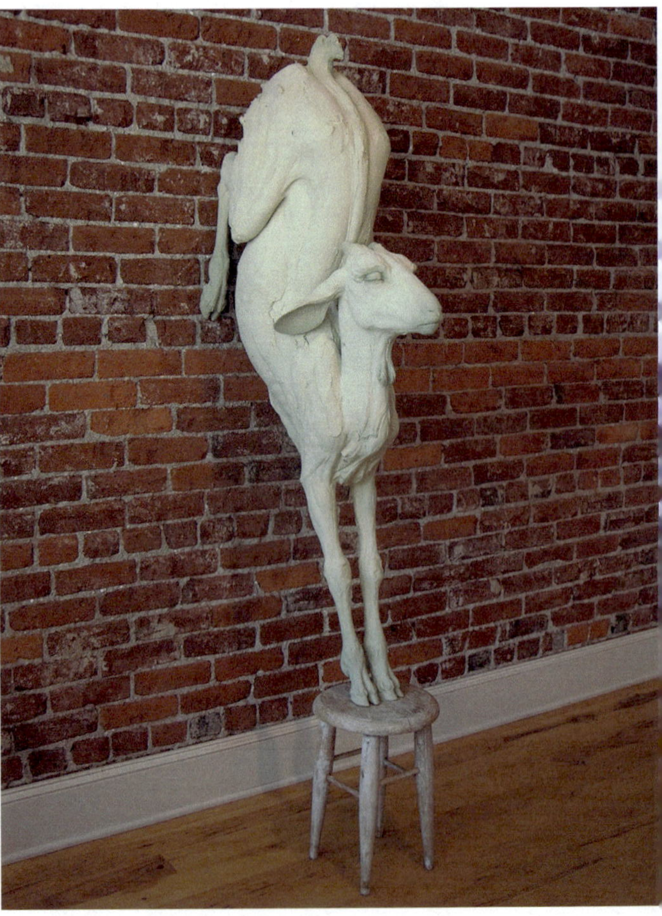

Beth Cavener Stichter, "Breathe"[3]

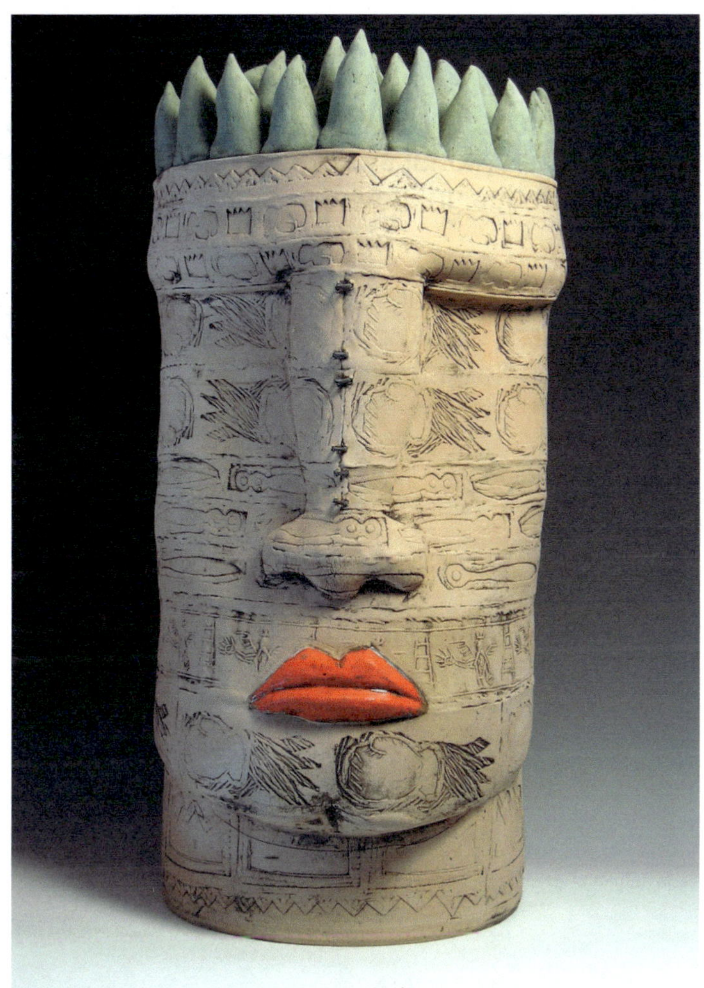

Paul Andrew Wandless, "Prize Fighter"[5]

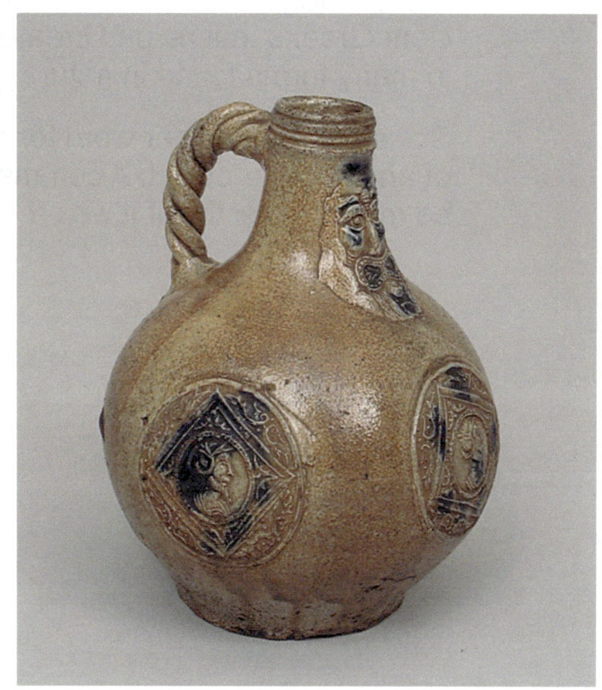

German saltglazed bottle[4]

Emphasis

Emphasis (also known as visual dominance) is the creation of visual importance through the use of selective stress. Parts of the image or object are differentiated from the other parts in order to enhance attraction and interest.

There are many ways to achieve emphasis, including contrasting or exaggerating size, shape, value, color, and texture.

Proportion / Scale

Proportion refers to *relative* size of an element measured against other elements or against some norm or standard. Proportion often refers to a ratio of the size of parts to the whole. The "Golden Mean" was a proportional system developed by the ancient Greeks that helped create harmony in design. It was based on and can be seen in many forms found in nature.

Scale can be another word for *size* in a work. Scaling can refer to changing the size of an image or object. A comment often heard during critique is that the object would be more interesting if it was a different scale (larger or smaller).

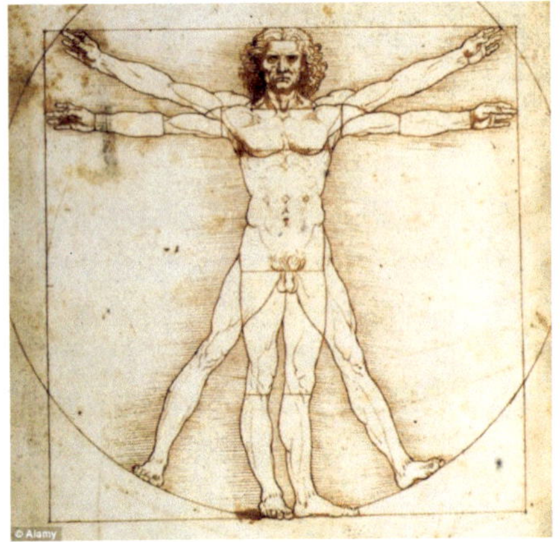

Leonardo Da Vinci"s drawing of "perfect" human proportions[6]

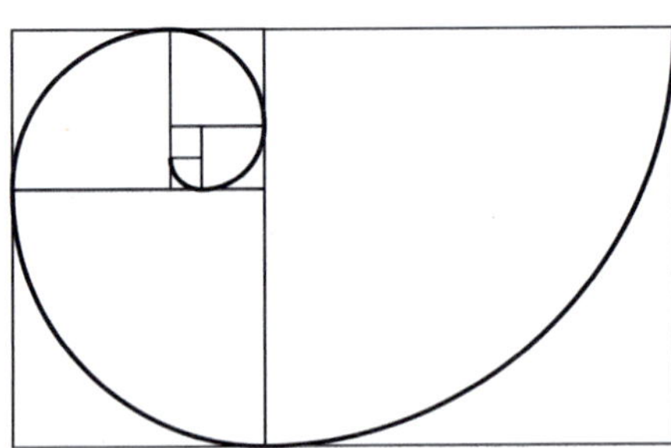

Golden Mean or Ratio[7]

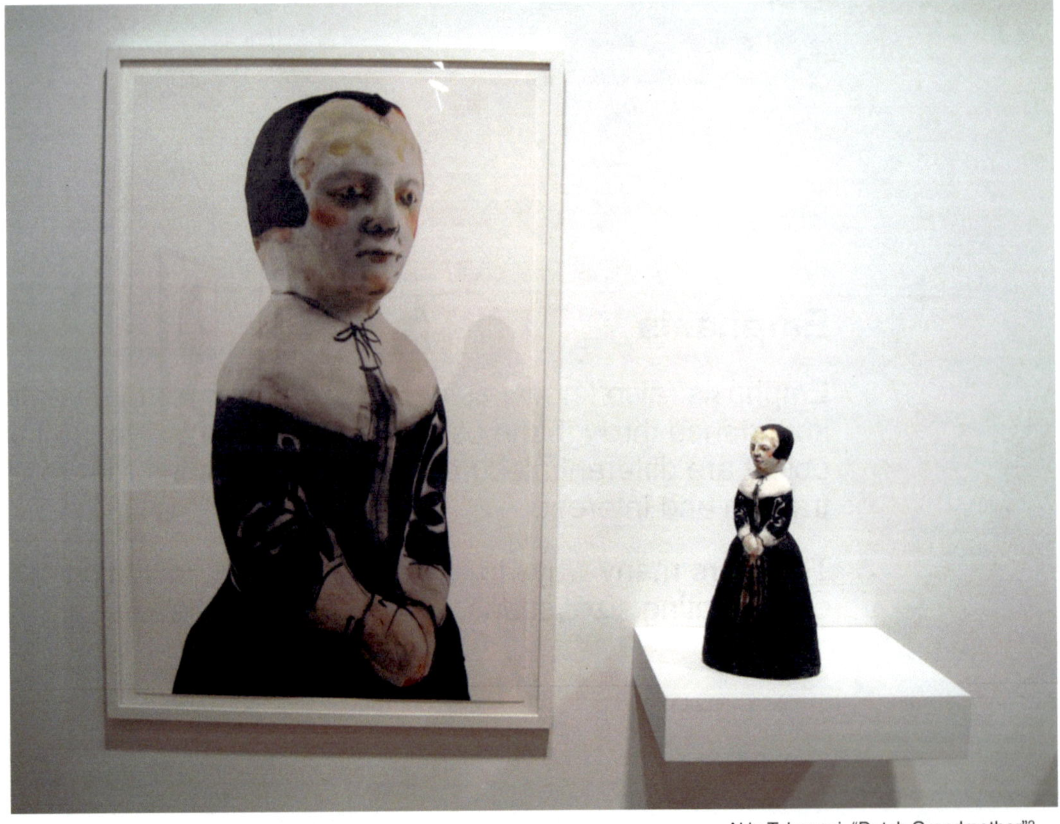

Akio Takamori, "Dutch Grandmother"[2]

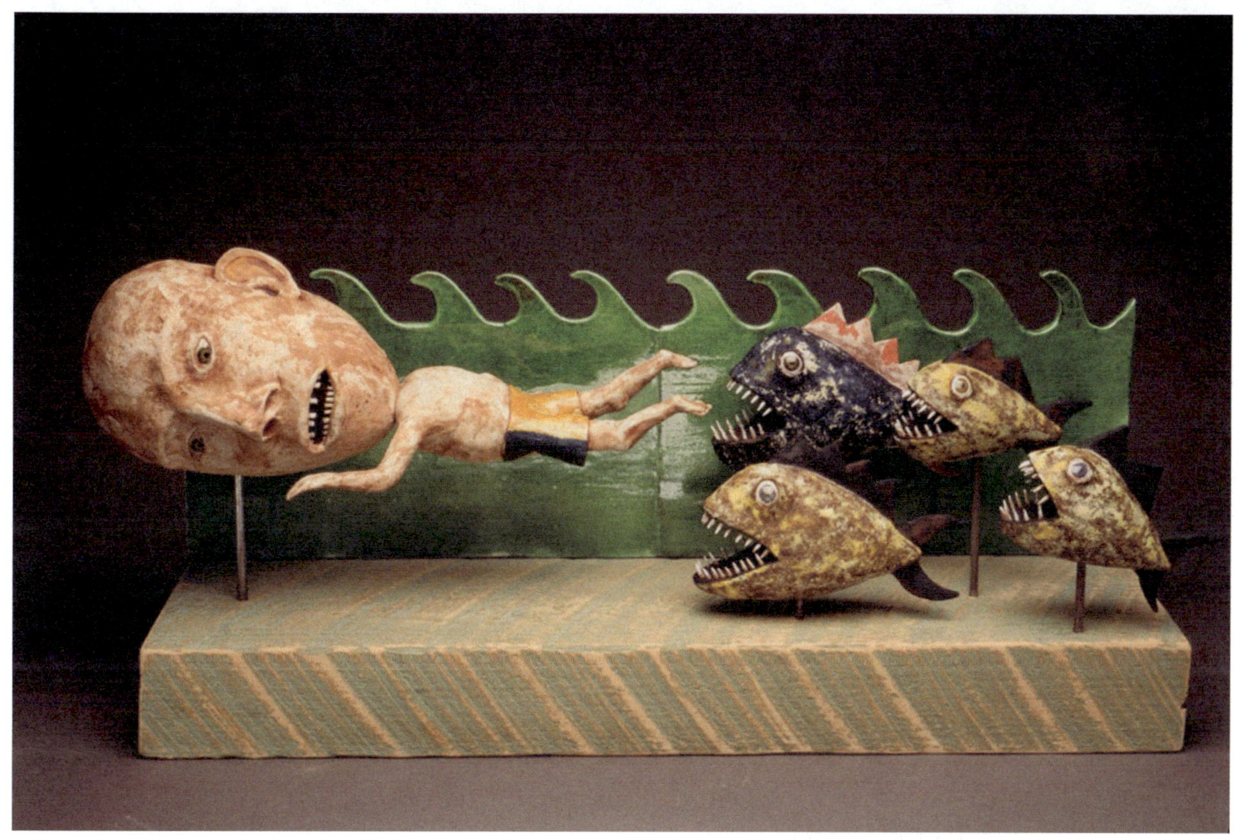

Wesley Anderegg, "Natsoulas 36"[3]

Movement

Movement (also known as directional force) is the direction and degree of energy implied by the art elements in specific compositional situations and directions.

Ways to create movement can include lines, repeated figures, blurred outlines, illusions of growth, and multiple images. An object with implied movement creates the sense that the object has momentarily stopped but will continue. Some three dimensional objects have actual movement (rocking, turning in response to the wind, wheels...) as part of their concept.

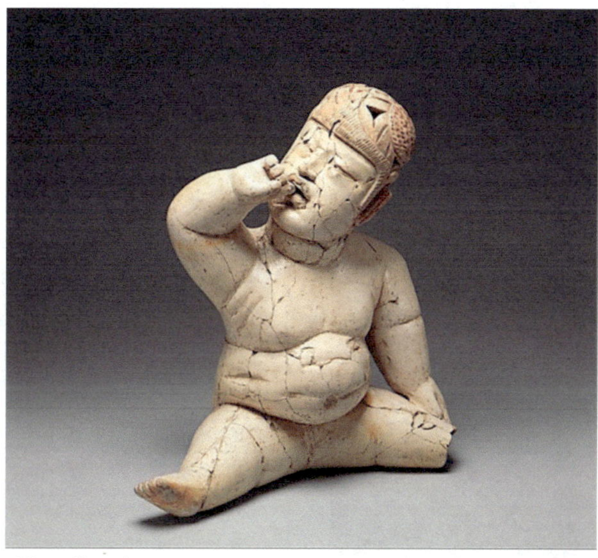

Olmec figure[4]

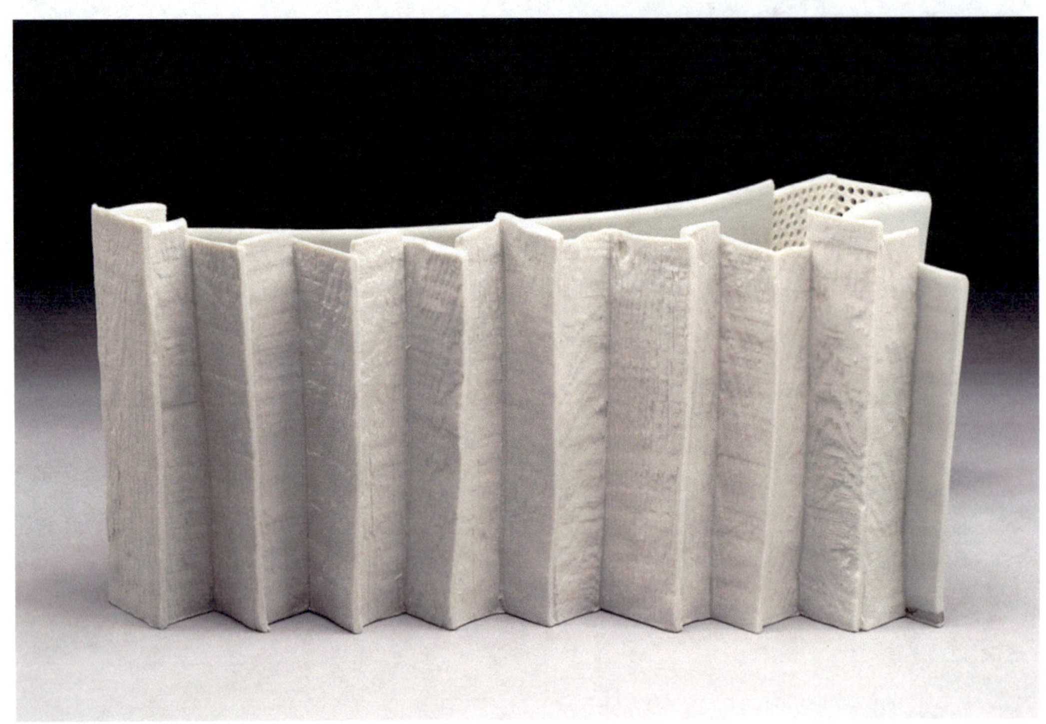

Bryan Hopkins, "Basket"[2]

Unity / Harmony

Unity is the presentation of an integrated image or object achieved through visual similarity.

A few ways to achieve unity include proximity of parts, coordination of all elements toward one concept, repetition of the same element in decoration, or a rhythm of slightly changing details. Unity can also be achieved by introducing an element of variety in parts that add up to an interesting whole.

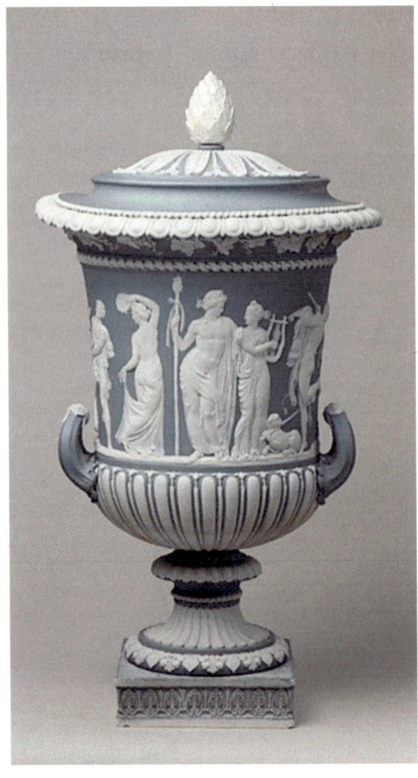

Wedgewood jar[4]

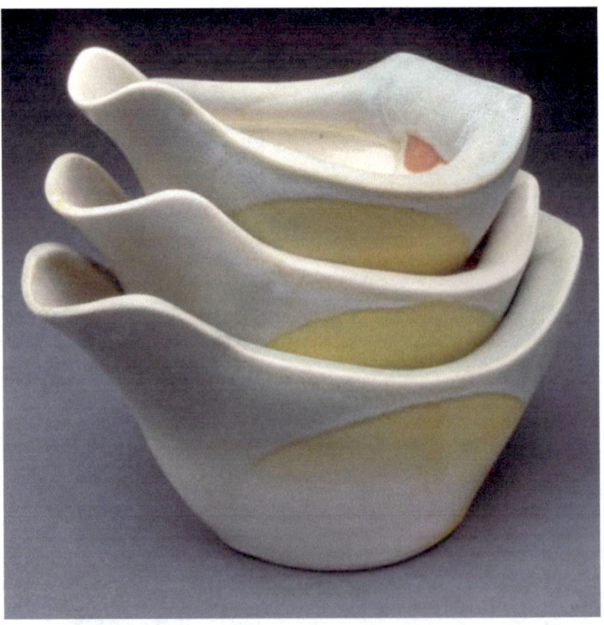

Deborah Schwartzkopf, "Pouring Bowls"[2]

Economy

Economy is the elimination of elaborate details leaving only the significant essentials of the image or object. The goal is to pare down without making the work monotonous. Economy is often associated with the term "abstraction" in which unnecessary elements are eliminated in order to show the essence of something.

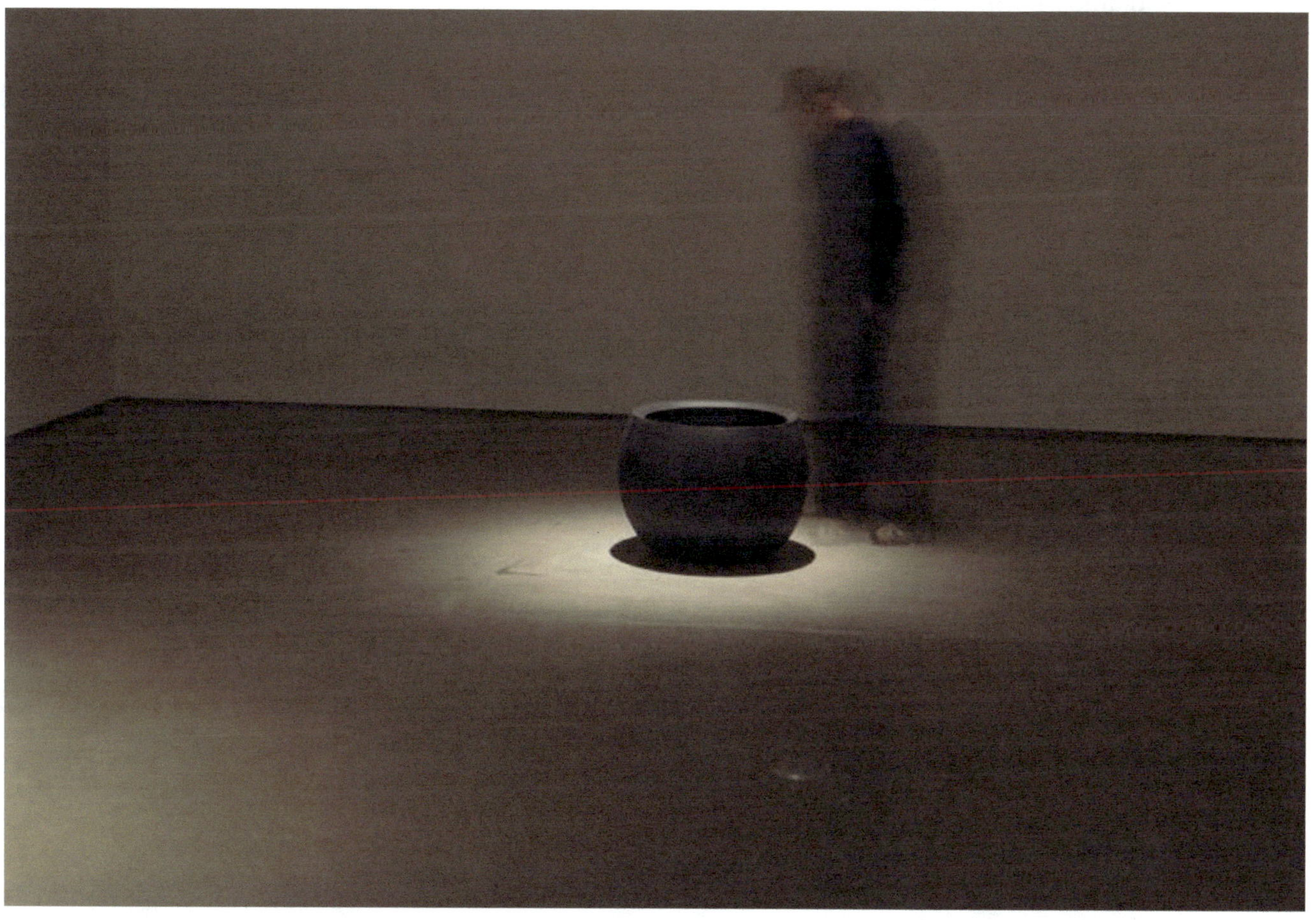

Shawn Murrey, "Crucible"[3]

Overall Concepts:

The creation of dynamic works of art is a complex exchange between idea, technique, and execution. For thousands of years, ceramic artists have been working to communicate with this material in a variety of ways. Outside of assigned projects, there are an infinite range of possibilities and concepts to explore. Here are some ideas to help get started.

Themes for Function:

eating, drinking, dining, presentation / ritual, lighting, utensils/tools, furniture, architecture / tile, music, souvenir, jewelry, fashion, trophies, containers for storage, serving, carrying, pouring, containers for plants / flowers, display

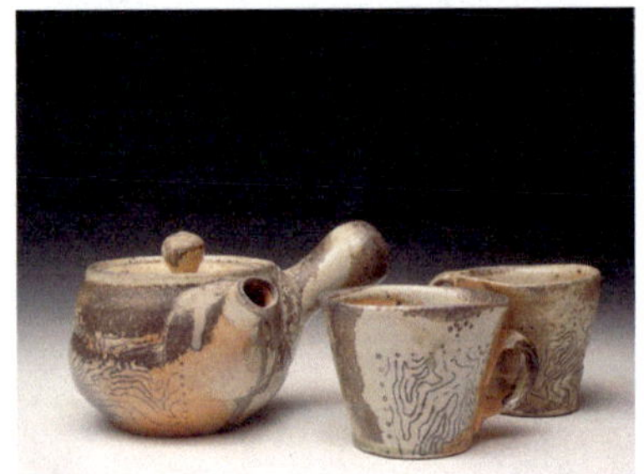

Ben Krupka[5]

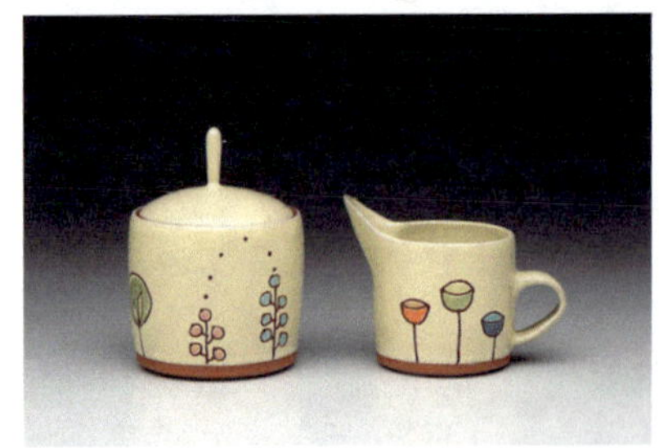

Courtney Murphy[3]

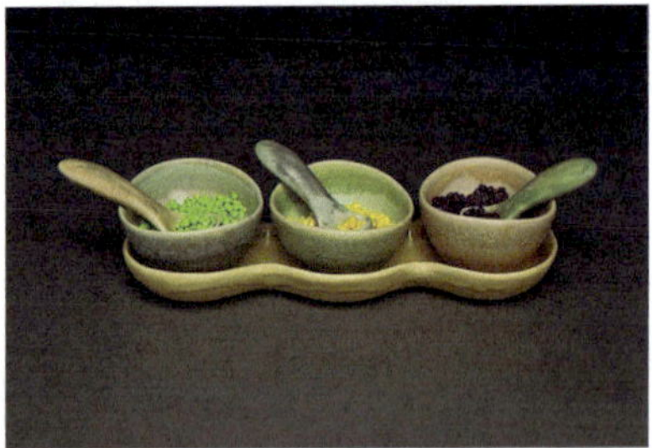

gwendolyn yopplo[3]

Themes for Sculpture:

transformation, multiples, layering, entrapment, modules, adornment, assemblage, enclosure, site specific, topography, light, nature, water, wind, sound, motion, place, identity, memory, community, the figure

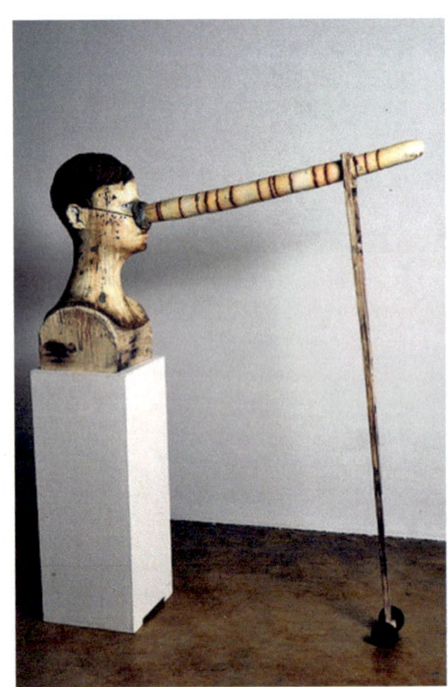

Thaddeus Erdahl[3]

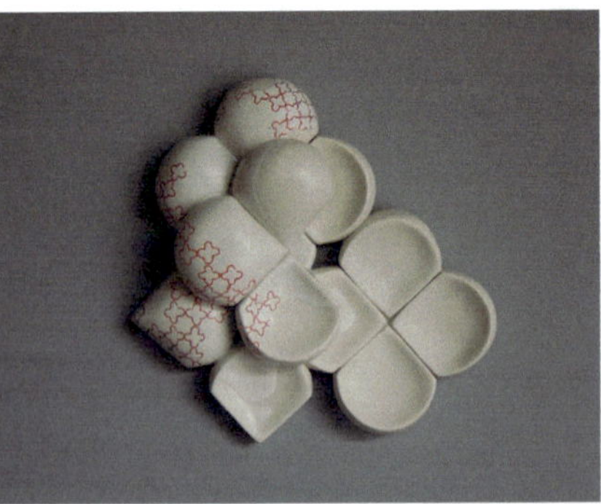

Elenor Wilson[3]

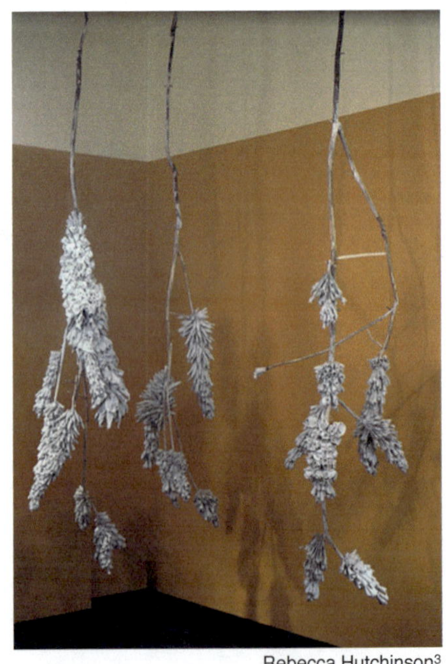

Rebecca Hutchinson[3]

If pots are to function well and also be visually appealing, a number of elements need to be considered. The entire shape must be created with technical skill and a sense for design. From the top down (or from the rim/lip to the foot), the object must work visually, technically, and physically. Here are some questions you should ask yourself as you are creating your work.

Overall Form / Shape
1. What is the function of the pot?
2. If it is a form to fit in the hand, does it feel comfortable?
3. Is it well balanced and not too heavy when in use?
4. Is it easy to clean?

Lip / Rim
1. What type of edge works best for the function of the piece?
2. Is it too thin or too thick to be comfortable to drink from?
3. Would the lip shape easily chip during normal use and washing?
4. Is it the correct sized opening for its function- can you reach inside the piece to take things out or to wash inside the pot?

Foot / Base
1. Does it sit on table in a balanced / stable way?
2. Should there be a hand cut foot or a wheel trimmed foot?
3. Does the proportion of the foot relate to how you want the shape to feel- wide and stable or narrow and delicate?
4. Does it elevate the form off the table or does it make it look bottom heavy?
5. Is the base smooth enough to keep the piece from scratching furniture?

Handles
1. Does it need a handle in order to fulfill its function?
2. Does the handle shape and size fit the proportion of the pot?
3. Is it easy to pick up from the table or use during pouring?
4. Is it attached well enough to stay on the piece during use?
5. Is the space inside the handle enough (or too much) to fit fingers inside?
6. Are the edges of the handle smooth enough to be comfortable?

Lids
1. Which lid style would fit the pot body best?
2. Does the lid need a handle or knob in order to pick it up?
3. Was it measured correctly so that it fits the body of the pot?
4. Is the edge of the lid strong enough to survive use?

Spouts
1. Does the spout size and shape fit the proportion of the body of the pot?
2. Does it pour well without dripping on the table?
3. Is the opening the correct size to constrict the flow of the liquid?
4. Is the spout placed higher than the highest liquid level possible in the body?

Glaze
1. Is the glaze food safe?
2. Does it have a glossy surface on the interior to help with cleaning and durability?
3. Does the glaze color make the food served on / in it look better?

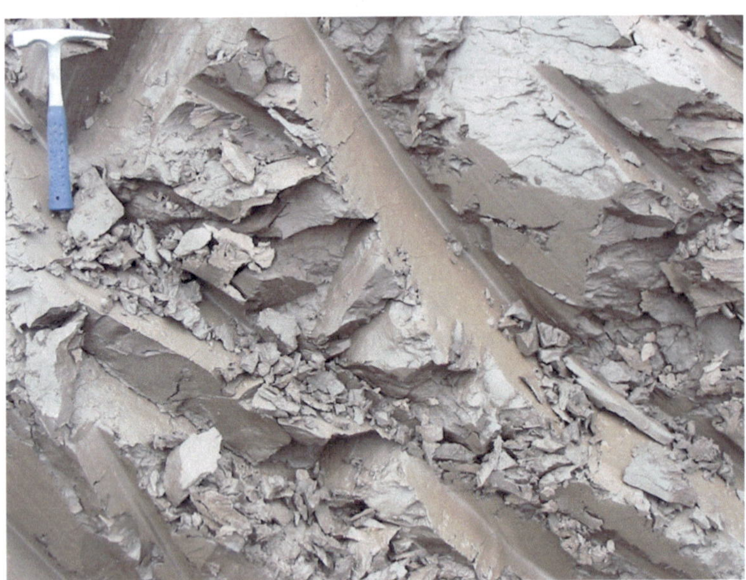

Excavating clay from a natural deposit.[9]

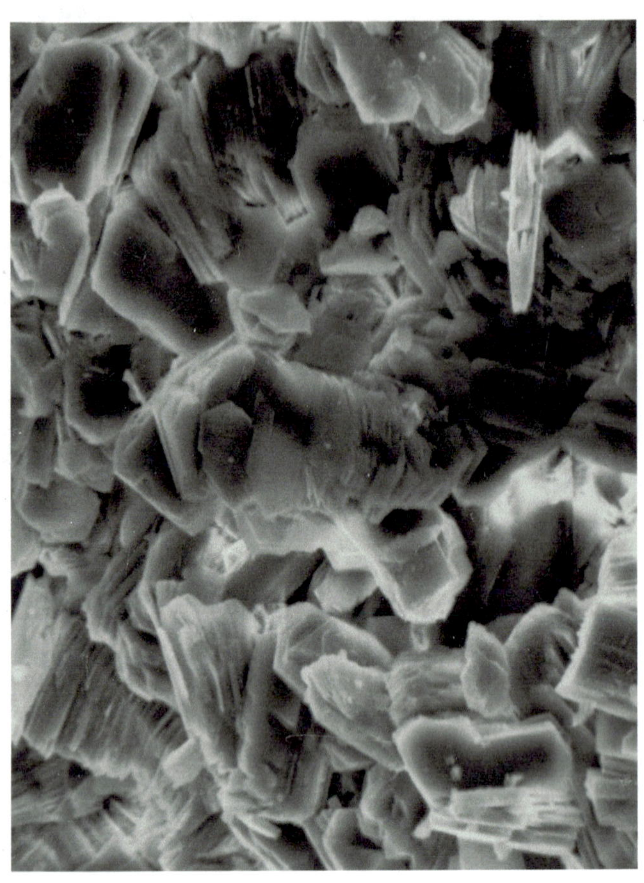

Photograph of microscopic kaolinite (clay) particles[8]

3

CLAYS
CLAYBODIES

$AL_2O_3\ 2SiO_2\ 2H_2O$ --- Chemical symbol for Clay

Clays are naturally occurring alumina-silica materials formed by the weathering of igneous rocks over millions of years. As these rocks were weathered, different types of clay were formed with each having particular characteristics. The two basic forms of clay are primary and secondary. Primary clays remained close to their source feldspathic rock after weathering. This means that they are relatively clean, pure, and often whitish. They are also more heat resistant than secondary clays. Secondary clays have been moved very far from their source. They may have been eroded by glaciers, washed away in rivers, or blown across deserts. The erosion process has changed the original clay particle size and shape and other minerals (most often iron and titanium) have been mixed in. This has created the variety of natural clays found across the planet. Over thousands of years of human history, clay has proven to be one of the most useful and important mate rials and that continues today. We are in a "ceramics / glass age" using a variety of high tech / high temperature materials in our computers, phones, and vehicles.

For the creation of ceramic objects, there are a number important characteristics possessed by natural clay. These properties include refractoriness (resistance to heat), the ability to become durable and dense after firing, mineral composition (contamination by other minerals), and plasticity (ease of shaping and ability to hold that shape). The plasticity in wet clay (one of its most important characteristics) is caused by a very fine particle size, the thin platelet shape of these particles, and the water moving between the particles (see the image on the previous page). After an object is shaped, it must be dried slowly to prevent cracks from forming and then fired to make it permanent. Once the piece is heated beyond 1,000 F (540 C), it has been turned into ceramic and is no longer a plastic workable clay. Clays found by prospecting in nature should be subjected to a variety of tests such as workability and firing temperature beforc being dug and used in large amounts.

See David Peters' website www.davidpetersceramics.com/process-gallery-test/ for an example of how clays can be prospected and used by studio artists.

Categories of Naturally Occurring Clays

There are a huge variety of natural clays found across the planet due to the diverse methods, locations, and situations of their formation. Geologists and ceramic engineers break these different clays into broad categories but it should be noted that since these are natural materials, some clays may fit into more than one area. Some brand names of these clays will go extinct or change as mines close or new more profitable sources of materials are found by the mining companies. There are five basic categories of natural clays, they are:

Earthenware (also known as surface clay)
These are the most commonly and easily found secondary clays. Earthenware was the first type of natural clay used by humans and required the simplest kiln technology and lowest firing temperatures. These fine grained clays are often red, orange, brown, gray, blue, black, or yellow in nature. This coloration is due to a high amount of mineral contaminants such as iron, titanium, and manganese mixed in during the long erosion process. Most of the clays found in this area of NY state are fine grained earthenwares. Some commercially available earthenware clays in the US are Red Art, Ranger Red, and Lizella Red.

Ball Clay
These are a large group of high temperature, contaminant free (very little iron) secondary clays. Ball clays are the most plastic of all types and have the smallest particle size which helps to create plasticity. One drawback of a small particle size is a high degree of shrinkage of the wet clay which

can cause problems with cracking. Ball clays are often used to increase the workability of a mixture called a clay body (discussed in the next few pages). Some commercially available ball clays are Kentucky OM#4, Tennessee #1, Spinks C & C, and XX Sagger.

Stoneware Clay

These are relatively refractory secondary clays that have a larger particle size than ball clays but are still very plastic. Stoneware clays are often found mixed with small particles of iron and some feldspar due to the erosion process. They usually fire tan, brown, or grayish and are also naturally occurring clay bodies that vitrify (becoming very dense and non-porous) at high temperatures. Some commercially available stonewares include Roseville, Gold Art, and Foundry Hill Creme.

Fireclay

These are highly refractory secondary clays with a very large, heavy, coarse particle size having been deposited early in the erosion process. Fireclays are not very plastic and they do not shrink very much during drying. Kiln bricks may be made from a large percentage of fireclay. Clay bodies formulated for large scale sculpture also have a large amount fireclay since the coarse particle allows thickly made objects to dry out more evenly. Commercially available fireclays include Hawthorn Bond and AP Green.

Kaolin

These are very pure white refractory primary clays. Since they did not move far from their source, few contaminant minerals were mixed in. Kaolins tend to be course grained and non-plastic clays. The name kaolin is derived from the Chinese word for "high ridge". These clays are necessary ingredients for making a porcelain clay body. Some commercially available kaolins include E.P.K., No.6 Tile Clay, and Grolleg (this kaolin is imported from the U.K.).

Notes:

Clay Bodies

Clay bodies are man-made combinations that blend a variety of clays and other materials. These mixtures are formulated for specific firing temperatures, forming processes, fired colors, textures and other issues. The most workable clay bodies are made from materials that have a wide variety of particle sizes.

There are three main clay bodies used throughout ceramics history. They are earthenware, stoneware, and porcelain.

Earthenware (also known as Terra Cotta)

This clay body has been used throughout history and by ceramic artists across the world. It is often a reddish orange color (due to its high iron content) and fired to the lowest temperature (around 1,800 F / 980 C) of the three clay bodies. It remains porous after being fired making it very effective for things like flowerpots. However, because of this characteristic, earthenware must be fully glazed if used to functional pottery or the food / drink will be absorbed into the pot surface.

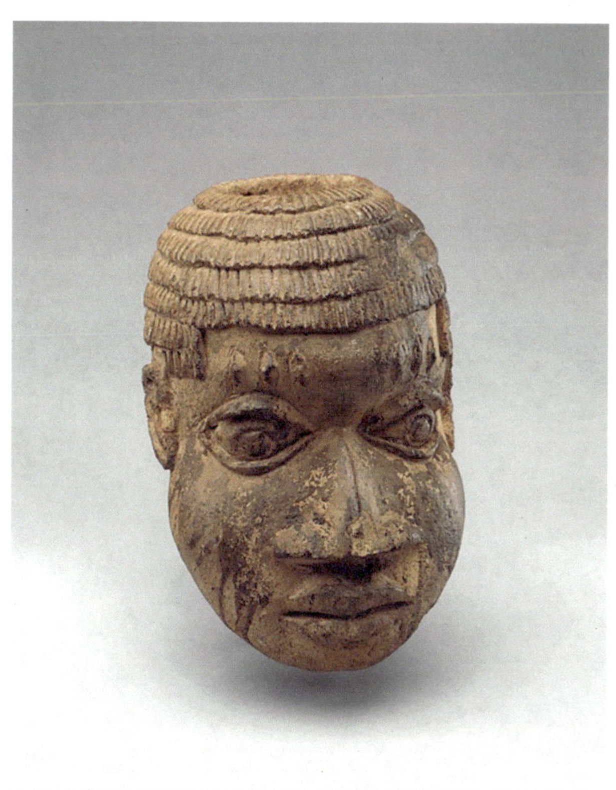

African Benin culture earthenware head[4]

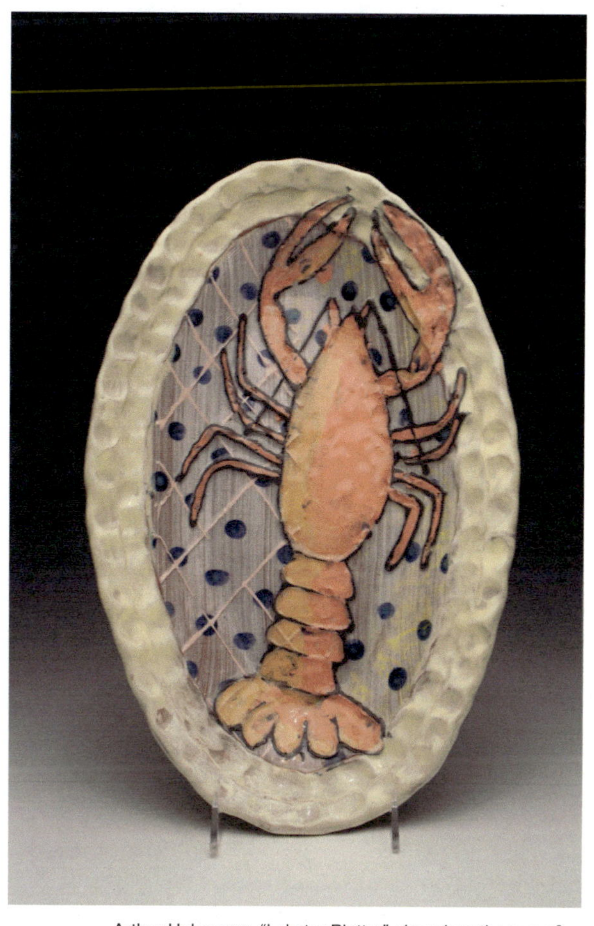

Arthur Halvorsen, "Lobster Platter" glazed earthenware[3]

Stoneware

This clay body needs to be fired to a high temperature (at least 2,150 F / 1,180 C) and often has a tan, brown or gray color. It becomes very dense after firing (vitrified) and has been used extensively for functional pottery. As the need for higher firing temperatures increased in ancient cultures, kiln technology advanced often alongside metal casting. Many of the kiln designs developed hundreds or thousands of years ago are still in use today. The CCC anagama woodfired kiln is based on an ancient Japanese kiln type used to fire stoneware ceramics.

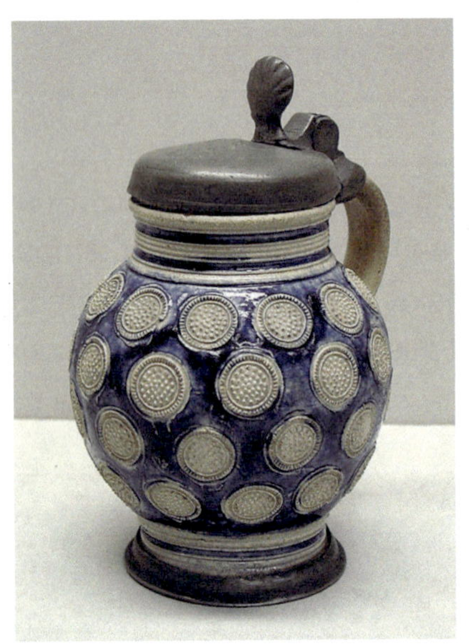

German Westerwald stoneware mug[4]

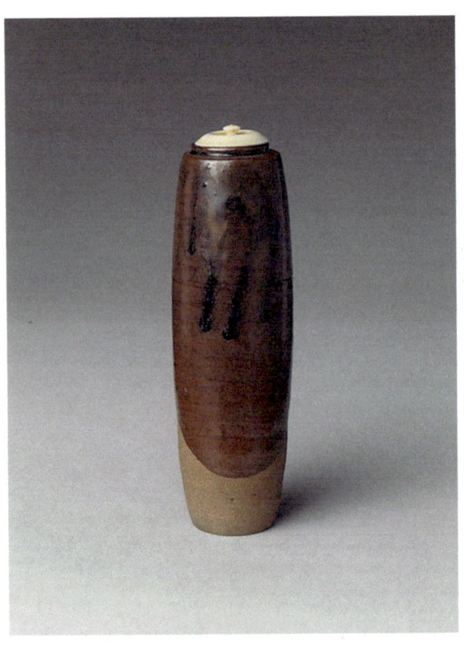

Japanese glazed stoneware tea ceremony jar[4]

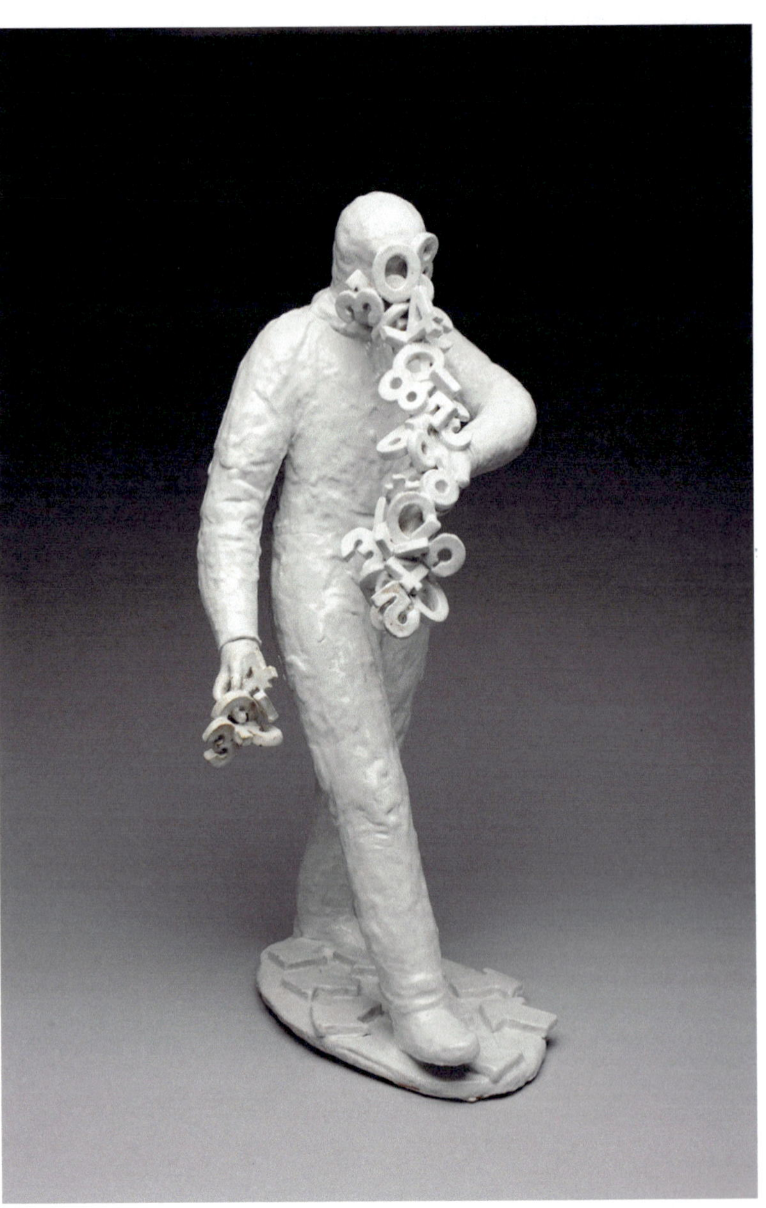

Paolo Porelli, "Excess", stoneware sculpture[5]

Porcelain

Porcelain is sometimes called "China" because of its country of origin. This smooth white clay body is fired to a very high temperature (close to 2,400 F / 1,315 C), after which it becomes very dense, glassy and sometimes translucent. Porcelain can be difficult to work with because of its relatively non-plastic ingredients. The whiteness of porcelain has allowed it to be the perfect surface to paint complex patterns and imagery.

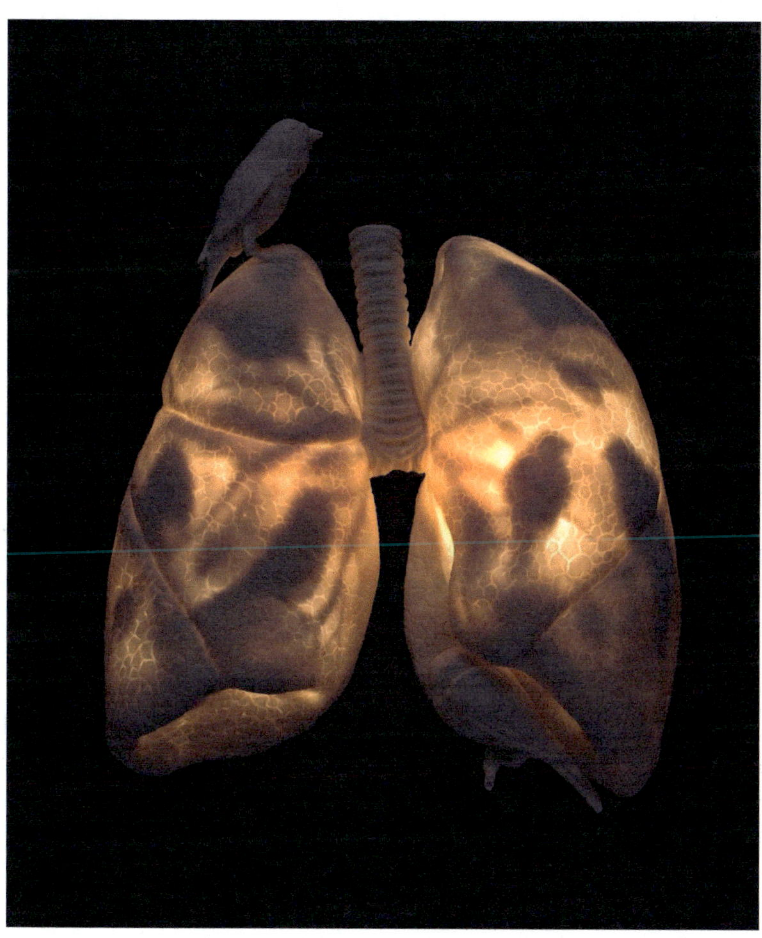

Kate MacDowell, "Canary" porcelain sculpture[3]

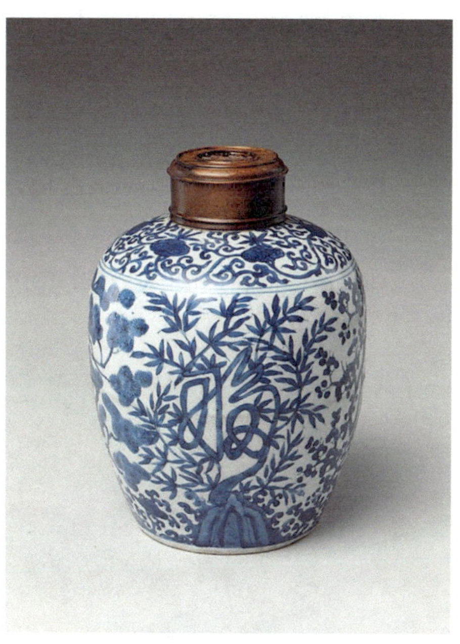

Chinese Ming dynasty porcelain jar[4]

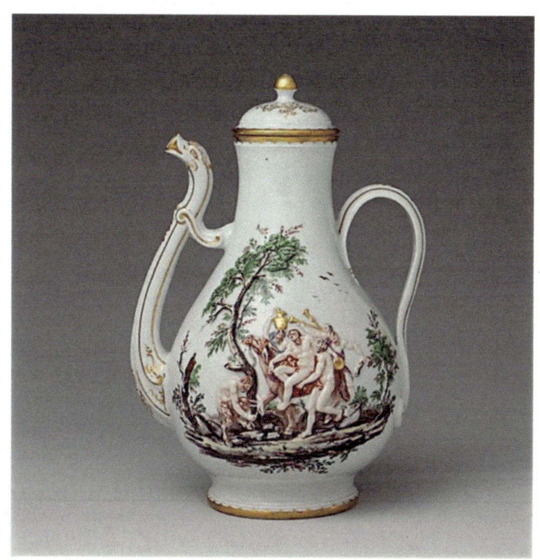

Italian Doccia porcelain coffepot[4]

Mixing Claybodies

Claybodies can be designed for a variety of functions. This helps to determine the types of natural clays and other materials selected to be mixed together to make a workable material. All ceramic materials are available from industrial suppliers and they often have helpful advice about claybody formulation. In addition, these suppliers sell commercially prepared claybodies eliminating the need for clay mixing equipment.

In the CCC studio, we use a clay mixer and a pugmill to mix our standard studio claybody which has been designed to be a general purpose stoneware. This stoneware is a dependable wheelthrowing and handbuilding clay that can be fired in both our electric kilns and the wood-kilns.

If desired, small sample test batches of new claybodies can be created by weighing out 1,000 grams of material and adding water to create a thick slip similar to cake frosting. This can be dried to workable consistency and used to make small test pieces for future firings.

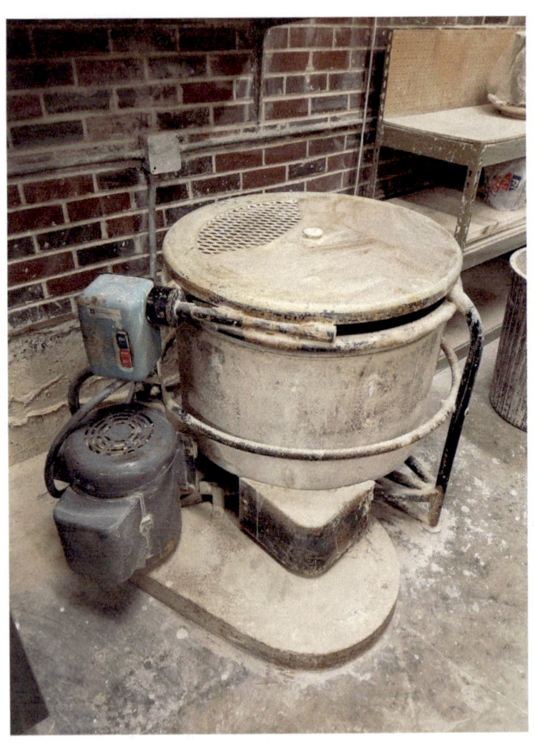

Soldner brand clay mixer[1]

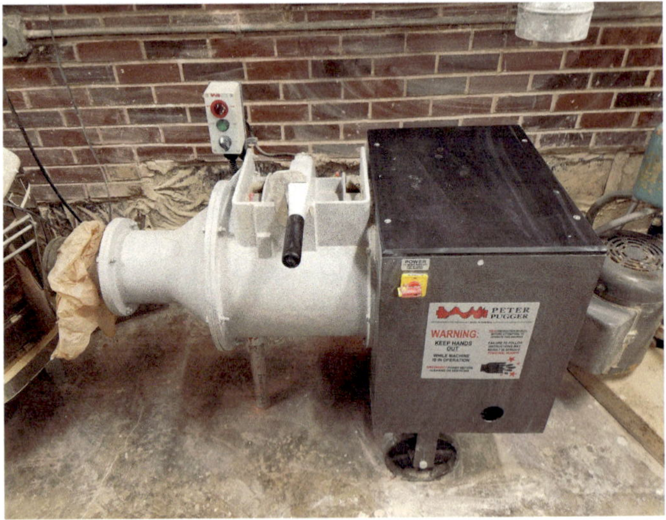

Peter Pugger brand pugmill / mixer[1]

Due to the potential danger of this equipment, no clay mixing will take place in the SUNY-CCC Ceramics studio without direct faculty supervision.

Process for designing and mixing a claybody

Clay

Select from the natural clays depending on firing color and temperature needed:

1. earthenware
2. ball clay
3. stoneware
4. fire clay
5. kaolin - needed for a porcelain claybody

then add a:

Flux

Fluxes are materials added to the clay body to help the clay particles and other materials fuse into a dense, strong structure. If too little flux is used, the clay body may be porous or brittle even if fired to a high temperature. The state at which the clay body has been fired to completion (or to the temperature required) is called "maturation".

Examples of common clay body fluxes are:

1. Feldspar- potash - for higher temperature bodies like stoneware and porcelain
2. Nepheline syenite - can be used for midrange to high temperature bodies
3. Talc- used for low temperature bodies

then finish with a:

Filler

Fillers are added to a claybody in order to increase its strength or density, provide texture, make it dry more evenly during forming, or to make forming easier. Some common filler materials are:

1. Grog - ground up fired clay
2. Silica - needed for a porcelain claybody
3. Sand
4. Paper fiber / organic materials

Sample claybody recipes:

Red Earthenware for Sculpture (cone 04 to 1)

Red Art clay	44 lbs
Fireclay	35 lbs
Talc	9 lbs
OM-4 Ball clay	9 lbs
Red Iron Oxide	4 lbs
+ Grog	9 lbs

SUNY-CCC Stoneware (cone 6 to10)

Fireclay	50 lbs
Ball clay	20 lbs
Kaolin	15 lbs
Custer feldspar	15 lbs
+ Grog	3 lbs

Porcelain (cone 9 to 12)

Grolleg kaolin	55 lbs
Custer feldspar	25 lbs
Silica	20 lbs

Notes:

Notes:

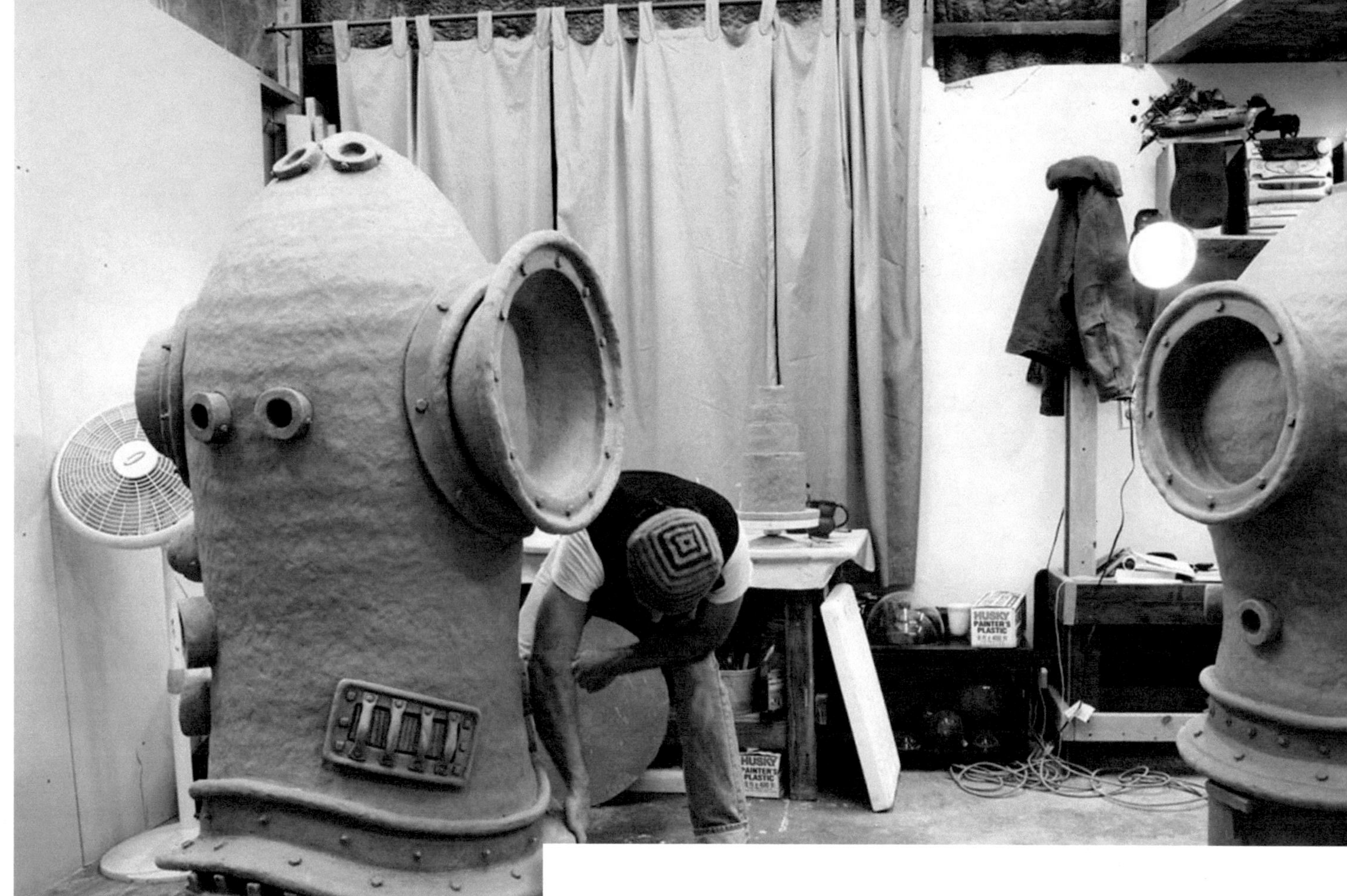

Jacob Foran working in his studio[3]

GETTING STARTED

The challenge of working in ceramics comes from the material itself. Clay is easy to shape but as it dries becomes more fragile. Patience and time management skills are developed as each process takes a certain amount of time. Ceramic objects must also be fired in a kiln to become permanent. The firing process has it's own set of challenges including getting the work into the kiln, heating to the correct temperature, and having the final product fit the artist's original design. The fired object can last thousands of years and can serve as future evidence of our culture.

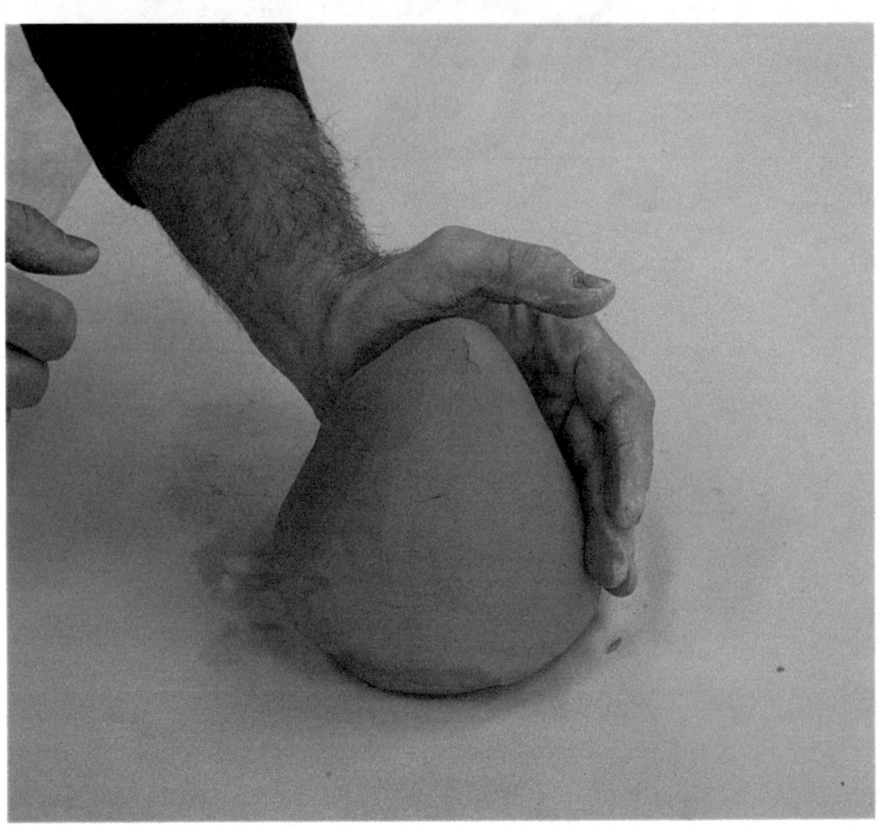
The finished product after wedging[1]

PREPARING TO WORK

One of great appeals of clay is the feeling of direct manipulation of the material. Every touch of hand or tool is recorded on the clay. Clay appeals directly to our tactile sense- one of our most powerful senses. Some of the first objects made by humans were sculpted using clay found in the caves near cave paintings. Finger prints can be found from the makers on pots thousands of years old.

Working with clay is working in three dimensions and fighting against gravity the entire time. A good habit to get into is to step back from your work and to rotate the object to view it from multiple perspectives. Try to be aware of how the weight of the work is affecting the overall shape. If things are getting distorted because the clay is too soft and heavy, look to prop it with paper or clay supports or use a hair dryer to stiffen the form until it will hold up its own weight.

The objects you make in clay are only limited to your imagination, the amount of material you have to work with, and the size of the kiln (and the assignments for class!).

One of the most important steps when you begin any project is to properly prepare your clay. This process begins with **wedging** the clay by taking a lump of clay out of the bin and bringing it to the table. On the canvas surface, you will repeated push the clay down and then rock it back on itself to force out any air pockets and also make the piece a consistent material. If the wedging is done correctly, you will be create a spiral in the clay. If we looked at the clay under a microscope after wedging, we would see the clay particles lining up so they can slide past and over each other. This allows the clay to stretch out and be more easily shaped.

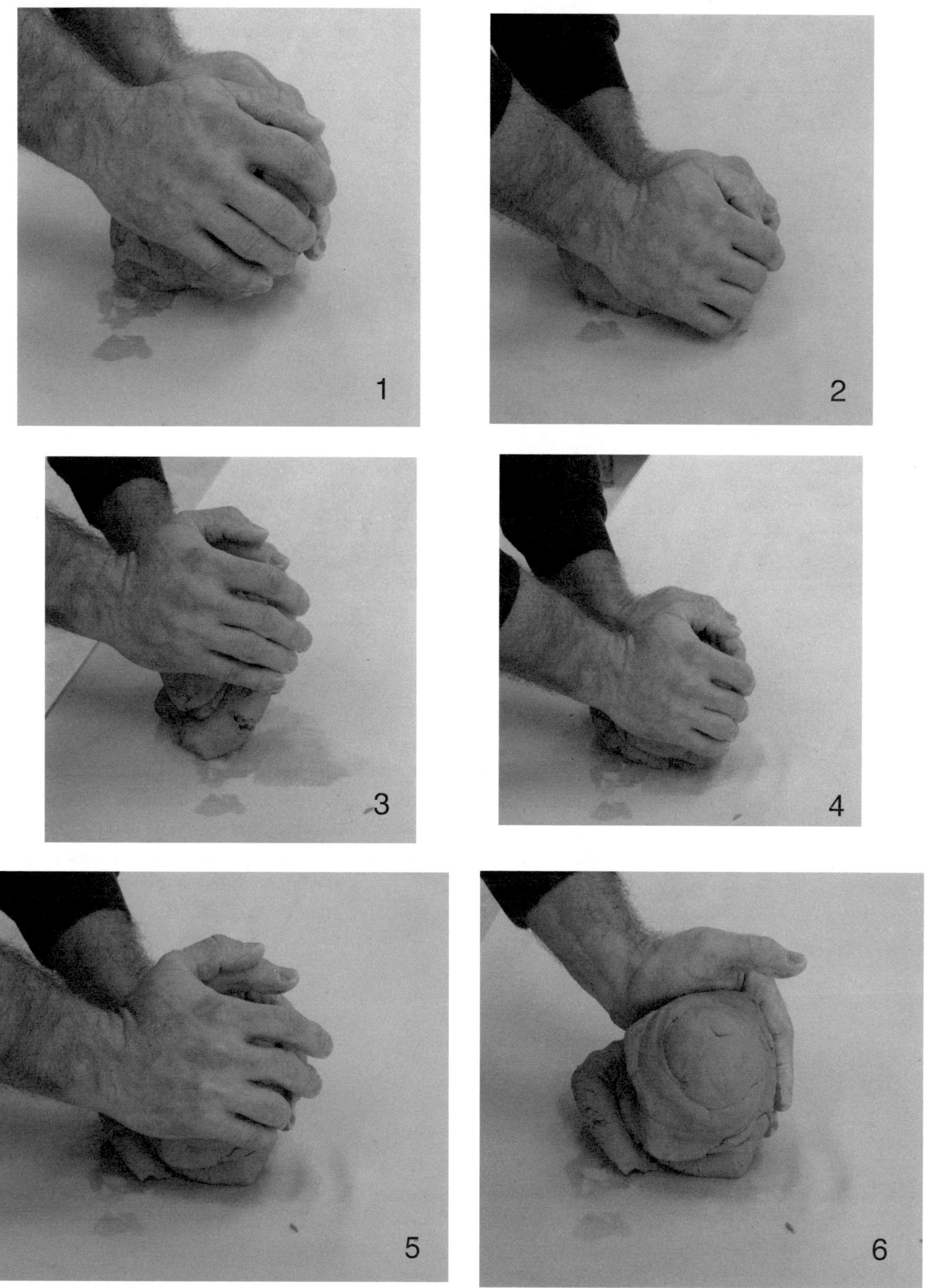

Steps in the wedging process. The rocking motion and a slight angle when pushing down allows the clay mass to move into a spiral. Continue wedging until it feels consistent and dense. You can also check by cutting the mass with a wire and checking for any air pockets or other inconsistencies.

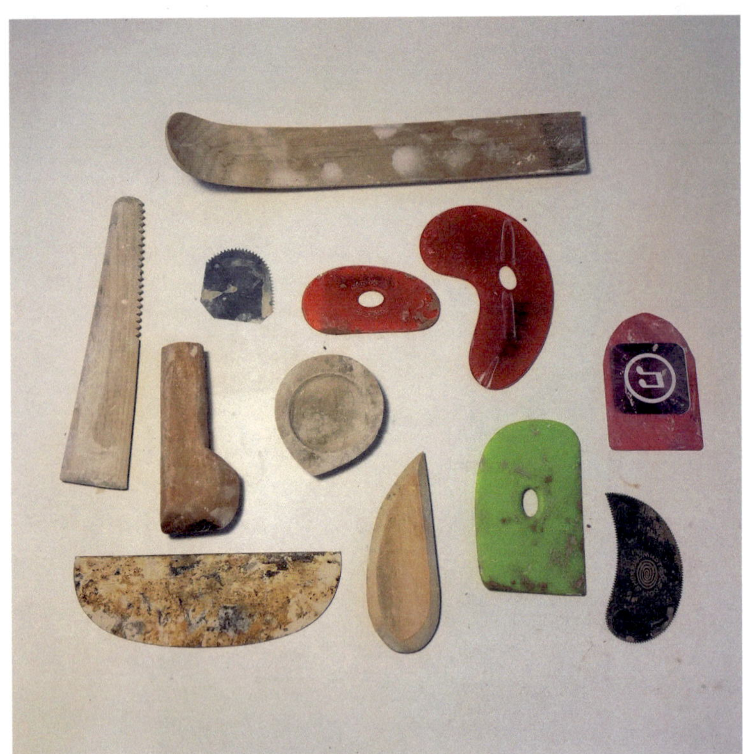

A variety of **ribs** used for shaping and smoothing. Wood, metal, and plastic are common materials. Unique shapes can be easily cut from old gift or credit cards[1]

CLAY TOOLS

Many tools have been invented, altered, and perfected over the thousands of years humans have been making ceramic objects. This process continues today as artists and manufacturers develop new materials and shapes. In addition, tools can be found in other areas (like cooking / baking or woodworking) that can be re-purposed for ceramics. Look at what's around, experiment, and make your own tools in order to create personal effects on your clay work.

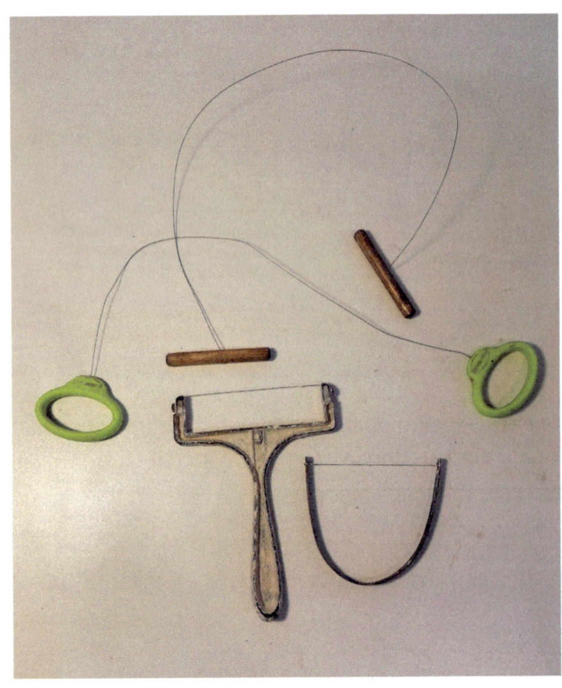

Cut off wires for cutting through blocks of clay. These can be braided metal wire or fishing line. A cheese slicer makes a very effective tool for cutting the top edge of work.[1]

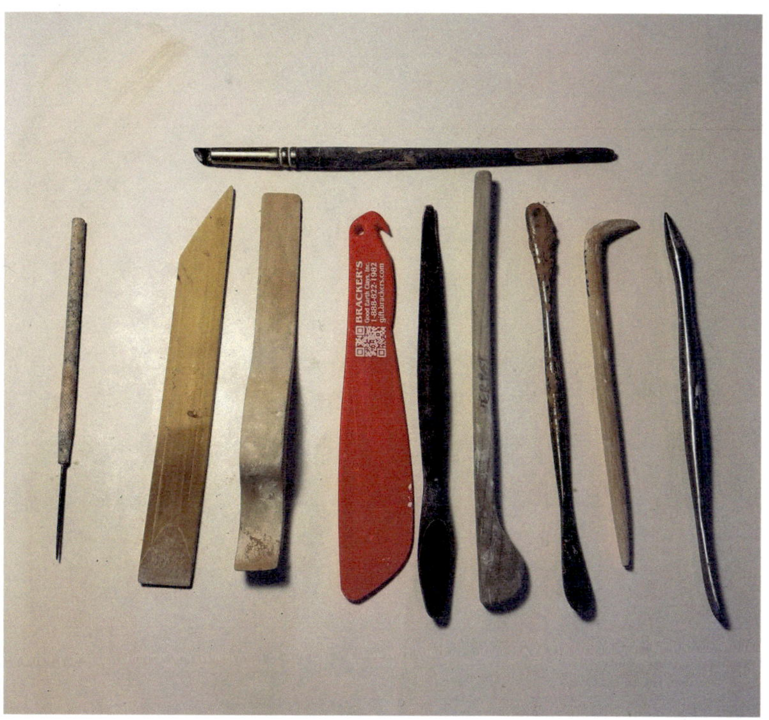

From left side: **Pin tool** (also called **needle tool**) for checking thickness or cutting through edges
Wood knife , next a variety of knife-like or dowel shapes for forming[1]

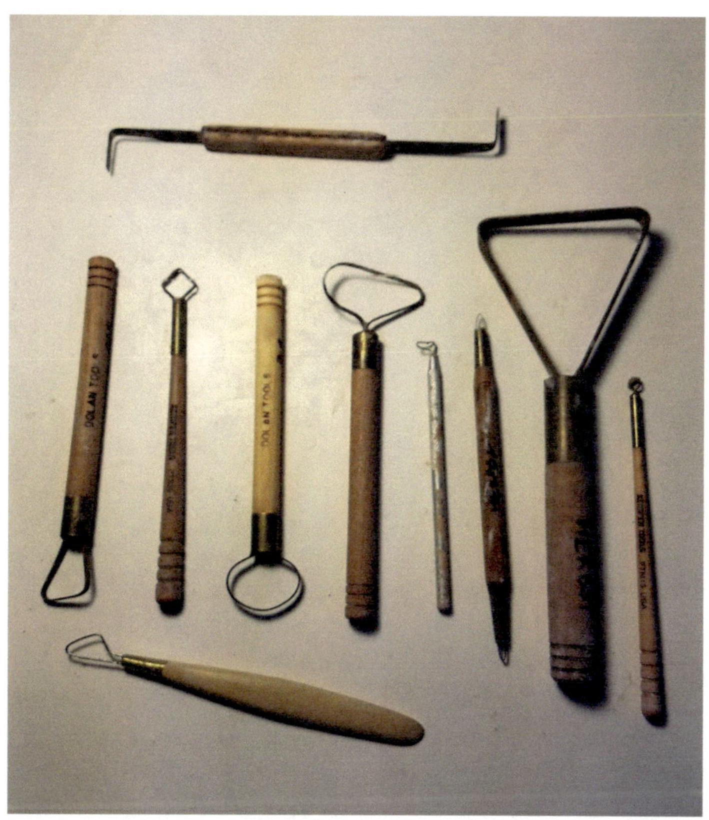

A variety of **loop tools** (also called **trimming tools**) for cutting or carving leather hard clay[1]

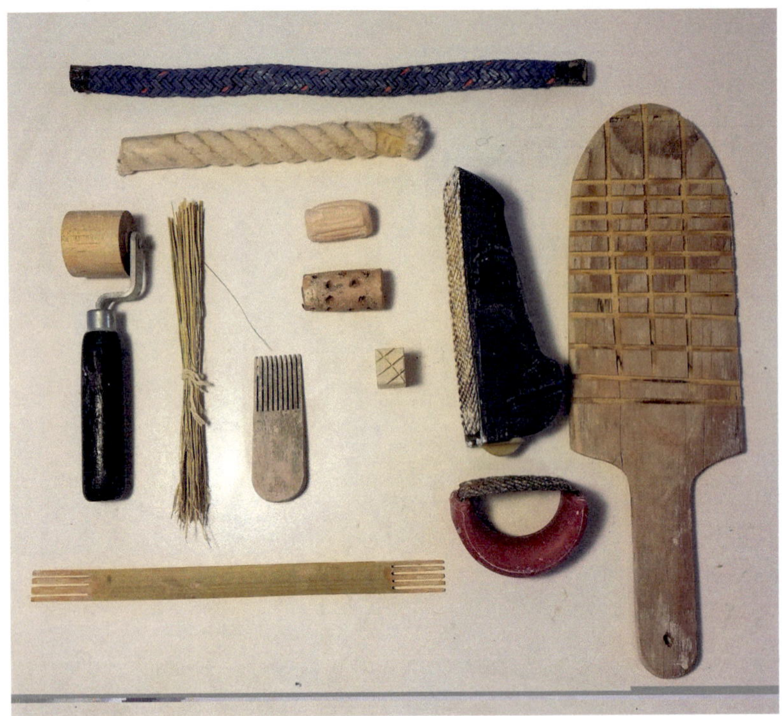

Tools for creating textures: a roller, a brush made from an old broom, bisque fired stamps, carved pieces of wine bottle cork and pieces of rope to roll over soft clay, two **rasp** tools for altering shapes, carved paddle[1]

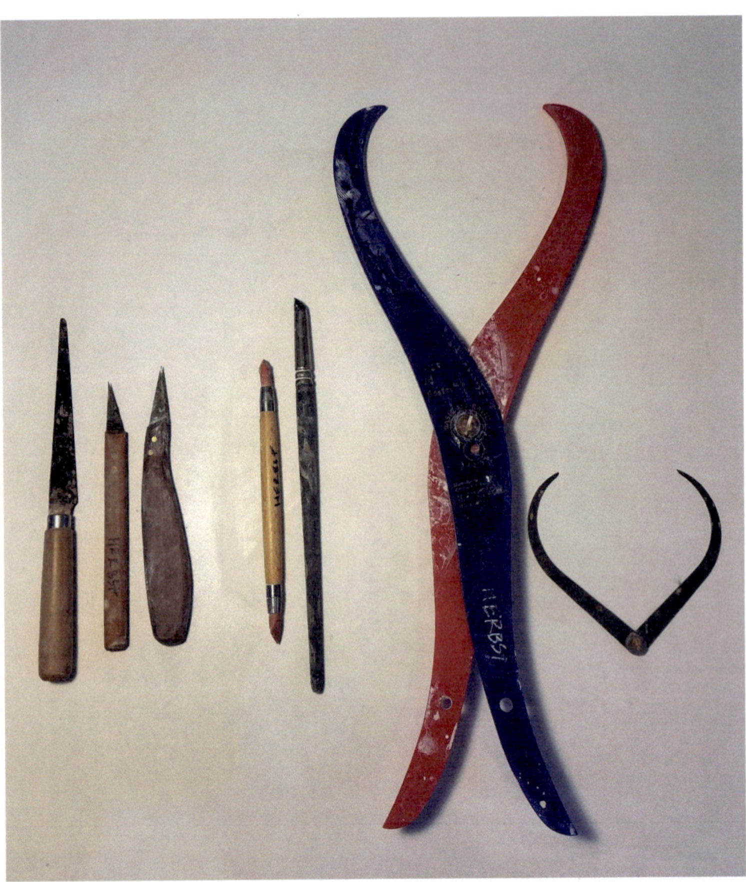

From left: **Fettling knife** and other knives for cutting, two soft tipped tools for shaping, two **calipers** for measuring [1]

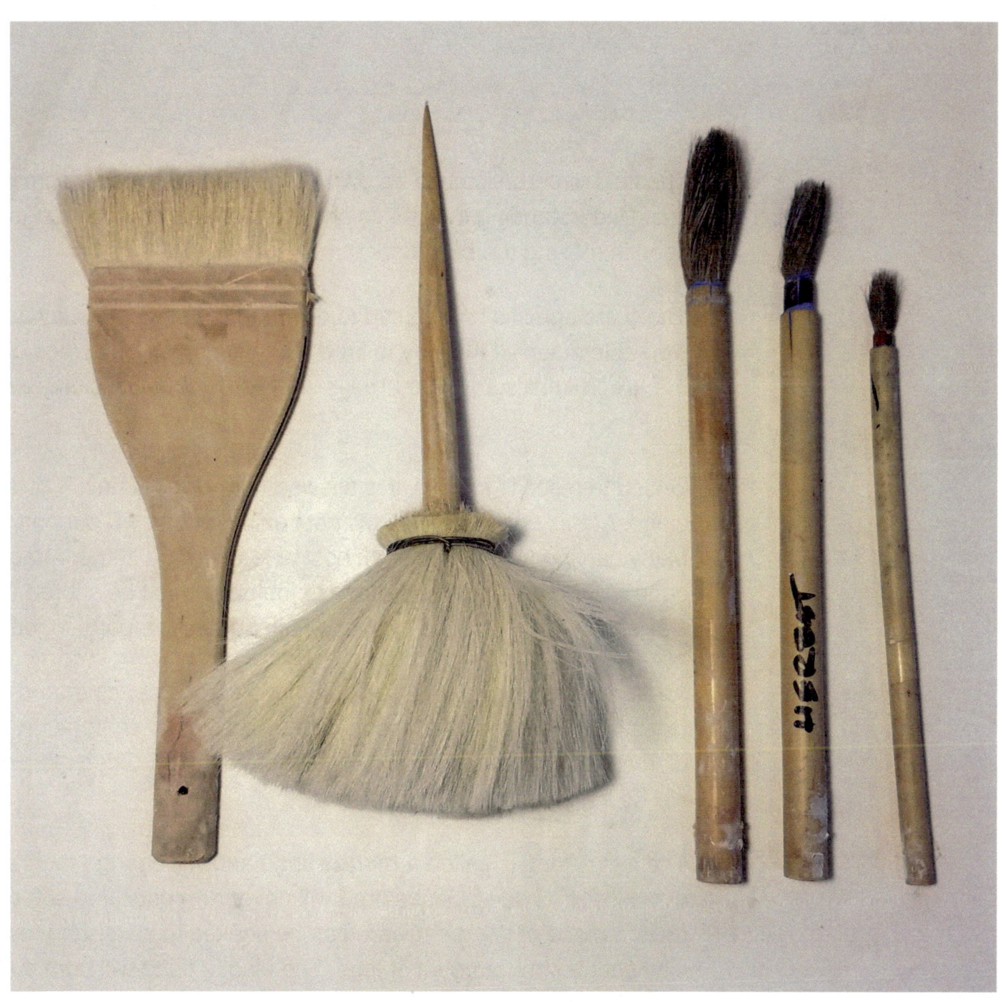

A variety of brushes for painting slips and glazes. The best brushes for ceramics are made from natural hairs and are often used for ink painting. These will hold ceramic materials better than synthetic brushes. Some artists make their own brushes from materials like deer or elk hair glued into a bamboo stem for a handle.[1]

STAGES OF CERAMICS

The field of ceramics has it's own vocabulary just like any area of study and practice. Understanding the basics of the material and its language will help you to succeed in making the best work possible.

There are specific terms used to describe the stages of clay as it goes from a soft workable mass all the way to fired ceramic object. Any piece of unfired clay is in the **greenware** stage. We always start with soft, plastic clay when building the work.

Once the piece is formed, it is allowed to dry slowly until it gets to the **leatherhard** stage. At this point, the clay will not flex much and will support its own weight. Many carving techniques work best at leatherhard stage. Attachments are often done at this point but the surface of the parts must be scored (scratched) and then wet with water or liquid clay slip to help adhere the parts together.

As it continues to dry, the piece changes to a lighter color and reaches the **bone dry** stage. The work is at the most fragile point when bone dry and must be handled carefully or it can easily crack or break apart. Once the piece is fully dried, it will be loaded into a kiln to be fired.

The initial firing is called a **bisque** firing and will change the clay into ceramic. A piece that has been bisque fired will never turn back into soft clay again. In contrast, a piece of dry greenware can be soaked in water and reworked into usable clay after a short amount of time. The bisque firing will burn out any organic material in the clay and also create a stronger, porous material that is easier to glaze.

After the bisque kiln is cooled and unloaded, the pieces will have a liquid **glaze** solution applied. The pieces are loaded into a kiln and fired (usually) to a higher temperature melting the glaze and fusing the ceramic body. When the work is finished it has been glaze fired and ready to be used and displayed.

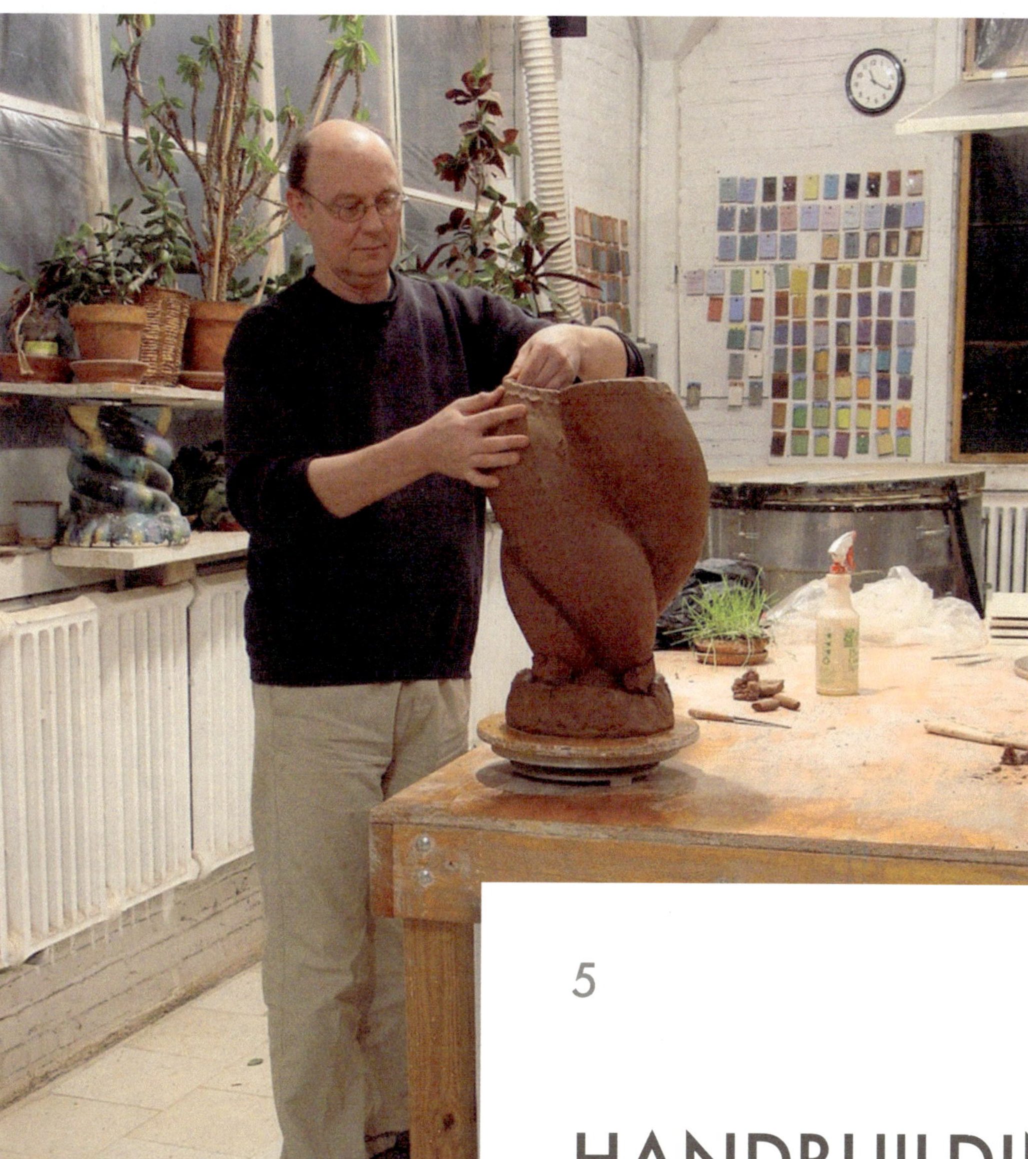

Gary Erickson coil building a sculpture in his studio[2]

5

HANDBUILDING

The processes of handbuilding in ceramics (pinch, coil, and slab) allow for a great deal of freedom and expression. Each method has advantages and disadvantages that the artist must deal with for the execution of their concepts and designs.

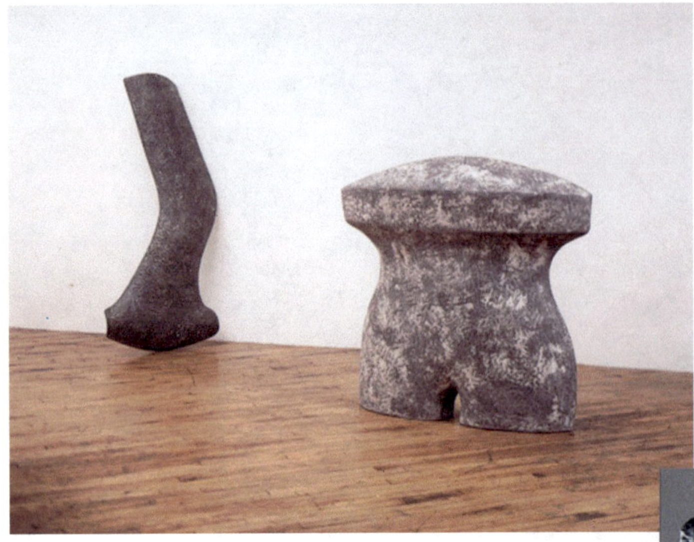

"Mock and Delude", Nicholas Kripal, unfired adobe over support armature, wax, and paint[2]

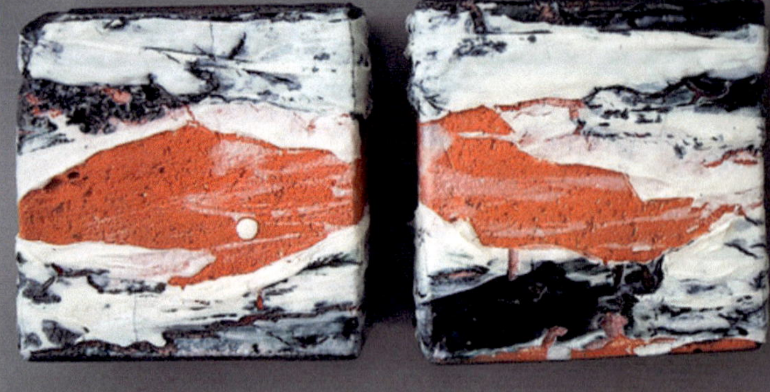

"Landscape Abstraction (red)", Liz Howe, altered kiln brick, slip, and mixed media[3]

breaking some rules

As an art form, ceramics has a long list of traditional "rules" that are taught to help students learn how to succeed with their work. For example, most clay objects are built hollow with an even wall thickness between 1/8" for small objects and up to 1" for large sculptural forms. This approach allows the material to dry out evenly and allows steam to escape safely during the heating process early in a bisque firing.

However in some cases, it is useful to build the object solid. This method is works well when creating small detailed shapes or for complex sculptural shapes that would be difficult to construct hollow. Building solid also allows you to use more force in the shaping process and not worry about the piece collapsing.

The difference is that as the object dries to leatherhard stage, the piece is cut open with a wire tool and hollowed out inside. Try to make your cut at a place that will be easy to repair when the object is reassembled. When hollowing out, it is important to make the wall thickness as even as possible to prevent the form from distorting or cracking during drying. Any areas that are extra thick should be pierced with a pin tool to create channels for steam to get out during firing. After the extra clay is removed, carefully score and apply thick slip to the areas that will be reattached. Press the object back together and reshape the seam to obscure the cut line. Dry and fire large, thick objects slower and for a longer time than usual.

Other rules can be broken or bent in order to create special effects on your pieces. New techniques and discoveries are being made all the time when traditional ideas are challenged. Use your sketchbook as a "research journal" as you work with this material and see what you discover as you develop your own way of working with ceramics.

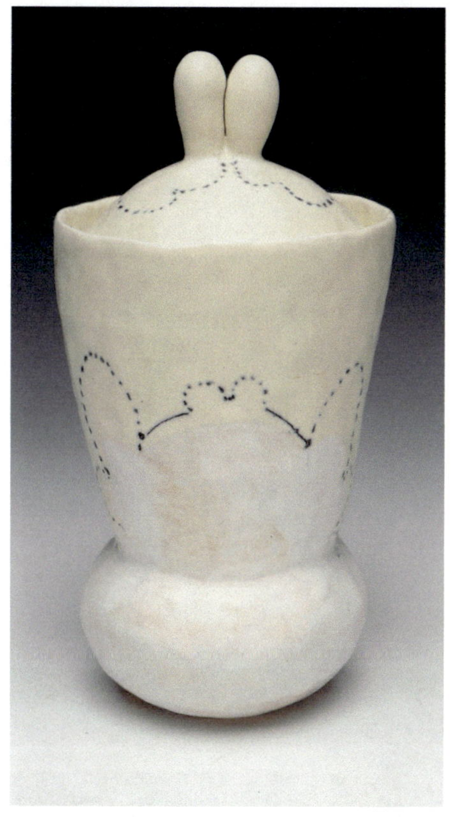

Emily Schroeder Willis, "Jar", pinched porcelain[3]

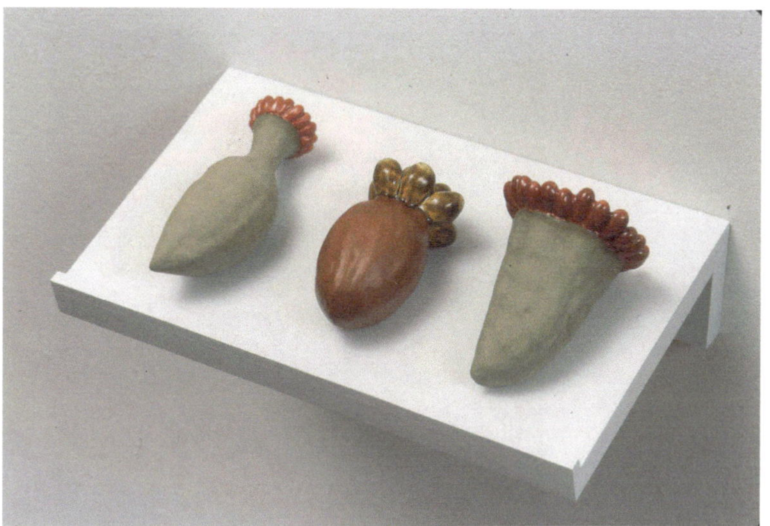

Julie Tesser, "Seeds", pinched earthenware[3]

PINCH

Pinch construction is one of the most direct and useful building methods. Starting with a solid mass of clay, you will slowing open and squeeze the walls between your fingers and thumb to create the shape desired and thin out the walls. The standard wall thickness for most clay work is between an 1/8" for small forms to a 1/2" for larger forms. You can also easily increase the size of your object by adding strips of clay to the top edge or by joining two separately pinched shapes.

The pinch technique will help to build your sensitivity to how clay reacts to your touch. Some artists prefer to leave the marks of their fingers on the work, others will spend a large amount of time smoothing or refining the clay wall to disguise the forming method.

To create any object using the pinch technique, start with a solid piece of clay (1). Push your thumb into this mass of clay (2) and begin to squeeze the clay between your thumb on the inside and your fingers on the outside (3). Slowly spin the clay and continue to squeeze / pinch the form as you thin out the walls (4) Depending on the shape intended, leave some areas thicker so that the clay can be carved away or manipulated later (5). Continue to work the form until the desired thickness, shape, and surface texture are achieved (6).

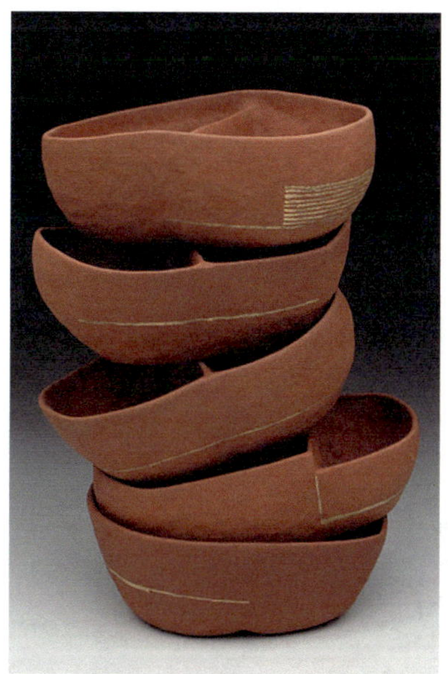

Lilly Zuckerman, "Untitled", pinched earthenware[3]

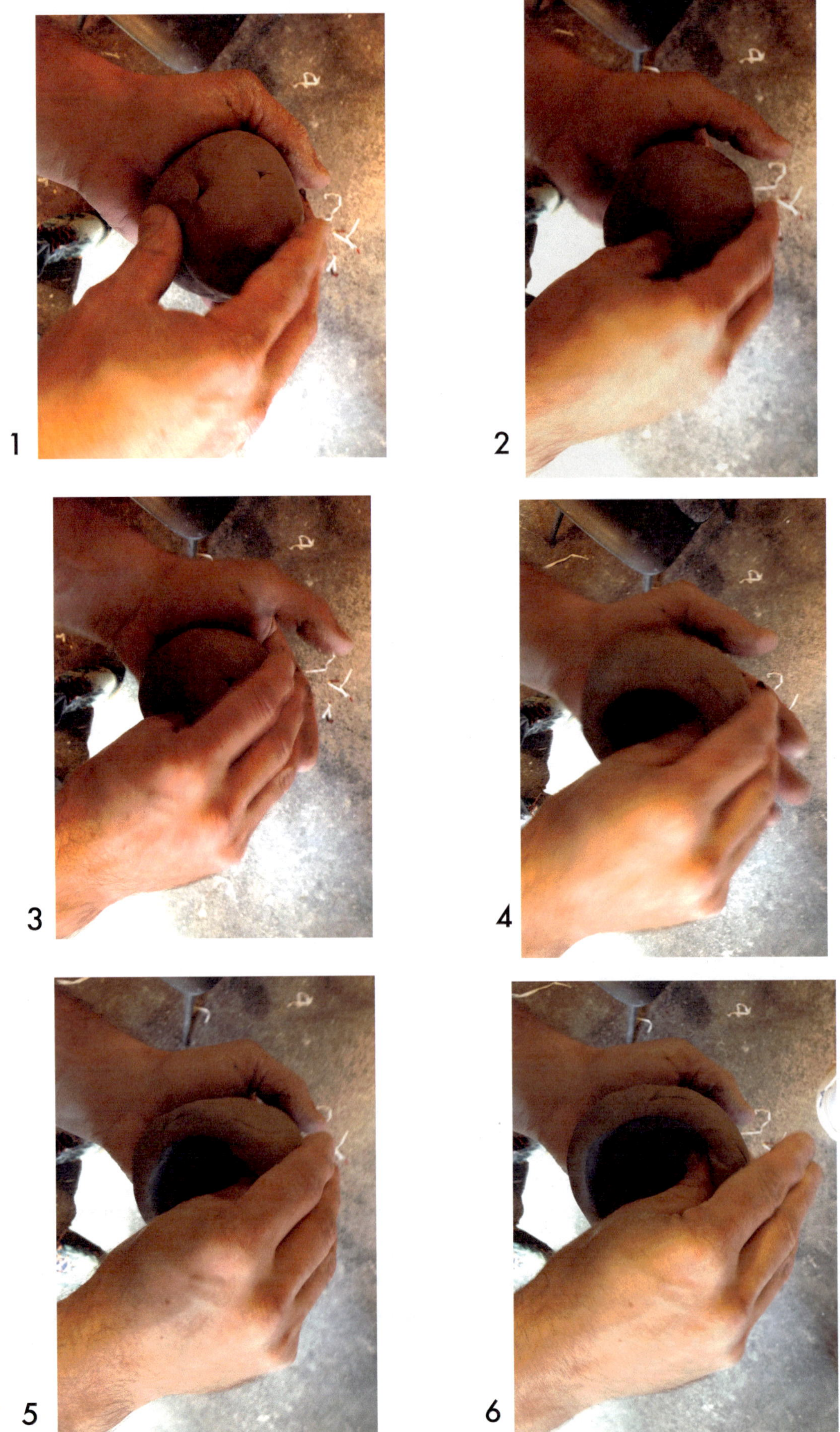

1
2
3
4
5
6

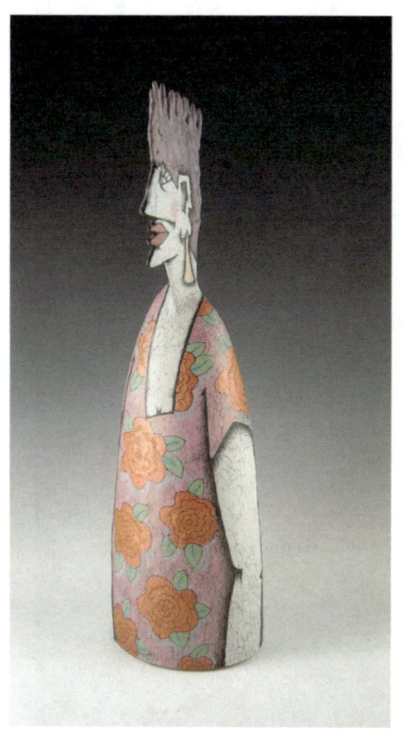

Rimas VisGirda, "BJT", coiled stoneware[3]

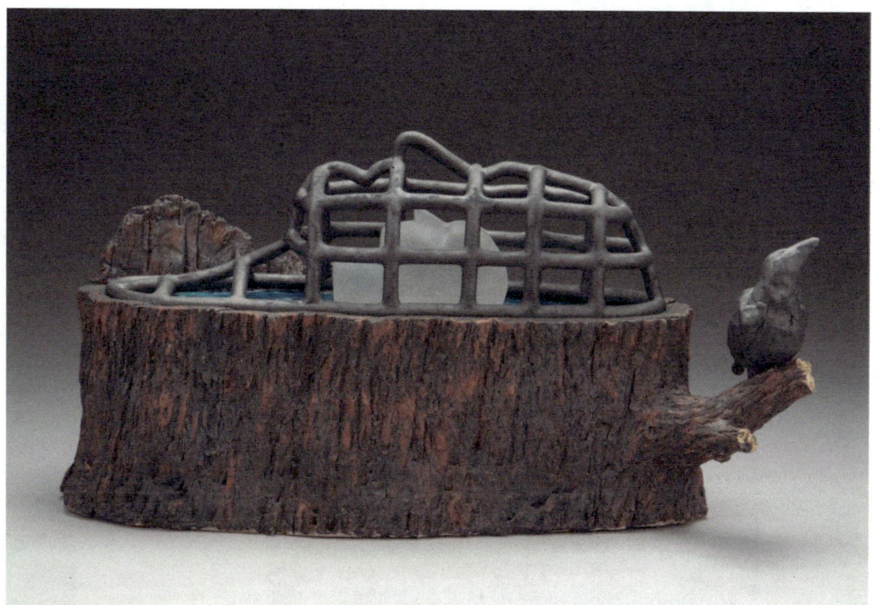

Ted Vogel, "Head Cage", coiled stoneware and glass[2]

COIL

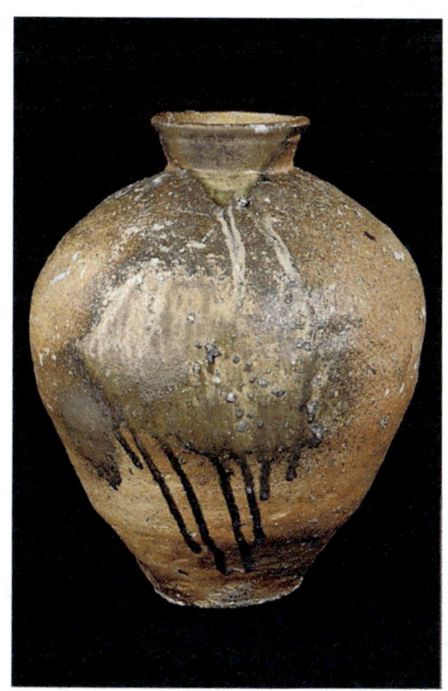

Japanese Shigaraki coiled stoneware jar[4]

Coil building can be a very useful technique for creating shapes at a larger scale. The method involves stacking and blending together layers of coils (both on the inside and outside) to build the form. Coils are made by rolling clay on the table or using the extruder to make multiple coils at one time.

This building method will take longer and each object will take multiple working sessions to complete. To prevent the piece from collapsing under its own weight, you must pause to allow the lower levels to dry just enough to help support the new clay. The drying process can be accelerated by using a hair dryer or fan, or putting the object in the sun.

When new coils are added to existing firmed up wall, the top edge must be scored (scratched) heavily and wet clay slip painted on. The new clay can then be blended on and smoothed. If sections aren't scored and slipped well enough, cracks will form or the piece may come apart.

Large forms may need to have some variation in wall thickness. Slightly thicker coils at the bottom of the piece will help support more weight above. Switch to thinner coils when nearing the top or completing the piece to reduce the overall weight of the object.

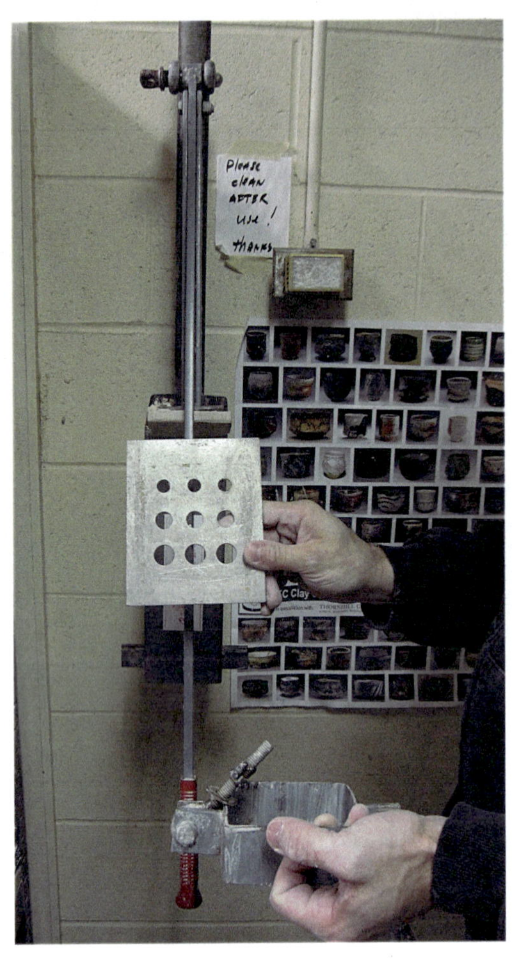

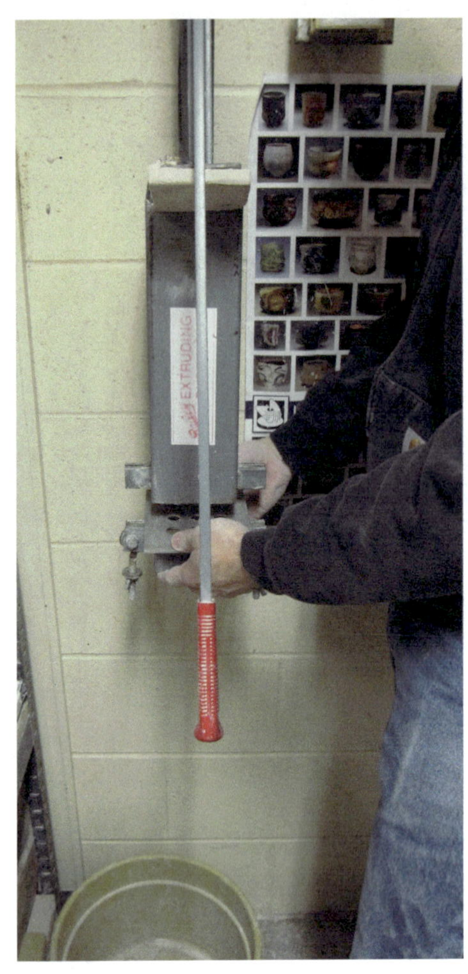

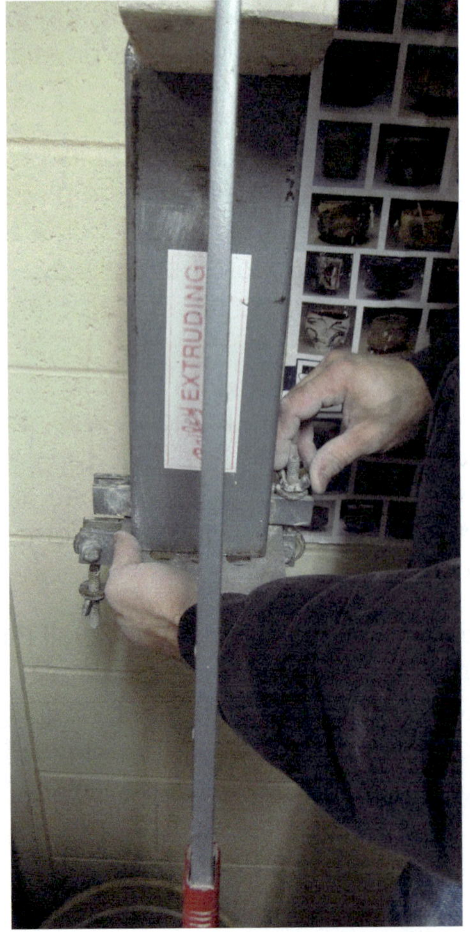

One way of speeding up the coil building process is to use the extruder. The extruder is a great tool for making a variety of shapes including solid coils, hollow tubes, and other geometric extrusions.

For coil building, the extruder allows you to make a number of coils at the same time. First select the coil die and attach it to the bottom of the tube. This is done by place the support ring under the die and tightening the wing nuts over the side tabs. Try to get the die to seal tight to the bottom of the tube.

On the next page, you will see that you then fill the tube with clay. Try to wedge and then block up the clay so it fits into the tube easily. Next, fit the plunging plate into the tube and use the bar to press it down. Continue to press down as the clay gets extruded out the bottom through the die. Tear off the coils and bring to the table before they break of and fall on the floor!

After you are done using the extruder during a class or wor session, take the die off the bottom and clean it off. Also use a stick or tool to scrape out all the clay inside the tube.

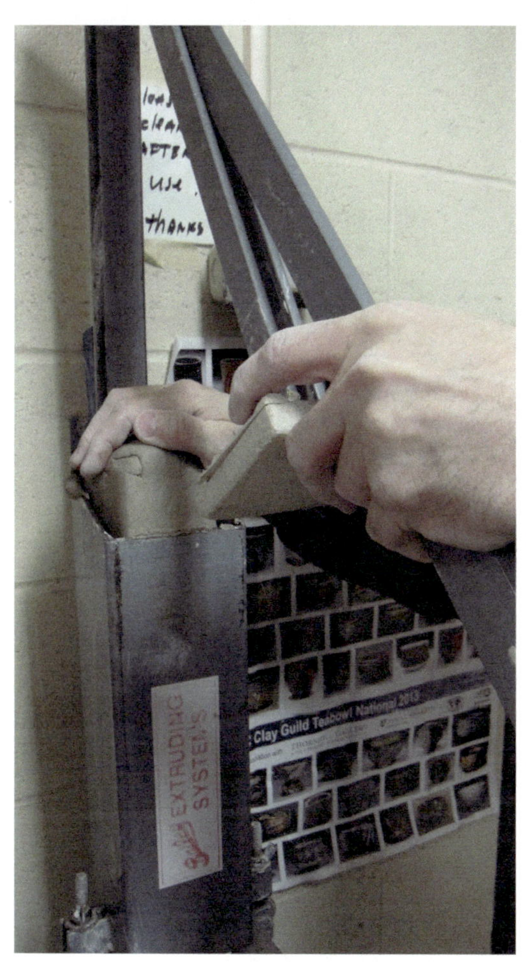

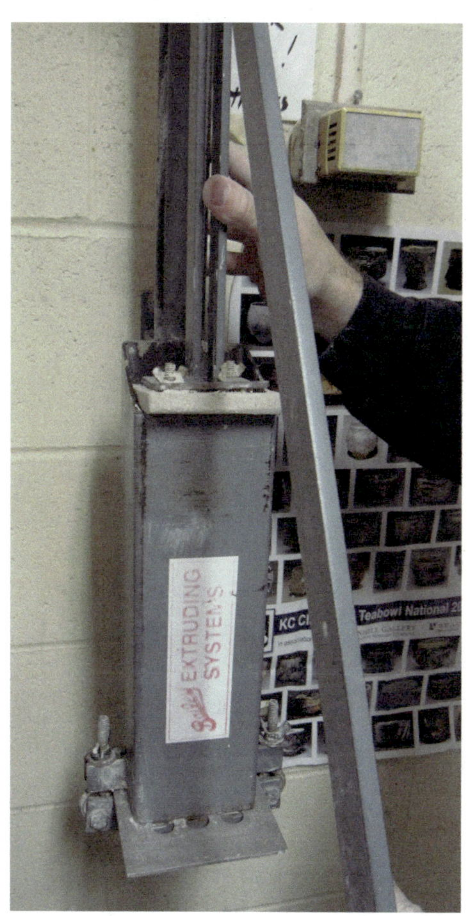

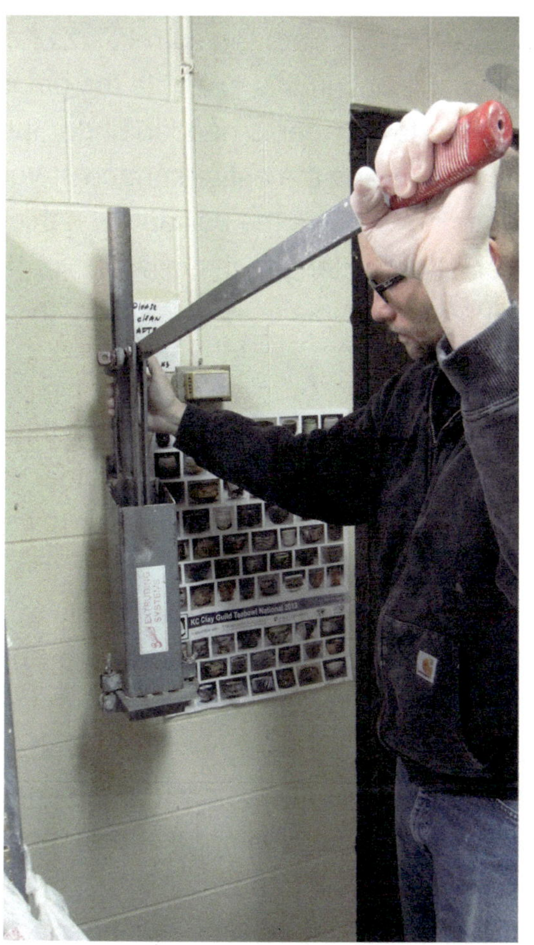

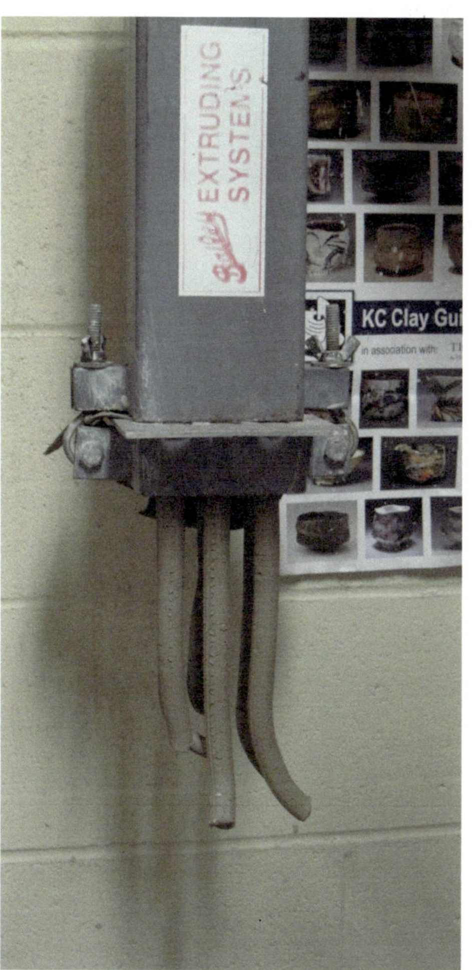

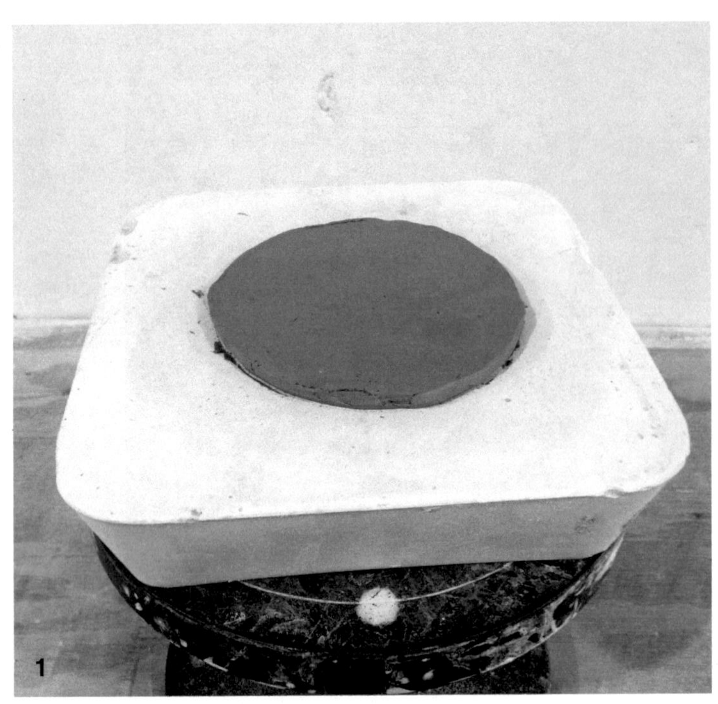

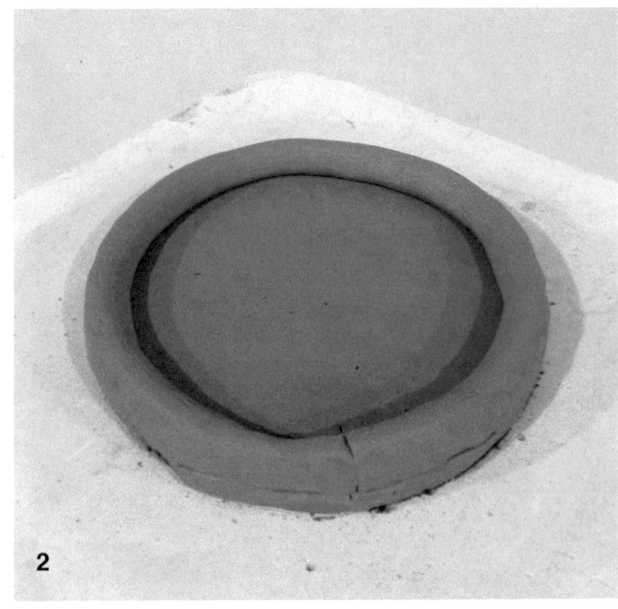

BUILDING WITH COILS

To start, make a solid sheet of clay (a slab) the correct size for the base (image 1). Build on top of a bat, in this example the pot is being built on a plaster bat so no newspaper is needed under the slab. Next, roll coils on the table using the entire surface of your hands (palms and fingers) trying to make the coil an even thickness and round shape over its entire length. If available, you should use an extruder to create multiple coils of identical thickness all at the same time.

Begin by stacking the first coil on the slab base (2). Pinch this coil down to the base. Continue to stack coils on top each other and pinch together to create the shape (3). After three or four rows, begin to blend all the coils together to make a strong, stable shape (4). A great tool to use for surface and shape refinement is a toothed rib. Work over the inside and outside of the shape (5), these marks will be removed later in the process. Continue to add coils as needed. If the form desired is a straight vertical wall, stack the next coils directly top of the ones below it. If the shape moves out, build the next coil on the outside edge of the one below (6). Stack, pinch, and join each row to develop the shape desired (7). If the shape needs to move in, build on the inner edge of

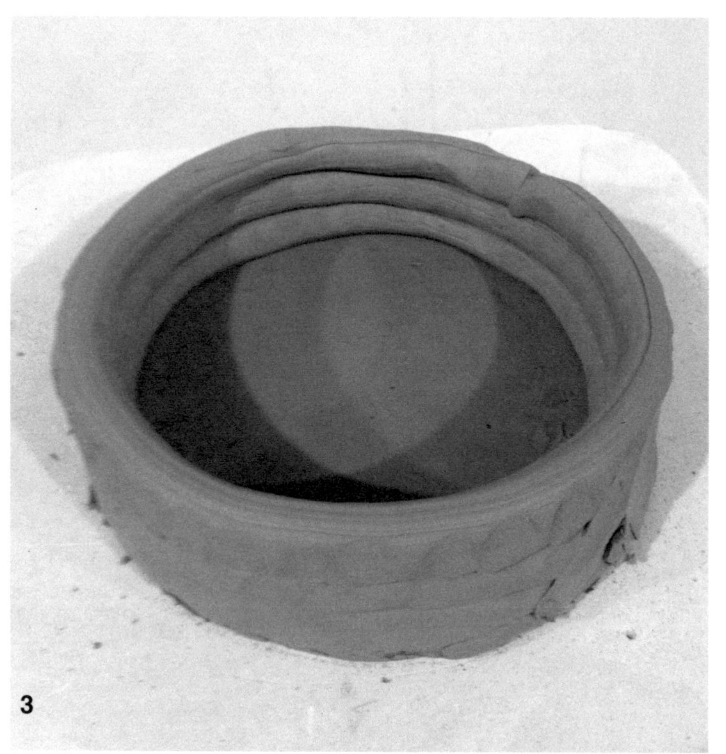

3

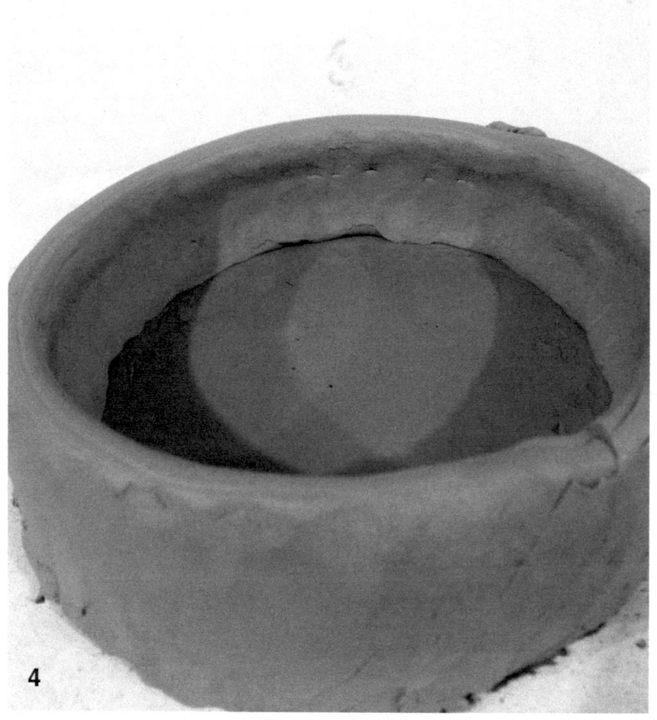

4

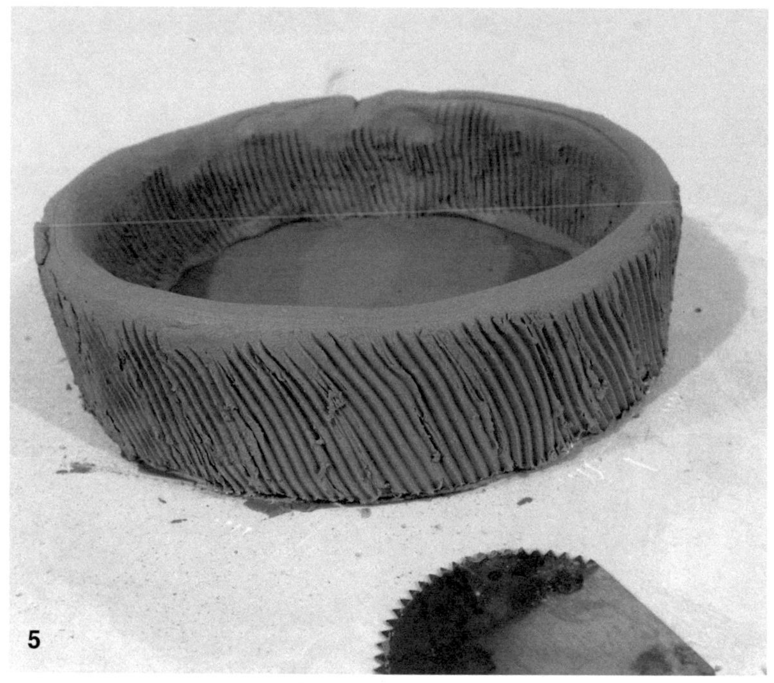

5

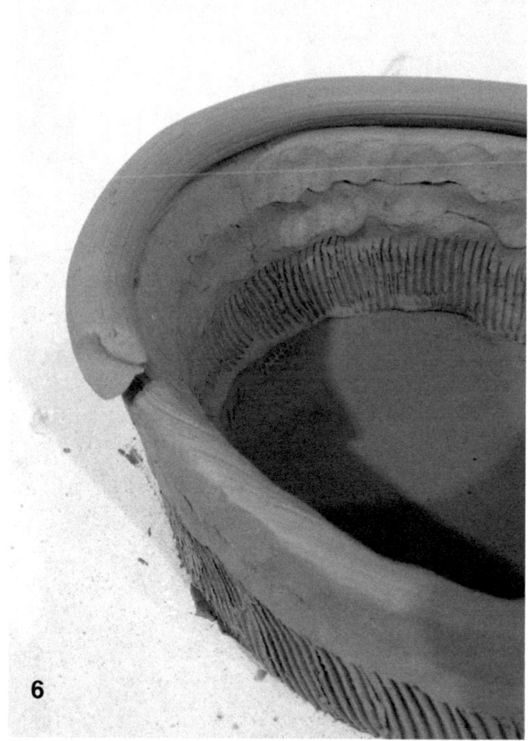

6

the coil below (8). Continue to build and blend coils together on the inside and outside (9). Make sure to check the shape and symmetry by spinning the piece on a turn-table and stepping away from it often. Begin to refine the overall shape by smoothing the toothed rib marks away from the inside and outside (10). As you finish the shape, make sure to cut a bevel on the bottom edge of the piece and also smooth out the top edge to create a fully refined shape.

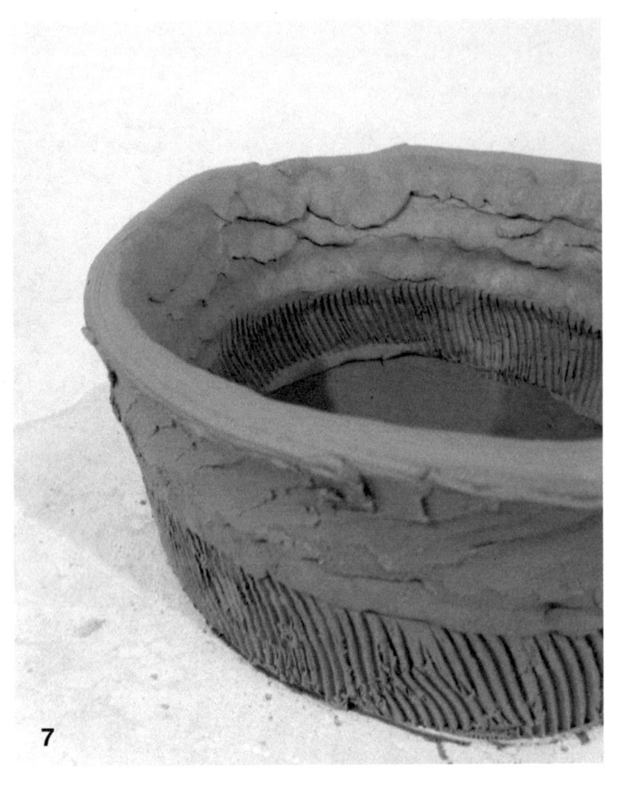

7

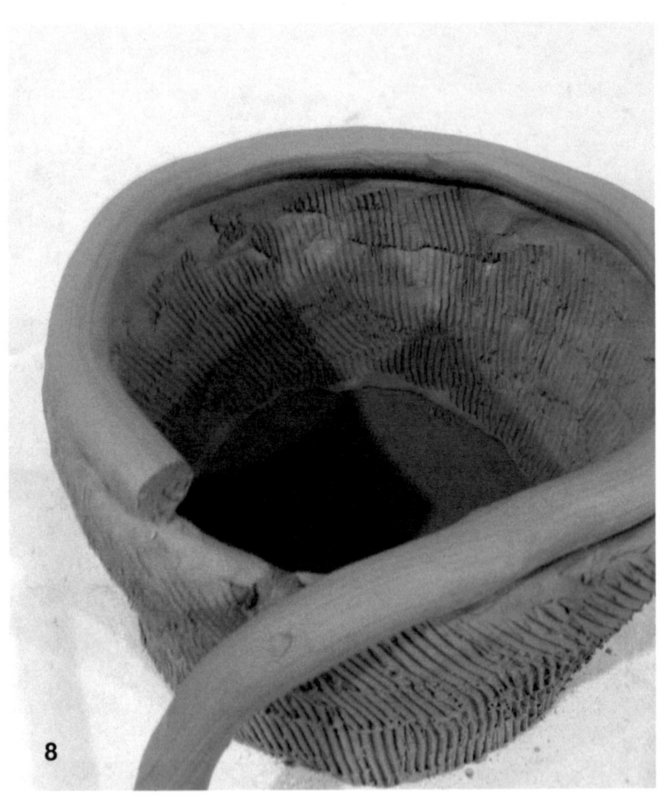

8

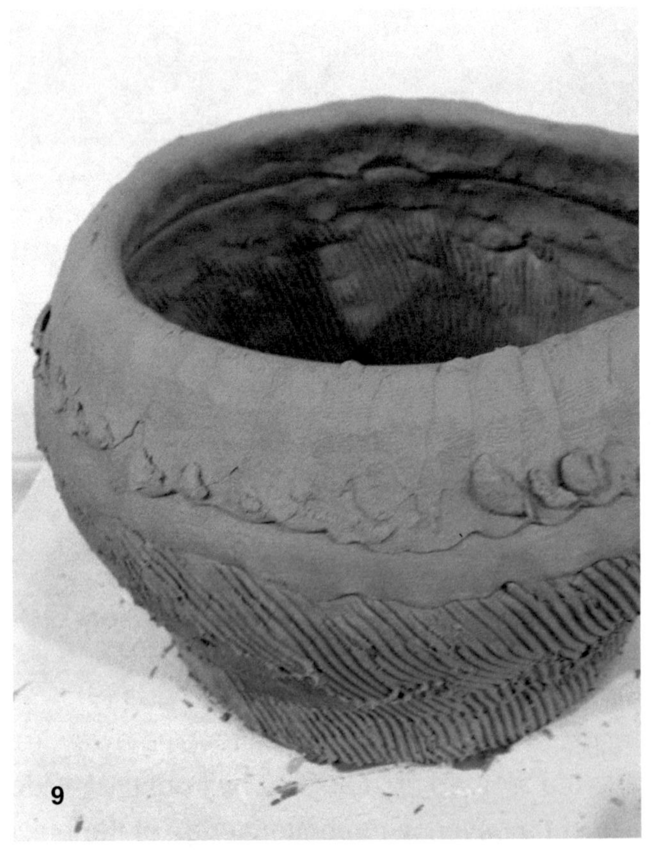

9

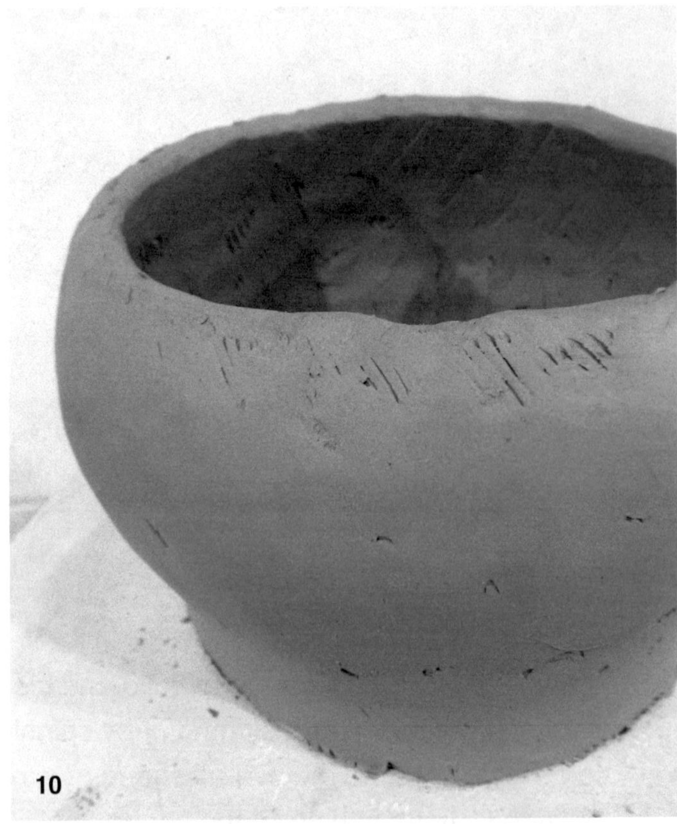

10

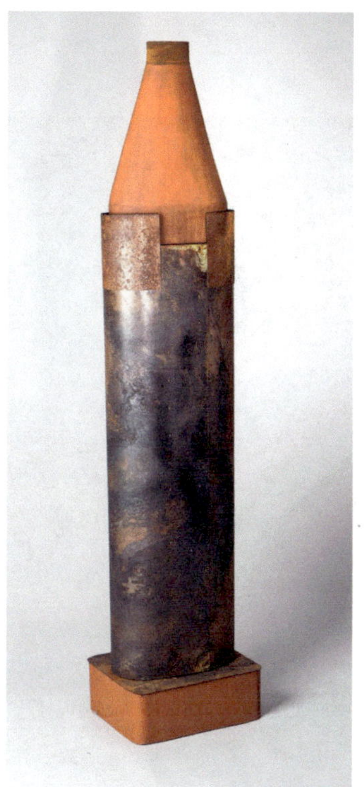

Lynn Duryea, "WRAP", slab earthenware and metal[3]

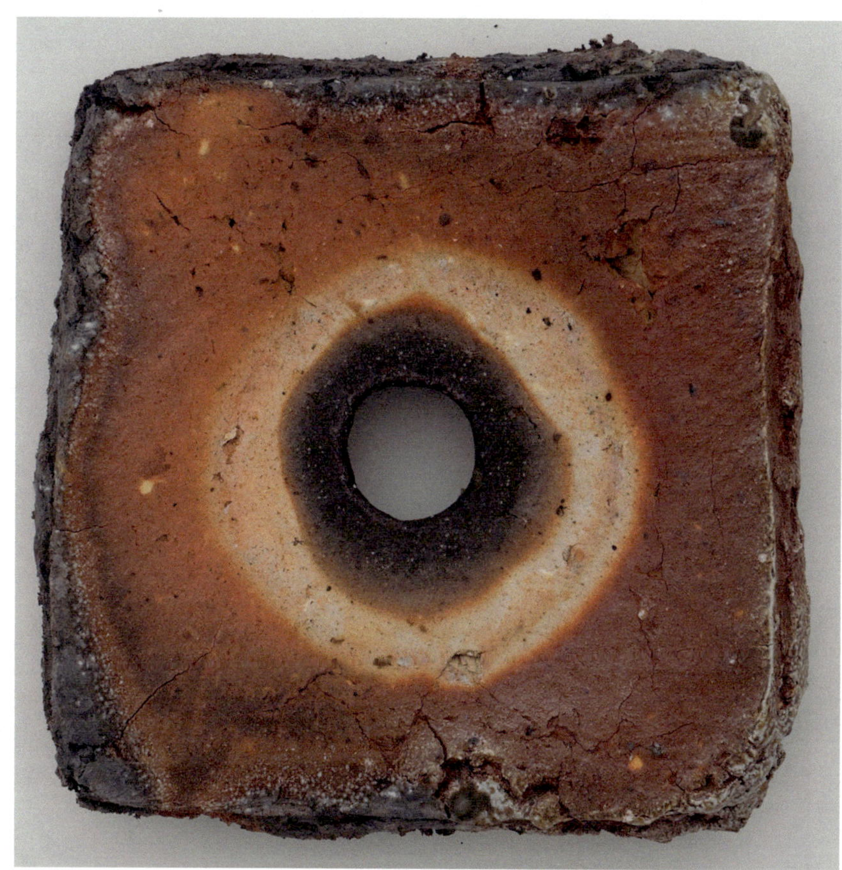

Jordan Taylor. "Square", slab woodfired stoneware[3]

SLAB

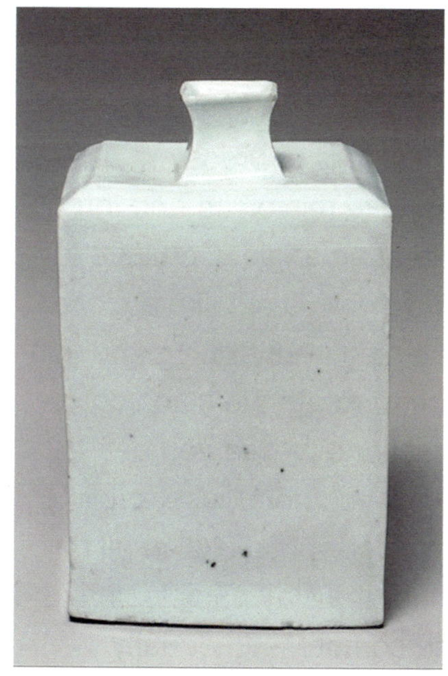

Korean slab porcelain bottle[4]

Slab building can be useful for making geometric forms or flat shapes. Slabs can also be used in conjunction with molds to create a variety of shapes. Slabs are most often made by using a slab roller machine, rolling pins, or throwing the slab out on a table like pizza dough. The process of creating the slab compresses the clay particles but it is a good idea to roll or stretch the slab in multiple directions to prevent any problems with cracking or warping.

There are two main slab construction approaches depending on when you use slabs and what your design requires. For "soft slab" construction and gestural/organic shapes, you will use the slabs soon after rolling them out. This approach is more useful for organic shapes but requires some type of support (molds, newspaper, tar paper, cardboard tubes) to hold the slabs in place as they dry.

The "stiff slab" method uses slabs that were rolled out and then allowed to dry to the near leatherhard stage. This approach is similar to building with wood or cardboard and allows for crisp geometric forms. It is very critical that when leatherhard slabs are joined, you carefully score and add slip to the seam. If this is not done well, the piece will crack apart during drying and/or firing. If possible, add a small coil into the seam to reinforce the connection.

One common and invaluable step is to make a paper or cardboard model of the object you plan to build. Tape this model together to get a sense of the overall shape and proportion. You can then take the model apart and use that as a patten to cut out your slabs.

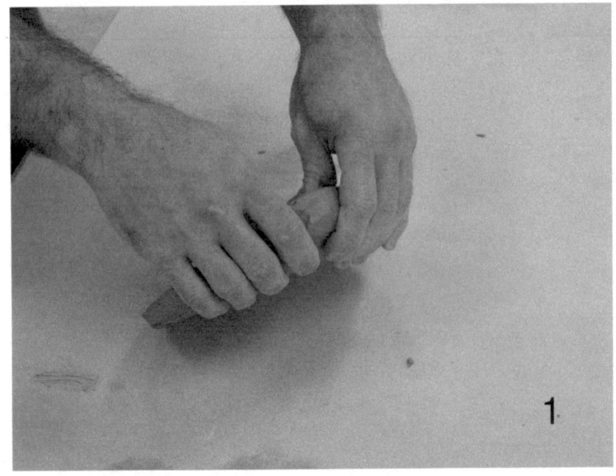

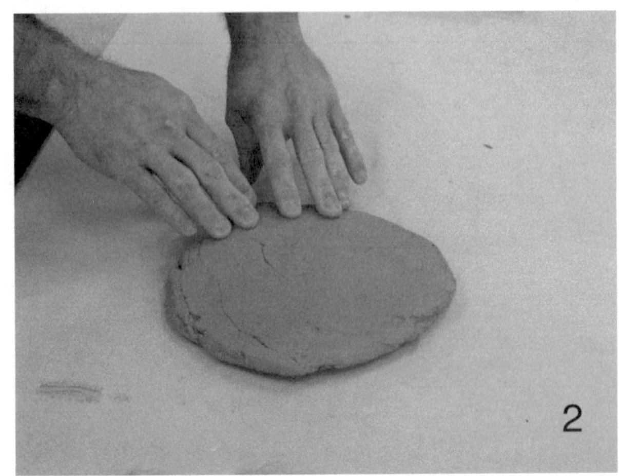

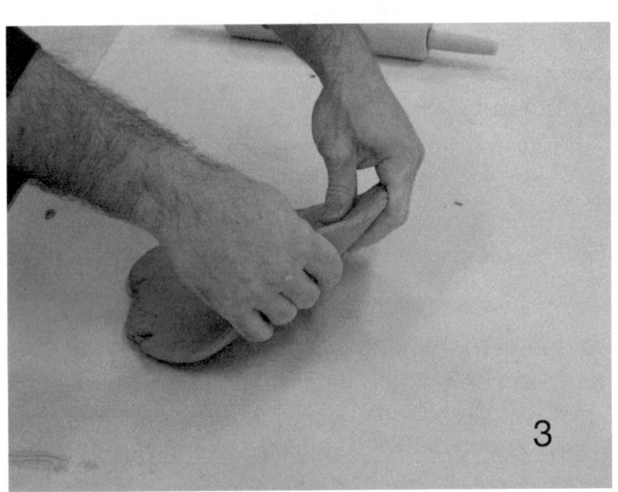

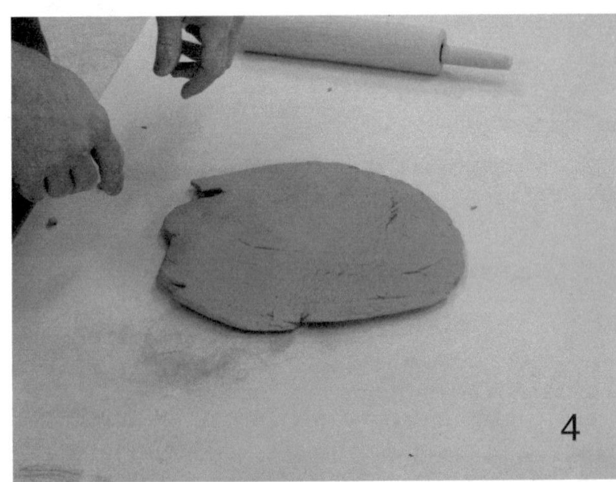

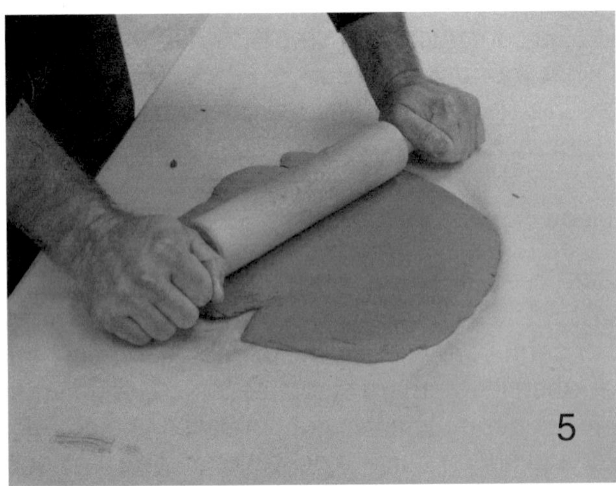

One way to make a slab is to press out a chunk of clay. Then take this piece and throw it down on the table at an angle. Continue to pick up the slab and throw is out like a piece of pizza dough. The clay is stretching and thinning out. Make sure to rotate the slab so it is stretching in all directions. When you get close to the thickness you need, use a rolling pin to even out any thick spots. Roll in all directions to make sure the clay particles have been stretched and compressed equally.

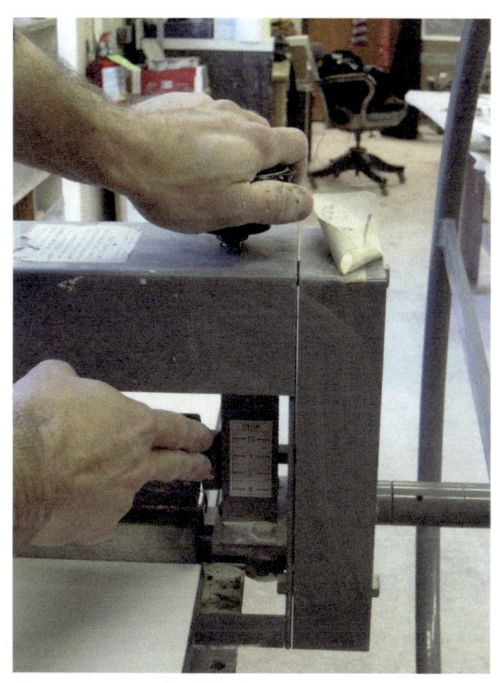
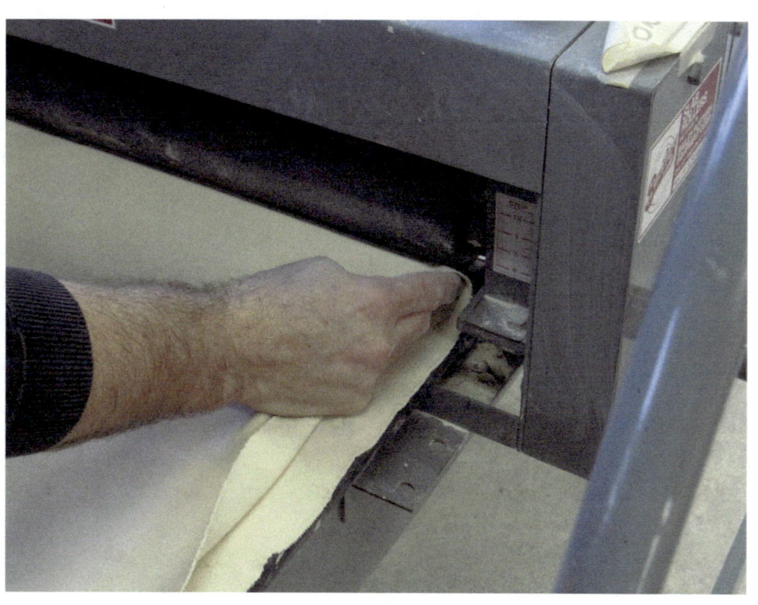
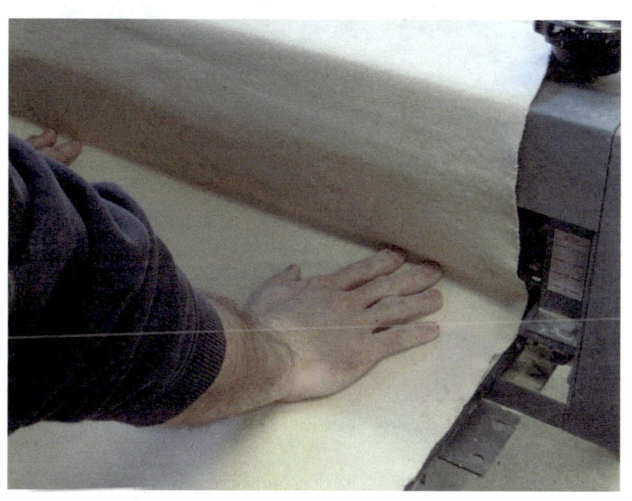
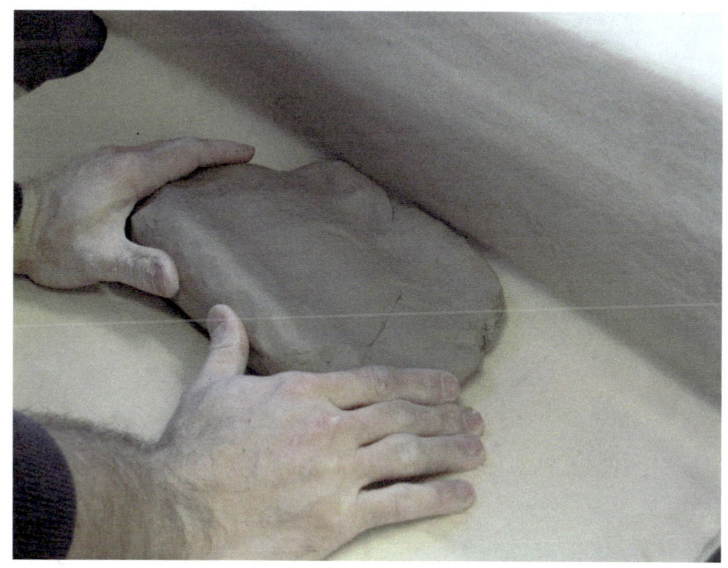
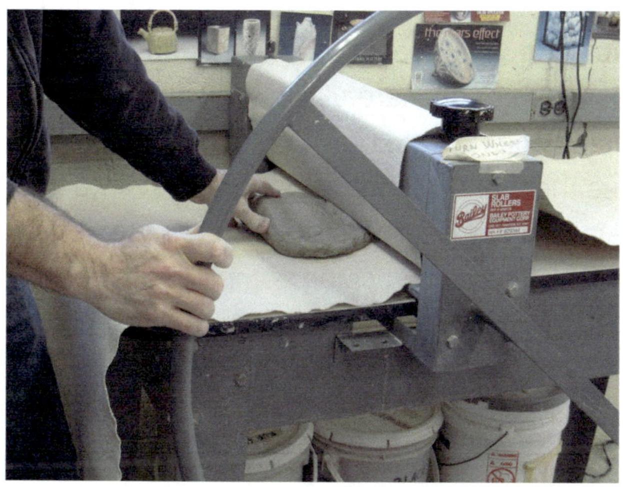

Another way of making slabs is by using the slab roller. The pictures on this page show the beginning of the process. First check and adjust (if needed) the thickness of the slab. For most things you need a slab around a 1/4" thick. Then fold the canvas in half and place the fold where the 2 rollers come together. NO CLAY should ever touch the rollers, only canvas should be in contact with the rollers. Next, take your lump of clay that is shaped into a rough wedge and place it up to the fold/rollers. Turn the gear wheel toward yourself to start the process.

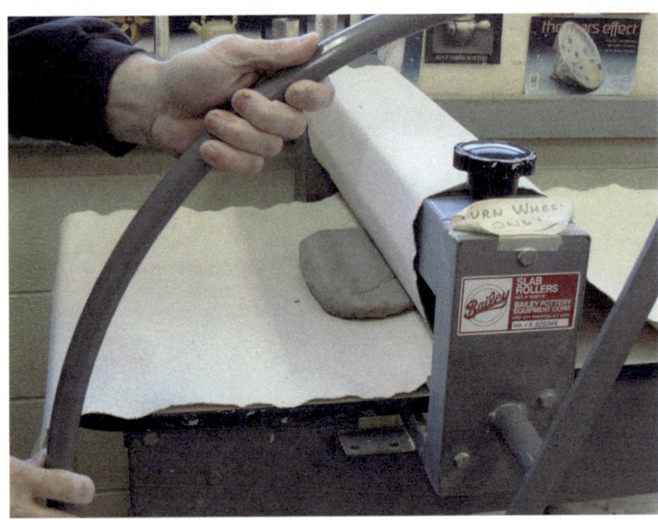

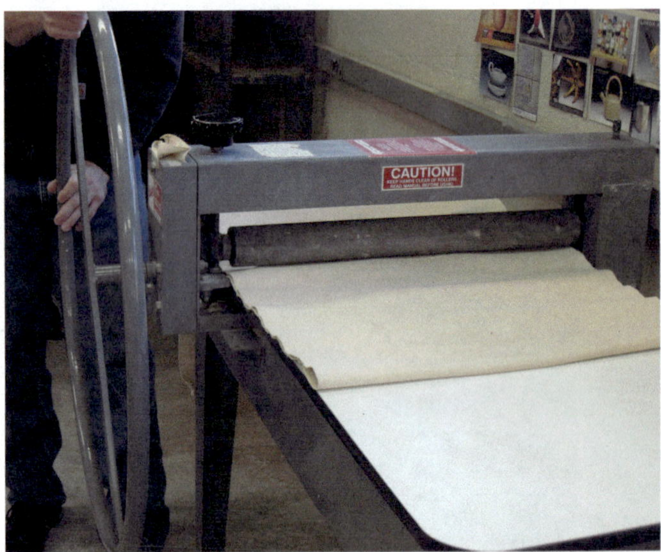

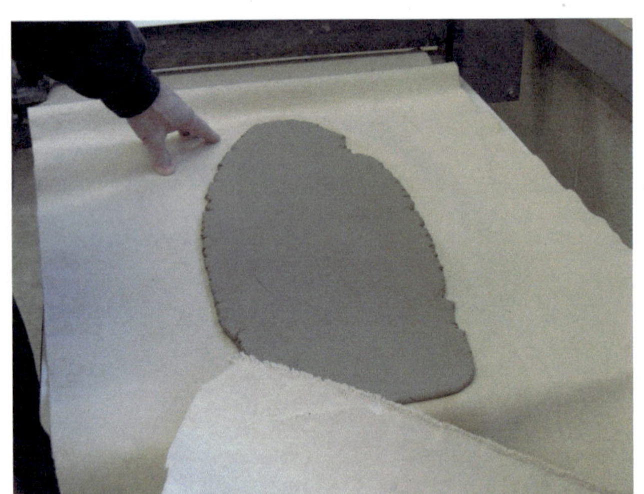

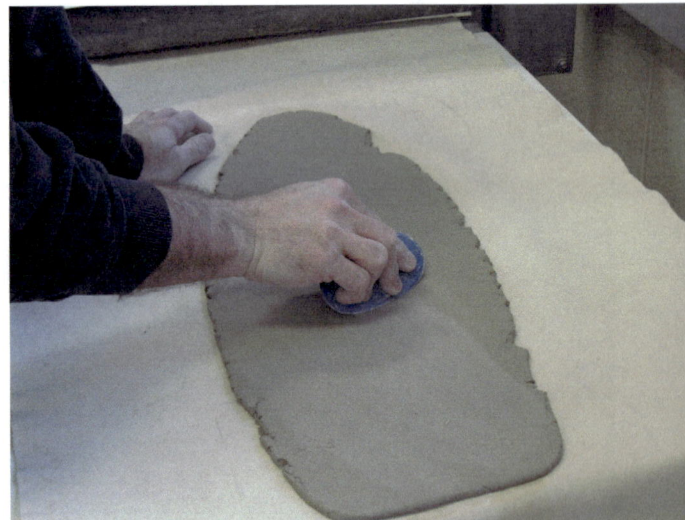

Continue to turn the wheel toward yourself to pull the clay into the rollers. The new slab will push out onto the table surface. Once all the clay has been pulled through, carefully pull the upper canvas layer off the slab. Use a soft rib to remove the canvas texture from the slab. You can use the canvas to move your slab over to the table to continue working. There is one major point to note about how this machine works. The slab is being compressed mostly lengthwise but not much in width. The best thing to do is make sure the block of clay you start with is wide enough for your needs before you begin to roll it through the machine.

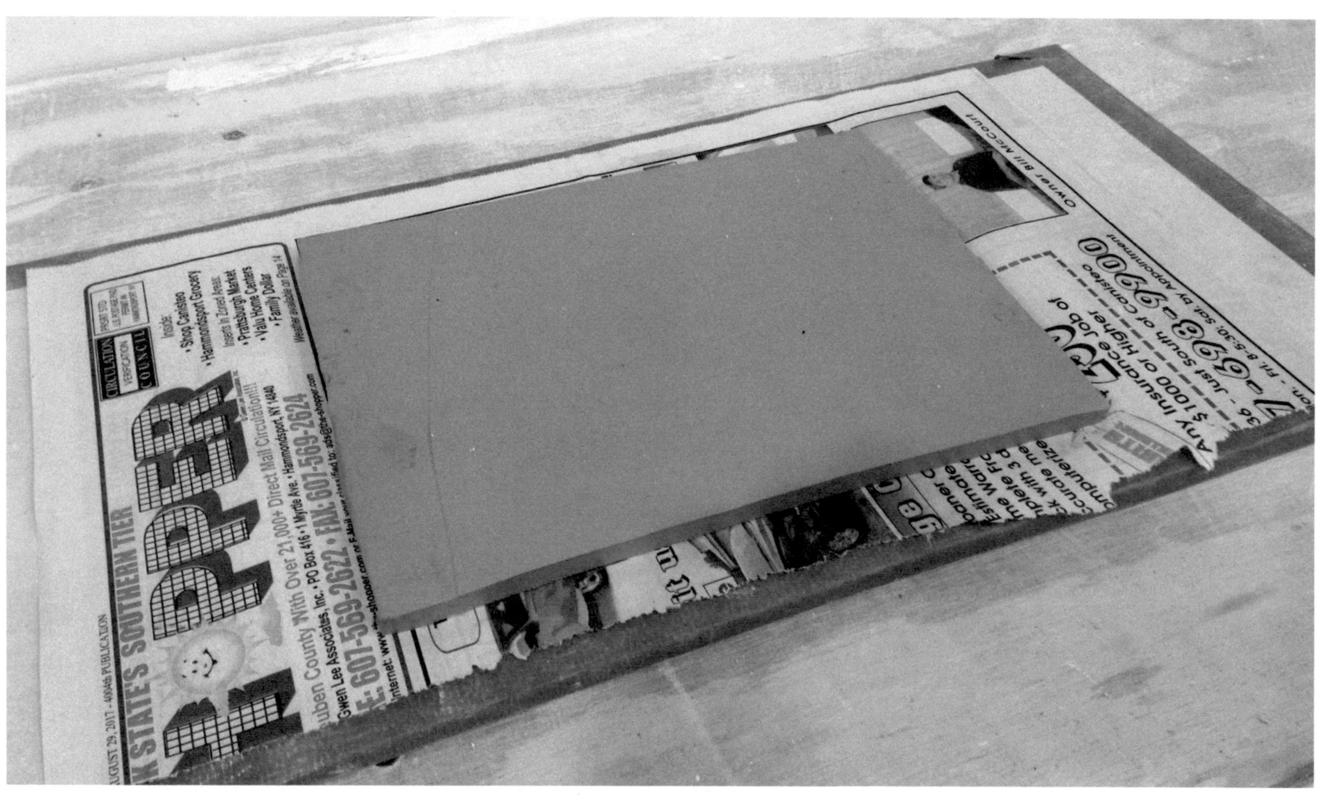

1

BUILDING WITH SLABS

Start with the base slab on a board with newspaper underneath. This example (a rectangular dish) is being built on a scrap piece of drywall (image 1). This material is used by many ceramic artists because moisture will be absorbed off the bottom of the object as it sits on the board. Scrap drywall pieces should have the edges taped so that the drywall powder does not get mixed into the clay.

This pot is being built with slightly dried slabs so that they have some flexibility but at the same time, will stand up well. Once the base is set, begin assembling the sides by scoring and slipping the seams and edges of the slabs (2). As you create corners, roll thin coils and blend them into the seams between slabs to serve as reinforcement (3). Complete the construction by attaching all the necessary sides making sure to blend and compress all the corners and seams between slabs (4). Continue to refine the sides, angles, and corners with ribs and other tools (5). Make sure to finish the top and bottom edges so that all elements of the object are well made.

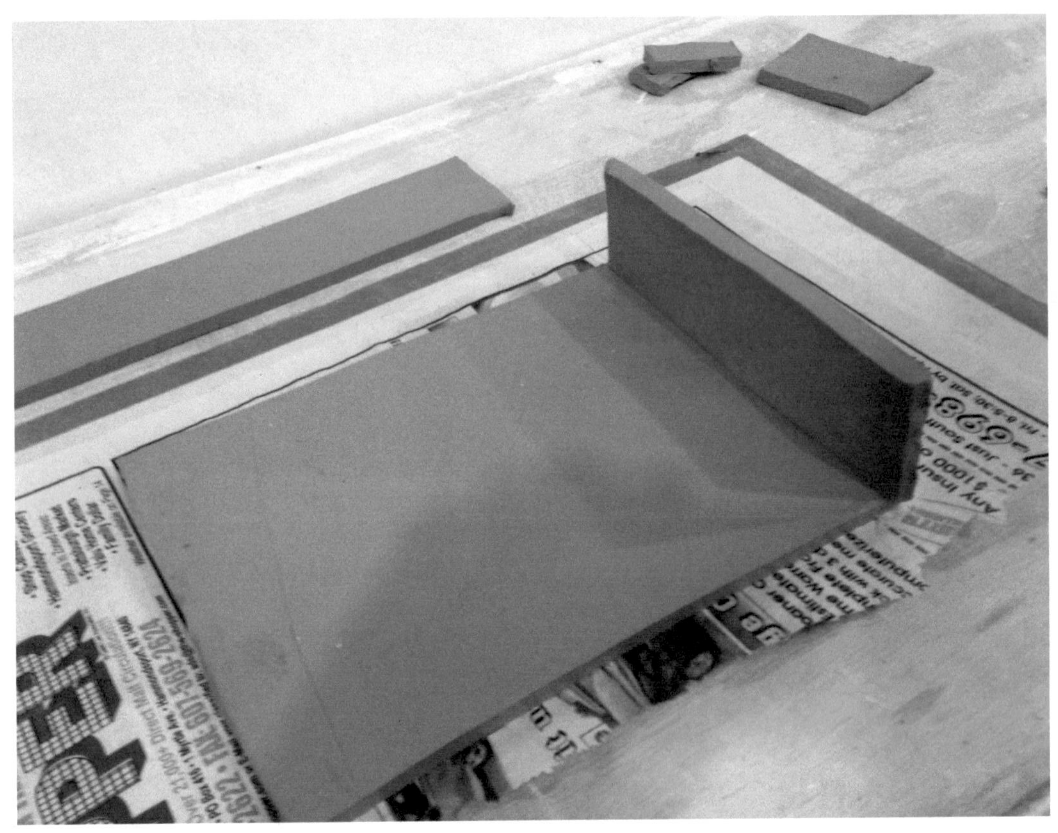

2

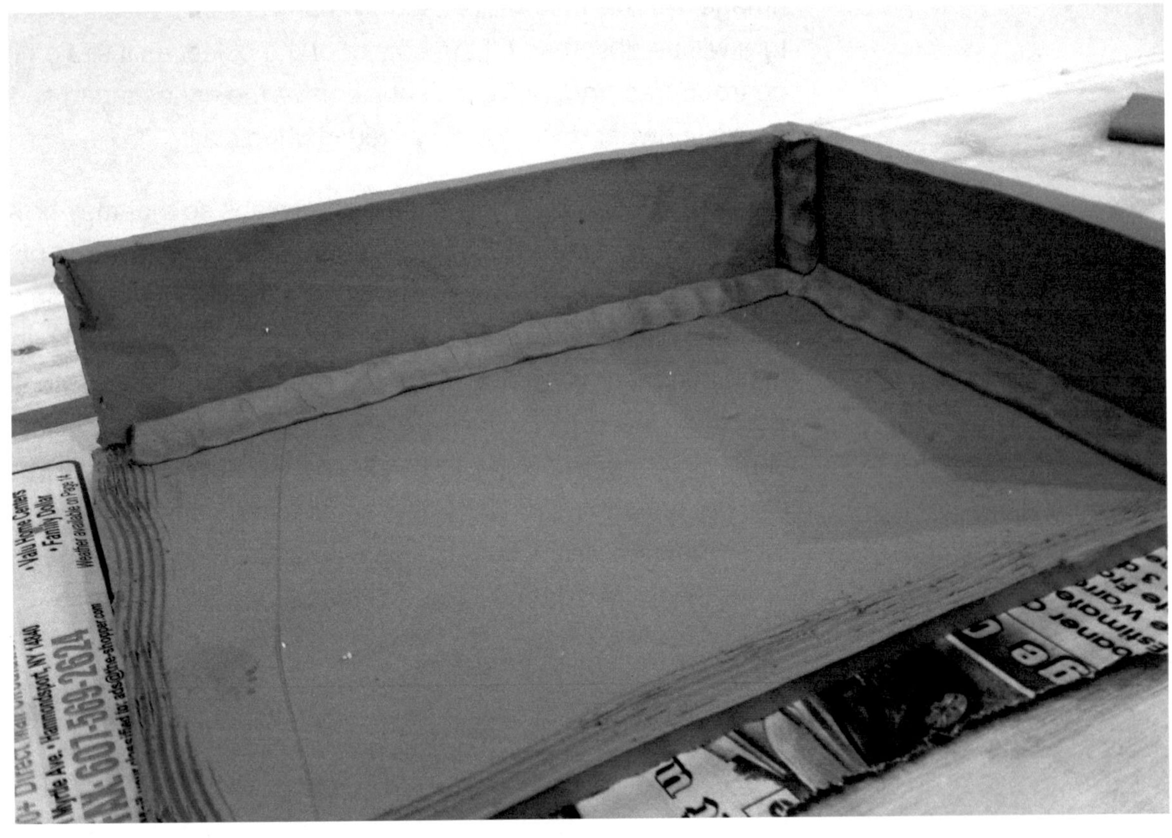

3

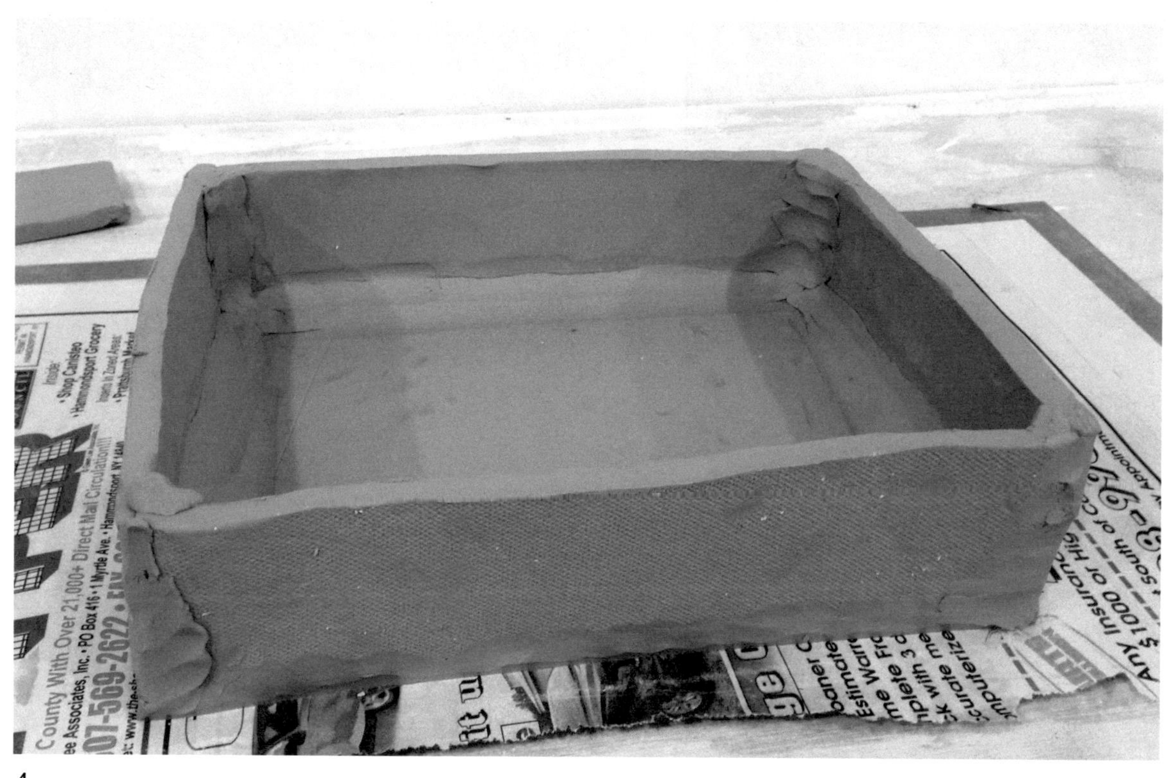

4

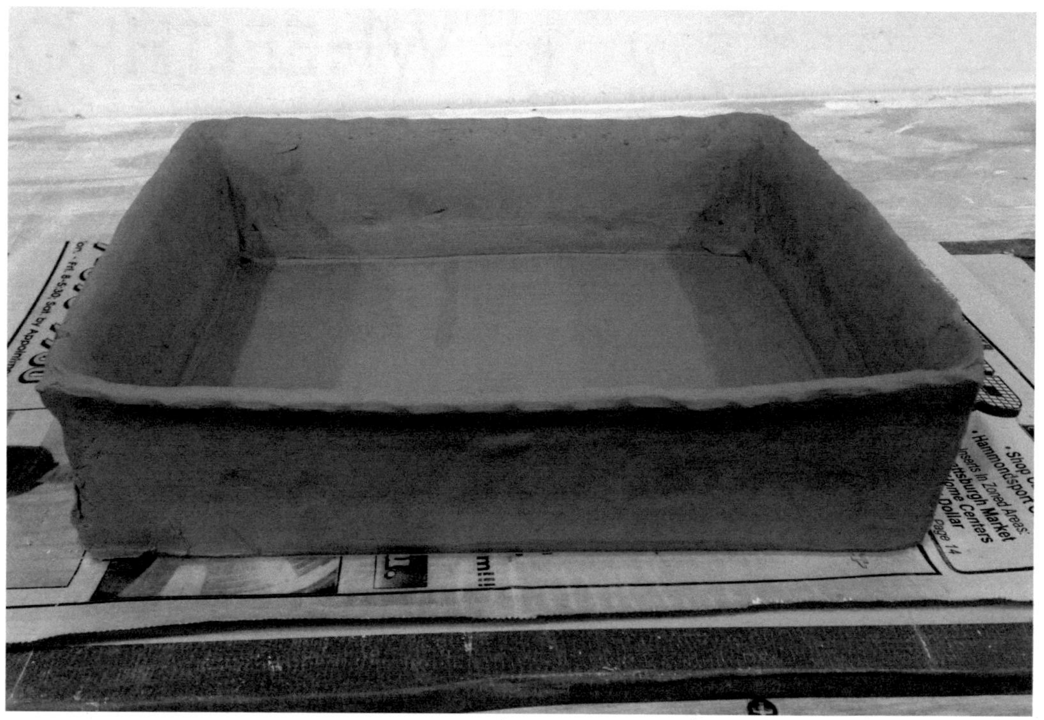

5

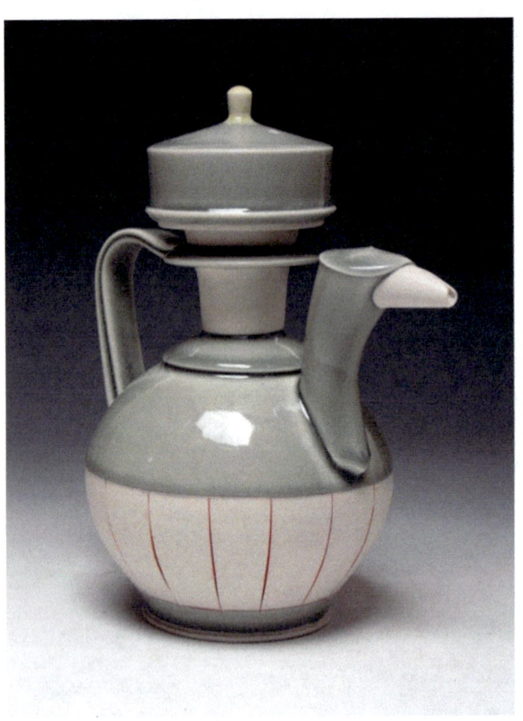

Shawn Spangler, "Ewer", wheel thrown porcelain[2]

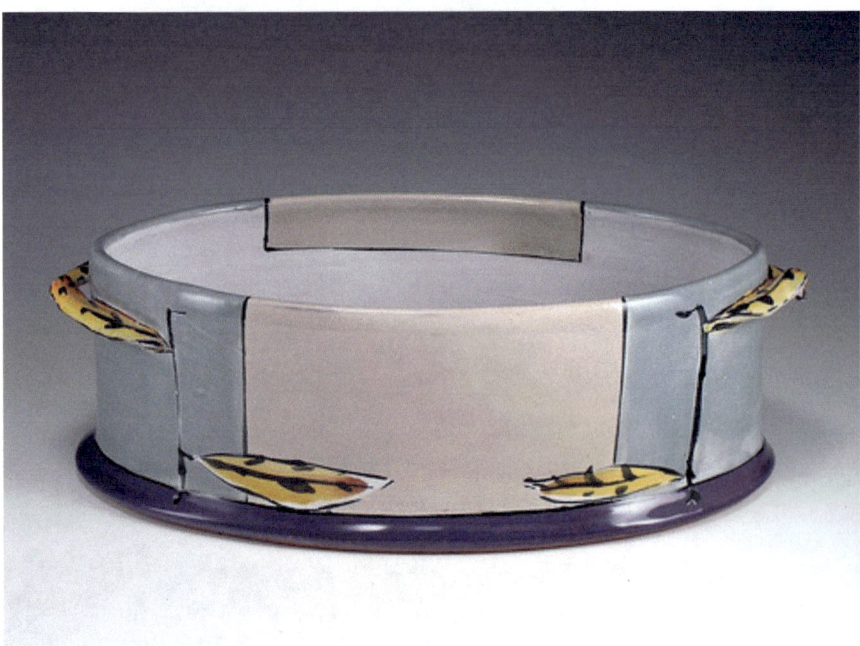

Linda Arbuckle, "Oval: Structure of Fall", wheel thrown and altered earthenware[2]

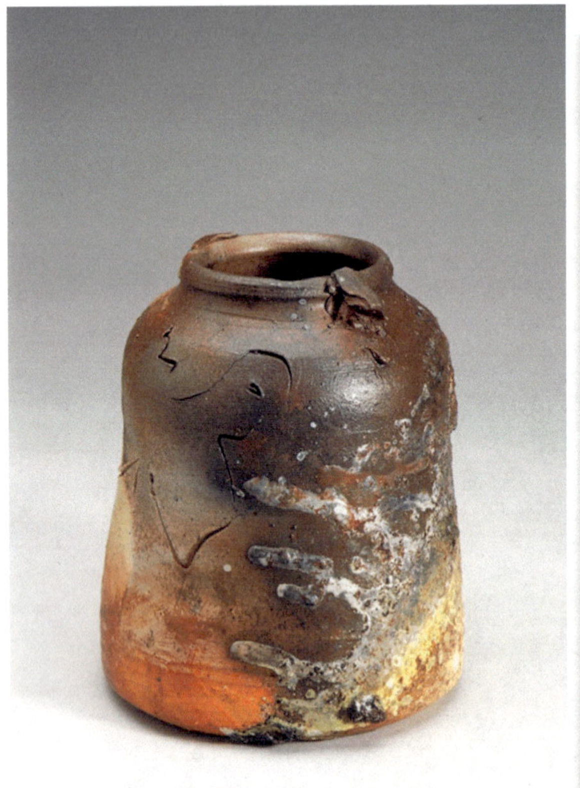

Janet Mansfield, wheel thrown woodfired stoneware[3]

6

WHEELTHROWING

The invention of the potters wheel revolutionized the production of ceramics. It is unclear where and when the potters wheel was invented but some theories are Egypt around 3,000 BCE, Mesopotamia (modern Iraq) around 3,130 BCE, or South Asia around 3,500 BCE. These ancient dates show that wheel thrown ceramics had a vital role in ancient ceramics history and that it remains a vital part of ceramics to this day.

There are some production advantages with the wheel. These include the ability to make symmetrical, thin, precise, rounded forms much more quickly than handbuilding. A disadvantage may be that the circular axis of the wheel can make it more difficult to create non-round forms.

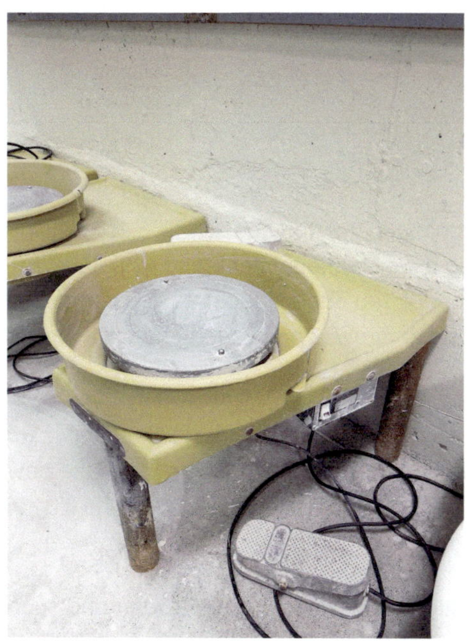

Brent brand electric wheel[1]

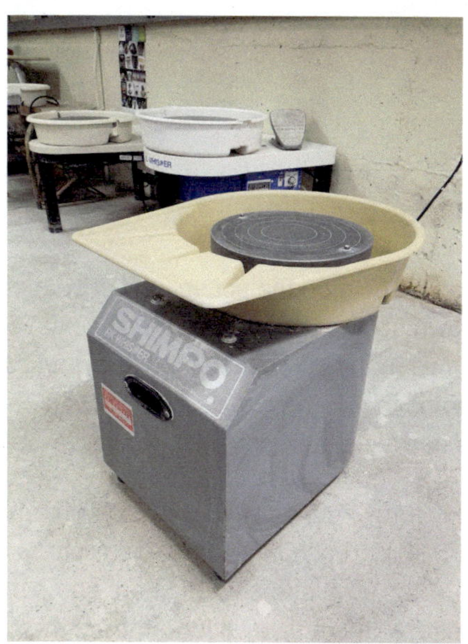

Shimpo brand electric wheel[1]

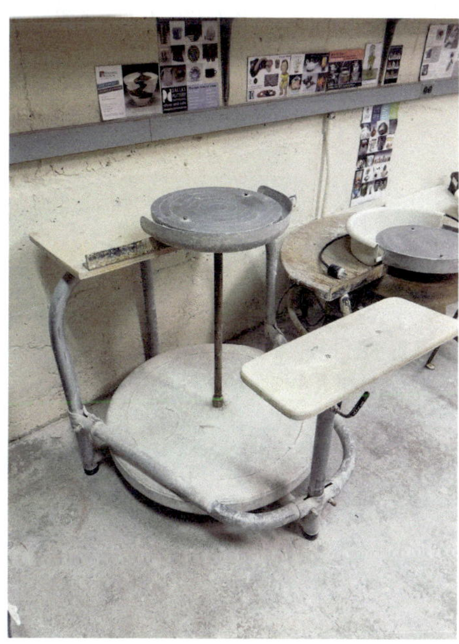

Thomas Stuart brand kickwheel[1]

WHEELS

There are a variety of potters wheel styles and formats. The earliest ancient wheels may have been a thick stone disk spinning on a peg set into the ground. From there, the tool evolved to become taller and include a fly wheel the potter kicked to spin the wheel head. This allowed for much greater speed and consistency. Today some potters continue to use kick or foot powered treadle wheels but most use electric powered wheels that give a good deal of speed and power control.

Regardless of the power method (foot or electric motor), the main goal is to spin the wheel head with controllable speed, torque, and stability.

All images in this section[1]

Steps for throwing-

All work thrown on the potters wheel starts with some basic concepts and body positions. Each artist will develop their own specific hand positions to achieve the goal of making a well crafted, interesting wheel thrown object. Watch as many different people throw (including a huge number of You Tube videos) as you can to see some variations that may work well for you. The only way to learn how to throw is practice, make mistakes, learn from those mistakes, and continue with more practice.

For any thrown object, you will start with one of two orientations. The vertical (cylinder) is first and is for forms such as cups, vases, teapots, and pitchers. The second is a horizontal (bowl) and is used to make bowls, saucers, plates, or platters. Both share some common hand positions but the cylinder is moving the clay in and up. In contrast, the horizontal form moves the clay out and up slightly.

To get started, make sure clay is wedged and prepared correctly. Get a small bucket of water and sponge, some plastic bats, a pin tool, a wood knife, a cut-off wire, and a variety of rib shapes. Pat the clay into ball shape and throw it down in the center of wheel. The wheel should be spinning counter clockwise if you are right-handed, some wheels allow a change in direction so make sure it's moving the way you want.

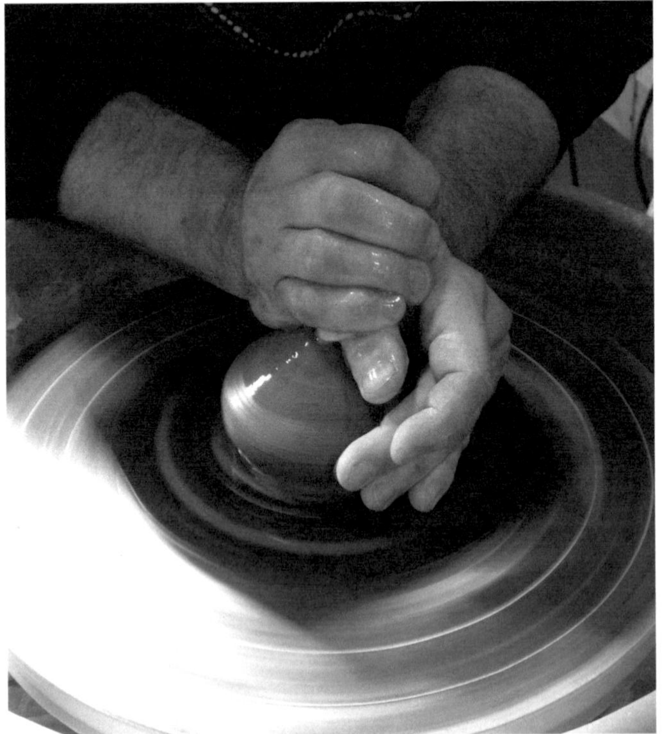
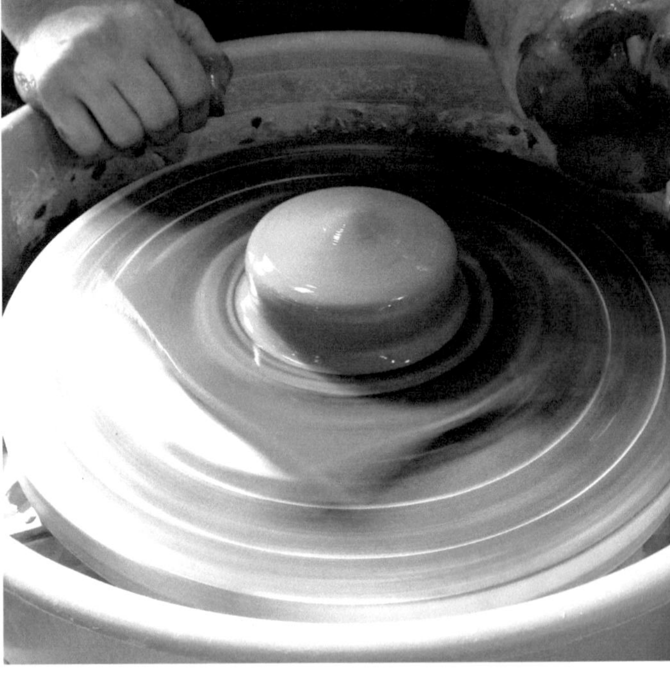

1. **Centering**- The wheel should be going very fast in order for the spinning (centripetal) force to help you move the clay into the center of wheel-head. The mound of clay needs to be pushed forward toward the center from behind with strong even pressure. Lock your elbows into your hips or body and lean forward just a bit to push into clay with heals of hands. Try to lock your hands together so they are working as a single unit. You are looking to have a perfectly symmetrical domed shape with straight side walls. Don't do anything else until the clay is fully centered. A variation of centering uses a motion called coning. Squeeze the clay up on the sides with even pressure to raise up a cone shape. Then push forward and down to bring the clay back into center.

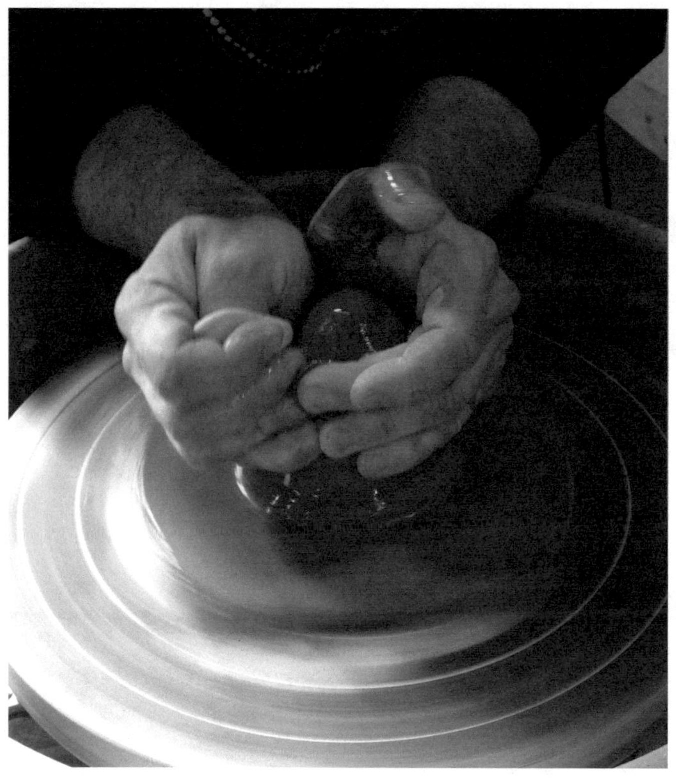

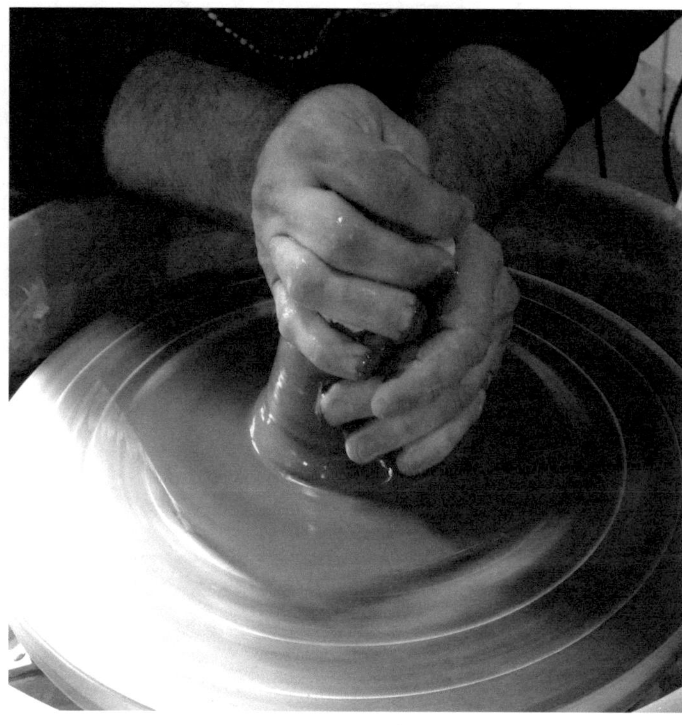

Steps for coning up the clay-
1. Squeeze in and up on the sides
2. Once you reach the top, start to push forward and down
3. Push down and away from you to center the clay

Coning may help you center if the clay hasn't been wedged very well.

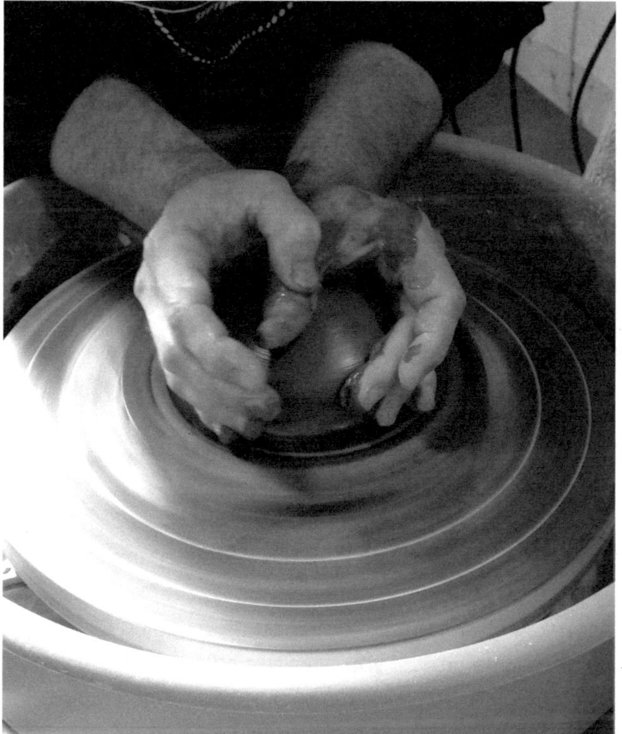

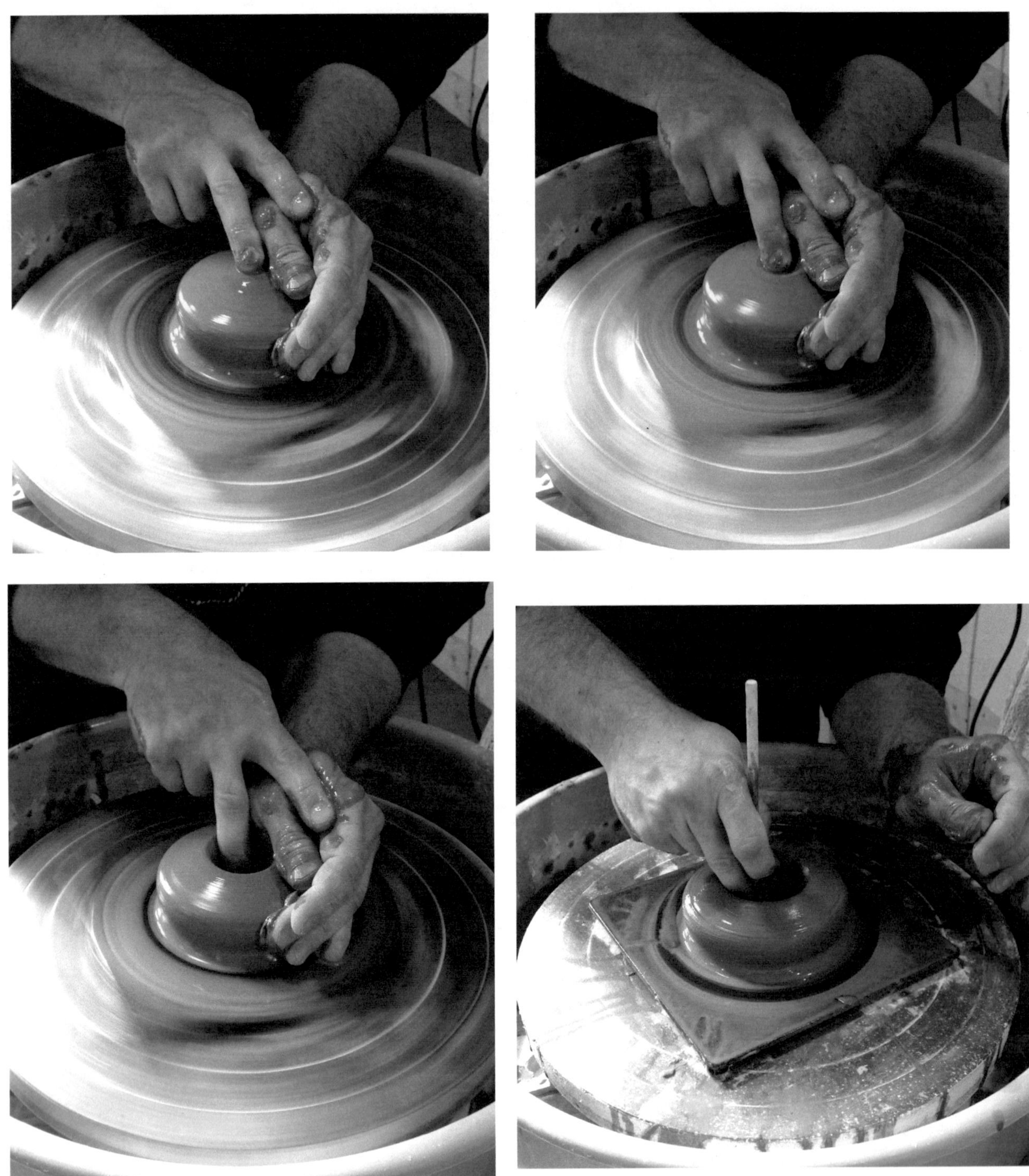

2. **Opening up**- After mound is centered, it is necessary to open the inside to shape the interior of the form and allow the walls to be raised. Keep your arms braced and slowly push down into the center of the mound with your fingers or thumbs. Push to within ¼" of the bottom, checking with a pin tool often to make sure you aren't going too deep. Flatten the bottom by pressing you fingers down and sliding out at the same time. If you are forming a cylindrical piece, make sure that the bottom is flat. Check to see that where the bottom joins the walls, there is a corner not a curve. The mound should now look something like a fat doughnut of clay. It should still be spinning symmetrically in the center of the wheel.

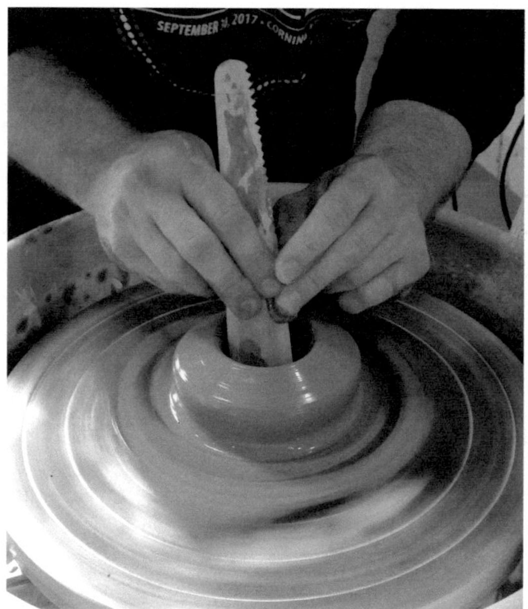

Compressing the inside bottom with a long rib after opening up.

3. **Pulling up the walls**- If you are throwing counter-clockwise, place your left hand inside the form and right hand opposite it on the outside at about 4:00 on the clock. Squeeze in starting at the bottom and move up the wall at the same time. You will make multiple passes from the top to the bottom in order to make the thickness of the clay move up into the wall and begin to shape your vessel. You will also need to adjust the amount of pressure you squeeze with as the clay begins to thin out. At the bottom, you will be able to squeeze harder than you will in the middle and at the top of your form. The wall of the vessel should be an even thickness all the way. You will also need to push in a bit as you pull up the walls to prevent the form from flaring out too much. After each pull, carefully press down on the lip of the shape. This will compress the clay edge making it stronger and slightly thicker. Smooth this top lip out with your fingers as the wheel spins. The goal is that you finish the pulling up process in 3 passes. This is usually not what happens!

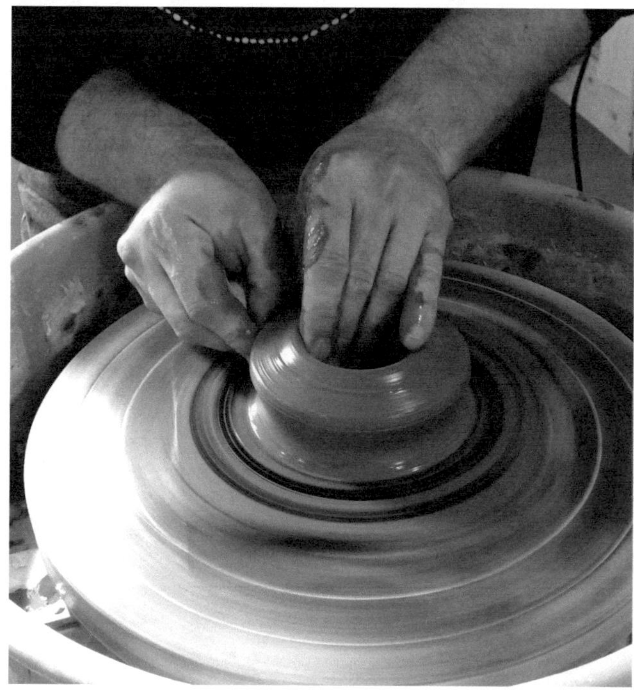

Pass 1

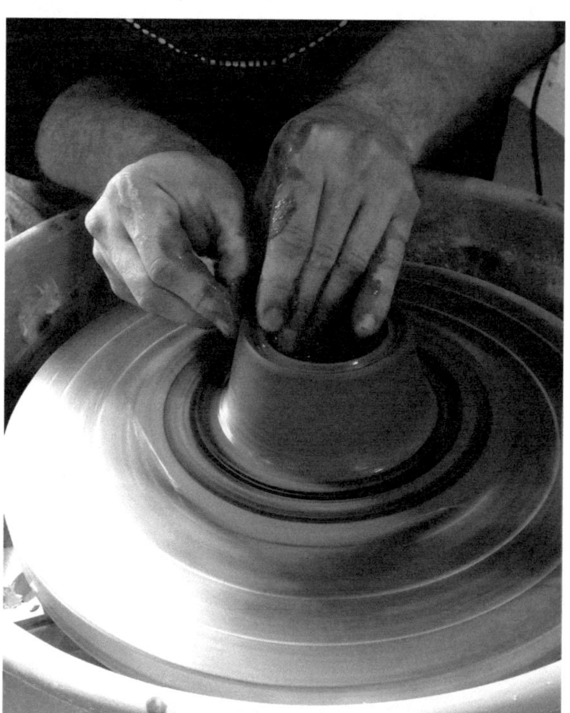

Pass 1

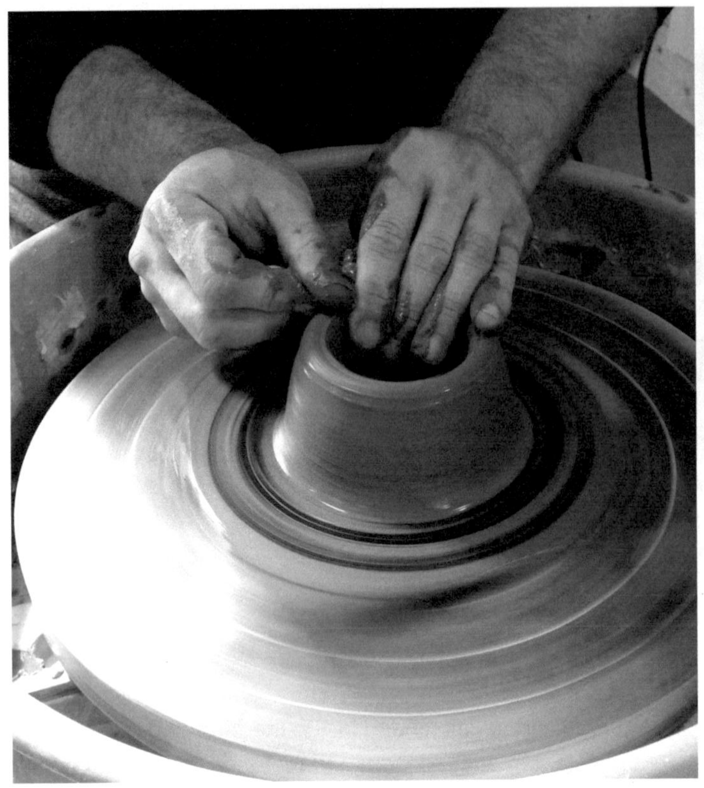

Pass 1

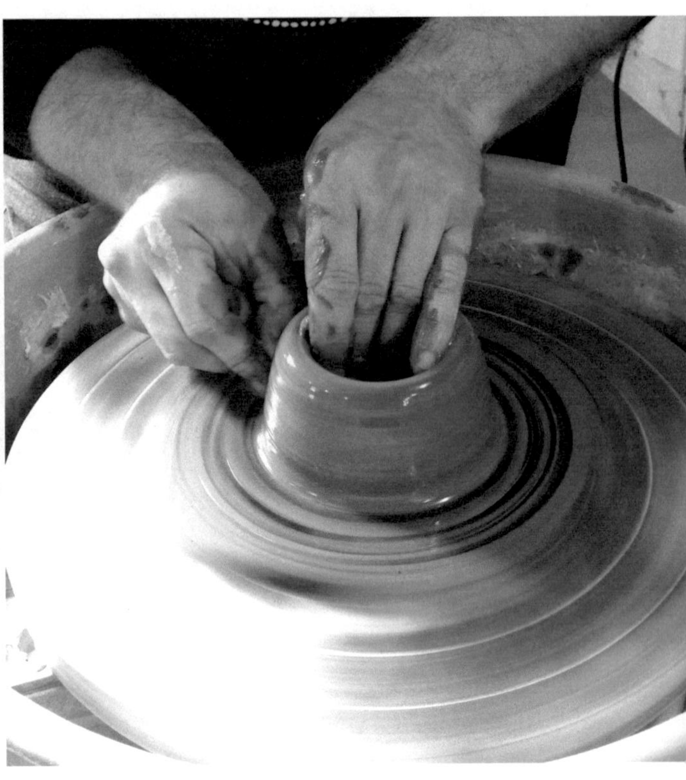

Pass 2

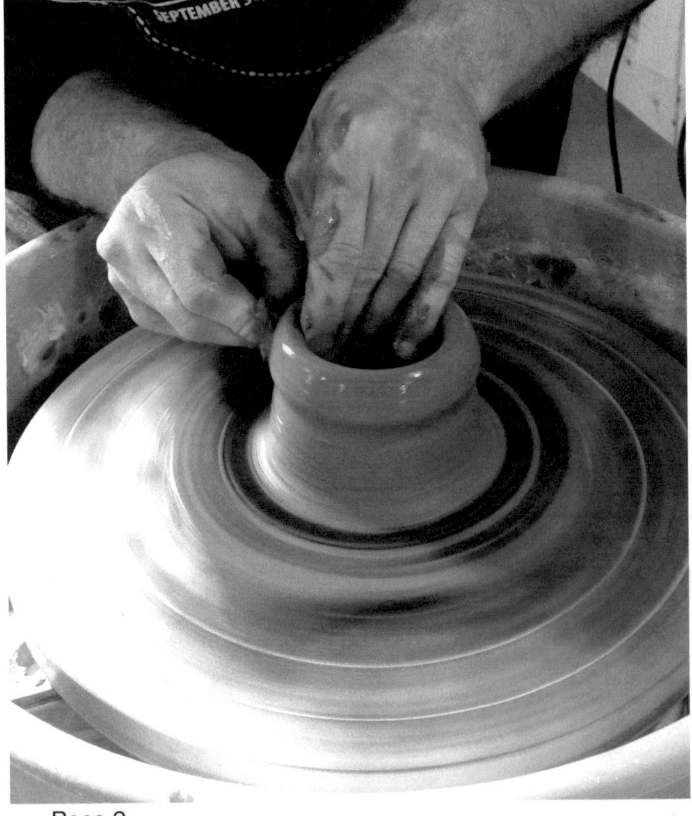

Pass 2

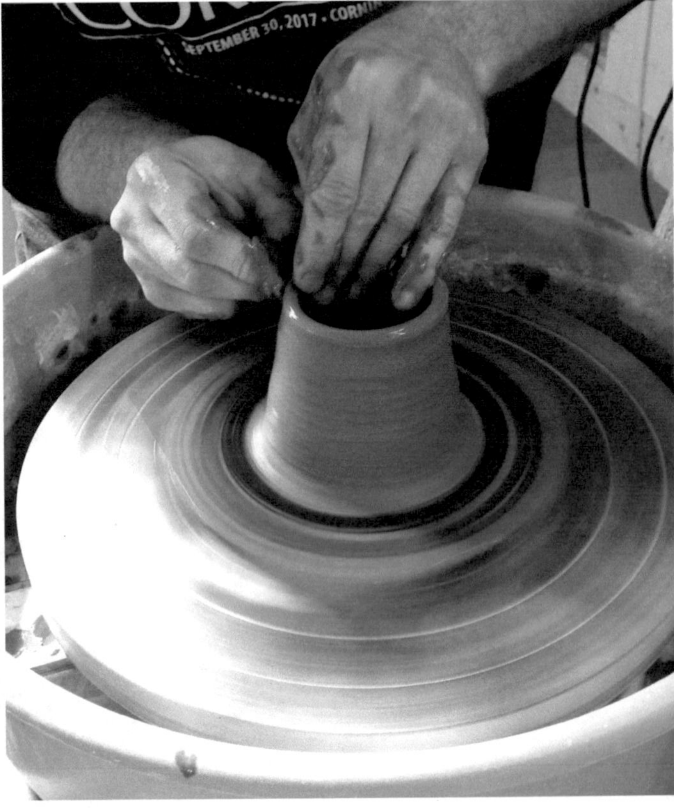

Pass 2

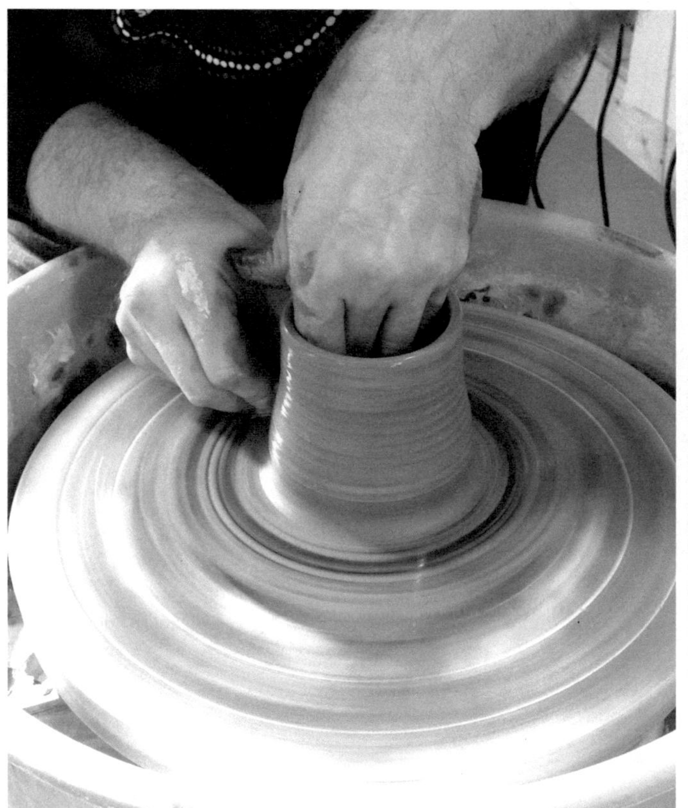

Pass 3

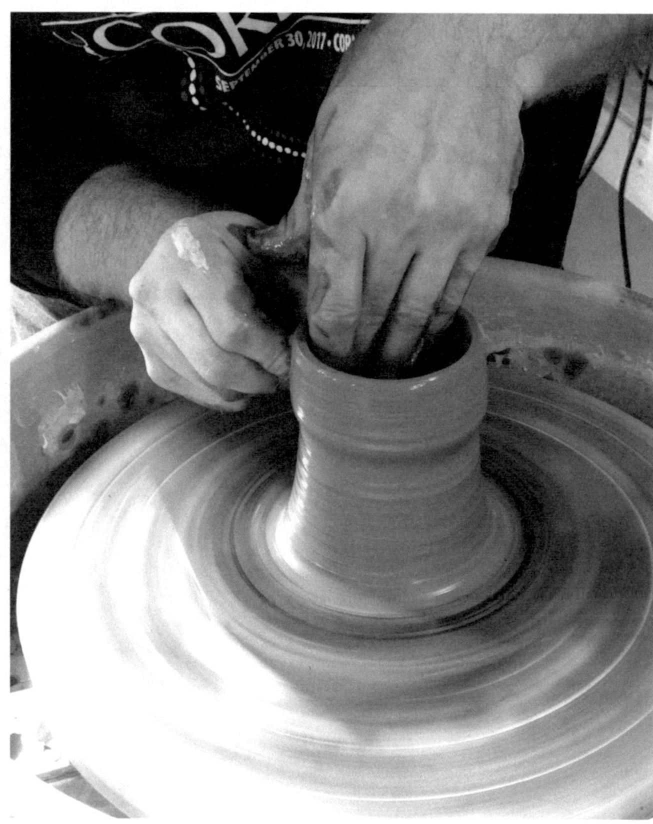

Pass 3

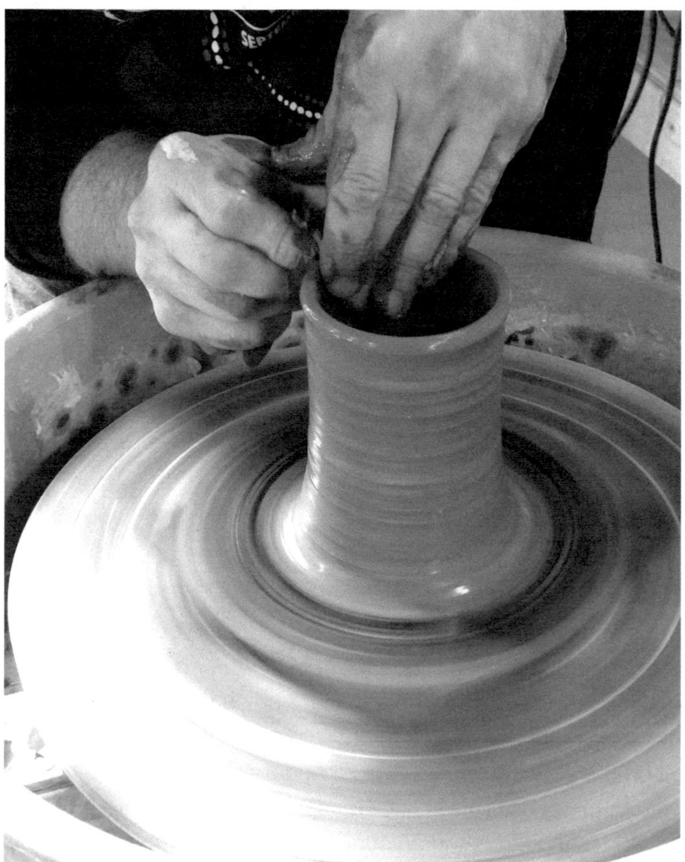

Pass 3

Before you move on to the next step, make sure that the wall thickness is even from top to bottom. Also, make sure that the top lip is compressed and smooth.

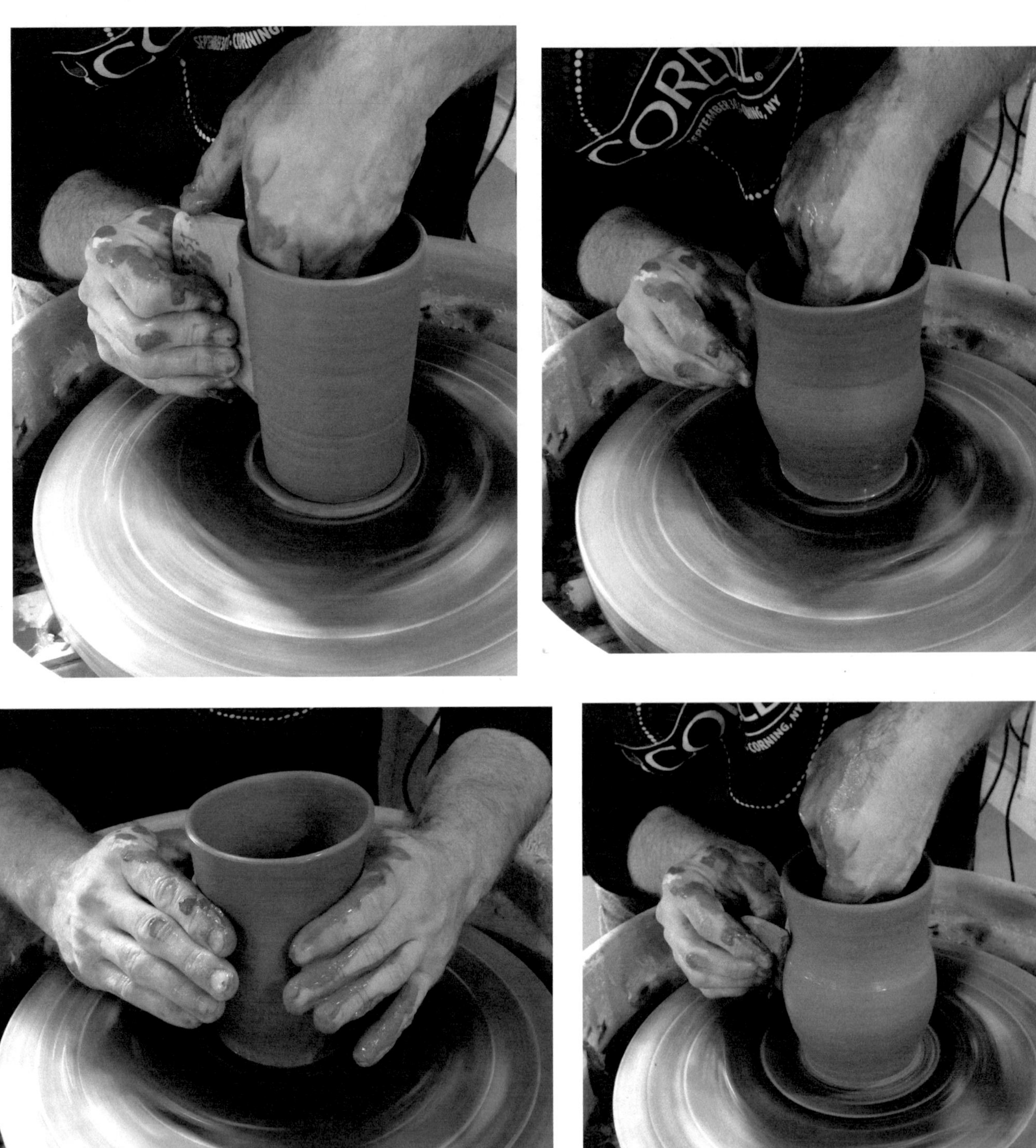

4. **Shaping**- After the walls are pulled up and are as thin as needed, use a rib to clean up the outside of the form. Make sure to support the pressure of the rib by having your left hand inside form. Move the rib from bottom to top compressing the clay wall, removing some of the excess wet slip from the surface, and cutting away the extra clay at the base. Now comes the most important part, the shaping of the vessel. In order to curve the form out, push harder with your inside hand (always supporting the wall on the opposite side with your fingers or a rib). If you want to move the shape in, carefully squeeze in and slide up with both hands. This is known as collaring. Be aware that as a shape is bellied out, the thickness of the wall thins where it is being stretched. In contrast, where a form is being collared the wall thickens and must be re-thrown to thin it back out. The variety of shapes possible is almost infinite just by alternating pressure in and out and by using a variety of tools.

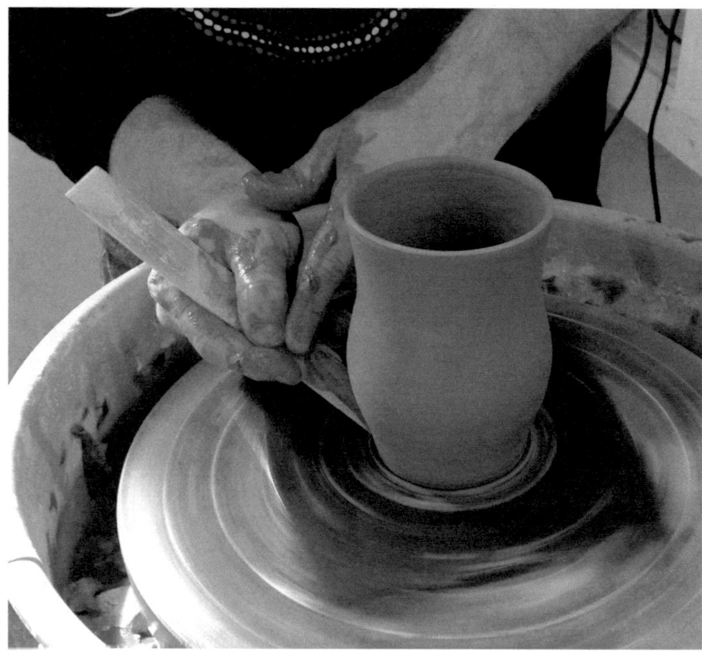 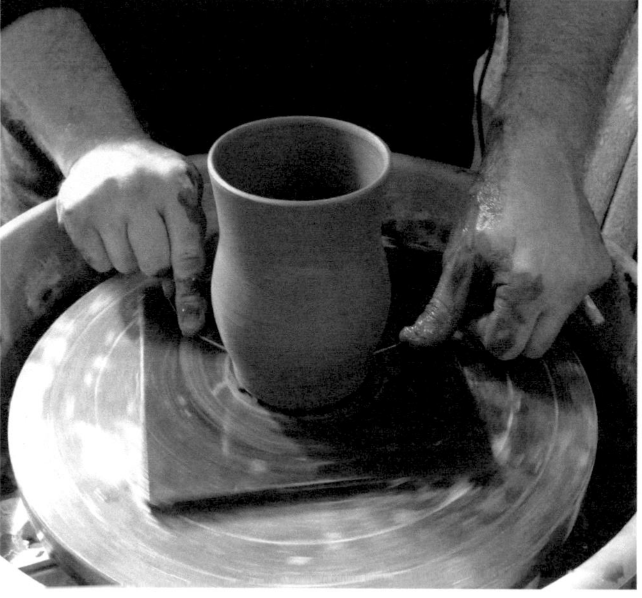

5. **Cutting bevel and cutting off**- After the form is shaped, you may want to carefully rib the outside one more time. Then use your wood knife to remove any extra clay at the very bottom and create a slight undercut bevel at the base. The last step is to cut the form off the bat by cutting under with your wire tool. Once cut off, the pot can be left on the bat to firm up to leatherhard or carefully taken off the bat and placed on board.

Horizontal / Bowl Forms:

When you are throwing a horizontal axis form, many of the steps are the same. The centering process is the same although you may want to center lower and flatter than the cylinder. The first difference is in the opening up. Open wider and at more of an angle, avoid creating a flat bottom on the inside. Make sure to leave more thickness in the bottom than normal since that will help support the shape and allow for a foot detail later. Start to pull the clay up and diagonally out to create the inside of the bowl.

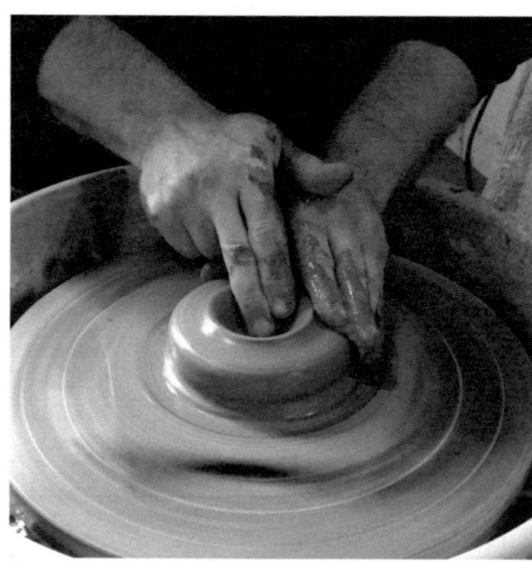 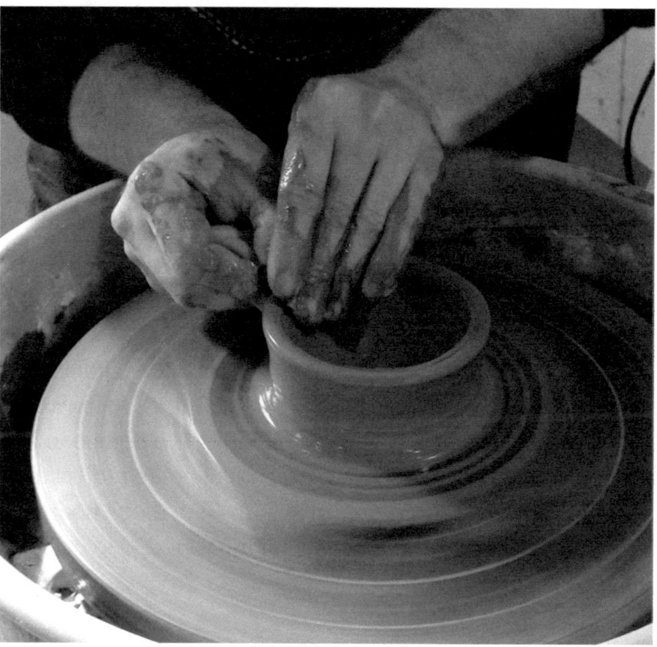

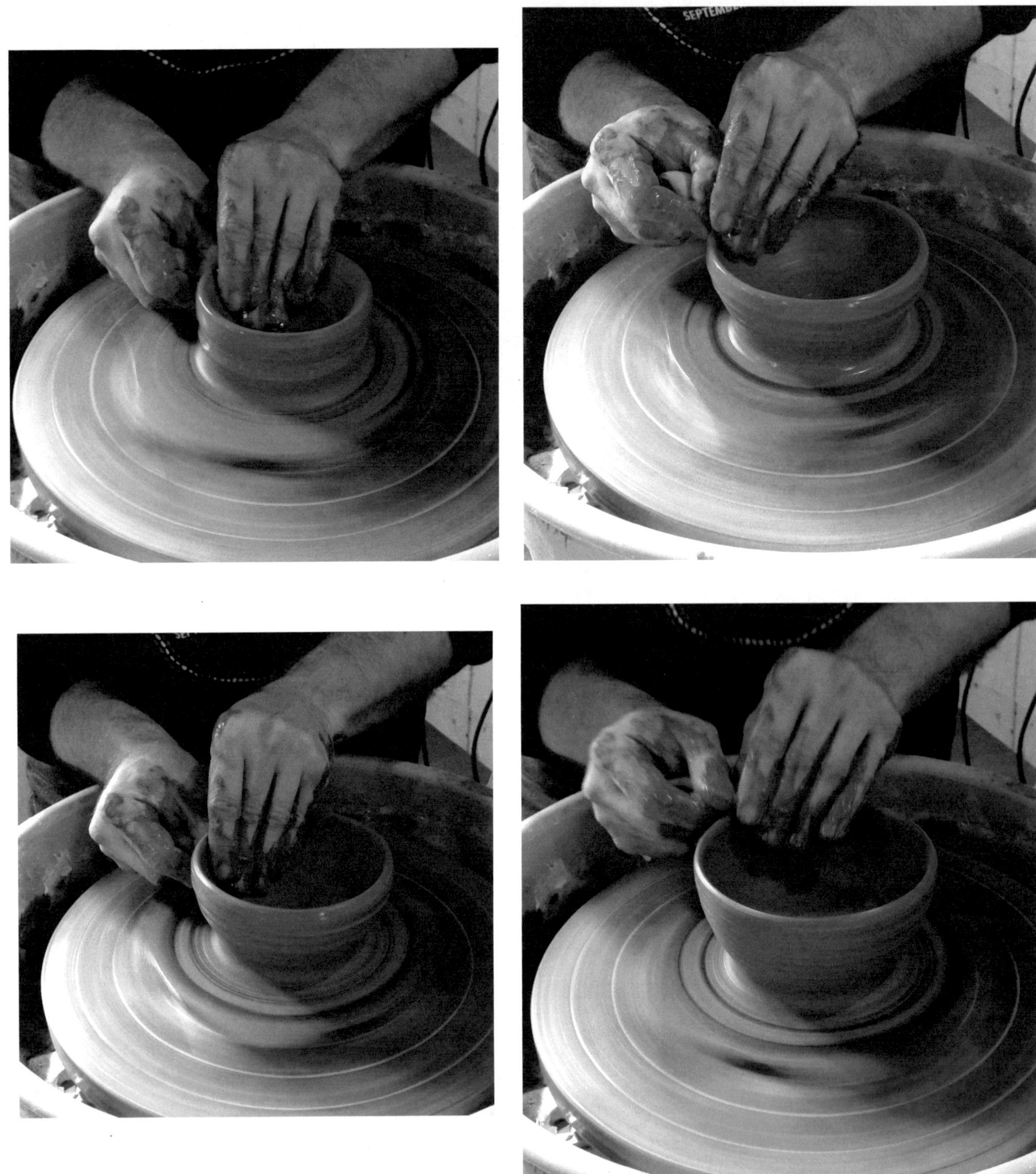

Continue to pull up and out thinning out the clay. You should also leave an extra thick wall at toward the bottom for support and the creation of the foot ring once the piece dries to leatherhard stage. After the wall is the correct thickness, shape the bowl using a similar process as the cylinder. Use a soft rib to compress the interior floor and base of the bowl. You can also rib the outside during shaping. Be careful not to project the bowl curve too far beyond the foot or the curve may collapse. Extra wall thickness is essential in making these horizontal forms, it will be cut away later during the trimming process. Use a wood knife to cut a bevel and the wire tool to cut the piece off the bat. Store on the bat until ready to trim the foot.

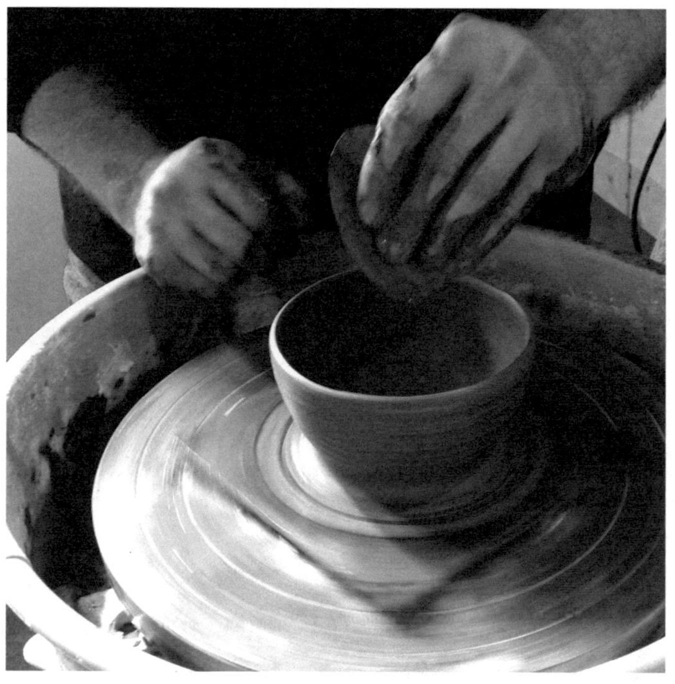
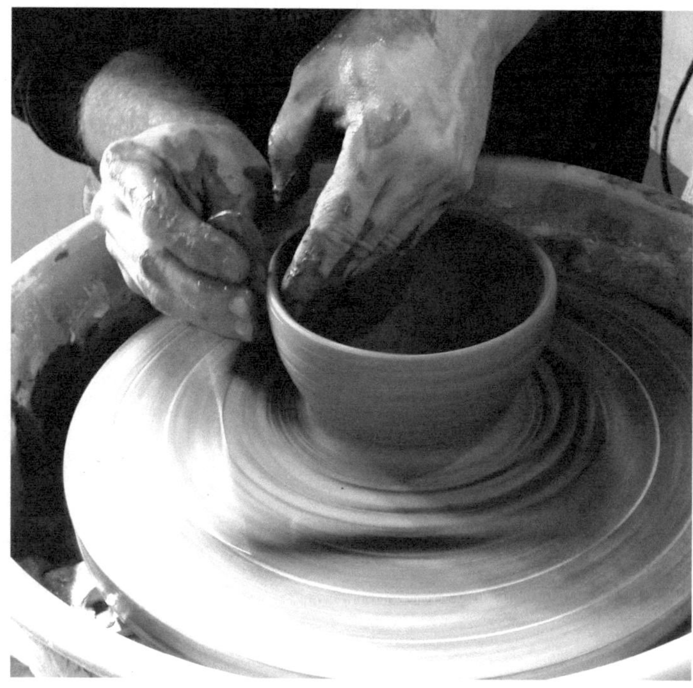
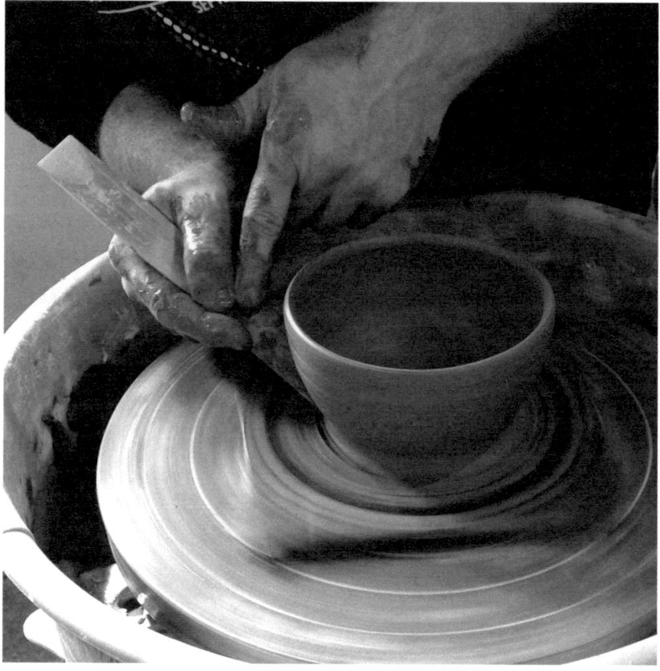
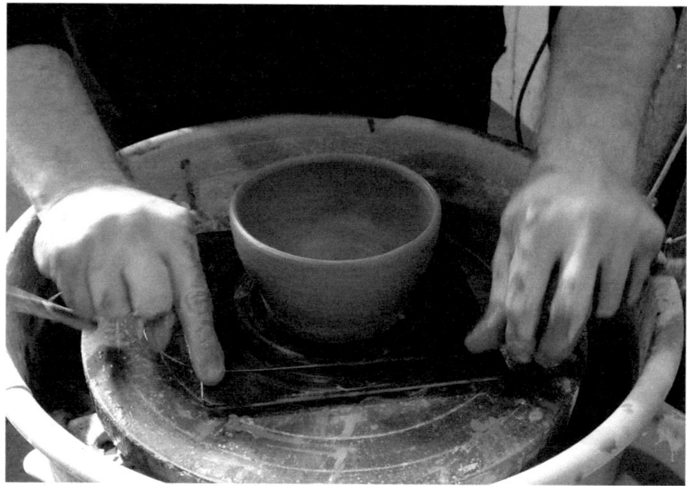

Trimming feet- After a form has dried to leatherhard stage, you may need to cut away extra clay at the base for pots like bowls and plates. Not all pots need to be trimmed but the process remains the same regardless of the shape. In order to cut the foot, you will turn your pot upside down on the wheel. Carefully recenter the shape and hold it in place with three fat coils of clay. Using a large loop tool, cut away extra clay on the outside of the bottom. You can change the curve of the shape by changing the angle that you are holding the trimming tool. Once the outside diameter is established, use a smaller loop tool to cut away extra clay from the inside bottom creating the foot ring. Be careful not to cut too deep as it is very easy to cut through the bottom of the pot. There are a large number of possible "feet" for you pots. Experiment with a variety of ring styles and cutting away or adding on elements.

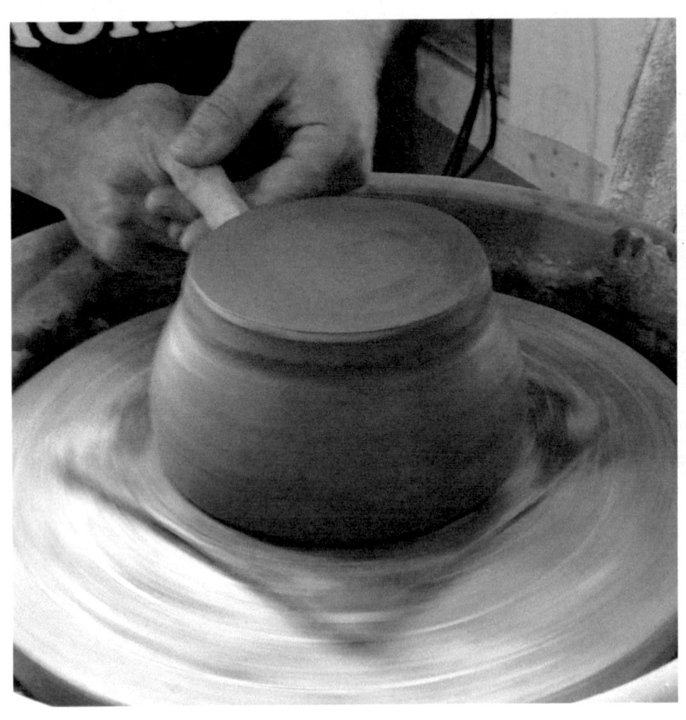

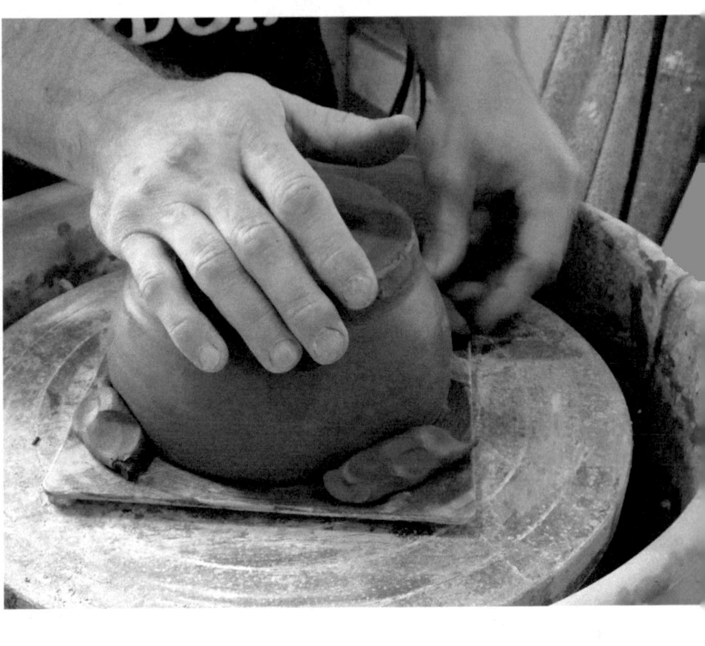

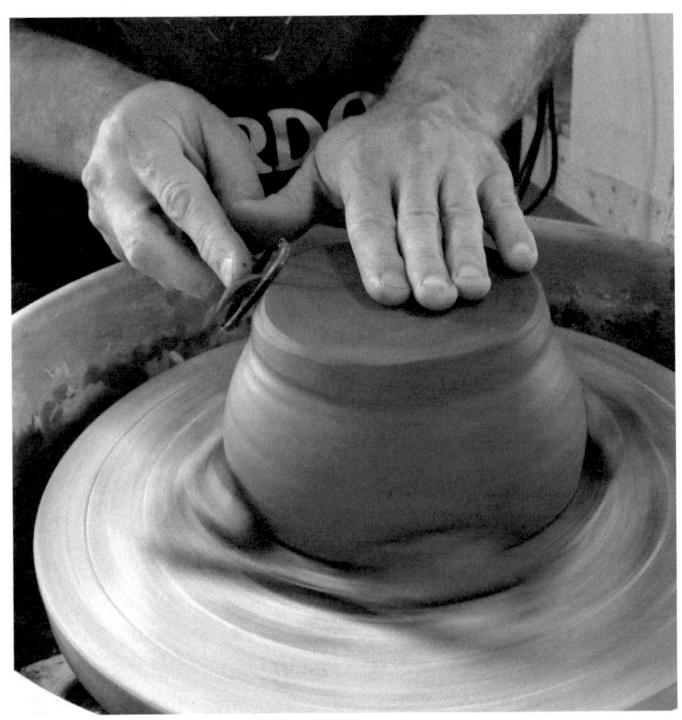

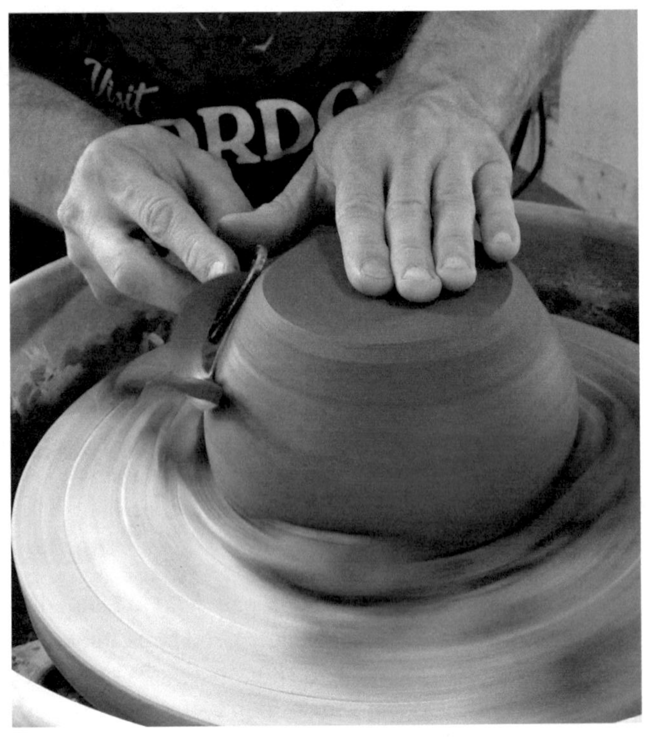

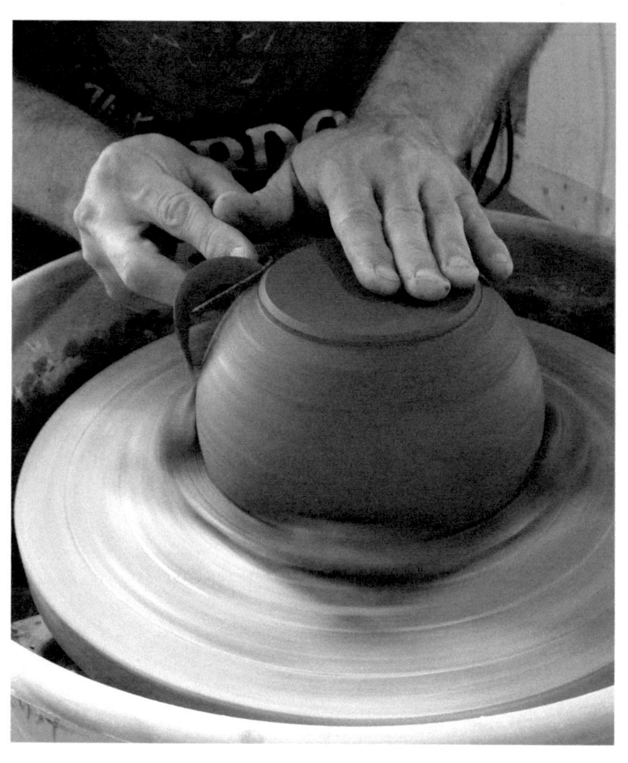

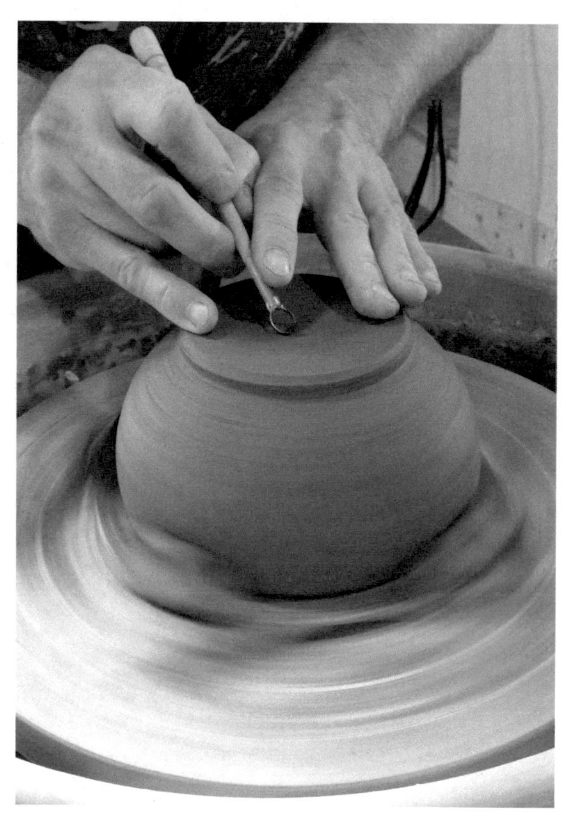

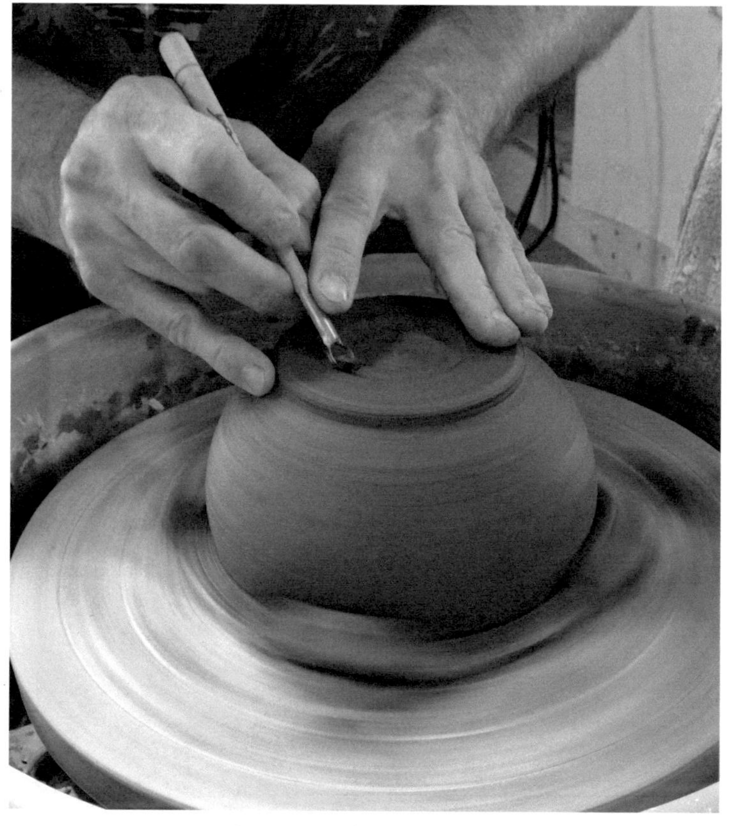

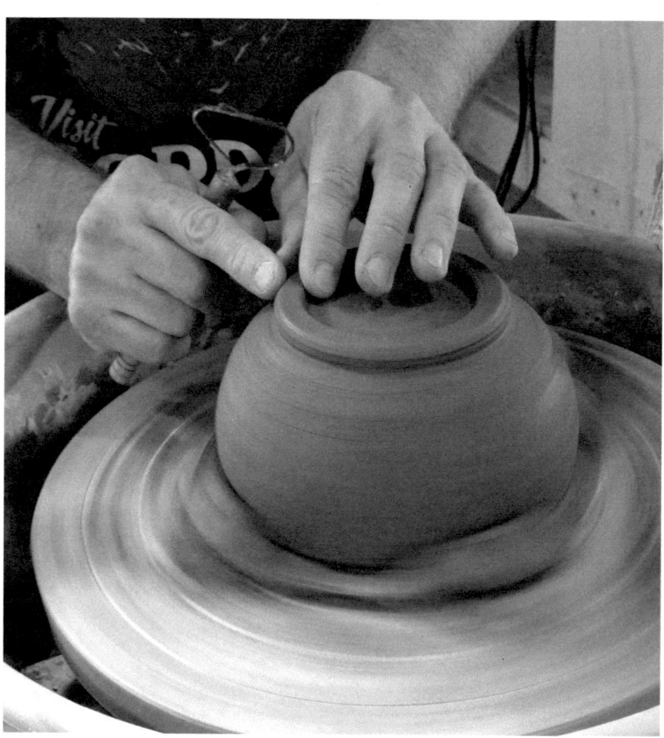

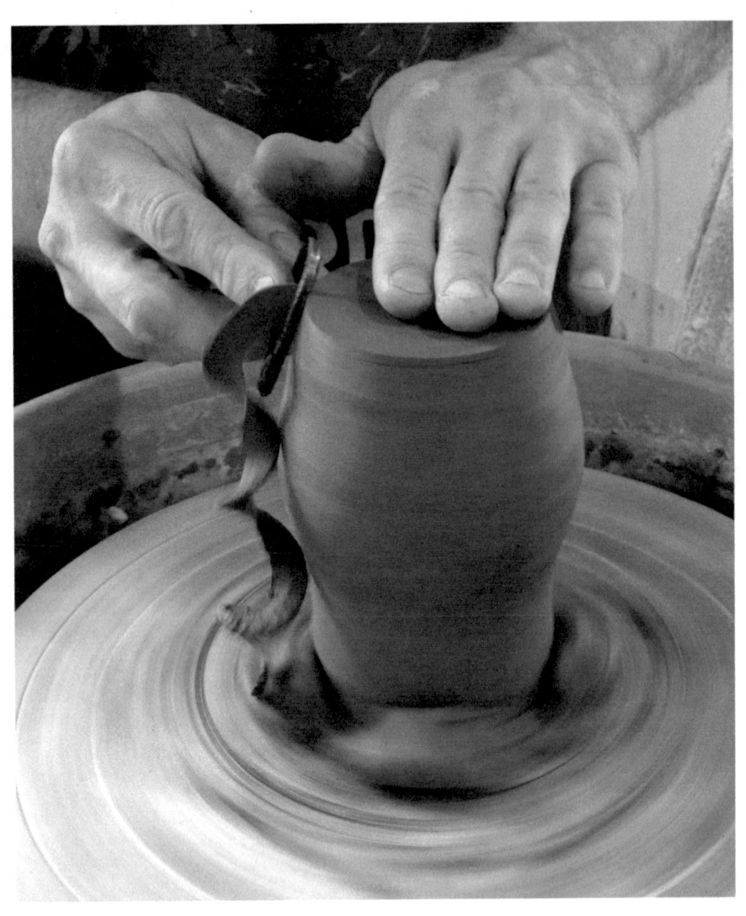

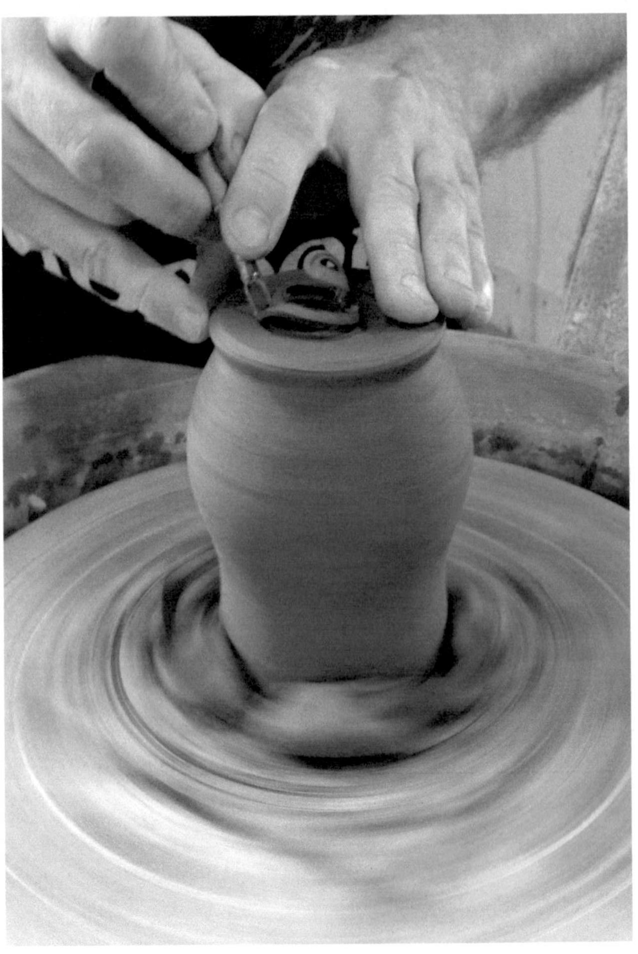

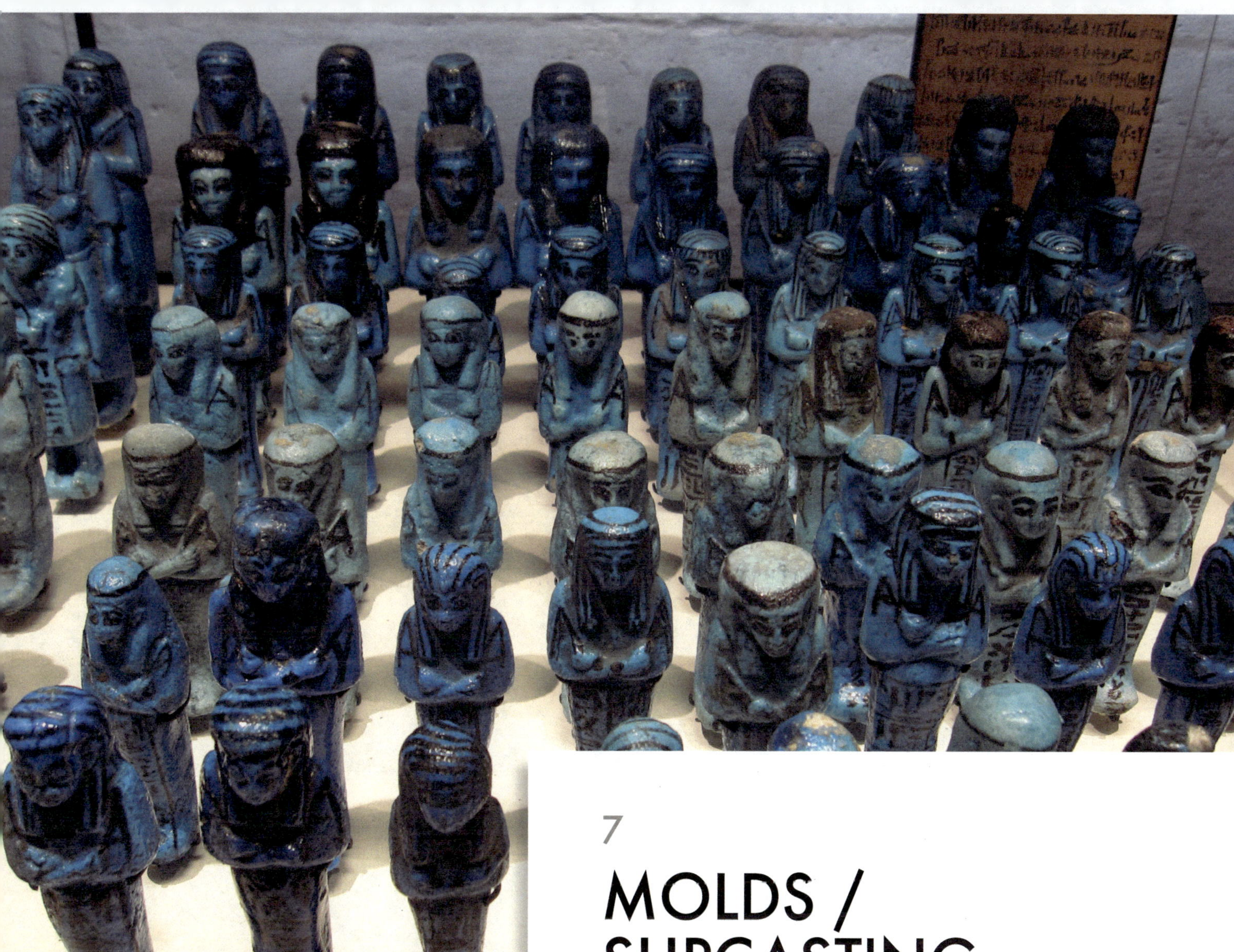

Ancient Egyptian press-molded ushabti tomb figures[1]

7

MOLDS / SLIPCASTING

Molds have been used in the production of ceramics since ancient times. The main advantage in the use of a mold is the ability to create a large number of identical pieces quickly. A variety of materials can be used to create molds, the most common being plaster, bisque fired ceramics, and wood. A common industrial production mold process called slip casting, has been in use for hundreds of years. Contemporary studio artists have taken the process and ideas of slip casting to new extremes in the production of their work.

One of the most useful materials for the production of molds is plaster. Plaster and clay will never stick together and the porous nature of plaster allows it to remove moisture from the clay surface.

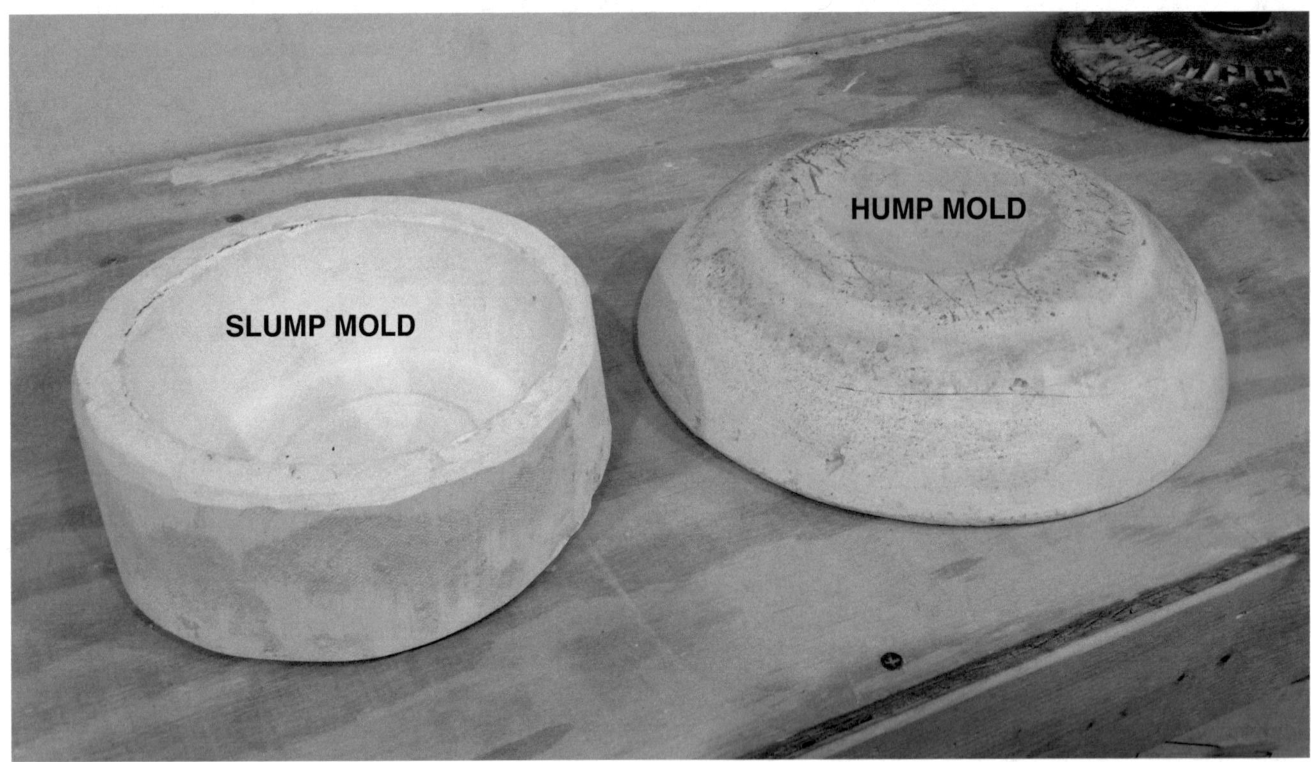

Types of simple one piece molds:

One of the most important concepts behind the use of molds is that it allows the repetition of shapes quickly and easily. This doesn't mean that you can mindlessly slap clay on a mold and expect success. Remember, clay is shrinking as it dries and this fact determines how you work with a mold. Some basic mold shapes in common usage are hump molds and slump (or press) molds.

Hump molds are used by draping a clay slab over the mold shape. If the mold has a hard surface (like plaster), the clay must be removed when it firms up but before it shrinks too much. If the clay is trapped on the form, it will crack apart as it continues to dry and shrink.

Slump molds are essentially the opposite of hump molds. In order to use a slump mold, you drape (slump) or press the clay into the mold. As the clay dries and shrinks, it will pull away from the mold on its own.

The type of mold you use is determined by what part of the shape (the inside or outside) you are trying to copy.

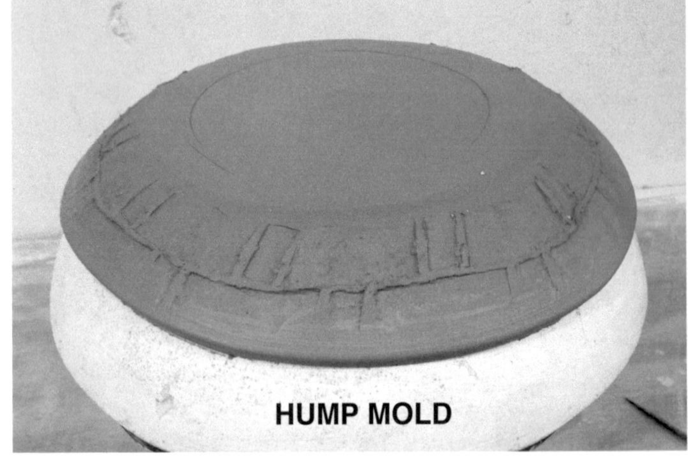

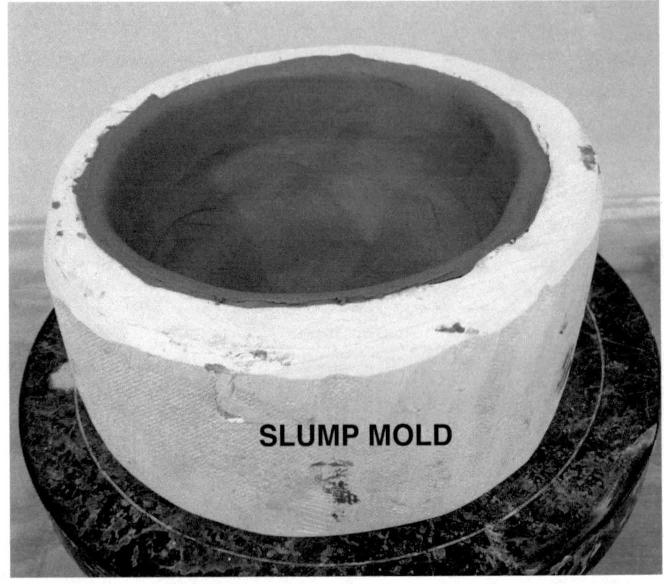

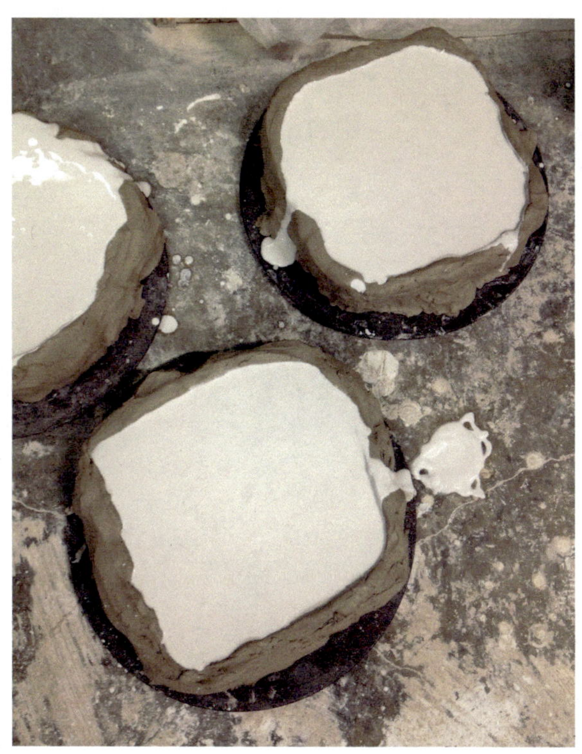

1

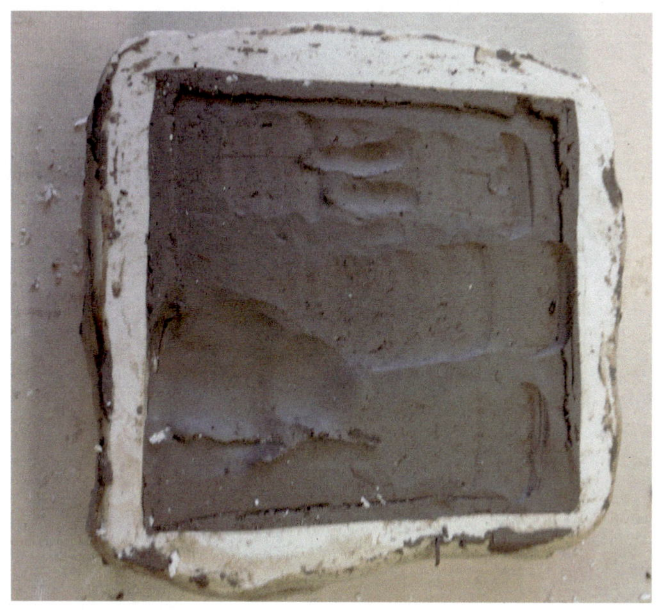

2

Making and using a one piece tile mold:

A common introductory experience with mold making is the production of a one piece tile mold. The first step is to sculpt the original in clay at slightly larger than the final size needed. This is done since the clay will be shrinking during the process when drying and firing. Once the original object is finished, a clay wall is built approximately 1" away from and 1" higher than the original. Plaster is mixed and poured into the "fenced" off area and allowed to solidify (Image 1). After the plaster has hardened, the mold is flipped and the original sculpted clay object is removed from the mold (2). The empty mold is then cleaned, sharp edges scraped off, and allowed to fully cure and dry (3). New clay is pressed into the mold. This will start shrinking away from the mold walls and should drop out of the mold as it is turned upside down. The finished mold can now be used to make a large number of identical copies of the original shape (4).

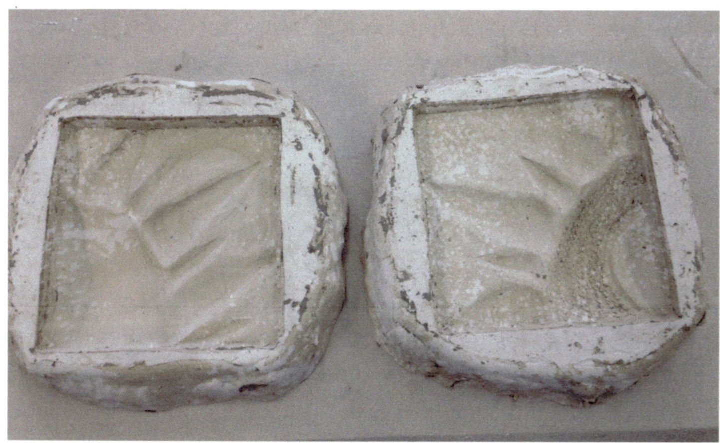

3

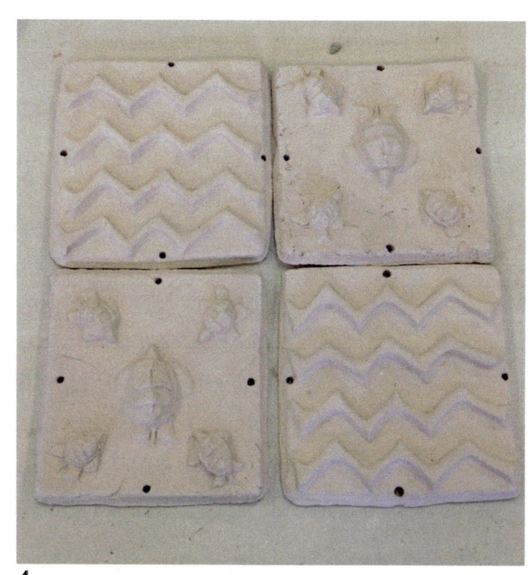

4

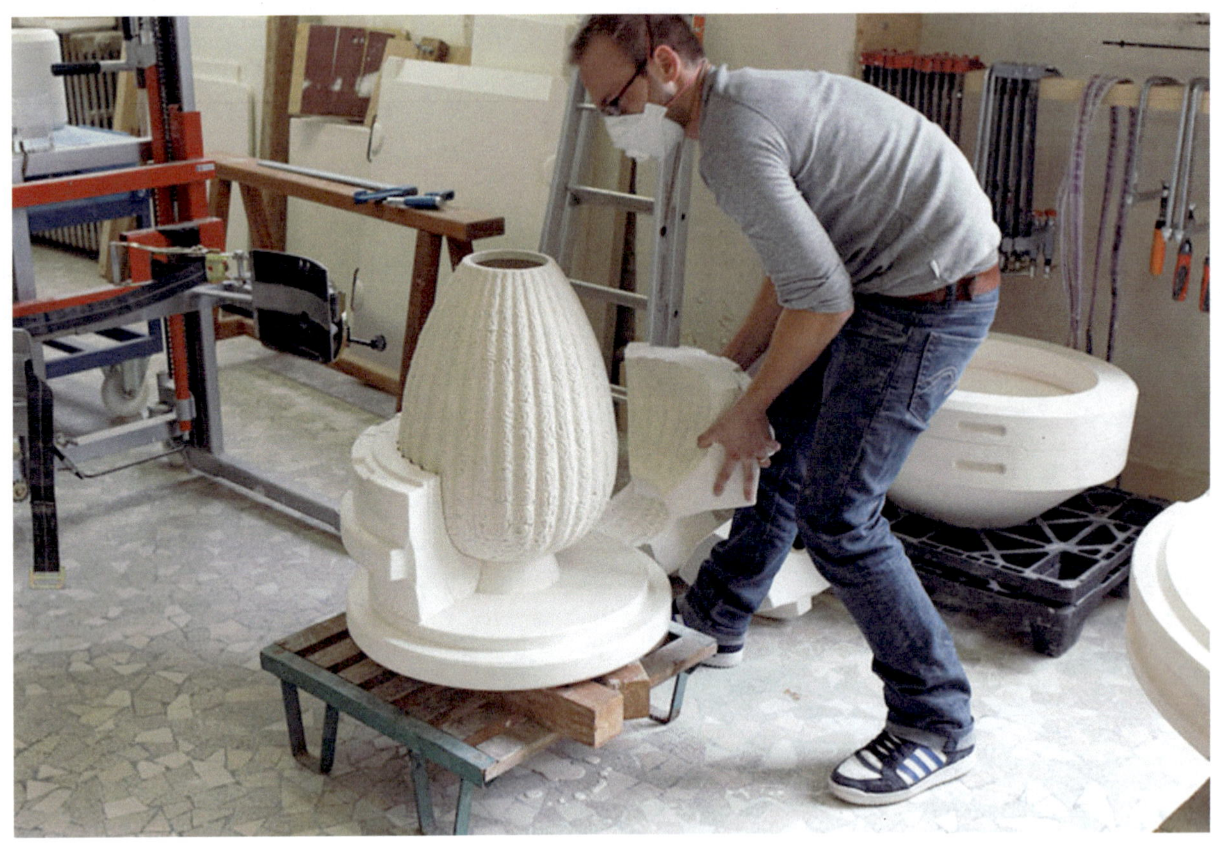

A small-scale slipcasting workshop of the Manufacture Nationale de Sèvres in France. The artist is removing plaster mold parts from a cast porcelain vessel. [12]

SLIP CASTING

Slip casting is a very important industrial process for making ceramics of all types. Most of the commercially made pottery and sanitary ceramics (sinks, toilets, urinals) we use every-day has been made using this process. Plaster molds (often with multiple complex parts) are assembled and a specially altered liquid clay slip is poured into the mold. The slip is left in the mold for an amount of time. The plaster mold starts to suck water out of the slip creating a sedimentary shell of clay against the mold wall. After the desired wall thickness is achieved, the excess slip is poured out of the mold and the object begins to dry. When the piece is stable enough to remove, the mold is disassembled and the object taken out. The mold is dried and can be used to cast a large number of repeat shapes. Complex objects can be cast in separate molds and then easily assembled later, for example teapot spouts cast in a small spout mold and then attached to the teapot body.

The clay slip used for this process is not just normal clay made more liquid. Casting slip has a special material added called a deflocculant. Normal clay particles want to stick together or flocculate (think of them as "flocks" of sheep) By adding a deflocculant, the electrical charge of the clay particles is changed and they begin to repel each other. This action allows the slip to stay fluid without using an excess amount of water. The correct consistency of this mixture is critical to having a strong cast object. The other vital part of this process is a skillful mold making practice and understanding of how to make complex, multipart molds.

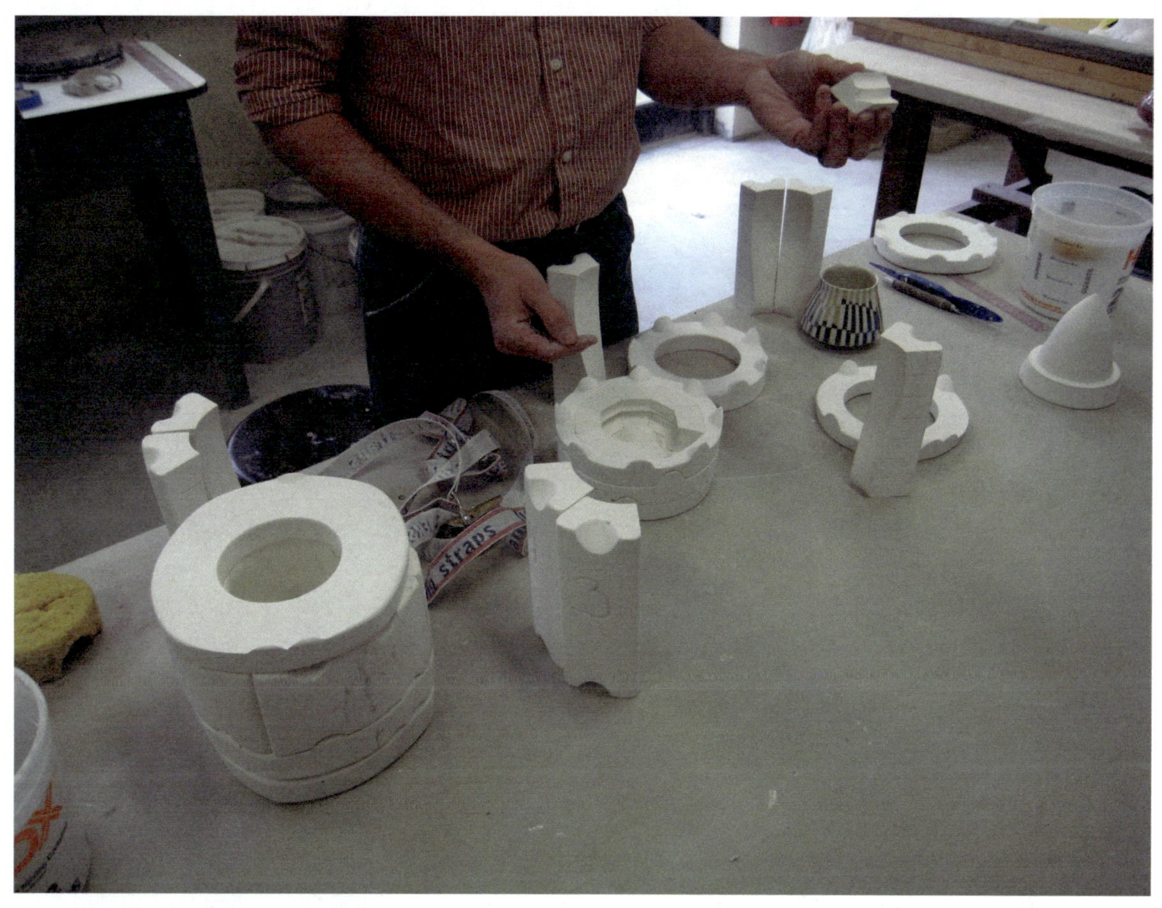

Visiting artist and RIT Ceramics professor Peter Pincus demonstrating his unique slip casting method at the CCC studio[1]

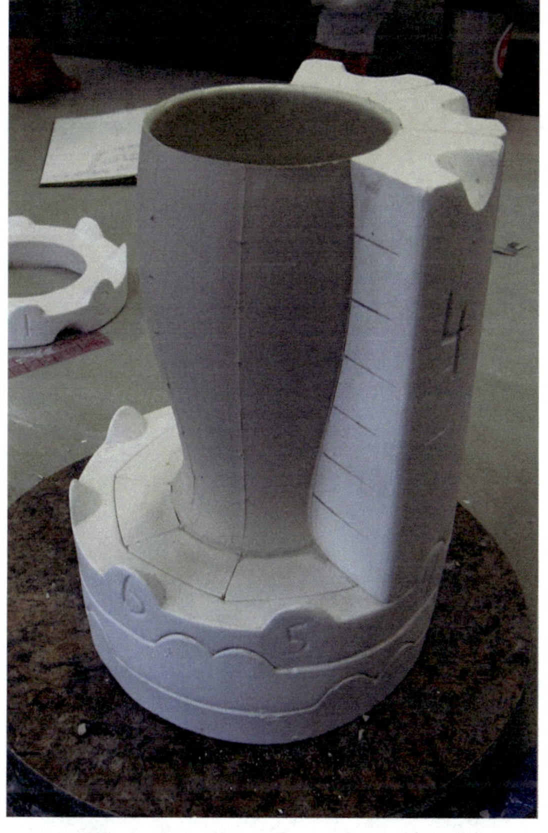

A finished cast form coming out of the multi-piece mold used by Pincus[1]

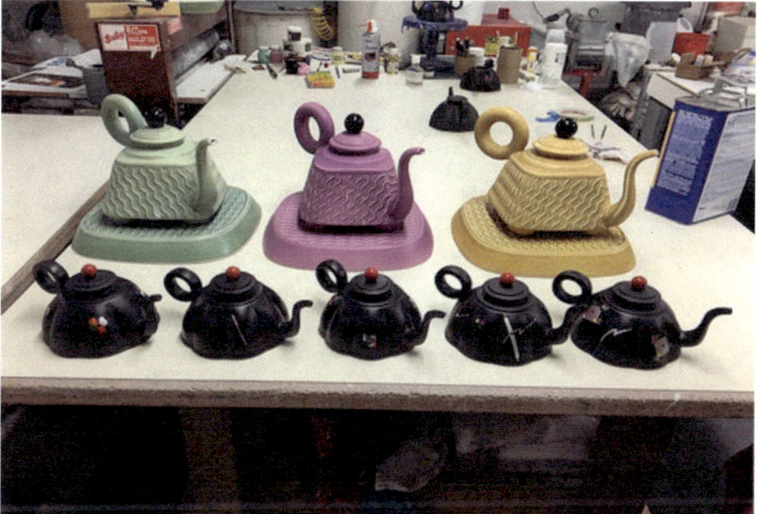

View of Jonathan Kaplan's studio with slip cast teapots[3]

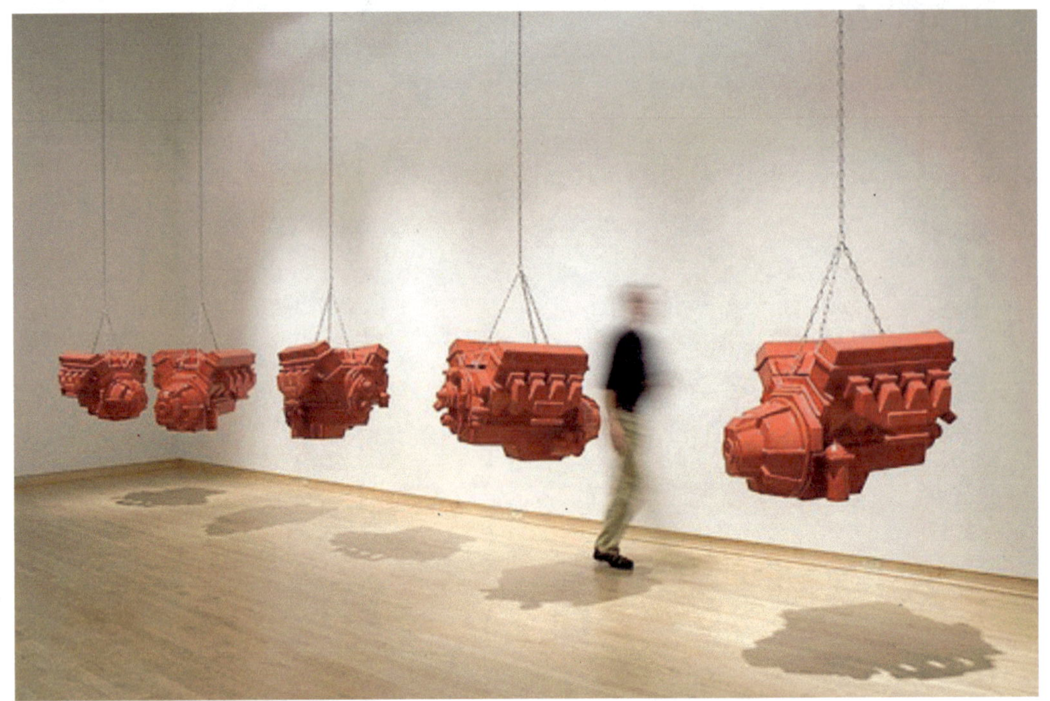

David Packer, "The Last of the V8's" slip cast porcelain[2]

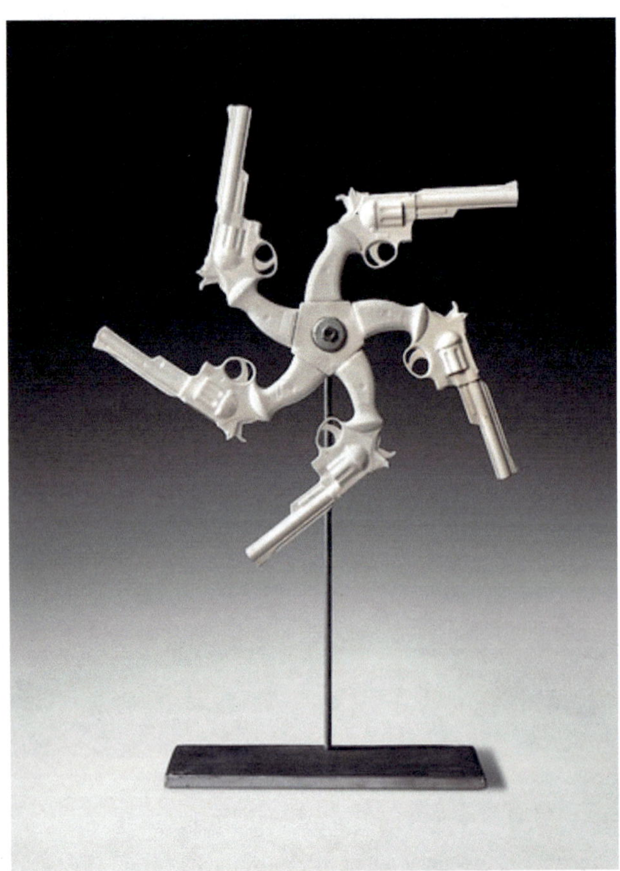

Linda Lighton "44 Magnum Mandala", slip cast earthenware[3]

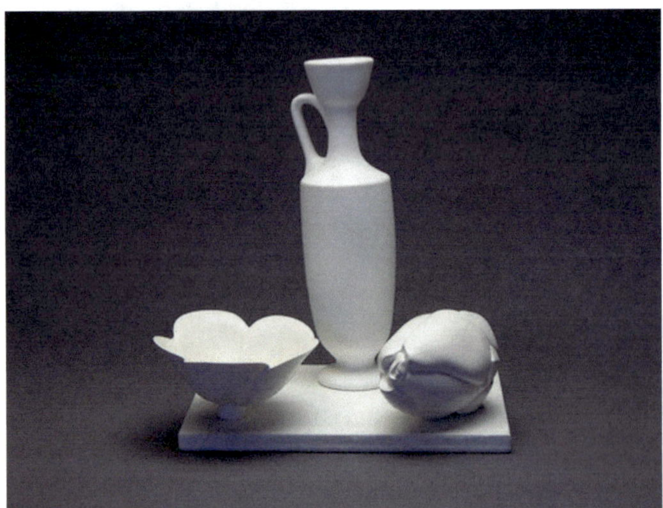

Anat Shiftan, "Still Life with Bowl, Bud, and Lekythos", slip cast porcelain[5]

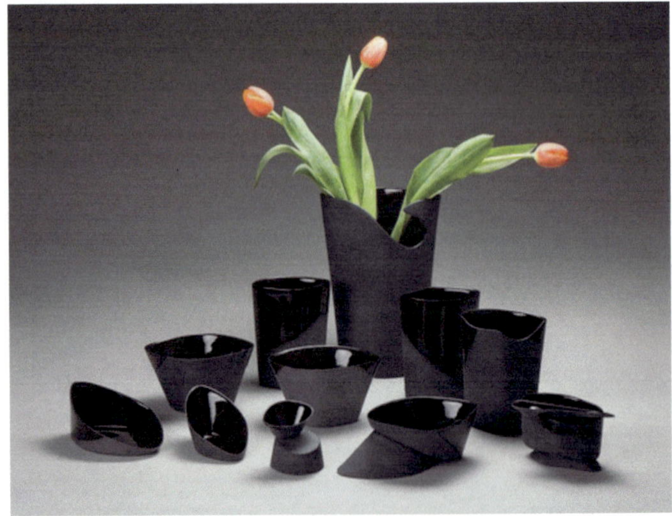

Heather Mae Erickson, "The Industrial Hand Collection", slip cast porcelain[3]

One of the best books on the plaster mold making process for ceramics. This book by Andrew Martin is available in the CCC Library.

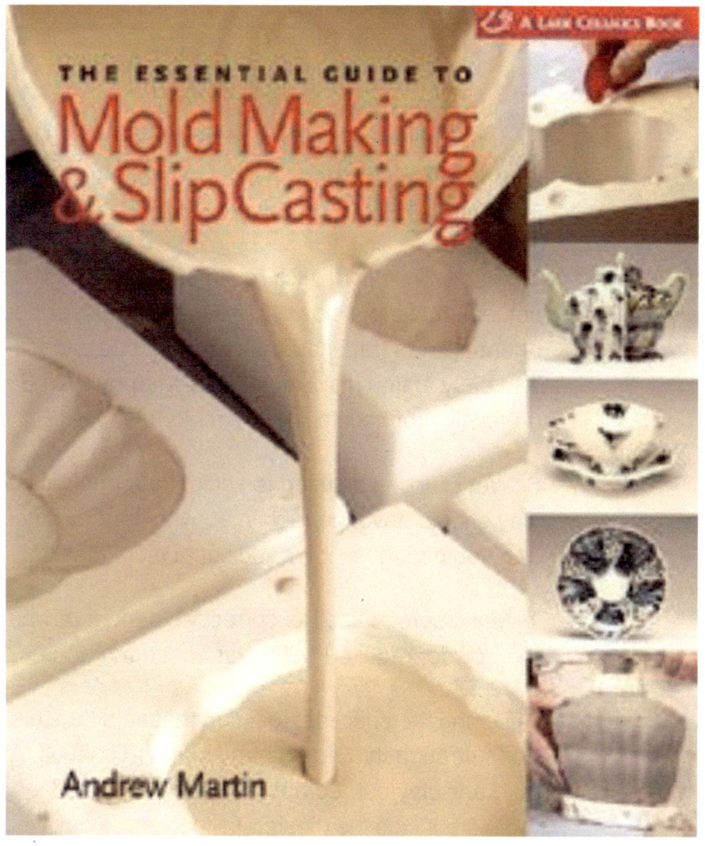

PLASTER
PLASTER MIXING

Plaster is made from naturally occurring gypsum which has been ground up, heated, and processed to become a very useful material for many industries. There are a variety of types and brands of plaster available for the ceramics artist but the most useful is called #1 Pottery Plaster. It is the best for general studio use and is easily purchased from ceramics suppliers.

Plaster has many advantages for ceramics production. The main being that you can create a liquid and pour that material to create molds and other shapes. Once mixed it will go through a chemical change that will harden the liquid into a solid block. This solid, cured piece of plaster will absorb moisture from the clay surface or liquid casting slip. Plaster can also be cast in solid blocks to sculpt into shapes that then can have a mold made of that shape.

There are some important tips to remember about mixing and using plaster in the studio.

1- Always add plaster powder to the required amount of cold water. Never use hot water and never add water to an amount of dry powder.

2- Keep your plaster powder in a dry place inside a sealed plastic container. Old plaster powder will absorb excess moisture from the air and start to solidify and forms lumps. Rotate your supply so that you are always using up powder so it doesn't sit too long.

3- Never wash mixed plaster, powder, or plaster chips down the drain. This will solidify and permanently block pipes. Pour excess material into the trash and keep a rinse bucket to wash your hands and tools. This bucket can then be dumped outside.

4- If possible, keep clay working space and plaster separated. In large studios, there is often a plaster room that prevents problems. If solid plaster chips get into wet clay and then are fired with the piece, the plaster will swell after firing and break your piece.

5- Liquid plaster will stick to almost everything except wet clay! If you are using wooden mold forms (called cottles), making molds of porous materials, or pouring liquid plaster on solid plaster, you MUST use a release agent applied (brushed on) to the porous surface to keep the new plaster from sticking. One of the cheapest and easy to find mold releases is Murphy's Oil Soap. Other releases include vaseline, cooking spray, or commercially produced sculpture mold releases.

6- Wet clay can be used to sculpt your original shape, as containment walls, or to seal wooden cottles. This clay should never be reclaimed with normal clay since it will contain plaster chips. Keep this clay wrapped up and you can reuse it for additional mold making.

7- Make sure to use the correct amount of powder for the water volume needed. Plaster mixed with less than the powder required will never set strong and be "punky" or extra weak.

8- During the chemical reaction that sets the solid plaster, it will heat up. Do not move your mold until it has gone through this change and starts to cool off. After the setting process, you can disassemble the walls and take any clay out. Scrape down any sharp edges and allow the mold to dry. Thick molds can take days for the moisture inside the plaster walls to come out. Plaster molds work best when dried and this can be sped up by setting the molds in front of a fan. DO NOT heat molds as this will break down the strength of the plaster wall.

Steps for plaster mixing:

1- Make sure to have your piece ready before you begin mixing plaster. Have your mold release applied if needed and the cottle forms sealed to the bottom board. The worst "plaster disaster" is when the pressure of the liquid plaster blows out your seal or clay containment wall. Overbuild your reinforcements.

2- Either calculate the overall mold volume needed or do a rough estimate of the water needed. The unscientific method will be using the "floating islands" method of mixing that uses observation and experience. The official manufacturers method will use specified amounts of water and plaster powder in order to get the correct volume.

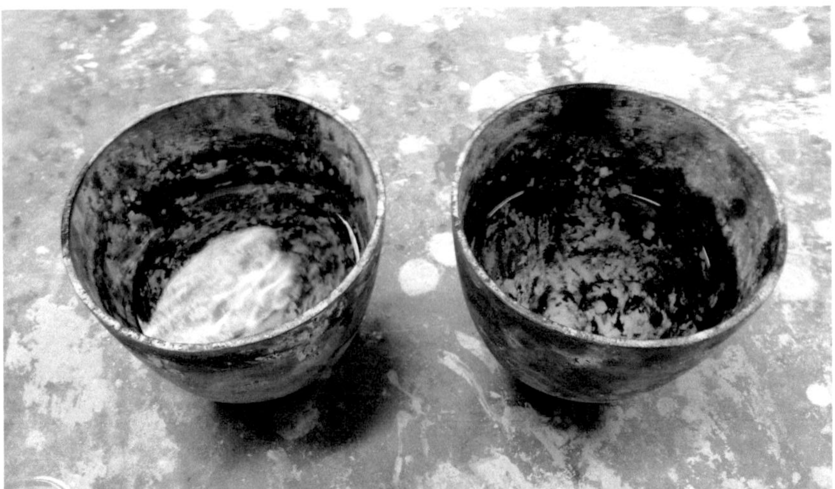

Flexible rubber bowls used for mixing plaster. These are filled 1/2 way for a small batch.

3- Fill mixing container with cold water about 1/2 the needed volume for floating islands or the correct amount for official method

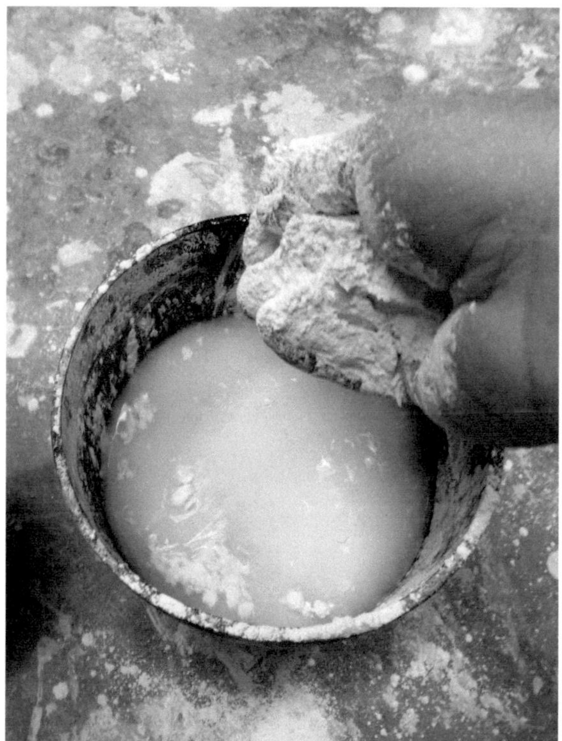 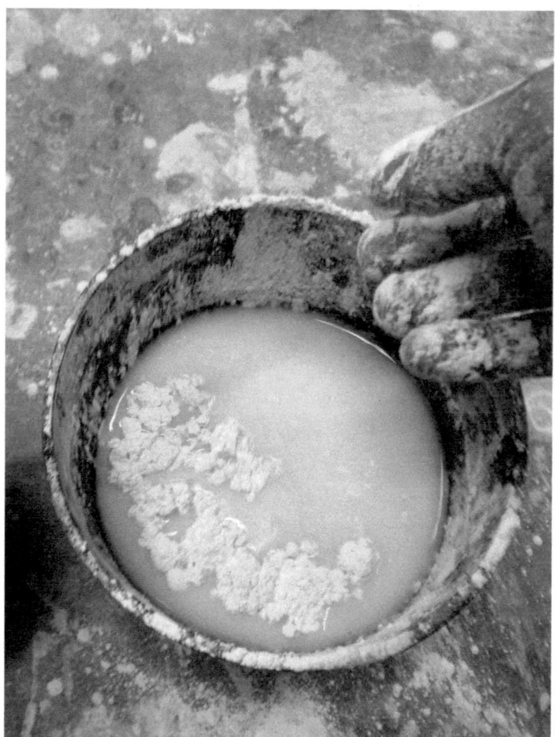

4-Carefully sift plaster powder into the water making sure to go all the way around the water surface. If all the powder is dropped into the middle of the container, the floating islands method will not work and the powder will not mix well.

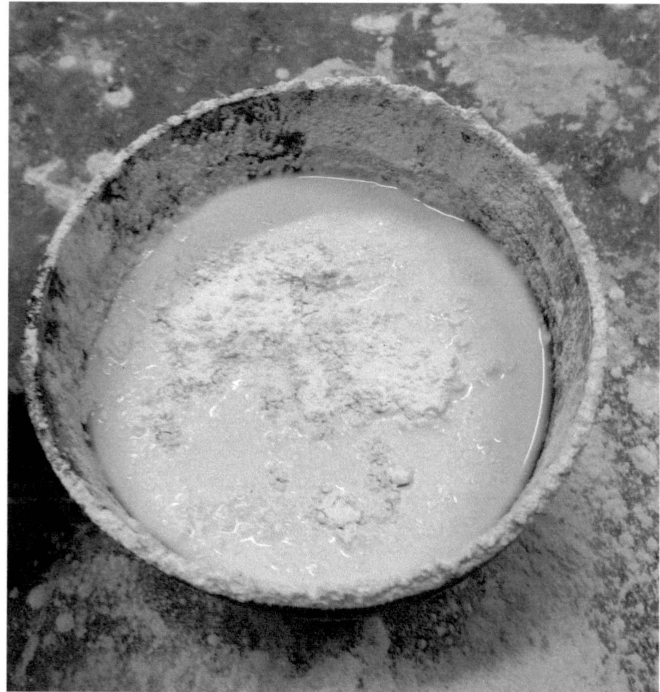

Correct amount of powder added for water volume= "floating islands".

5- If using the floating islands approach, watch the surface as the powder is added. When the correct amount of powder is reached, it will not drop into the water as quickly.

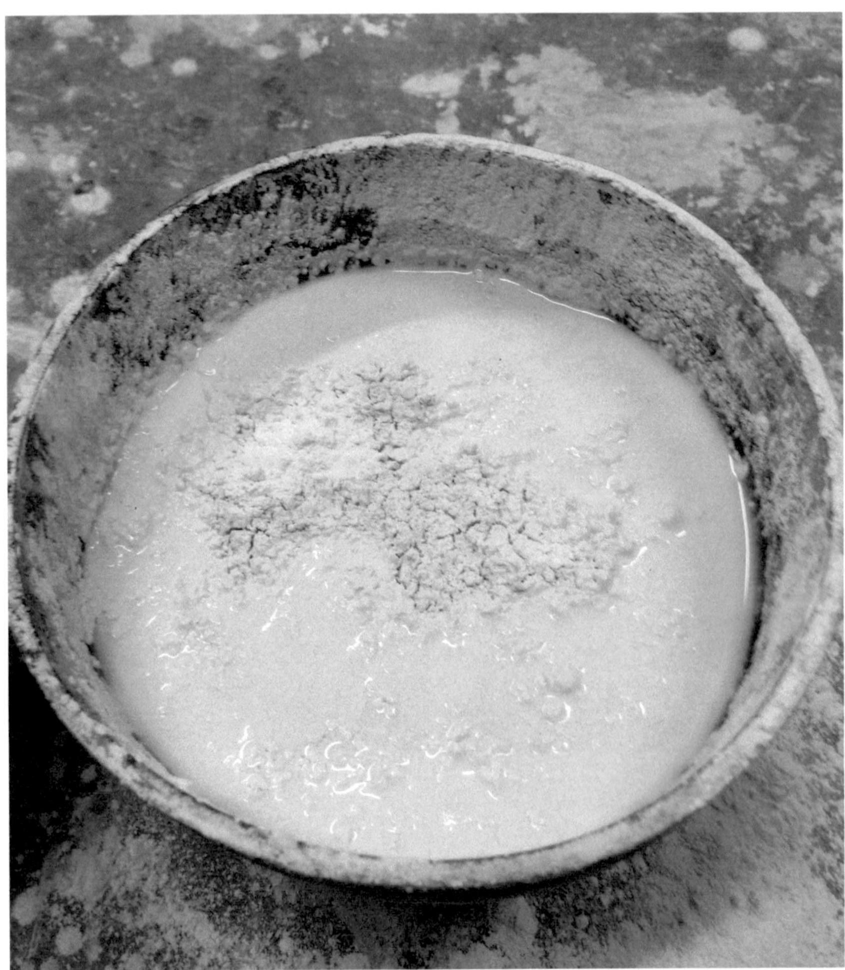

Allow powder to fully soak into the water. This creates less lumps in the mix.

6- Once all the powder is added, allow it to soak for about 3 minutes or until all the dry powder at the top is wet.

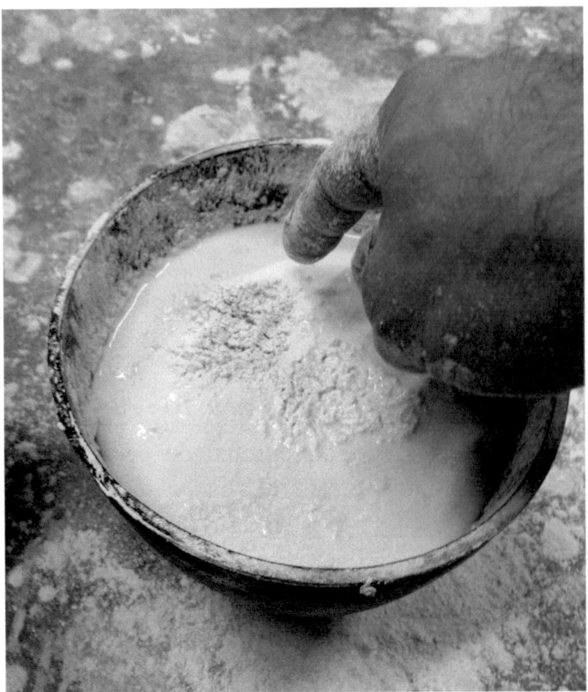

7- Carefully push your hand into the plaster, stir, and squeeze any lumps in order to mix the liquid to an even consistency. For larger amounts, you can use a drill mixer to thoroughly mix the plaster. Once you have mixed and agitated the liquid, the timer begins as the chemical reaction has started. You will have about 2 or 3 minutes to pour your molds before the mix starts to thicken. It will go from cream consistency to solid is about 8 to 10 minutes.

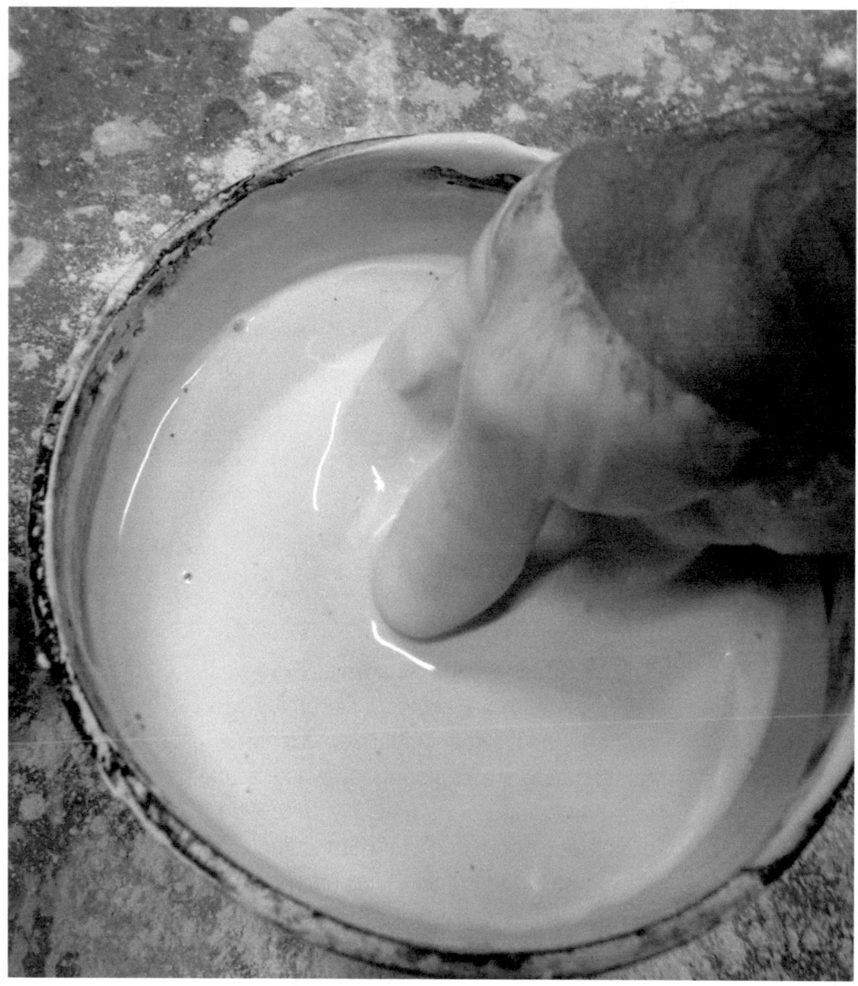

8- After the liquid is poured, make sure there are no mold blowouts that need plugging. Dump extra plaster into the trash and use rinse bucket to clean your hands and the mixing container.

9- Wait until the plaster has heated and cooled (usually about 30 minutes total) before you move and disassemble your new molds.

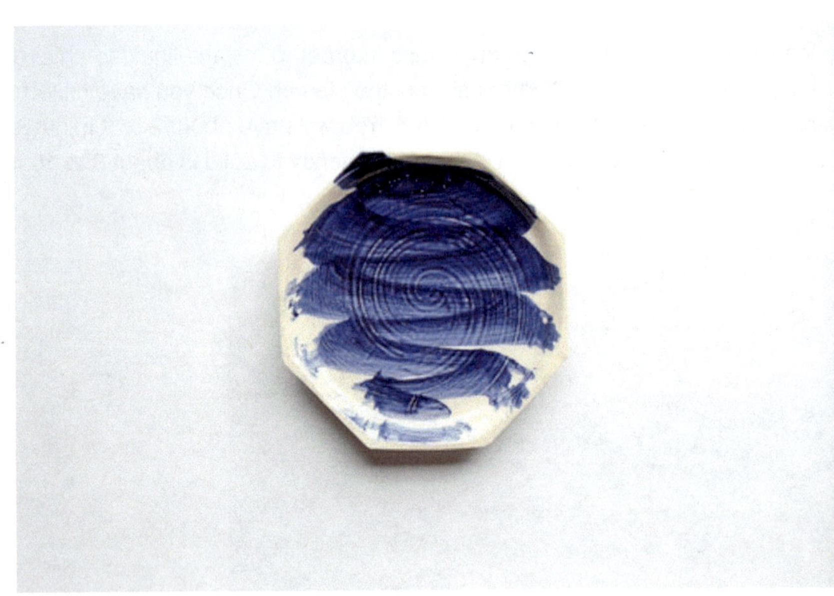

Adam Chau, "Digital Calligraphy" series, CNC decorated porcelain[3]

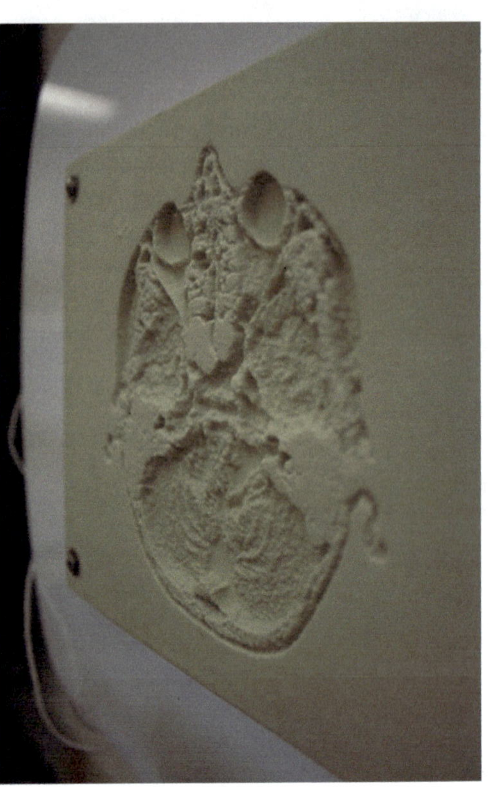

Bryan Czibesz, "Diagnostic: Myopia", CNC milled porcelain[13]

NEW
TECHNOLOGY

The ceramics world has always been on the cutting edge of the newest technological and material advances. Ceramics can easily be a blend of some very old methods and the newest cutting edge technologies. One of the avenues that many ceramic artists are exploring today is the use of computer modeling (CAD), 3-d printing, and computer numerically controlled (CNC) tools. Some artists are modeling their pieces on a computer first using CAD software and then using that as a pattern to build the piece. Other artists are utilize the new tools of 3-d printing in order to have the machine build the object they modeled on the computer (or then making a plaster mold of the object) or use milling machines to cut plaster molds. These techniques have great potential to give the artist freedom to invent and construct unique types of ceramics objects.

Resources
Free CAD software: SketchUp: www.sketchup.com
TinkerCAD: www.tinkercad.com

Artists using digital technology to produce their work:
Bryan Czibesz: www.bryanczibesz.com
Del Harrow: www.delharrow.net
Olivier Van Herpt: www.oliviervanherpt.com
Jonathan Keep: www.keep-art.co.uk/index.htm
Adam Chau: www.adamchau.com
Brooks Oliver: www.brooksoliver.com

Data Clay group: www.data-clay.org

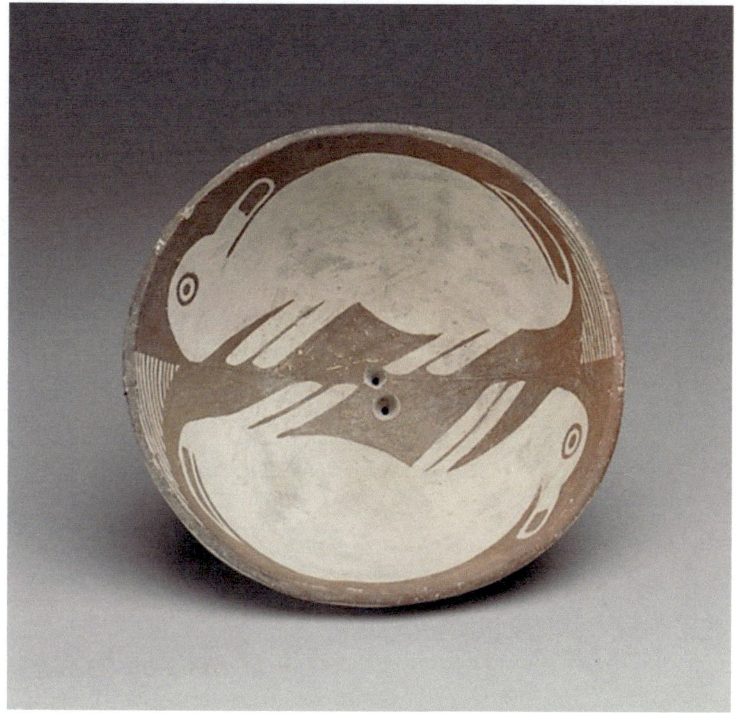

Native American Mimbres culture slip painted bowl[4]

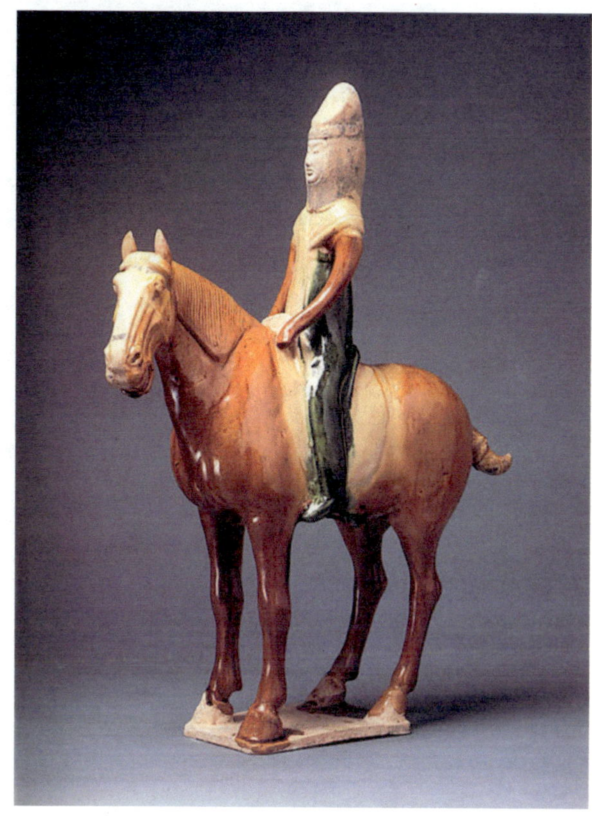

Chinese Tang Dynasty lead glazed tomb sculpture[4]

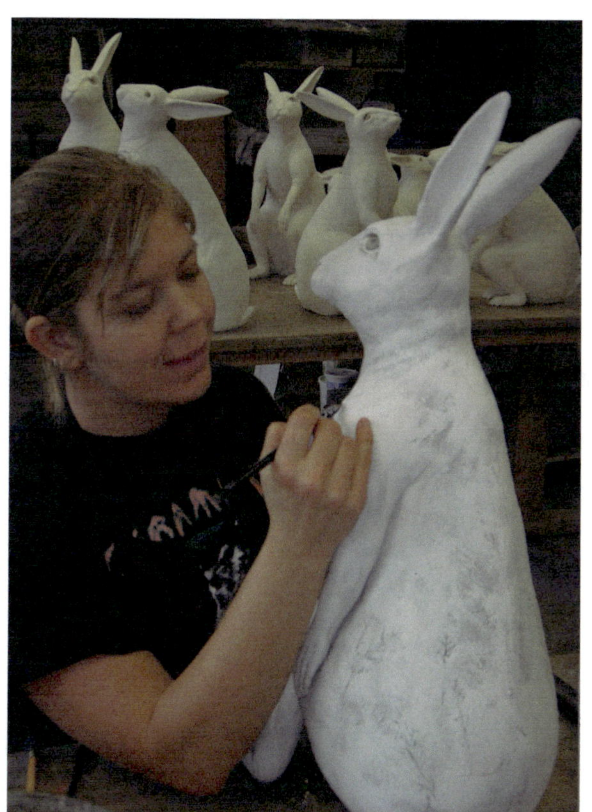

Kelly Connole in the studio developing the surface on her work[2]

8

SURFACE DECORATION

As a plastic material, clay allows for a wide range of surface decoration techniques. One of the key factors in the success of any technique is understanding the best time to utilize it. For example, some approaches work best at the leatherhard stage, some at bone dry, and some can only be done on bisque.

One way to think of the surface of your work is as a skin of the material. It will record the mark of finger, tools, stamps, or brushes in very interesting and effective ways. Use this natural characteristic of clay to your advantage.

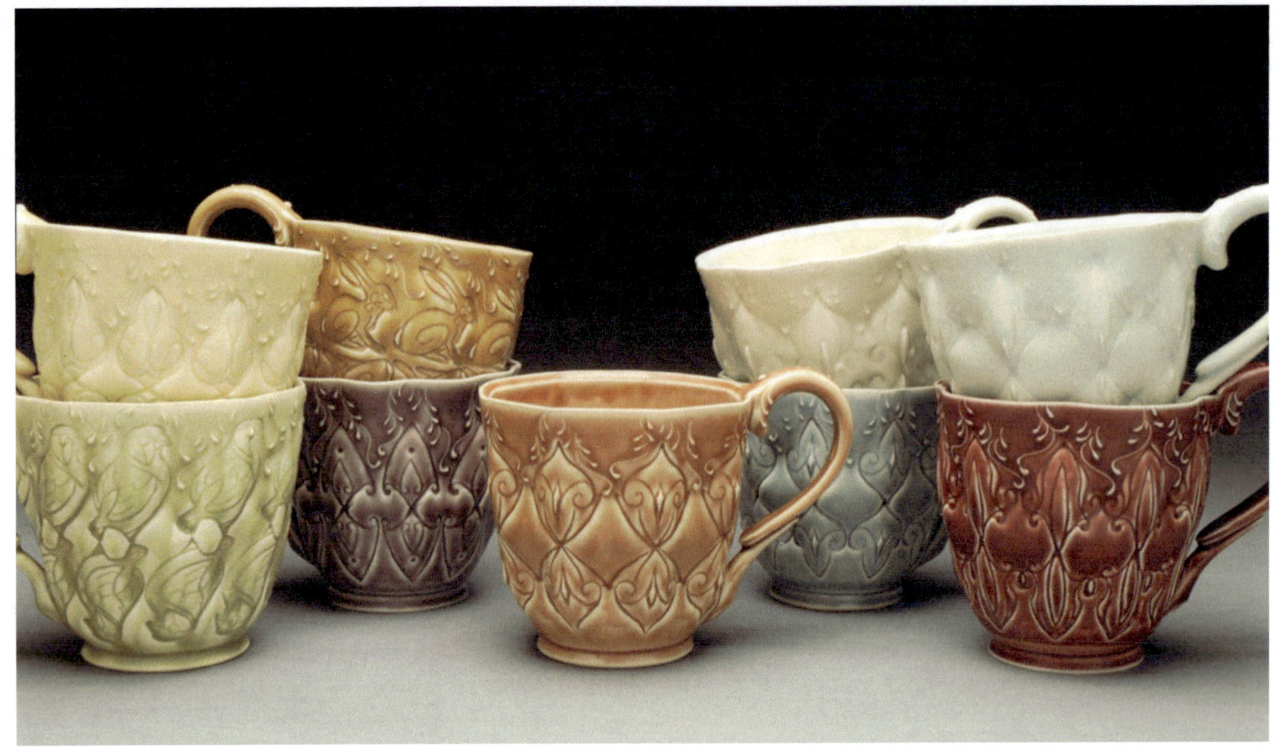

Kristen Kieffer, "Stamped Cups"[3]

SURFACE TECHNIQUES

Stamping

A variety of materials can be pressed, rolled, or stamped into the surface of a piece. Often the best time is just before leatherhard stage when force can be applied to push in the stamp without creating too much warping or danger of breaking the piece. Some materials include: rolled rope, thick grasses, woven mats, the bottom of shoes, rubber craft stamps, metal gears, and carved pieces of wine bottle cork. A good way to develop personal textures is to make your own bisque fired stamps for marking your work or creating complex patterns.

To make your own stamps, pinch or roll out a coil. Then texture the ends to create whatever pattern you need. Remember that anything pushed into the clay will become a raised surface on the final work when stamped in. If you create letters, make sure to write then backwards on the stamp or it won't work correctly. You can also texture the side of a coil to make a roller.

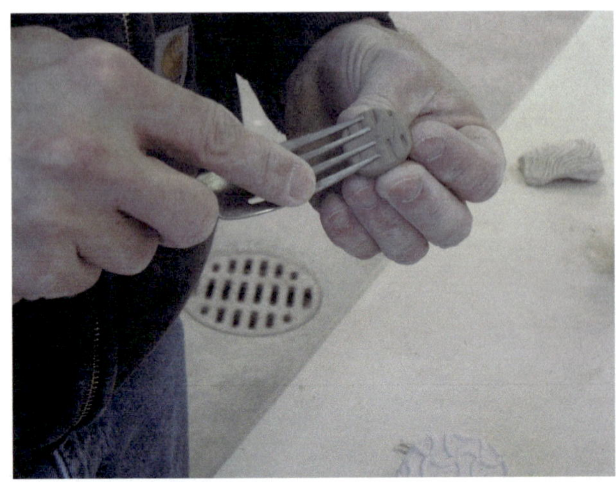

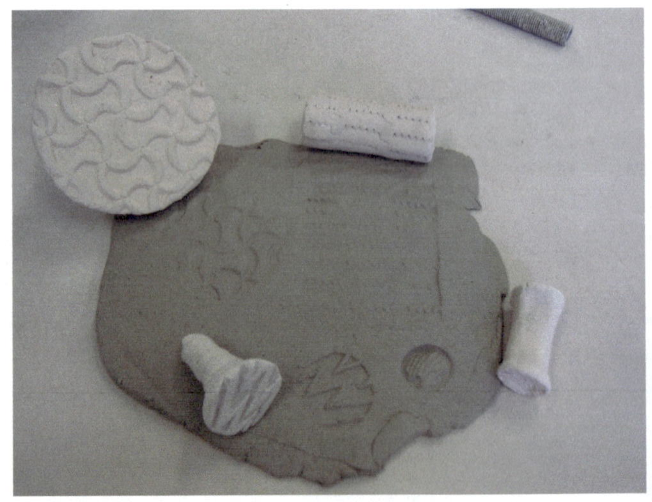

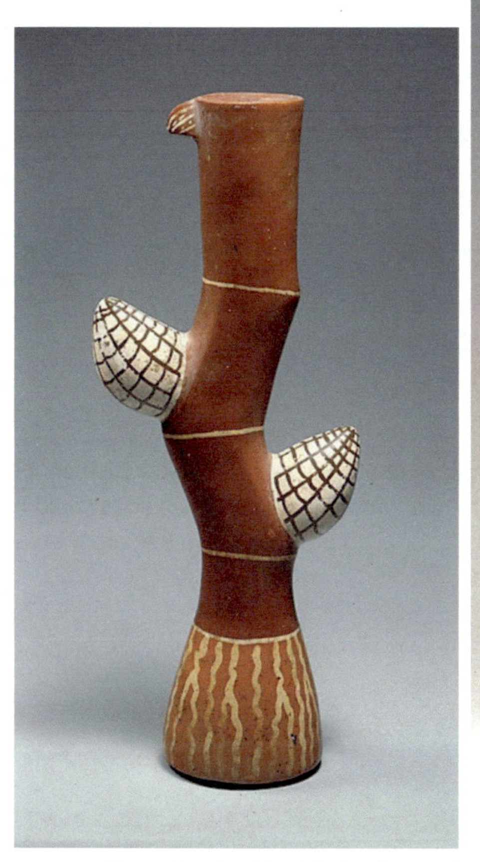

Nazca slipped and burnished earthenware[4]

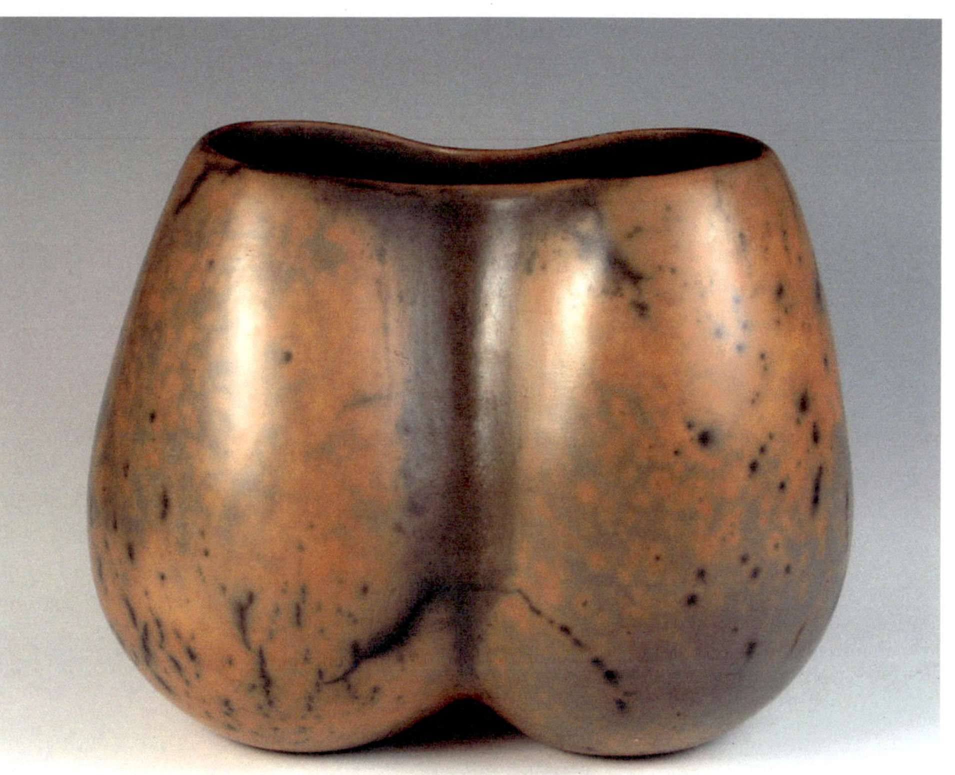

Roland Summer, "Brown Object" burnished[2]

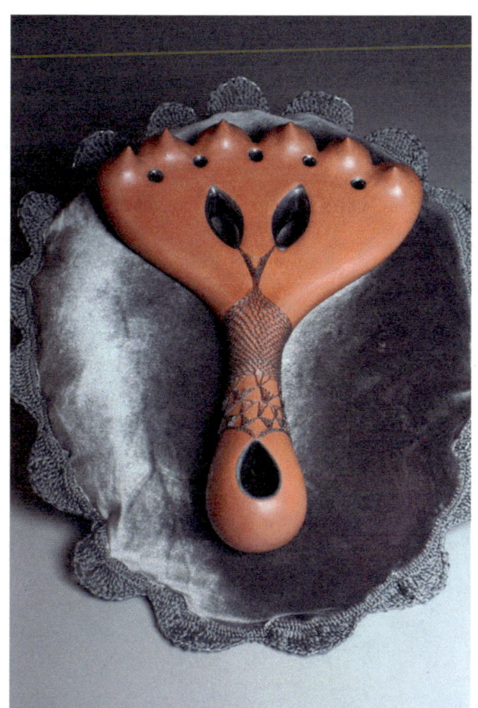

Stephanie Lanter, "Rubberscratcher", burnished earthenware with fabric[3]

Burnishing

Burnishing is one of the oldest surface techniques. It is done by carefully rubbing over the bone dry surface (with a smooth river stone, piece of horn, or back of a spoon) in order to compress and flatten out the clay particles on the surface of the object. If done well, it creates a silky smooth surface on pot that also makes it less porous.

Burnishing is also often done in conjunction with a slip material called terra sigilata. This specially prepared fine clay slip is painted over the piece and then burnished to a high polish.

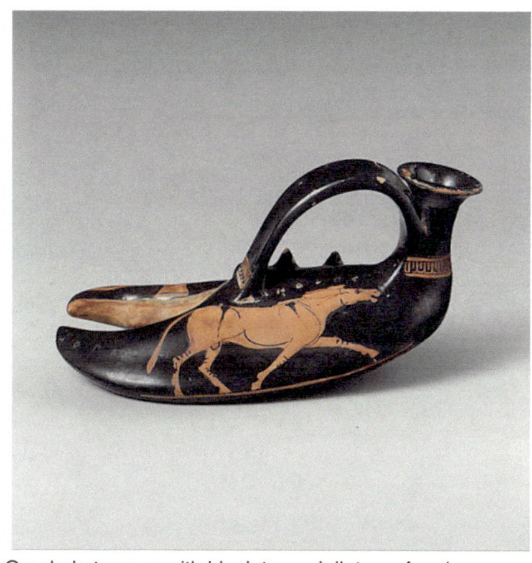

Greek rhyton cup with black terra sigilata surface[4]

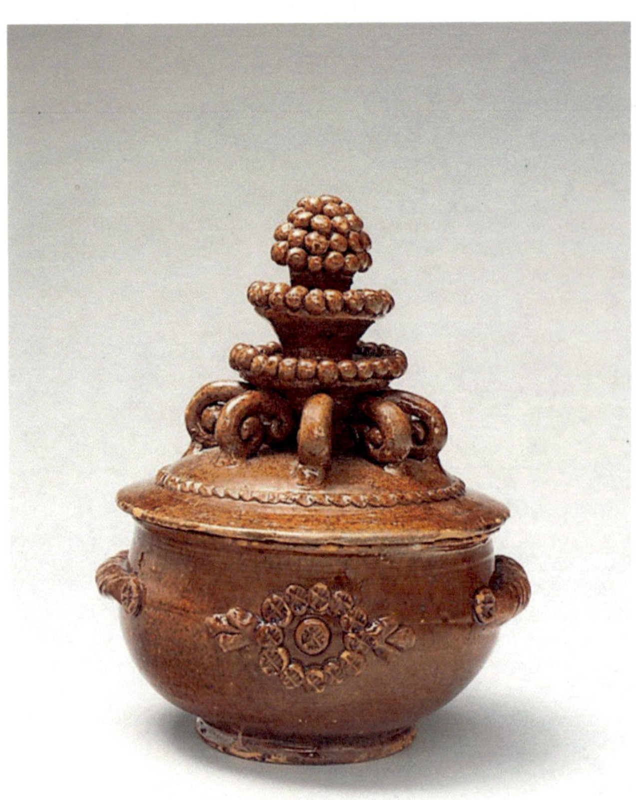

Early American pot with sprigged details[4]

Sprigging

Sprigging is a process of applying smaller decorative shapes to a larger piece at the leatherhard stage. These pieces could be small bits, raised symbols, or mold pressed forms that are then attached to the larger work.

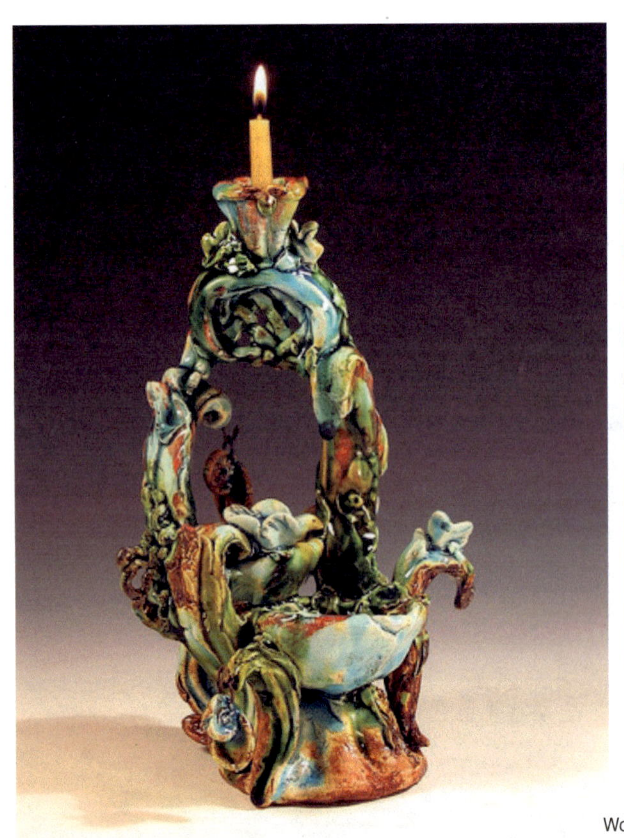

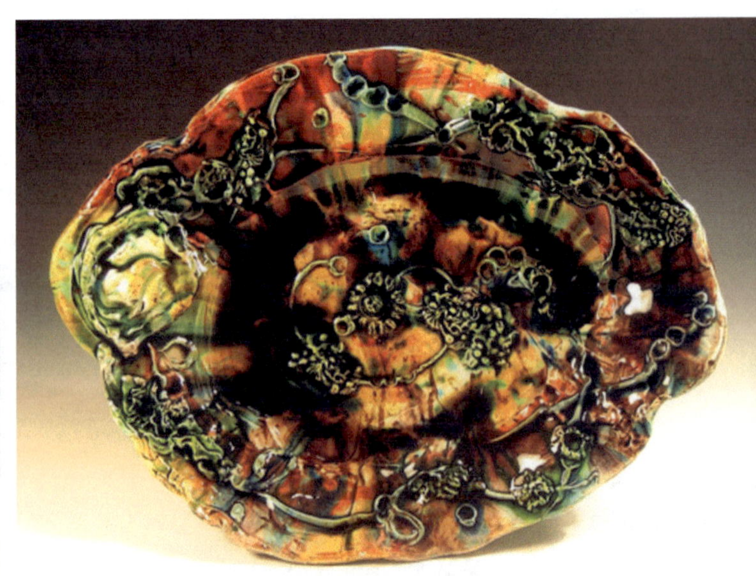

Works by Lisa Orr using a variety of pressmolded, handbuilt, and sprigged surface details[3]

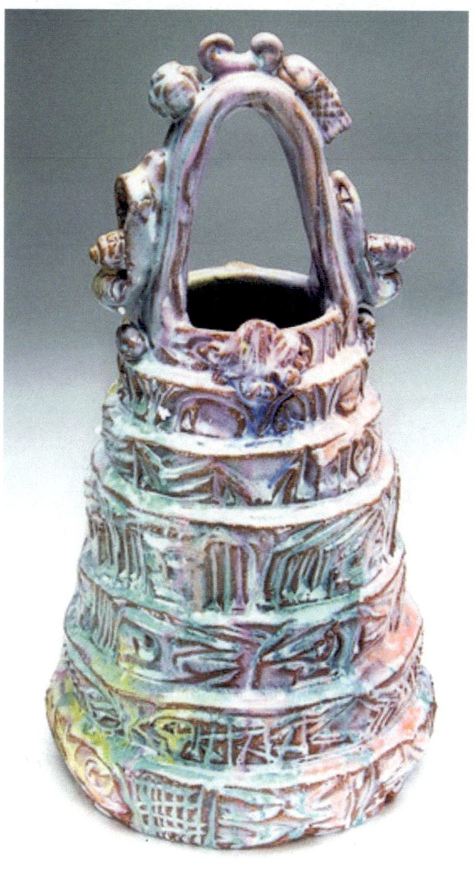

"Boat Ziggurat", Kirk Mangus, carved earthenware[3]

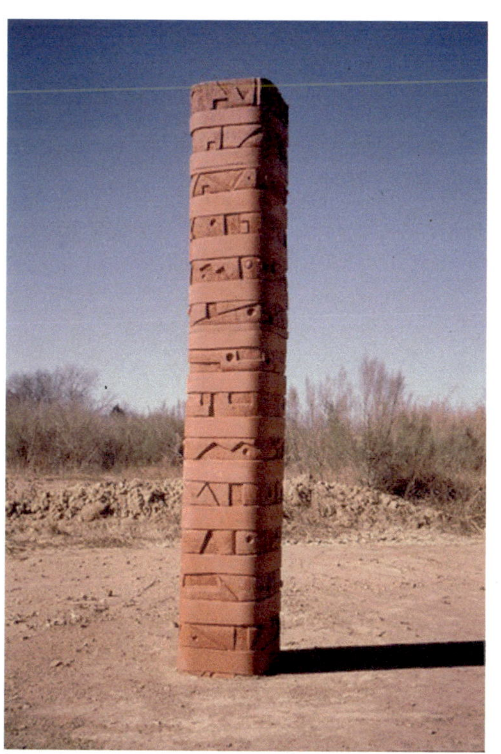

"Marker", Francisco "Pancho" Jiménez, carved earthenware[3]

"Interrupted", Carla Potter, carved porcelain[3]

Carving

Carving into the surface of a piece is a very common way to create pattern or designs. Most often, the best stage for carving clay is at the leatherhard stage when the marks will stay crisp and at the same time, not cause the work to collapse.

There a variety of tools that can be used for surface carving. Commercially made or hand made tools offer a wide range of sizes and shapes to make the process easier, more effective, and more personal.

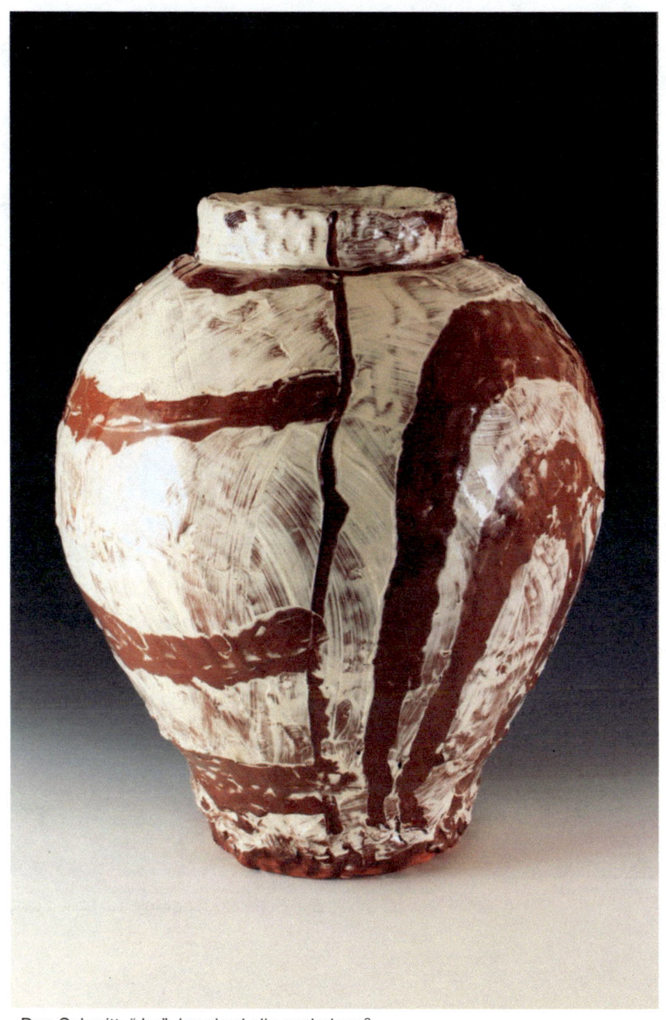

Dan Schmitt, "Jar", brushed slip and glaze[2]

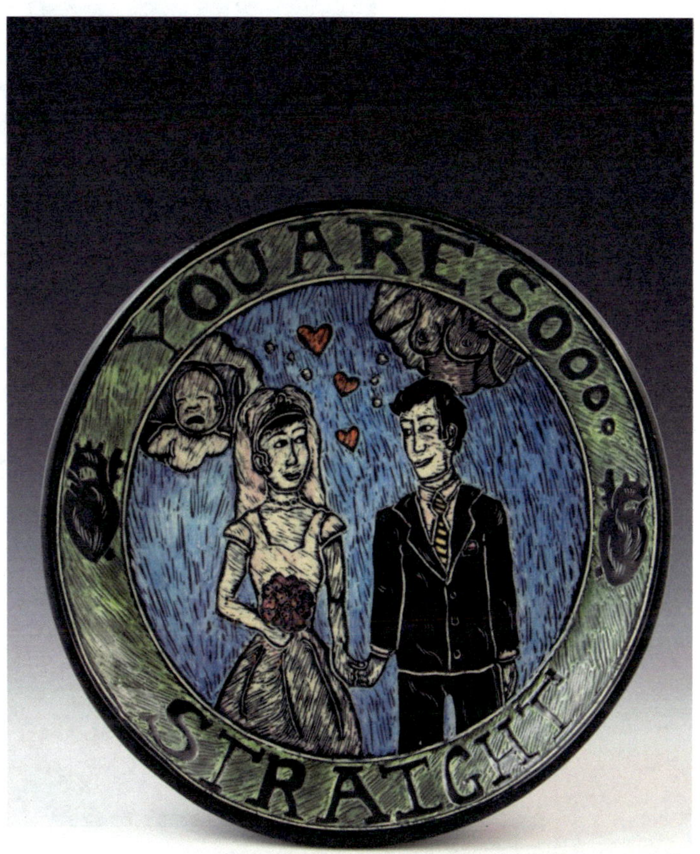

Kathy King, "You are Sooo Straight", underglaze with sgraffito, glaze, and china paint[3]

SLIPS
UNDERGLAZE

Slips used for decoration were originally called "engobes". They were whitish slips that covered the majority of a work made from a dark claybody. Today, most artists use the term slip to talk about a liquid colored clay material used in a variety of ways to decorate the surface of ceramics. This decoration is then most often covered with a clear glaze to brighten the fired color and give the work a glossy surface.

A newer kind of material that can be used in similar ways to slip is called underglaze. Underglazes are commercially prepared liquid mixtures of ceramic materials that come is a range of colors and are useful at a wide range of firing temperature. The main drawback with underglaze is the cost of material compared to studio prepared slips.

Slips are most often applied when the piece is wet clay through leatherhard stage. Some slips and underglazes can be used all the way through bisque stage. Most often, a clear or translucent glaze is applied over the slip to intensive the color and make the surface glossy. There are a variety of slip application techniques to work with. The most direct is to apply the slip on the surface with brush like paint. Additional techniques follow:

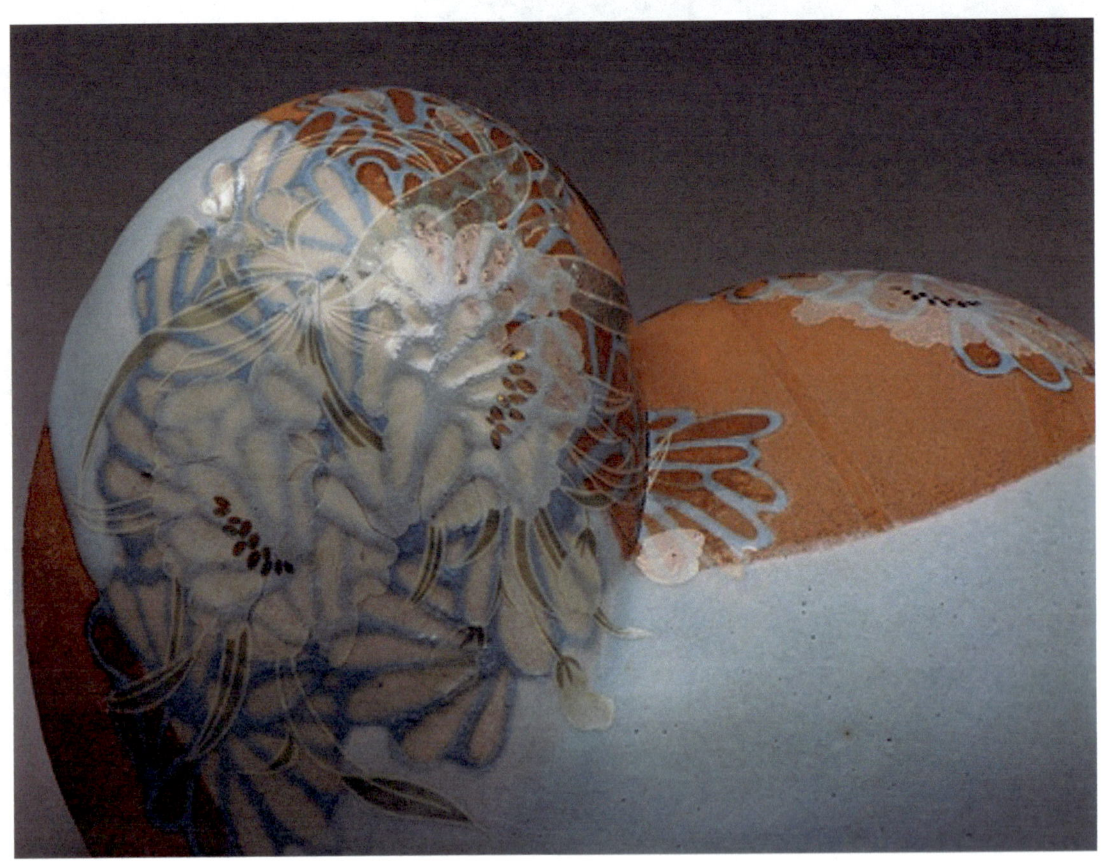

detail of "Accordance", Erin Furimsky, showing slip trailed detail[2]

Slip trailing

Slip trailing uses a bottle with a thin needle-like nozzle to apply the material in dots, lines, and curves. The result is a raised line of material on the surface of the work.

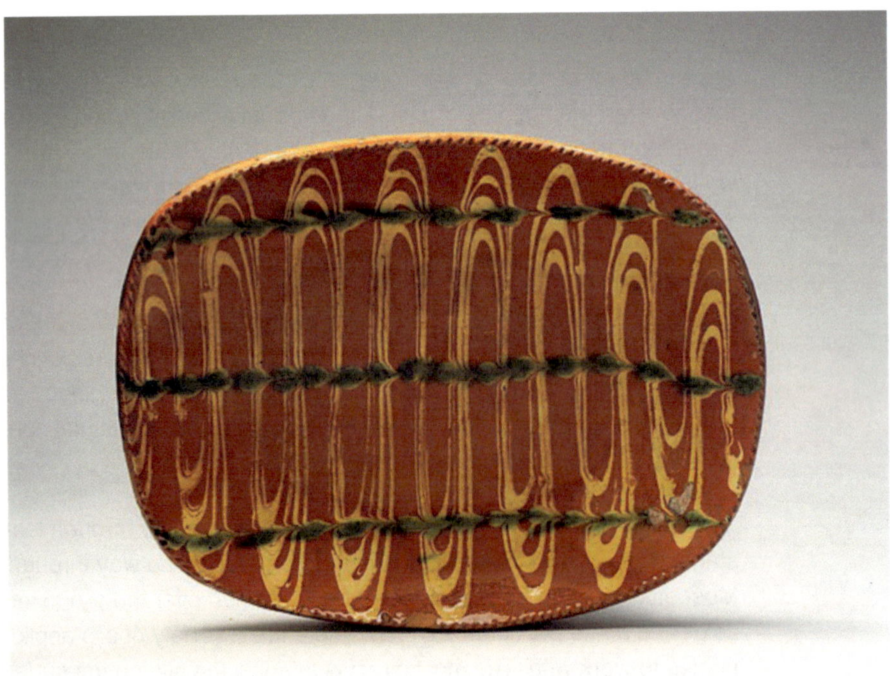

Early American earthenware dish with slip trailed decoration[4]

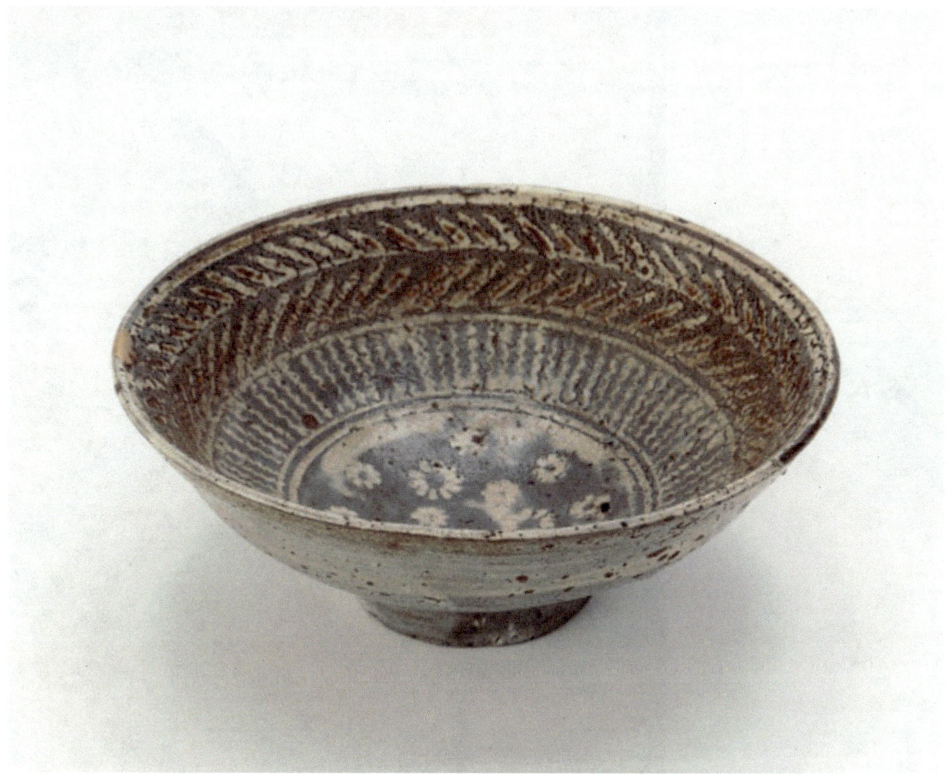

Japanese bowl with Mishima surface design[4]

Slip Inlay / Mishima

The process for slip inlay (also called mishima) requires a design cut or stamped into the surface of the clay. Then liquid slip or underglaze is painted on in order to fill the cut or depressed area. After the slip dries a bit, the excess material is scraped or shaved off the surface leaving the slip "inlaid" in the body of the work.

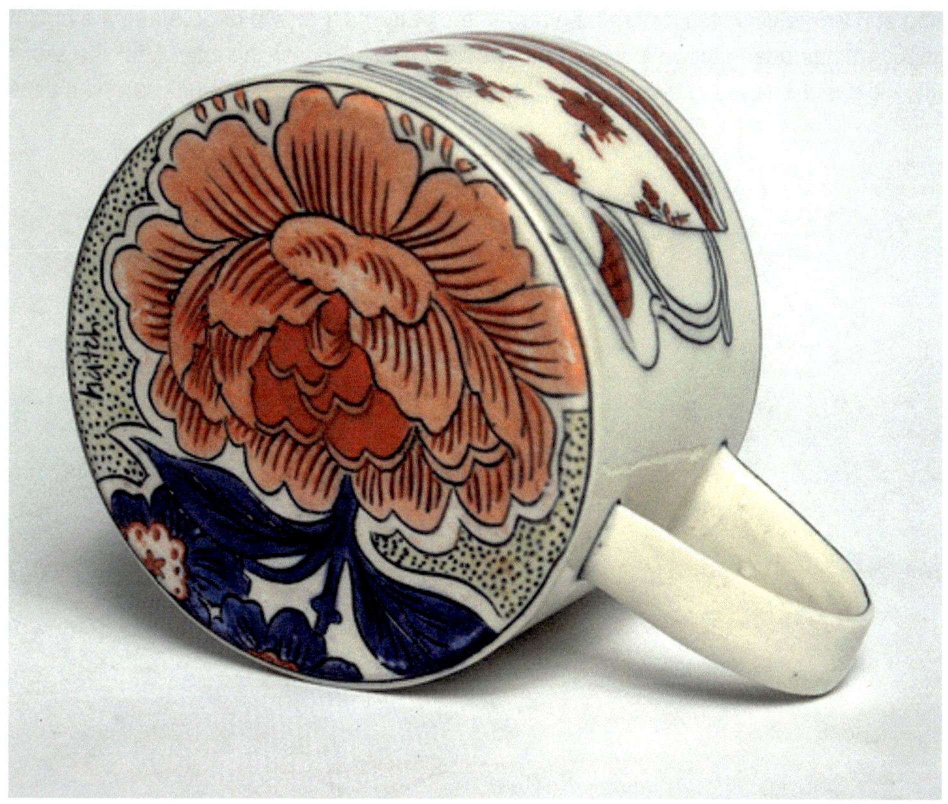

"Cup Painting: Cup on Cup Base", Molly Hatch, porcelain with mishima underglaze and slip[3]

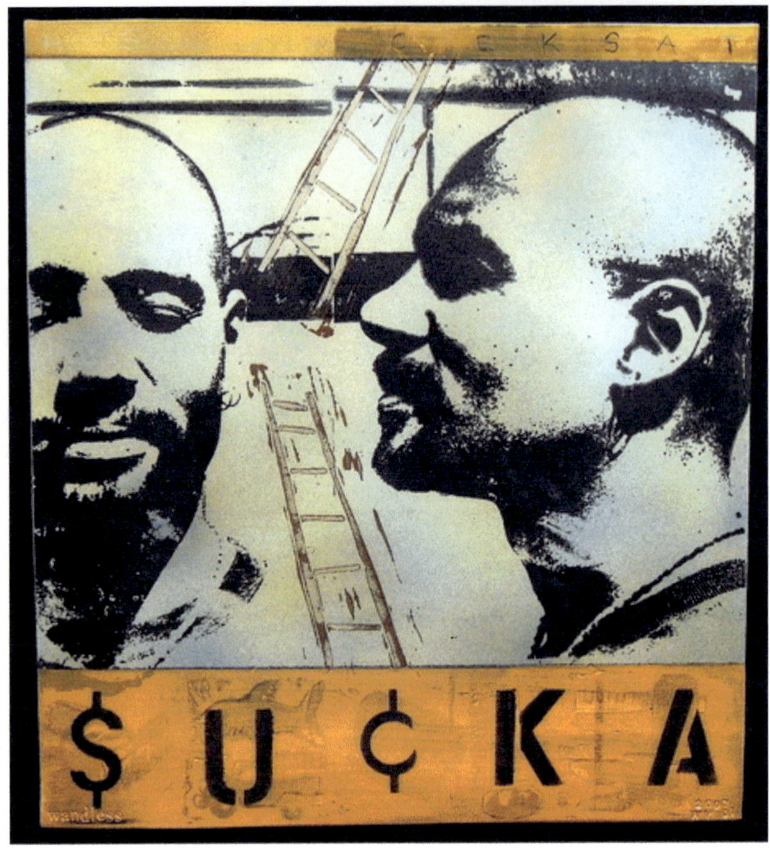

"$u¢ka", Paul Andrew Wandless, stenciled, screened,and linocut underglaze[5]

Slip resist / Stencil

In slip resist, a shape is placed on the surface of the work and then slip is painted over. This technique works just like stenciling and works very well for creating geometric patterns. For slip decoration, the best material to use is a paper shape that has been dipped in water and pressed carefully onto the clay. After the slip is applied and dried slightly, the paper shapes can be pulled off and any bleeds under the stencil can be cleaned up.

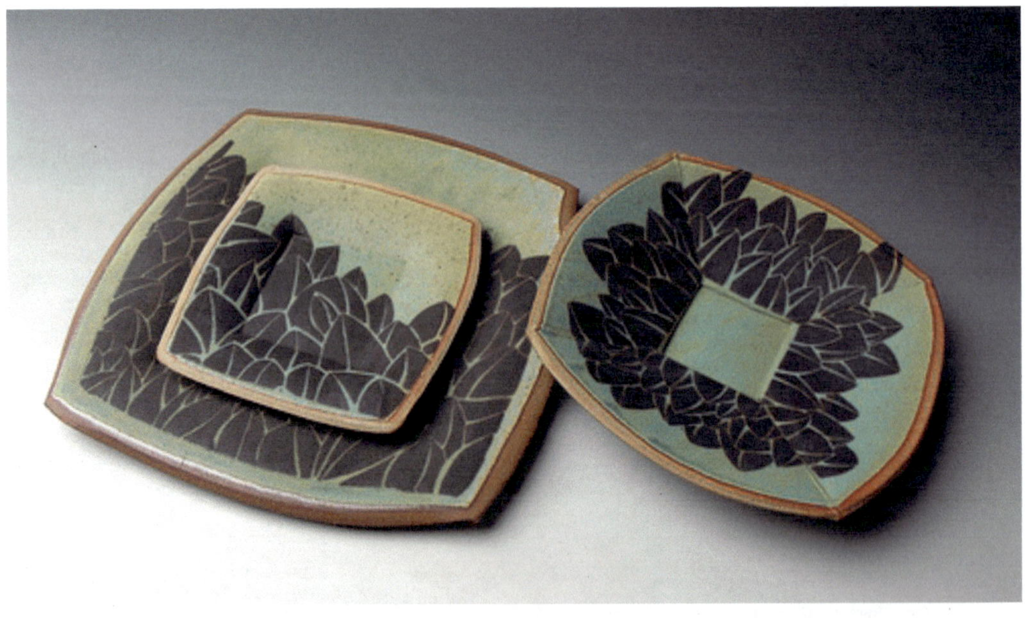

"Leaf Dinnerware", Hayne Bayless, stoneware with stenciled black slip[3]

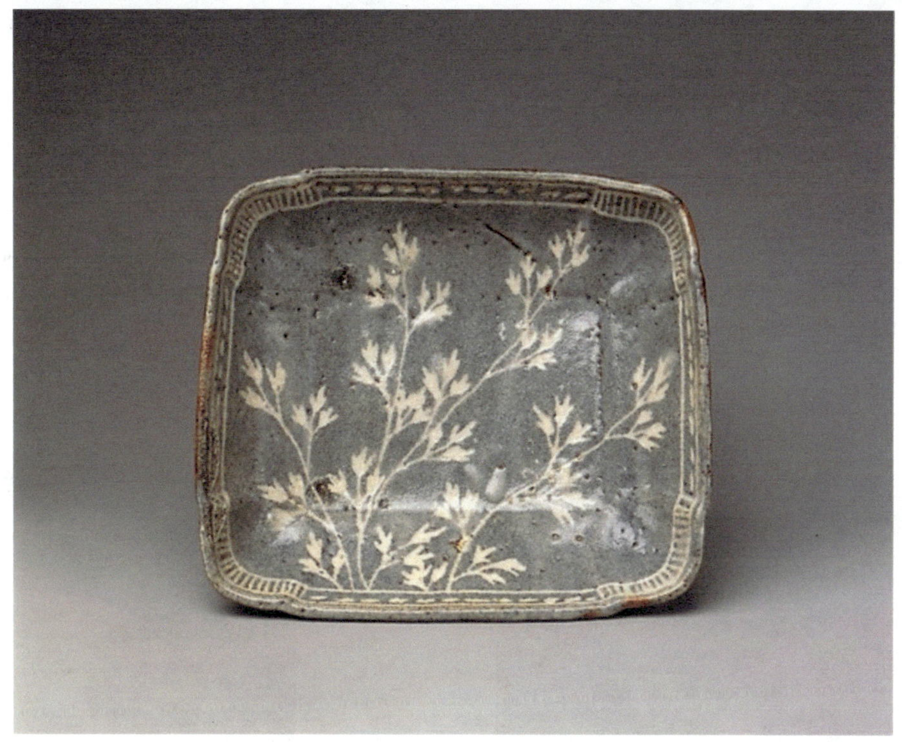

Japanese Shino ware dish with sgraffito decoration cutting through a dark slip into the whitish clay underneath[4]

Sgraffito

Sgraffito is a traditional technique using a layer of slip or underglaze applied to the piece. When the liquid material dries, a sharp tool cuts or scratches into the surface breaking through the layer of material on top. This reveals the color of the clay underneath.

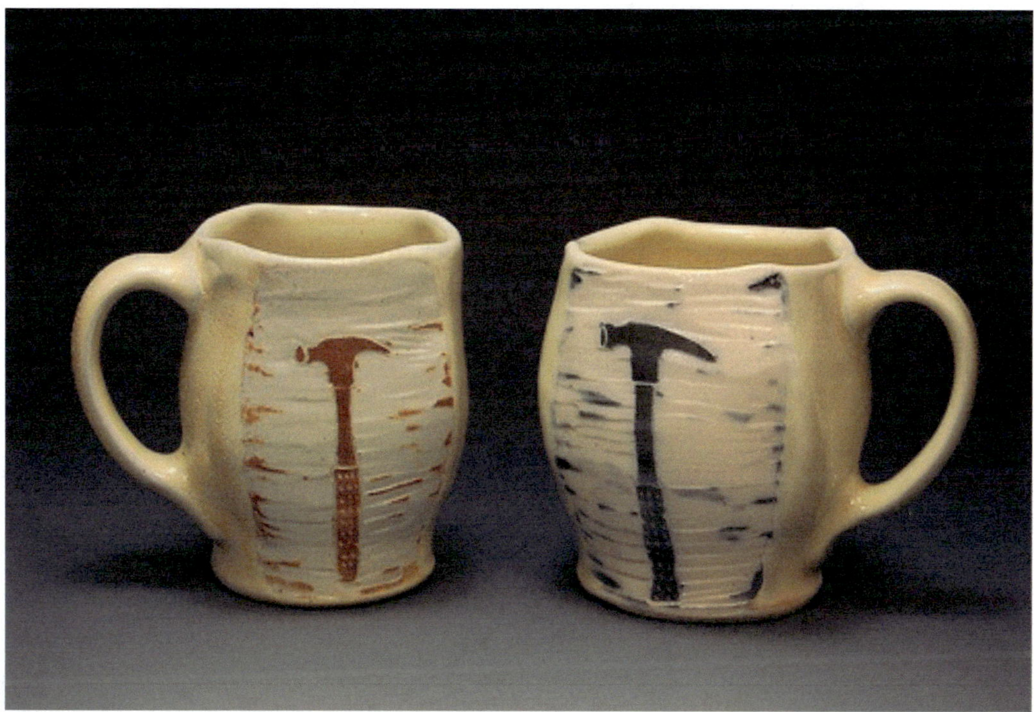

"Hammer Mugs", Kowkie Durst, porcelain with sgraffito[3]

Other Slip techniques

Flashing slip
A flashing slip is used when firing work in a wood, soda, or salt fired kiln. This very thin coating of clay and other materials (applied to bisque) makes the clay body more receptive to the atmosphere inside the kiln and usually creates orange, red, or yellow colors on the surface.

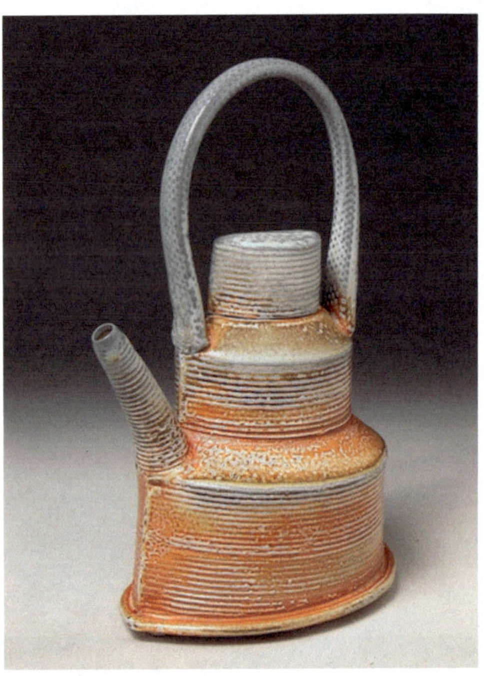

Richard Burkett, soda fired stoneware with flashing slip[5]

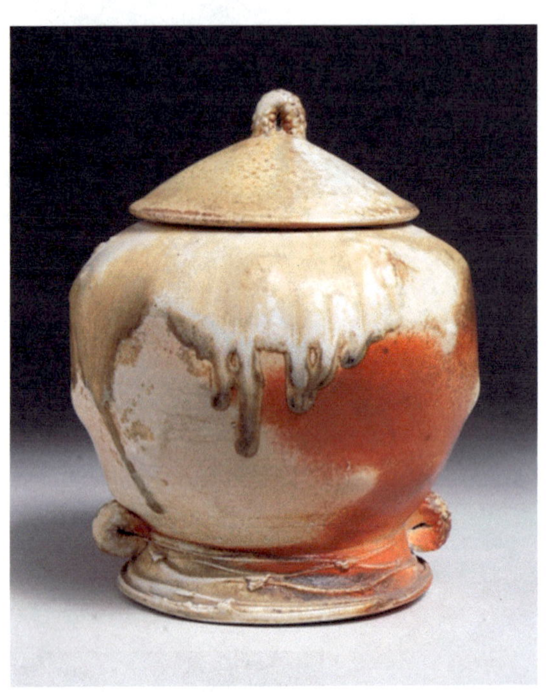

Richard Burkett, woodfired porcelain with flashing slip[5]

Terra sigilata
This very fine grained clay slip is created by chemically altering the clay particles in a liquid solution. The solution settles into layers of particle sizes and the fine layer is siphoned off to use. The "sig" is then brushed onto a dry piece and burnished down to make a silky smooth surface on the clay. This material was used by the ancient Greeks to create some of the masterpieces of ceramic and art history.

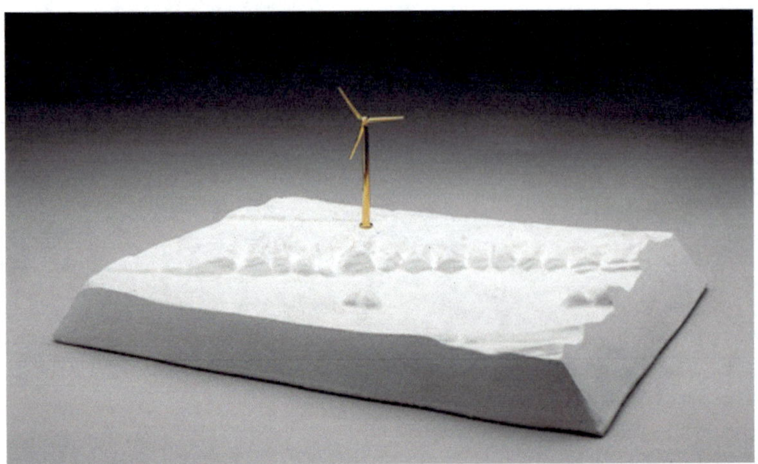

"Wind Turbine", John Williams, slip cast earthenware with terra sigillata[3]

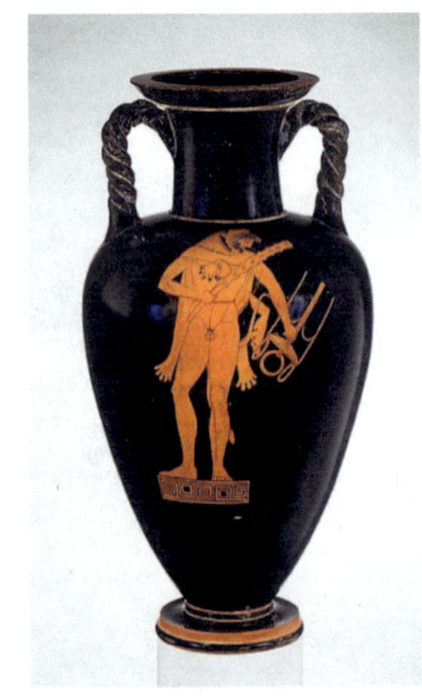

Greek amphora with black and red terra sigilata[4]

Slip Recipes:

-Most slips work best from wet clay to leatherhard stage
-Some slips can be applied to bisqueware if mixed very thin
-Most base recipes are white or off-white
-Color can be added with minerals or commercial stains
-Some slips are designed to be fired in specific kinds of kilns

Mangus Slip (cone 04-9)

EPK kaolin	25%
Ball clay	25
Silica	25
Nepheline Syenite	13
Gerstley Borate	12

Val's All Purpose Slip (cone 6 -10)

EPK Kaolin	15%
Tile #6 kaolin	30
Ball clay	25
Nepheline syenite	15
Silica	15

Hess White Slip (cone 6 - 10)

EPK kaolin	50%
OM#4 ball clay	10
Silica	10
Nepheline syenite	30

Birdie's White Slip (cone 6-10)

Grolleg kaolin	17%
Calcined kaolin	19
OM#4 ball clay	17
Custer feldspar	19
Silica	19
Borax	4
Zircopax	5

Bede's Crackle Slip (for bisqueware in woodkiln)

EPK Kaolin	15.3%
Calcined kaolin	21.4
OM#4 ball clay	15.3
Custer feldspar	21.4
Silica	21.4
Borax	5.1
Zircopax	5.1

McNamee Flashing Slip (for bisqueware in woodkiln)

McNamee kaolin	70%
Helmer kaolin	5
OM#4 ball clay	5
Silica	10
Nepheline Syenite	10
Bentonite	1

Lobster Red Flashing Slip (for bisqueware in woodkiln)

Grolleg kaolin	12.1%
Tile #6 kaolin	26.4
EPK kaolin	19.3
Ball clay	12.2
Nepheline Syenite	30
Soda ash	4
Bentonite	3

Ted's Orange Slip (for bisqueware in woodkiln)

Grolleg kaolin	42%
OM#4 ball clay	42
Zircopax	10.5
Lithium Carbonate	5.5

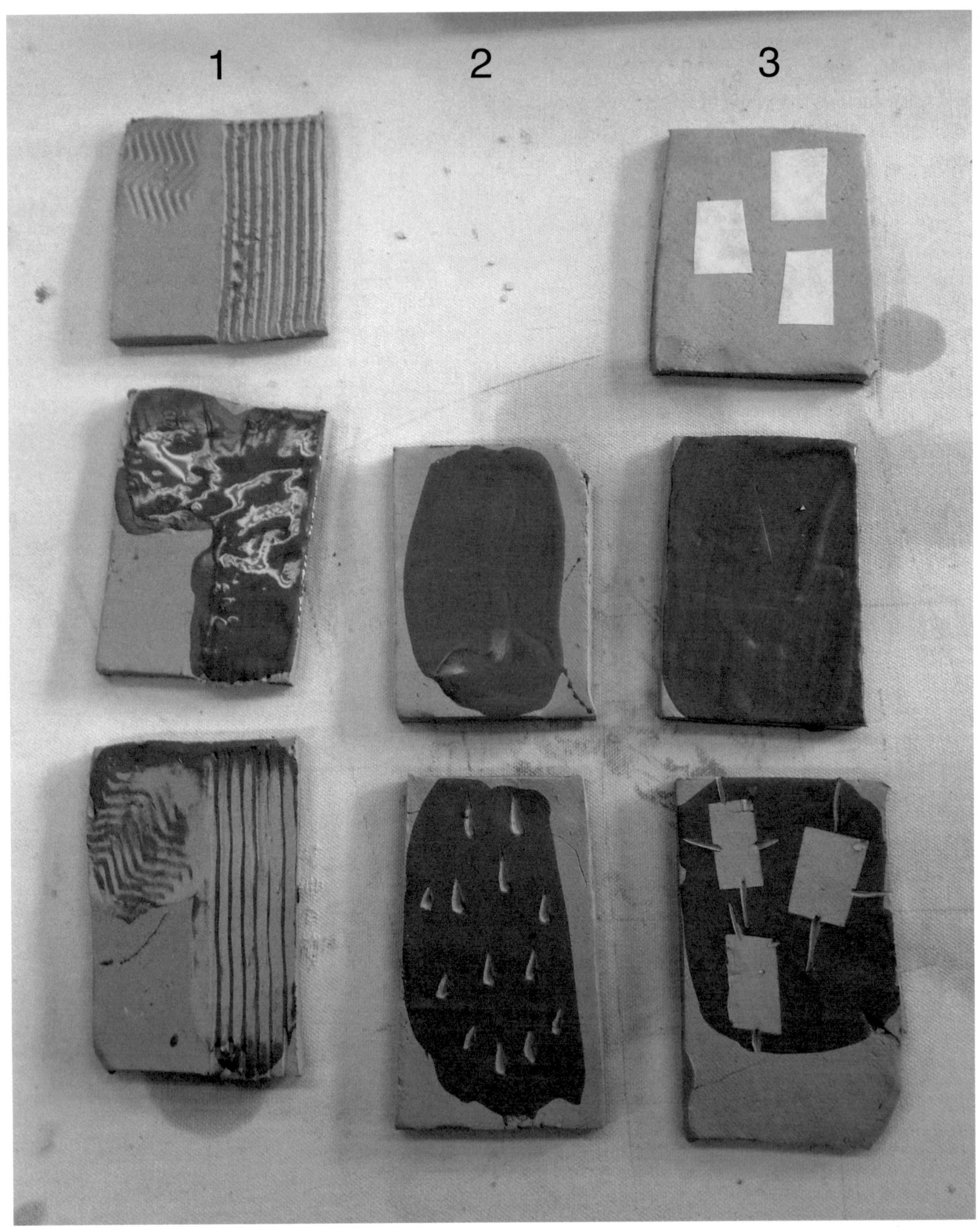

Steps for slip decoration techniques.[1]
Column 1: **Inlay (Mishima)**- Impress or carve into the clay surface, fill with liquid slip and let dry, scrape excess off surface
Column 2: **Sgraffito**- Paint on slip and let dry, carve design through slip layer to reveal the clay underneath
Column 3: **Slip Resist**- Cut out paper stencil shapes, wet paper and apply to clay surface, paint slip over, remove paper stencils

Notes:

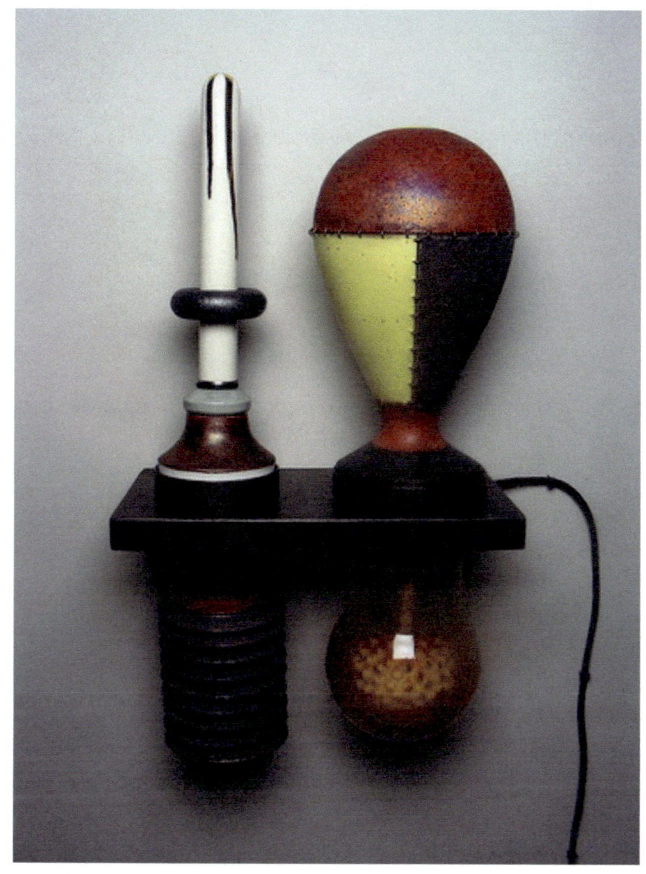

"Surrogate", Matt Wilt, glazed porcelain and mixed media[3]

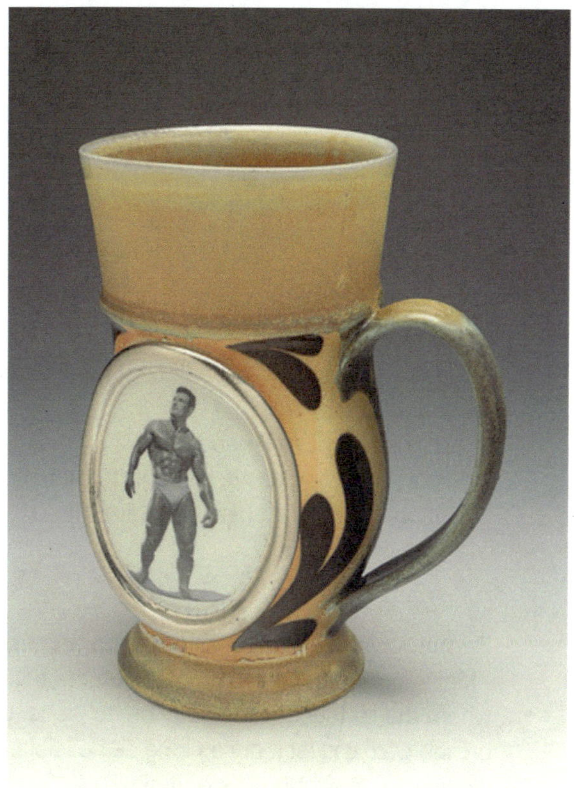

"Yelena's Stein" Bethany Benson, soda fired glazed stoneware with decals[3]

GLAZE

A glaze is a glassy coating of minerals and clays fired onto the surface of the ceramics and is very common surface technique. This liquid mixture is most often applied to bisque ware using a variety of methods such as dipping, brushing, spraying, or sponging. Once the glaze application is dry, the work will be fired a second time in order to melt this material and fuse it to the clay body. Additional firings can be done in order to apply other materials or other glazes. The temperature of these firings depends on the melting temperature of the material with the hottest firing done first and then progressing to lower temperature each time. For example, a high fired glaze on porcelain first, then a lower temperature glaze next, and finally a very low temperature firing for gold luster or decals.

All glazes can be described using the following four characteristics with the idea that glaze is like a glass and has similar properties. They are:
1- Color: Glazes can have a very wide range of colors but this is influenced by the materials used, the kind of kiln used, the temperature of the firing, and other factors.

2- Fluidity: As a molten mixture during firing, the glaze can move down a piece. Some glazes are formulated to be fluid others to be totally stable.

3- Surface: Glazes all have a finished surface related to their chemistry and how the piece has been fired. Some glazes are meant to be dry matte surfaces, while others to have a high gloss, glassy finish. Some sculptural glazes can look like rust, lichen, or even dried mud.

4- Opacity: Just like glass, glazes can have a range of opaque to transparent light transmission. Some glazes are totally opaque and do not allow any of the clay surface to be seen. Pieces with complex slip or surface patterns most often have a clear transparent or translucent glaze covering.

Steps for applying glaze
1- Rinse bisqueware in sink
2- Stir glaze in bucket
3-Dip piece in bucket or if painting- paint on one coat, then let dry and paint on second coat in different brush direction
4-Let dry
5- Apply other glaze if needed
6- When finished glazing, wipe glaze off bottom of piece until bisque shows
7- Put on the correct shelf to be glaze fired, write down glazes used and in what order

Reminders for successful glaze application:
- Make sure that there is no glaze on the bottom of the piece. If it has parts like a lid, make sure that there is no glaze where the lid touches the body of the piece. Liquid wax can be used to resist the glaze from getting on those parts. Apply the wax and let it dry as long as possible. Then make sure to wipe any glaze dots off the wax after glazing or simply use a wet sponge to clean glaze off.

-You can glaze within an 1/8" from the bottom. This gives the glaze a small space to move into if it is fluid. If there isn't enough space left, the molten glaze will flow down, stick the piece to the kiln shelf, and ruin your project.

-Always mix the liquid glaze thoroughly to get all the heavy ingredients into the mix. If glaze isn't mixed, the application will be too thin and result in incorrect colors and surfaces.

-If using more than 1 coat of glaze, make sure to allow the first glaze to dry completely. Waiting at least 1/2 hour is minimum, some potters glaze the insides of their work one day and the outside the next.

-If you used slips and underglazes for decoration, you need to apply a glaze (most often a clear glaze) to intensify the color and smooth over the surface of the slip/underglaze.

-Masking tape on clean bisqueware and liquid wax over glazed sections can be used to create resist patterns in the glaze application. Tape can also be used to mask out areas / shapes on the bisque for later brush patterns.

-Pay attention (and write it down) to the order in which you applied your glazes. The result will differ depending on which glaze was on top. When you layer glaze, your are mixing molten minerals not mixing pigments like paint. For example, a white glaze on top of a black glaze does not create a gray color.

Additional glaze techniques

There are a number of glaze possibilities outside of applying individual glazes and finish firing the piece a single time. One traditional technique is to use precious metals in a solution (called **luster**) painted onto a previously glaze fired piece. The work is then re-fired to a lower temperature, around 1,000 F, in order to fuse the solution onto the glaze surface. The luster material must be handled carefully since the solution is toxic and during the firing, the kiln must be vented well. After firing, the luster is safe and is often used as decoration on fine porcelain dinner ware.

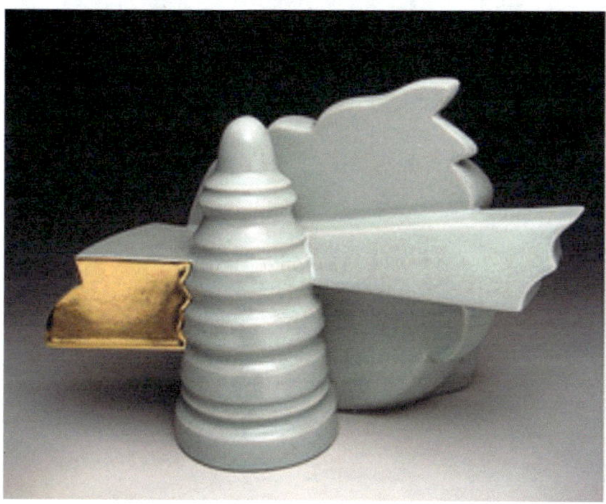
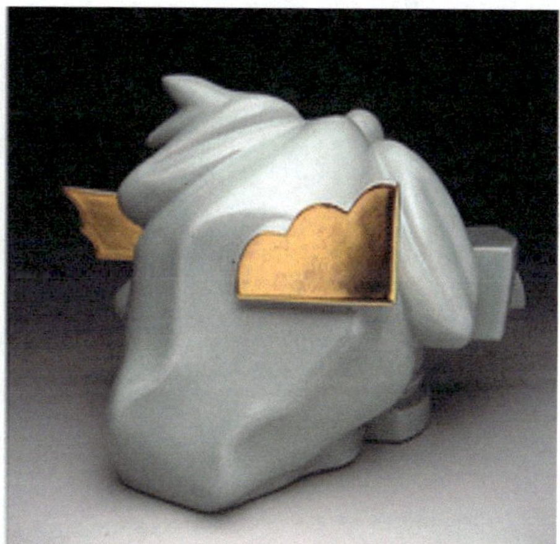

"Born Tree", William DePauw, glazed porcelain with gold luster[5]

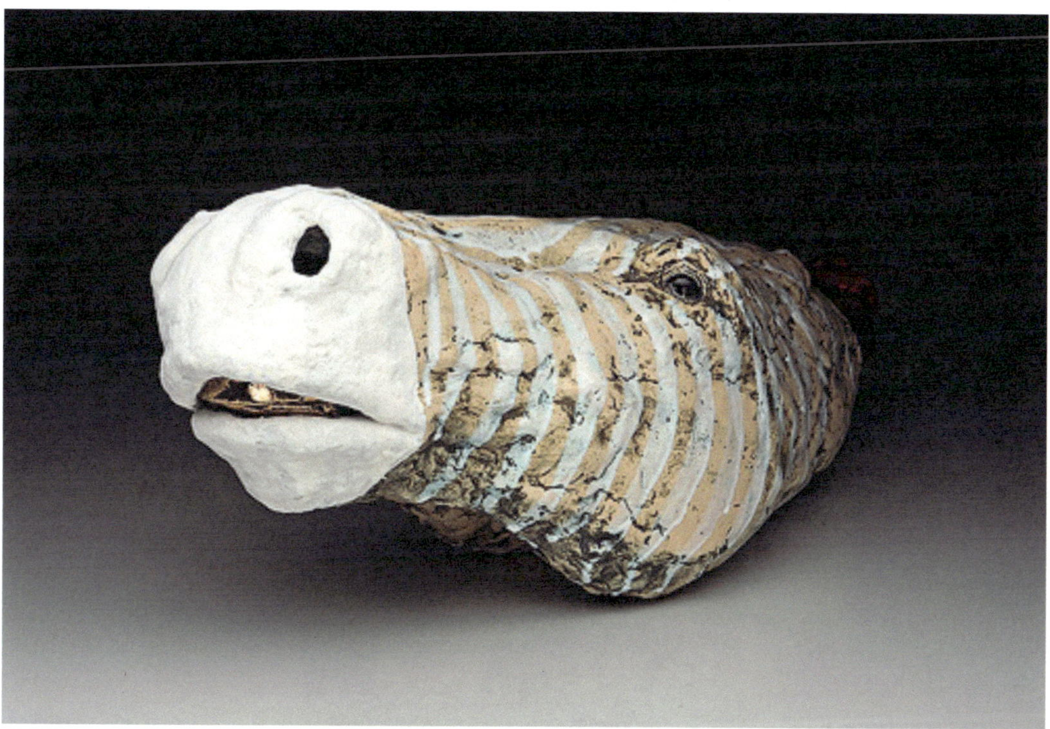

"Ouroboros", Roxanne Jackson, earthenware with slips and gold luster[2]

Ceramic **decals** are pre-printed patterns / images that will be fired to the surface of a glazed piece at a low temperature. The decal is soaked in water, slipped off the backing paper, and applied to the glazed surface. The piece is then re-fired. Many artists today are using the decal process to apply photography or digitally created images to their work.

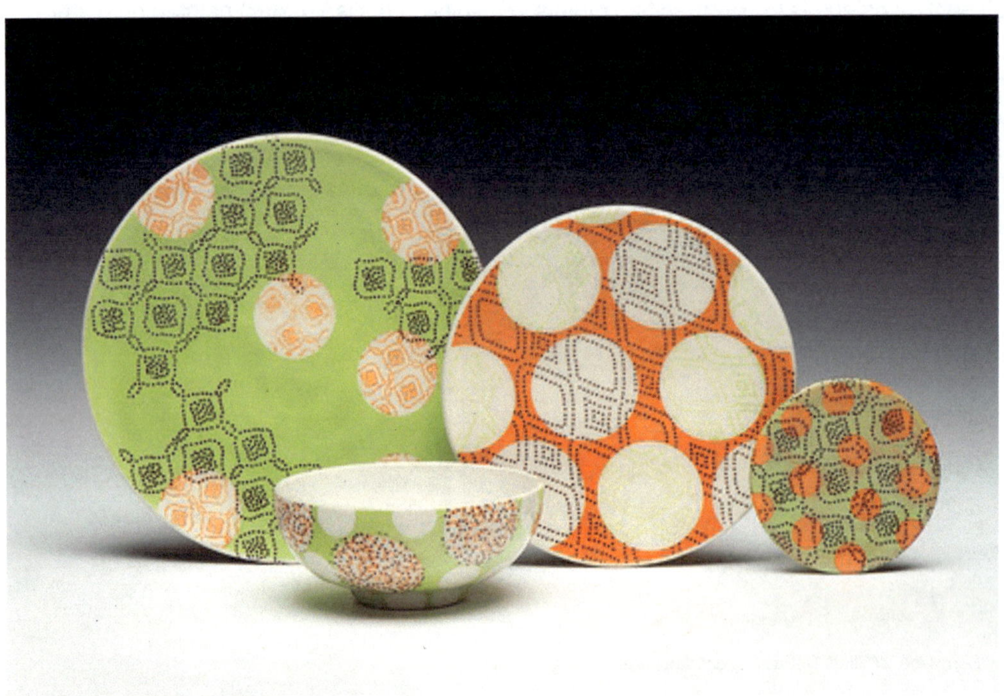

"Dinner Setting", Meredith Host, porcelain with screen printing and decals[3]

Finally, a material seeing a revival in use by artists is one that was once isolated to use by "hobby" painters is **china paint** (also known as overglaze). This water or oil based enamel material is painted onto the glaze of a fired piece. It is then re-fired to between 1,100 and 1,350 F to melt the color onto the glaze.

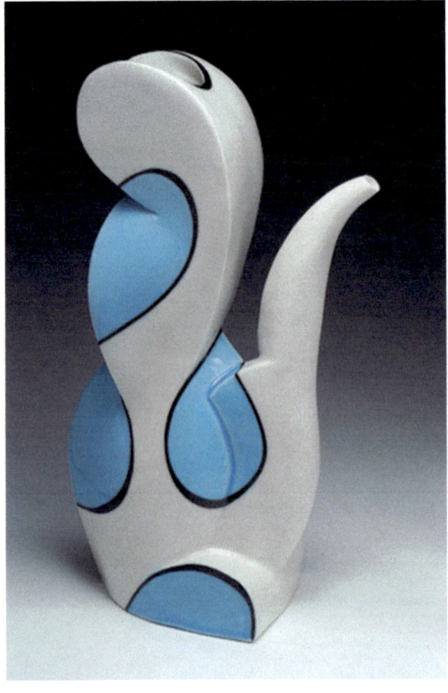

"Ewer", Sam Chung, glazed porcelain with china paint[2]

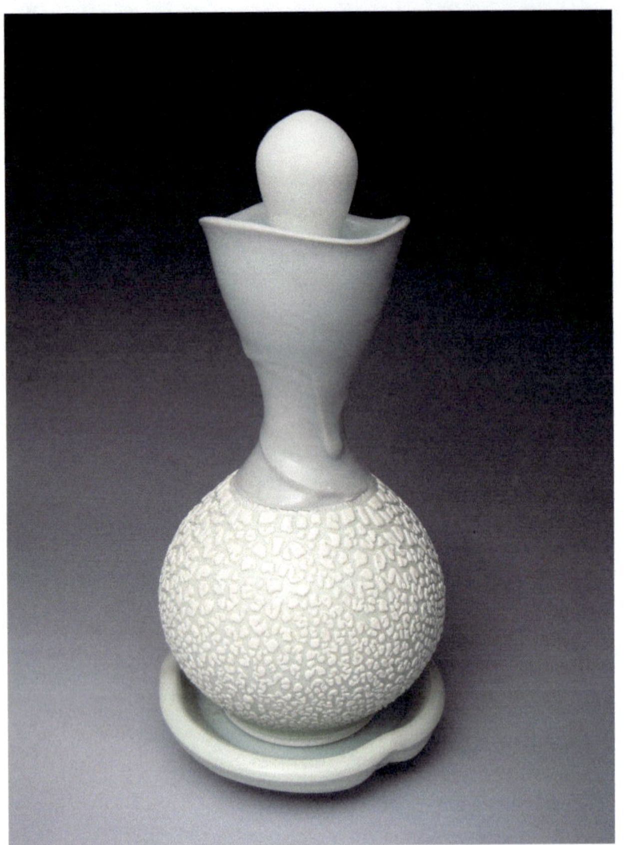

John Oles, "Bottle", cone 10 glazed porcelain[3]

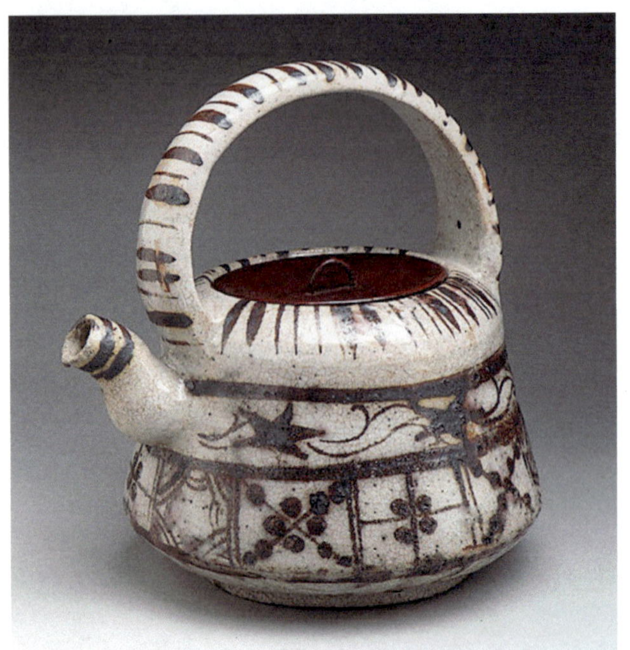

Japanese Mino ware pouring pot[4]

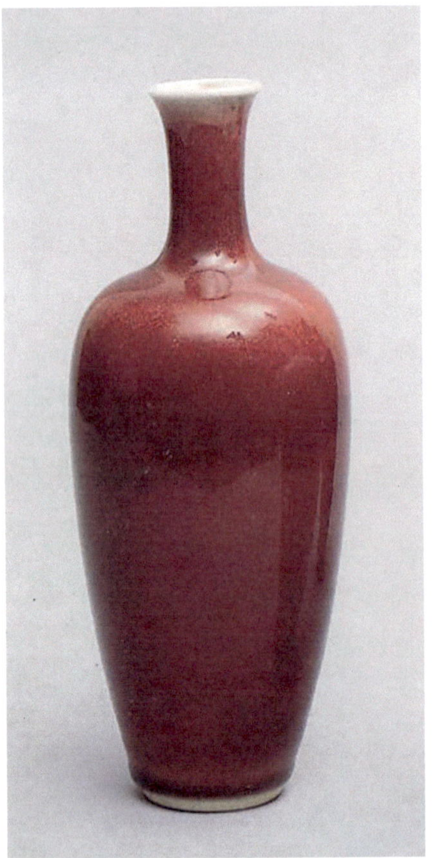

Chinese Qing Dynasty copper red glazed bottle[4]

9

GLAZE CHEMISTRY

Glazes were developed thousands of years ago in order to decorate the surface of ceramic objects and also to make them more functional or decorative. This coating is a mixture of elements like silica, alumina, sodium, calcium, potassium, zinc and other minerals. Using glaze is not like using paint, colors and surfaces come from the mixture of molten minerals interacting with clay, heat, and the atmosphere inside the hot kiln. With experience, surface designs on your work can be developed like a composition for drawing, design or painting.

Glazes can have a variety of surface textures from high gloss to dry matt and be transparent like window glass all the way to completely opaque.

The History of Glazes

Current research shows that the first glazes were developed in Ancient Egypt around 10,000 years ago. This was most likely an accident when a salty sand mixture melted into a fused glassy material in the heat of a fire. This material became known as "Egyptian Paste" and is still used today. In the Middle East around 5,000 BCE, potters were creating true low temperature glazes using a variety of ceramic materials. By around 1,500 BCE, Chinese potters developed the kiln technology to fire ceramics to a very high temperature (over 2,200 F) with wood and coal and create stoneware and porcelain ceramics. Near the end of the Ming Dynasty (around 1644 CE), Chinese artists had developed the majority of the ceramics knowledge we continue to use today. The development of glazes had been a process of curiosity and trial and error up until the 19th century. A German chemist named Hermann Seger developed a way to work with glaze chemistry that utilized precise molecular weights of the elements. This allowed ceramic industry and artists to have more control and predictability in this difficult process. Today glaze chemistry software takes most of the hand calculations out of looking at the chemical makeup of glaze recipes and allows the artist and engineer to look at the "bones" of a glaze and get a sense of how it might work in the kiln. Glazes still have surprises for the user and even after years you can discover new ways of using just a few.

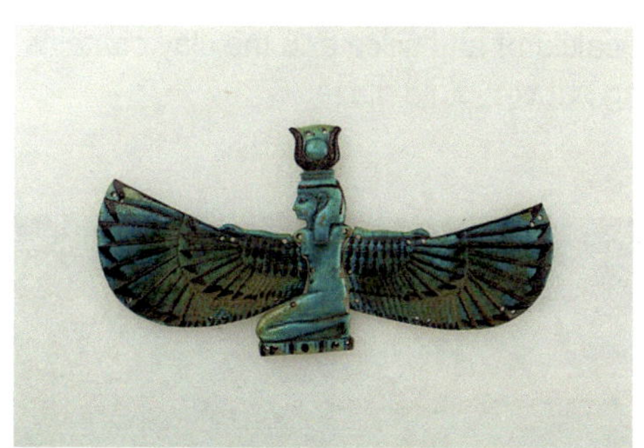

Egyptian Paste amulet[4]

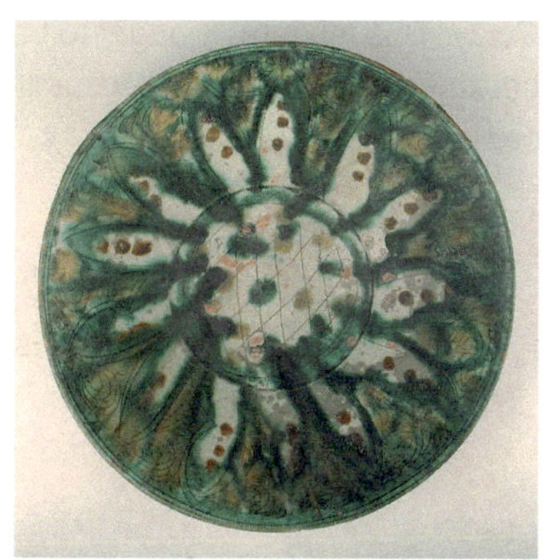

Nishapur bowl from Iran[4]

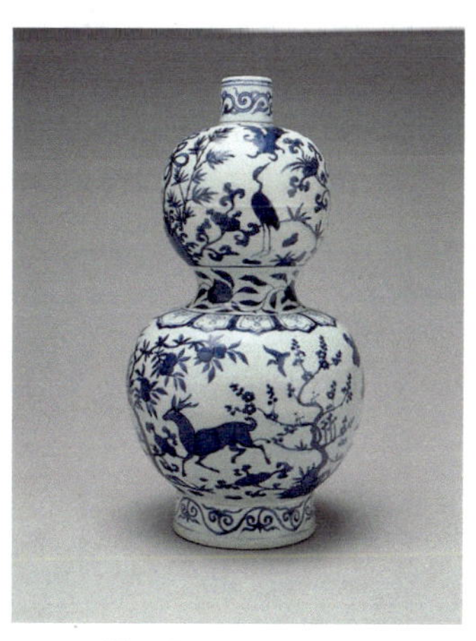

Ming Dynasty porcelain bottle[4]

Basics of Glaze Chemistry

Any glaze can be broken down into three main parts. These are:

1- *Glass formers*- These materials form the glassy structure of the glaze when the correct temperature is reached. Silica, or silicon dioxide, is the most important glass former in ceramics (and glass making), one of the building blocks of clay, and it's the most common element in the Earth's crust. When formulating glaze recipes, silica can come from adding pure silica, clays, feldspars, and other silicate materials based on their chemistry. Other glass formers sometimes used in glazes are Boron oxide and Phosphorous oxide.

2- *Fluxes*- Pure silica melts at a very high temperature- nearly 3,000 F. This temperature is much too high for making ceramic pots and sculpture so something is needed to help lower the melting temperature of the glaze mix. A *flux* material helps the glaze melt. The mixture of different materials in a glaze creates a reaction during heating called a *eutectic*. This interaction lowers the melting point of the materials below their individual melting temperature.

The fluxes used in glaze making are often very complex alkaline oxide (lithium, sodium, and potassium), alkaline earth oxide (magnesium, calcium, strontium, and barium), and metallic oxide (lead and zinc) elements.

In addition, man-made materials called *frits* can be used as a flux in the creation of glazes. Frits are manufactured mixtures of specific fluxes and silica that help to make things more predictable, eliminate problems with handling, and make some materials less hazardous.

***3-Refractories*-** A refractory (alumina oxide) component is very important as a stabilizing element in a molten glaze mix. Once the flux has helped to melt the silica, the melted glaze can become very fluid. The refractory helps to slow the movement of the glassy material and prevent it from running off the side of the object. The most common refractory in a glaze recipe is clay. The type of clay most often used is kaolin since it is white and doesn't contain an excess of minerals (like iron) that might affect the glaze color. Adding clay to a glaze also helps keep the liquid mixture from settling in the bucket as the glaze is stored.

One of the most common fluxes for higher temperature glazes is a form of feldspar. This type of rock contains alkaline oxides, silica, and alumina. In essence, this one material contains all the chemistry needed to make a high temperature glaze on it's own. From personal experience, it does work but it is ugly! A nicer looking simple glaze mixture is the combination of 50% fireplace ash and 50% clay. This mixture, thought to be one of the first high temperature glazes, works because wood ash contains a complex mixture of flux elements (especially calcium) and silica and the clay contains the refractory alumina and silica. So with two ingredients, you can get a working but very fluid glaze.

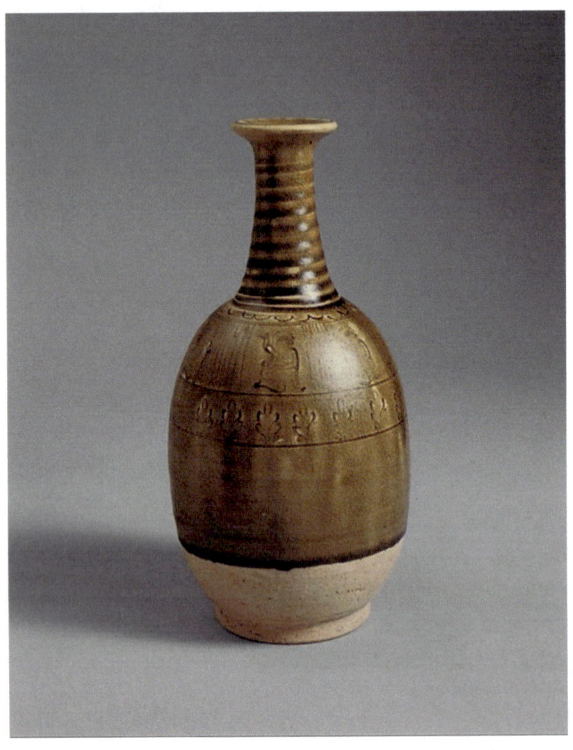

Chinese Sui Dynasty (581-618 CE) stoneware bottle with applied glaze containing wood ash[4]

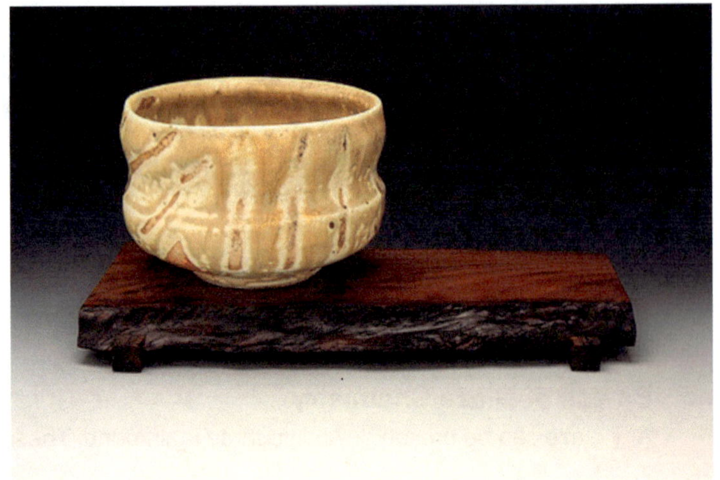

Heidi Kreitchet, "Teabowl with Wooden Base", 2013, stoneware bowl with wood ash glaze[5]

Glaze color is a very complex issue. In general, the colors achieved in the fired glaze depend on the materials used, how they were applied and to what clay body, how the piece was fired, if there were glazes overlapping, and other factors. Any base glaze can be made more opaque (most glazes will be gray, white, or semi transparent with no additions of colorants) by adding an opacifier or have color with the addition of certain minerals or commercial stains.

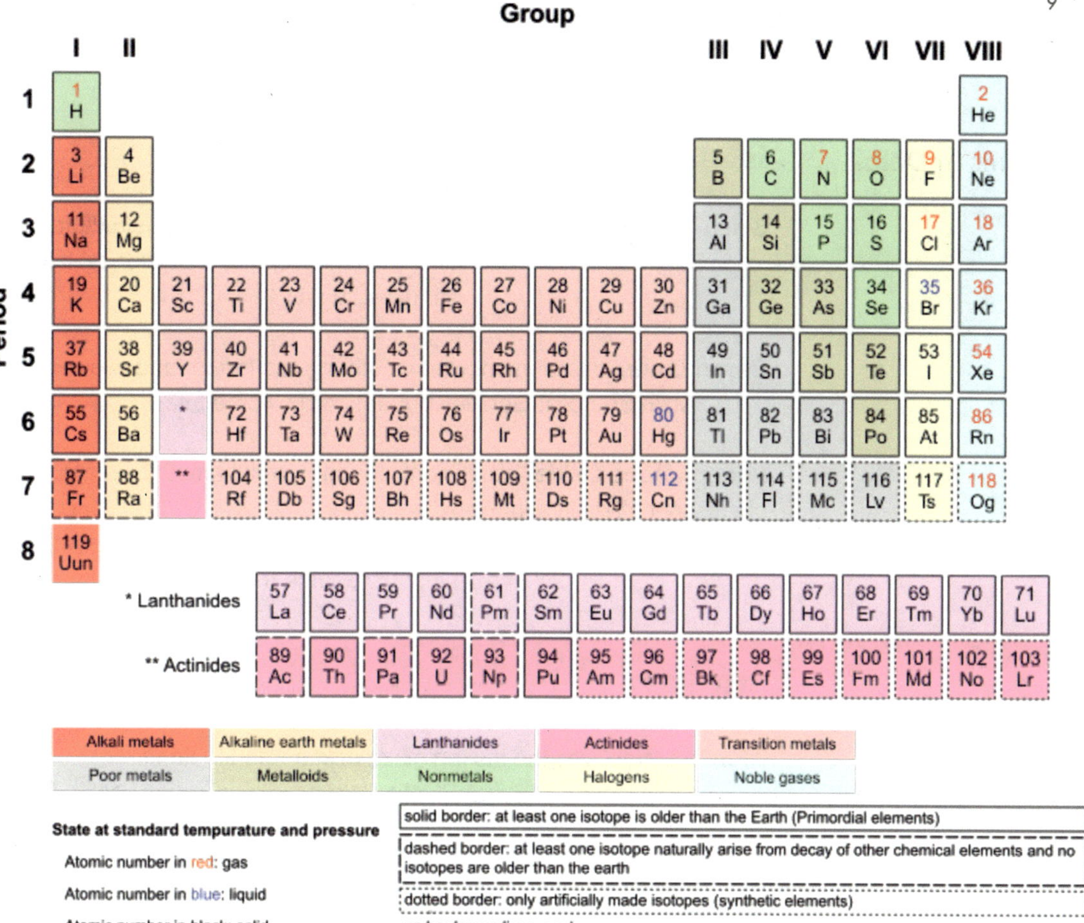

CERAMIC CHEMISTRY

A basic familiarity with chemistry will help you understand how glazes and other ceramic materials work. We use a relatively limited range of elements compared to the total on the Periodic Table. The most important elements are near the top of the table and can be broken into 5 categories.

Glass formers (RO_2)
Silica- SiO_2
Boron- B_2O_3 - also a strong flux
Phosphorous Oxide- P_2O_3

Stabilizer (R_2O_3)
Alumina- Al_2O_3

Fluxes
Alkaline Oxides (R_2O)
Lithium- Li_2O
Potassium- K_2O
Sodium- Na_2O

Alkaline Earth Oxides (RO)
Barium- BaO
Calcium- CaO
Magnesium- MgO
Strontium- SrO

Metallic Oxides (RO)
Lead- PbO
Zinc- ZnO

Elements in Detail

Glass Formers

Silica- the most important element in creating the glassy structure of glaze.
> Main Sources: silica, all clays, all feldspars, wollastonite, talc, bentonite, various frits, sand, wood ash

Boron Oxide- this element works both a glass former and a lower temperature flux.
> Main Sources: Gerstley borate, borax, some frits

Phosphorous Oxide- usually only found in small amounts in a glaze. Can create a bluish opalescent effect in some glazes
> Main Sources: Bone ash (calcium phosphate) or TCP (synthetic bone ash), wood ash, plant ash, some frits

Stabilizer

Alumina- stabilizes the molten glaze mixture during firing.
> Main Sources: Edgar Plastic Kaolin (EPK), Grolleg kaolin, OM#4 ball clay

Alkaline Oxides: Primary Fluxes

Lithium Oxide- the most powerful of the alkaline fluxes, creates strong colors, and promotes crystals in glaze
> Main Sources: Lithium carbonate, Spodumene, Petalite, some frits

Potassium Oxide- has a wide melting range and creates a durable glaze surface
> Main Sources: Custer potash feldspar, Cornwall Stone, Plastic Vitrox (PV) clay, wood ash, volcanic ash, some frits

Sodium Oxide- acts in similar ways to potassium. Can create issues with crazing (crackling) and too much fluidity in the glaze
> Main sources: Kona F-4 soda feldspar, Minspar soda feldspar, soda ash, Gerstley Borate, Nepheline Syenite, wood ash, some frits

Alkaline Earth Oxides: Secondary Fluxes

Barium Oxide- produces strong colors, crystals, and soft matte surfaces. Toxic material.
> Main Sources: Barium carbonate, some frits

Calcium Oxide- produces durable surfaces from cone 6 and above. When used in large amounts, produces a runny surface similar to wood ash glazes
> Main Sources: Whiting, Wollastonite, Dolomite, some feldspars, some frits, Gerstley Borate, Bone ash, wood ash

Magnesium Oxide- produces satin matte surfaces and when used in high amounts a lichen-like surface. Can make glaze more opaque
> Main Sources: Magnesium carbonate, Dolomite, Talc, some frits

Elements in Detail Continued

Strontium Oxide- similar to barium and calcium. Can be used as a substitute for toxic Barium in a glaze - use 75% of the amount needed.
> Main source: Strontium carbonate

Metallic Oxides

Lead Oxide- a very effective low temperature flux with a long history of use. No longer used in most locations because of its high toxicity.
> Main sources: White lead, Red lead, some frits

Zinc Oxide- a strong secondary flux from cone 6 and above. Can opacify a glaze and create crystals
> Main sources: Zinc oxide, calcined Zinc Oxide

Opacifiers

These elements are added to make the glaze more translucent to fully opaque. Adding a large amount of these materials to a glaze will usually create a fully opaque white glaze. An opacifier is not necessary if other colorants will be added to a glaze since those colorants will usually make the glaze less transparent.

Tin Oxide- the most effective opacifier with a very long history of use. It does have some refractory character helping to stabilize a glaze.
> Main source: Tin Oxide, Black Tin Oxide

Titanium Oxide- develops small crystals in the glaze that make it opaque. Usually creates interesting surfaces because of this.
> Main sources: Titanium dioxide, Rutile (combines iron and titanium),
> Ilmenite (coarse iron and titanium)

Zirconium Oxide- a very refractory material that will not fully melt in a glaze. This creates opacity in the glaze glass because of the floating zirconium particles.
> Main sources: fritted zirconium materials - Zircopax, Ultrox, Opax

Colorants

Color in glaze can be achieved in many different ways but the most common is to add a metallic colorant oxide to the base glaze recipe. Many of these colorants will react in different ways depending on the base glaze chemistry, how the piece is fired, and if other glazes are layered together. **Nearly all metallic oxides are dangerous to handle and precautions against skin, dust, and firing exhaust exposure must be taken.** If large amounts of colorants are added to glazes intended for functional pots, fired glazes should be tested for safety against leaching out of the glaze from food acids.

Chrome Oxide- a very strong colorant that usually produces strong green colors but can produce reddish colors when combined with tin oxide.
> Main sources: Chromium oxide, Iron chromate

Cobalt Oxide- the strongest (and most expensive) mineral colorant that usually creates blue colors in glazes. Only small amounts are needed starting at 1/4%, 1% in a glaze will create a very deep blue black.
> Main sources: Cobalt oxide, Cobalt carbonate, Cobalt sulfate

Copper Oxide- usually produces greens and/or reds, and in high amounts black, very influenced by the firing atmosphere inside the kiln
> Main sources: Copper carbonate, copper oxide

Iron Oxide- one of the most common, safest, and versatile colorants. Depending on the amount and how the glaze is fired, it can produce yellows, greens, browns, blacks, blues, greens, and reds.
> Main sources: Red iron oxide (RIO), Black iron oxide, Illmenite, Rutile, Crocus
> Martis, earthenware clays, Yellow ochre

Manganese Oxide- can create deep brown/black colors and sometimes very metallic surfaces. Great care must be taken when handling and firing glazes with manganese.
Main sources: Manganese dioxide, Manganese carbonate

Rutile- Rutile is a naturally occurring combination of combination of the oxides iron and titanium. Rutile can produce a wide range of colors from yellow to blue. It also creates a very dynamic surface texture in the fired glaze.
Main sources: Rutile, Illmenite

Commercial Stains- these are produced by industry as a fritted colorant to make them more stable and reliable. They also make minerals safer to handle since the fritting process locks the element into a glass. There are drawbacks including cost of material and sometimes the flatness of color in the glaze.
Main sources: Mason, Cerdec, Spectrum

Glaze suspender- over time, a liquid glaze will begin to settle in the container. This makes the glaze difficult to mix and apply correctly. An additive can be used to prevent the glaze from settling and make the remixing process easier.
Main sources: Bentonite, Macaloid, Epsom salts

Notes:

An effective way to build understanding of how glaze recipes and ingredients work is to review the parts of some sample recipes.

Ron Meyers Clear glaze (cone 08-04)

Ferro Frit 3124	72.7 %	primary flux- high calcium commercial frit
EPK kaolin	18.1	stabilizer and some glass maker
Silica	9	glass maker
bentonite	2	glaze suspender

Floating Blue (cone 6)

Nepheline Syenite	47.3%	primary flux and some glass maker
Gerstley Borate	27	primary / secondary flux
EPK kaolin	5.4	stabilizer and some glass maker
Silica	20.3	glass maker
bentonite	2	glaze suspender

colorants:

Red Iron Oxide	2	darkens color
Cobalt Carbonate	1	creates blue color
Rutile	4	creates visual texture in glaze

Sea Slug (cone 9-10 for woodkiln)

Custer feldspar	33.3%	primary flux, stabilizer, and glass maker
Whiting	14.5	secondary flux
Talc	7.3	secondary flux
Bone ash	2	secondary flux
EPK kaolin	9.3	stabilizer and some glass maker
Silica	30.22	glass maker
Titanium dioxide	3.1	opacifier

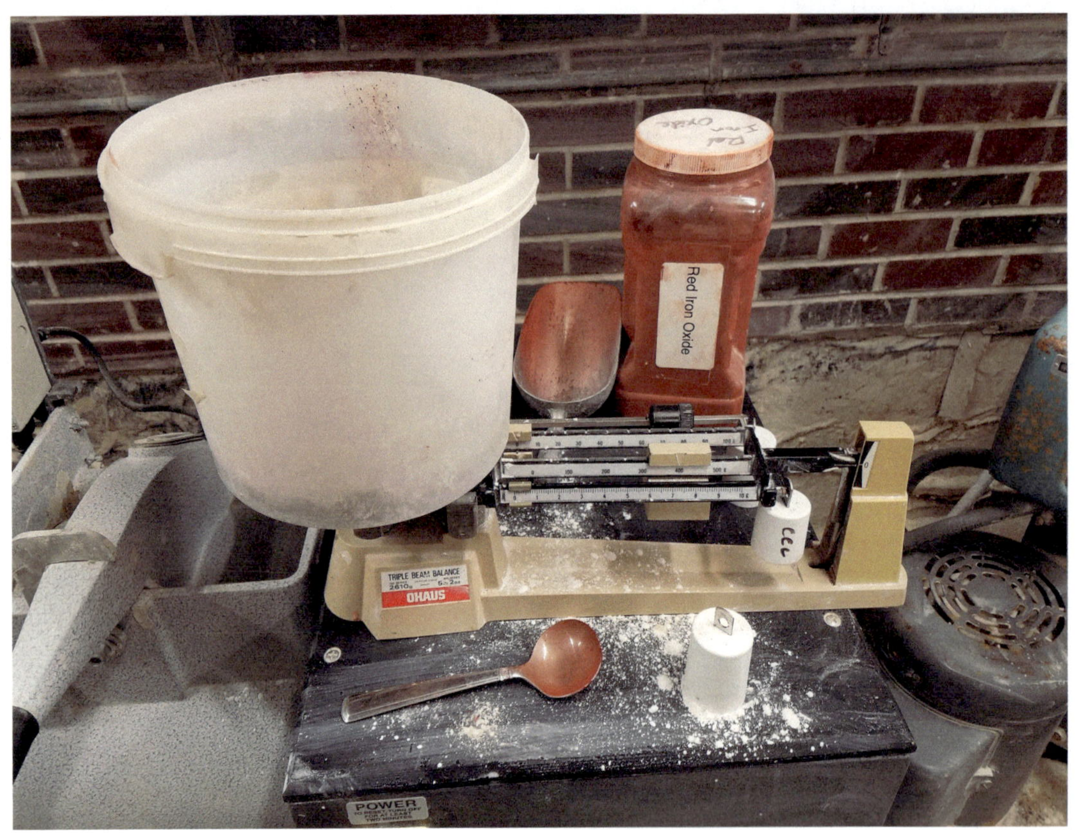

GLAZE EXPERIMENTS

One of the best and most important ways to build understanding of glazes is to mix and test a variety of recipes. The easiest way to begin is to find existing glaze recipes, weigh out a small 200 gram batch, and make it into a liquid glaze to dip on sample tiles. Observations can then be made about what happened in the kiln when compared with the recipe. Since every kiln and studio are different, published recipes may look different in each situation. This is why testing and careful note taking is so important. The goal is to find, use, and improve glazes that help you make the best work possible.

Sources for glaze recipes to test:
There are a number of books in the CCC library about a range of glaze types and firing temperatures. Start in the TT 900's section.
Ceramics Monthly, *Pottery Making Illustrated*, *Ceramics Technical* are also in the library in the magazine section

There are many online sources and a quick search will return more than you will ever need! A very good glaze database is Glazy (glazy.org) which has thousands of recipes that is searchable by firing temperature, color, and other factors.

This is a simple exercise that can develop a wide range of glaze possibilities for cone 6 electric firing. For each of the 3 glaze bases, pick a different material from the specified category. Weigh out the required materials in order to make 1,000 grams of each base glaze. Dry mix this powder as much as possible. Divide this by reweighing the dry mix into five 200 gram test batches. If needed, add colorants to the new smaller (200 gram) dry batches in the stated percentages below. Wet mix, dip onto a test tile, and label the tile carefully.

Glossy Glaze Base

Main Flux	400
Secondary Flux #1	150
SecondaryFlux #2	150
Clay	100
Silica	200

Satin Glaze Base

Main Flux	300
Secondary Flux #1	150
Secondary Flux #2	150
Clay	250
Silica	150

Matte Glaze Base

Main Flux	200
SecondaryFlux #1	150
Secondary Flux#2	150
Clay	400
Silica	100

Main Flux options

1. Custer Potash feldspar
2. Soda feldspar
3. Nepheline syenite
4. Cornwall Stone
5. Gerstley Borate

Secondary Flux #1 / #2 options

1. Whiting
2. Dolomite
3. Talc
4. Strontium Carbonate
5. Magnesium Carbonate
6. Zinc oxide
7. P. V. Clay
8. Spodumene
9. Ferro Frit #3110
10. Ferro Frit #3124
11. Ferro Frit #3134
12. Wollastonite

Clay options

1. EPK Kaolin
2. OM#4 Ball clay

Colorants added to one of the five 200 gram batches:

1- Base glaze with no colorant

2- Copper Carbonate 3%

3- Red Iron Oxide   4%

4- Rutile   3%

5- Cobalt Carbonate 0.5 %

Glaze Recipes tested:

Notes:

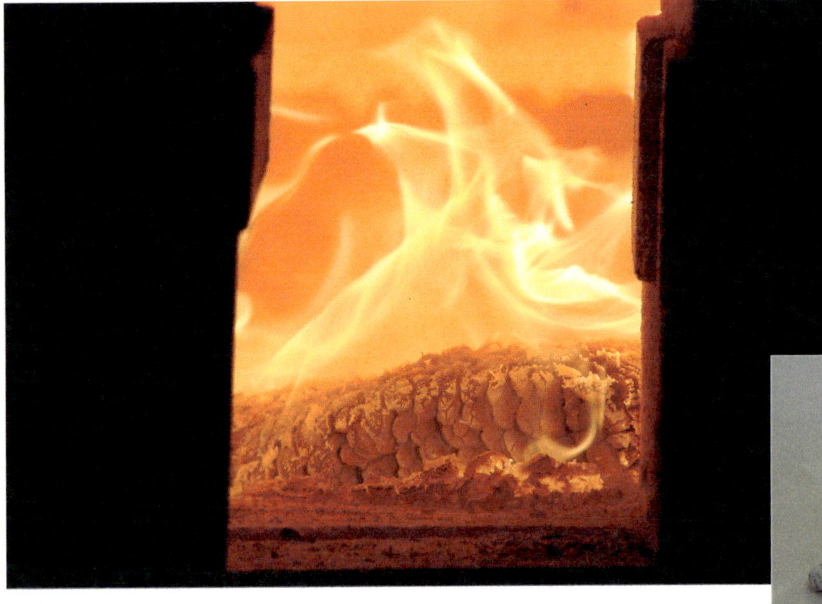

View inside CCC woodkiln firebox[1]

Pyrometric cones used for reading temperature during firing[1]

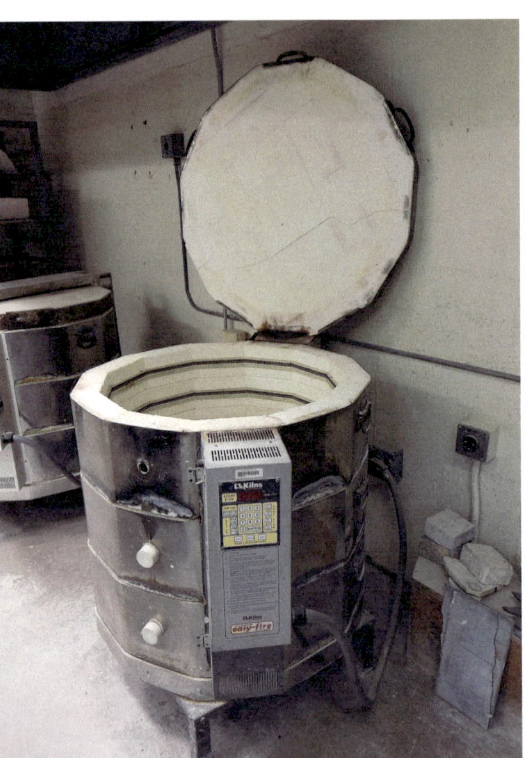

L&L brand electric kiln[1]

10

FIRING

The heating or "firing" of ceramic objects is a critical step in the process that makes our work permanent, dense, and durable. Researchers believe that the first fired ceramics may have been created by accident. Ancient people would often smear wet clay inside baskets in order to seal them. A basket left too close to a bonfire may have burned and heated hot enough to harden the clay. As with most human discoveries, this simple event turned into a "happy accident" that led to advanced technology.

In the beginning of human ceramics production, most objects were fired by being piled up and then having bonfire burn over the objects heating them. There are some people who still practice this method.

One of the problems with this method is that many pieces will break and heat unevenly. As a result, a variety of **kilns** were developed in order to make the firing process more reliable. In general, these designs moved the fire into a chamber that vented heat into a space that contained the ceramics. This simple idea helped ceramics production become one of the most important art-forms in history.

Main firing types

When talking about firings done in ceramics there are two main types. The first is the **bisque firing** in which the dry clay pieces are heated to around 1800F. During this initial firing process, the clay pieces undergo physical changes to become more dense and yet still porous. The clay body is now no longer clay, having been changed into ceramic by the heat. After the bisque is cooled, the work is removed and then a liquid glaze is often applied. The pieces are then loaded into a second firing known as the **finish or glaze firing**. This can take place with a variety of types of kilns, firing processes, and temperatures. The options are often constrained by the type of clay body used in the work, what kinds of kilns are available, and the aesthetic goals of the artists.

Ways to monitor temperature inside a kiln

In the history of ceramics production, a number of methods have been developed in order to see how hot the temperature is inside the kiln. Most ceramic artist rely on more than one way to read kiln temperature. These include:

Visual color inside kiln chamber

As heat builds inside the kiln, the color of the space will change from dark black to dull red. As the heat continues to climb the color continues to get brighter moving from orange to yellow and finally yellowish white at the highest temperature end for most art ceramics at around 2,400 F. It is good safety practice to always wear shaded glasses when looking into a firing kiln in order to protect your eyes. The light intensity of a high firing kiln can damage your eyes.

Draw rings / tiles

Small rings of clay (made from the same clay the pots are made from) are often covered with slips and glazes that have been applied to the work. During the firing, the rings are periodically removed from the kiln with a metal bar to see the melt of the glazes and the maturity the clay body. This method is most often used in salt or soda firing to see how the clay surface glaze is developing. Draw rings should never be used in an electric kiln since touching an electric element with a metal bar during firing is deadly.

Pyrometric cones

Formulated from the same materials in clays and glazes, cones are special shapes designed by and for ceramic industry. The cones are designed to melt and bend or fall down at specific temperatures. Multiple cones are used in a "pack" that gives a reading of range of temperature. A cone melting and tipping over gives an indication of how both the climbing temperature and amount of time of firing is affecting the ceramics in the chamber. Looking inside a firing kiln and "reading" the cones is one of the most common methods used today.

Pyrometer

A pyrometer is a very high temperature thermometer used to read the current temperature inside a kiln with a probe called a thermocouple. Pyrometers can be not very precise at high temperatures but will still show if the temperature is climbing or falling. A pyrometer should always be used in conjunction with pyrometric cones.

As experience with firing a particular kiln builds, the ceramic artist often develops a sense of how far along the firing should be at specific times. In addition, careful notes should always be taken in the form of kiln logs (noting things like time, temperature, cones fallen, gas pressure settings, or chimney damper settings) so that good firings can be repeated. As with everything in ceramics, a notebook/sketchbook filled with notes, sketches, and details of production go a long way toward building a successful studio practice.

Effects of Heating / Firing on Ceramics

Cone	Temperature C/F	Color in Kiln	What Happens
-	0 / 32	-	water freezes
-	100 / 212	-	water boils
-	100-300/212-572	-	chemical water in clay burned off
-	470 / 878	dull red	color begins to be seen inside kiln
-	573 / 1063		Quartz crystal expansion and contraction
O22	605 / 1121		lowest cone / luster firing temperature
O19	683 / 1261		overglaze enamel firing temperature
O16	792 / 1458		carbon burns out of clay
O12	884 / 1623	bright red	Raku temperature
O6	999 / 1830	orange	average bisque temperature
O4	1060 / 1940		lowfire glaze firing temperature
6	1186 / 2167	yellow	mid range glaze temperature
9	1280 / 2336	bright yellow	high temperature stoneware clays mature wood ash melts during woodfiring
11	1315 / 2399	yellow white	porcelain clays mature

Important Firing Concepts

Greenware should be bone dry before being loaded into a kiln to be bisque fired. Larger work needs a longer period of drying and firing than thin wheel thrown pieces. A long pre-heat (5 to 6 hours) hold on a computer controlled electric kiln should allow time for moisture to get out of the work. If the thick or damp pieces heat too fast, the steam pressure inside the wall will cause the piece to explode.

Most bisque firing is done in electric kilns because of the ease of controlling temperature. The majority of newer electric kilns have computer controllers programed with specific heating cycles to make firing simpler.

In a bisque firing, work can be made of any clay body (earthenware, stoneware, and porcelain) and most bisque firings are done to around 1800F. The pieces can be stacked or touch the kiln since the surface of the piece doesn't melt at this temperature. The pieces will shrink a good deal during the firing so be careful when stacking work.

At approximately 1063 F, the silica crystals in the clay and glazes will go through a process called **quartz inversion**. During heating, the crystals will quickly expand and then quickly contract at the same temperature during the cooling cycle. If the kiln moves through this temperature range too rapidly, the pieces may crack.

In some types of kilns, the atmosphere can be controlled in order to create specific effects on the work. Electric kilns only allow for the work to be fired in **oxidation**. This firing atmosphere is one where the level of oxygen is similar to our normal atmosphere. During most firing cycles, the kiln will be in oxidation up to a certain point. The other common firing atmosphere is called **reduction**. The reduction process is controlled by increasing the amount of fuel going into the kiln, closing in the chimney damper, reducing the amount of air going into the kiln, or any combination of those controls. The reduced level of oxygen inside the kiln creates a chemical reaction with the elements in the clay and glazes used on the work. In general, this causes a shift or dramatic change in the glaze and clay body colors. This explains why certain glazes will look very different when fired in both oxidation and reduction.

A final important safety note: All kilns must be ventilated carefully in order to remove fumes and heat produced from interior spaces.

Types of glaze / finish firing

In the CCC studio, we have access to electric kilns for oxidation firing and woodfired kilns for woodfired reduction. There are a large number of other finish firing options that have been developed. Some types of kilns are commonly purchased from ceramic suppliers and kiln companies. Other types are most often custom built (like the CCC woodfired kilns) with high temperature refractory materials. There are a number of books and online resources available on the process of designing and building a kiln.

Gas fired kilns
Due to important safety issues with natural gas and propane, gas kilns are most often purchased as a completed system with the structure and burners designed and built by a manufacturer. Gas kilns can fire in both oxidation or reduction.

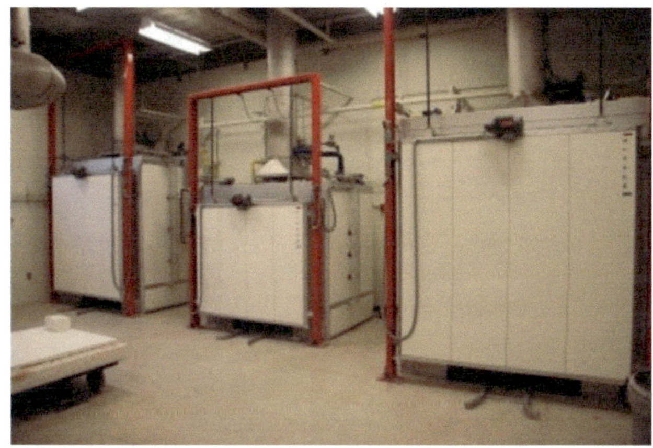

Blaauw gas fired kilns[10]

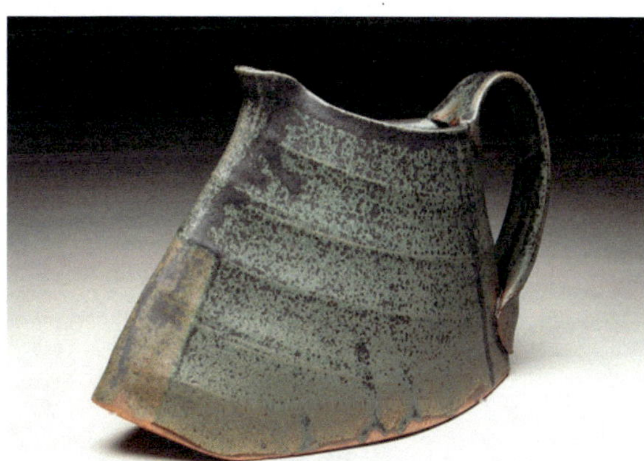

Sequoia Miller, "Altered Pitcher", stoneware, cone 10 gas fired in reduction[3]

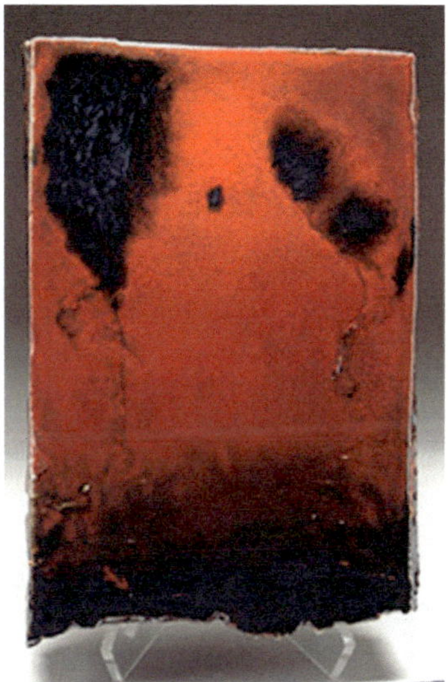

Charles Timm-ballard, "Flattop", stoneware, cone 10 gas fired in reduction[3]

Types of glaze / finish firing
continued

Electric kilns

Electric kilns are also most often purchased from a number of kiln manufacturers. These kilns are the very popular and relatively easy to use. The work is heated by electric elements that radiate a large amount of energy into the chamber. All electric kilns fire in oxidation and usually are limited to firing to a maximum of cone 8. Special higher temperature electric kilns can fire to cone 10 but must have heavy duty electric elements and thicker kiln walls.

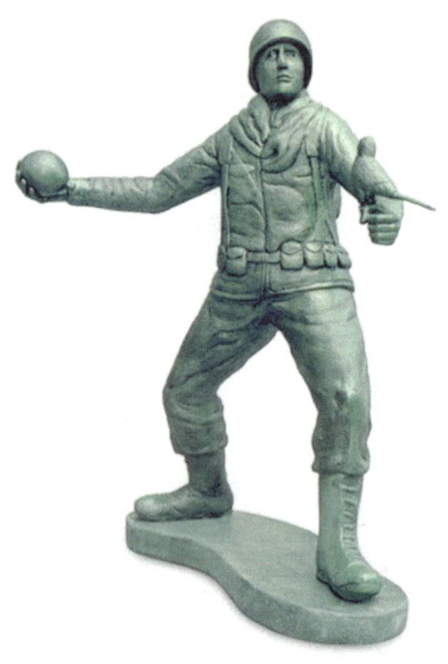

Monica Van den Dool, "Army Man with Water Balloon", oxidation fired earthenware[2]

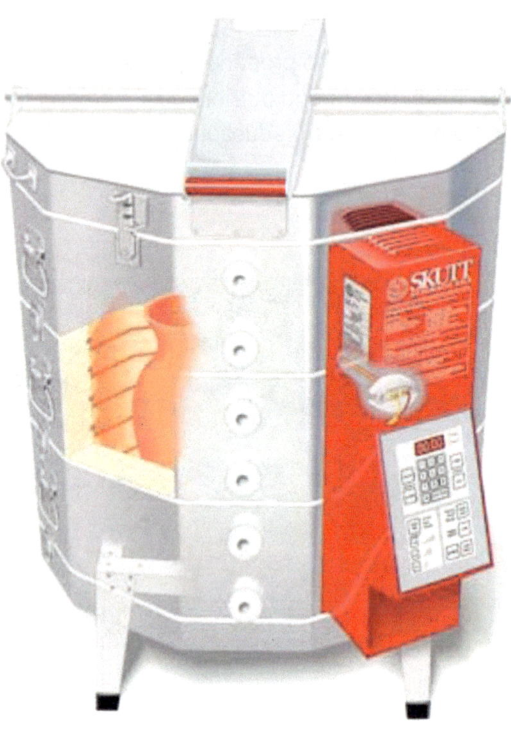

Cut away view of a Skutt electric kiln[11]

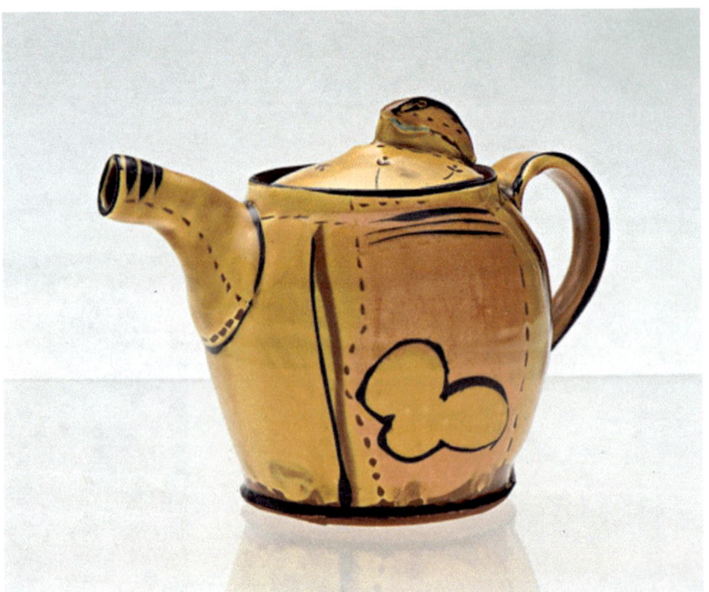

Victoria Christen, "Yellow Teapot", oxidation fired earthenware[2]

Types of glaze / finish firing
continued

Woodfiring

Firing ceramics with wood fuel was the most common method up until the Industrial Revolution. In the most direct woodfiring kiln design (both the CCC woodkilns are of this type), a large firebox contains burning wood and the heat, vapors, and ashes move across the ceramics on the way to the chimney. The vapors interact with the chemistry of the claybody creating organic patterns on the surface called **flashing**. The ashes coming off the burning fuel lands on the ceramics and at a high temperature melt into a glass.

There are variety of woodfired kilns designs that make certain effects easier to achieve. For example, some artists do not want a large amount of ash glaze on their work and as a result, use a kiln design that prevents this from happening.

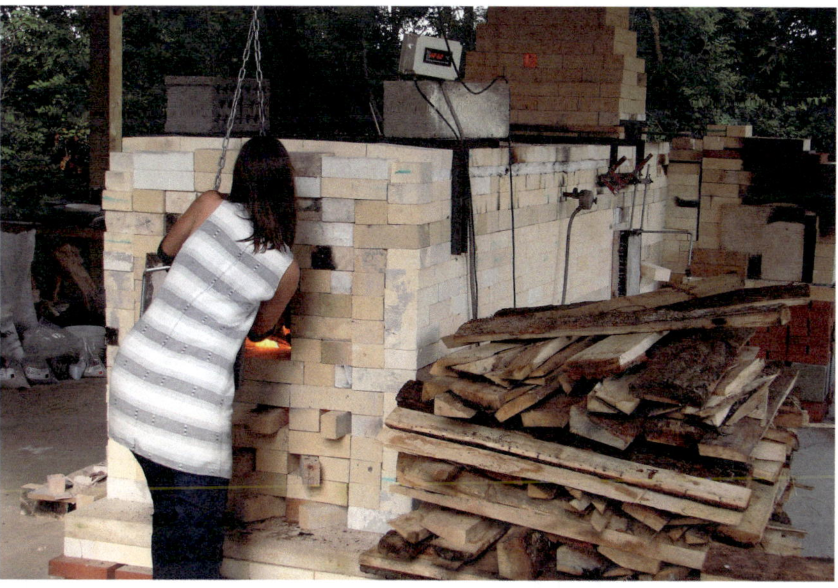

A student at Domaine de Boisbuchet in France stoking wood into the kiln design first developed at CCC that allows for firing ceramics and blowing glass at the same time.[1]

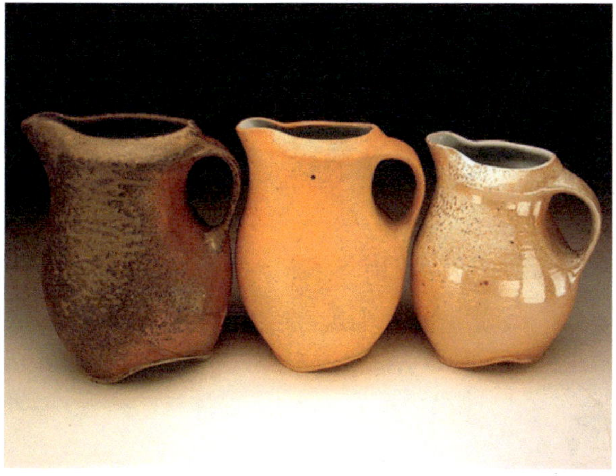

Thomas Rohr, "Three Pitchers", woodfired stoneware and porcelain[3]

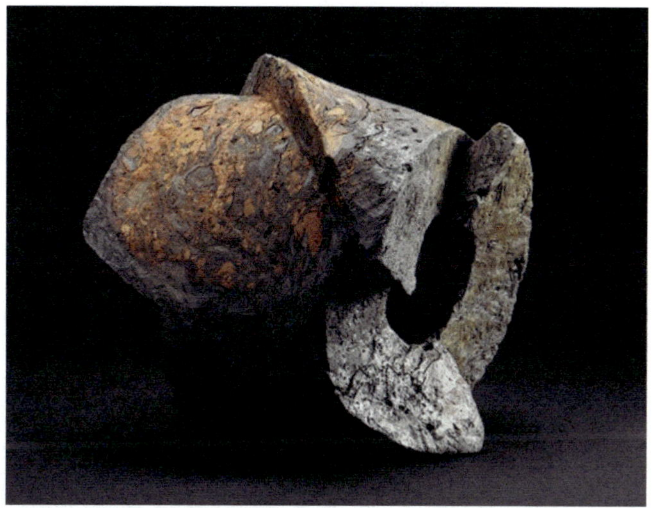

Tim Rowan, "Object 103", woodfired stoneware[2]

Salt firing

The process for salt firing ceramics was developed in Germany during the Middle Ages. This **atmospheric firing** (a process where a special atmosphere in the kiln affects the ceramics, woodfiring is also atmospheric) technique is done by heating a kiln with gas or wood to around 2200F (cone 8) and then throwing salt into the kiln. The salt instantly vaporizes and this sodium vapor combines with the silica in the clay body to create a glossy surface. Many times, the surface has a slightly pebbled texture like an orange peel. Glazes and slips that have been applied to the work are also affected in unique ways. The vapor released during the firing is dangerous so a respirator filtering vapors must be worn when working around the kiln.

Types of glaze / finish firing
continued

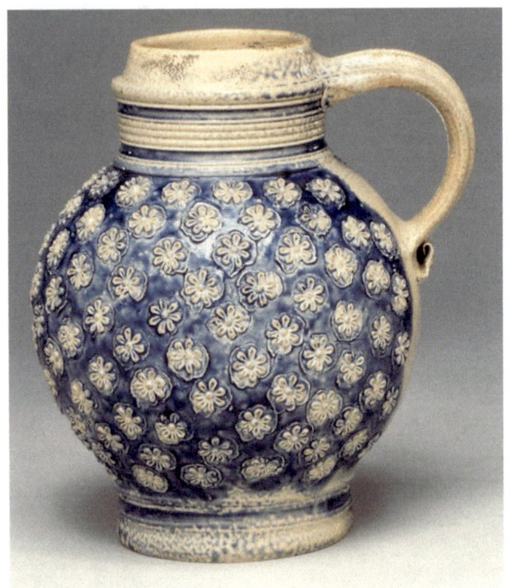
German salt glazed tankard from 1680-1700 CE[4]

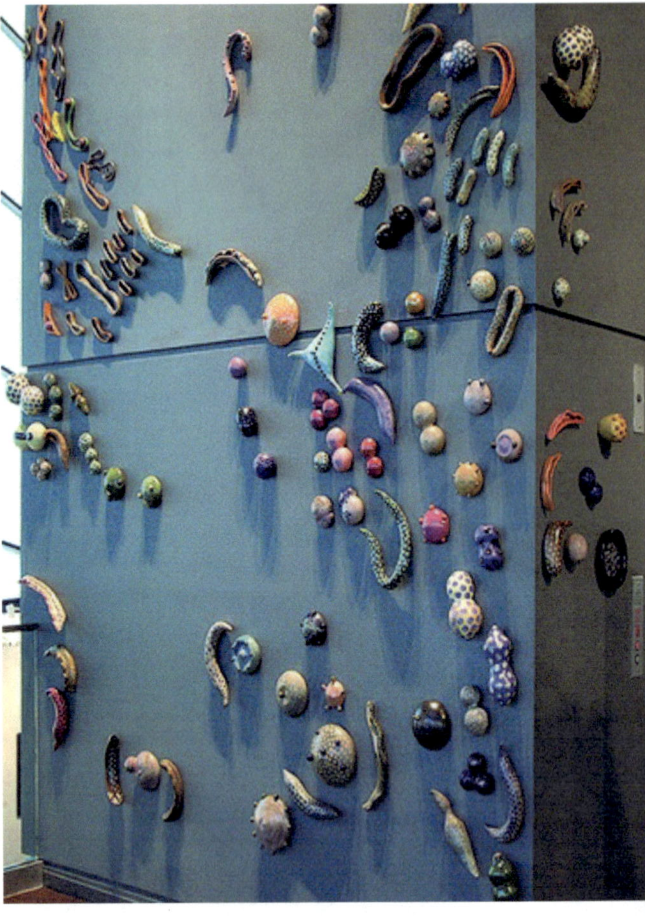
Eva Kwong, "Bacteria, Diatoms & Cells", salt glazed stoneware and electric fired elements[3]

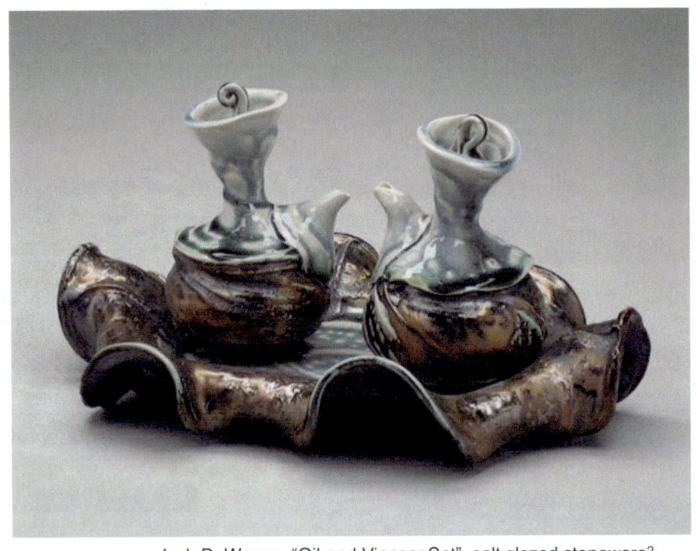
Josh DeWeese, "Oil and Vinegar Set", salt glazed stoneware[2]

Soda firing

Soda firing, another atmospheric firing method, was developed in the 1970's at Alfred University because of growing concern about pollution created during salt firing. The firing process is done in a very similar way to salt firing except that a different sodium material is used. Instead of salt, soda ash and/or borax is introduced into the kiln to create the vapor. This is most often done by dissolving the material in water and then spraying this solution into the kiln. Once again, the vapor combines with the silica in the clay to create a glossy surface.

All work fired in an atmospheric (wood, salt, soda) kiln must have special clay pieces applied to the bottom to prevent it from sticking to the kiln. This material, called **wadding**, is made from very refractory materials and sometimes things like sawdust and sand. The flashing marks left by the wadding is an obvious sign that a piece has been fired in an atmospheric kiln.

Types of glaze / finish firing
continued

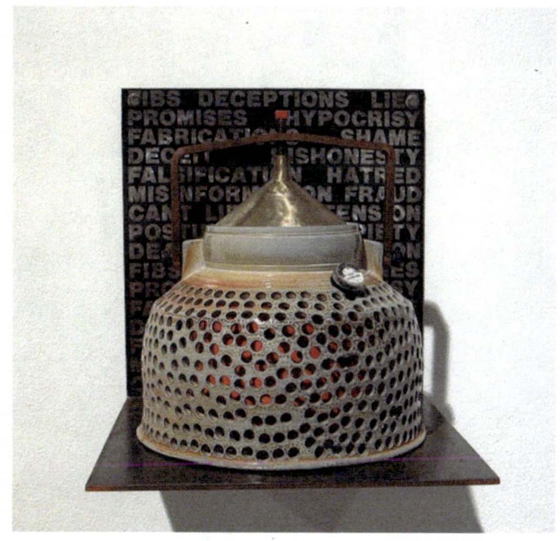

Richard Burkett, "Red Core", soda fired porcelain and mixed media[5]

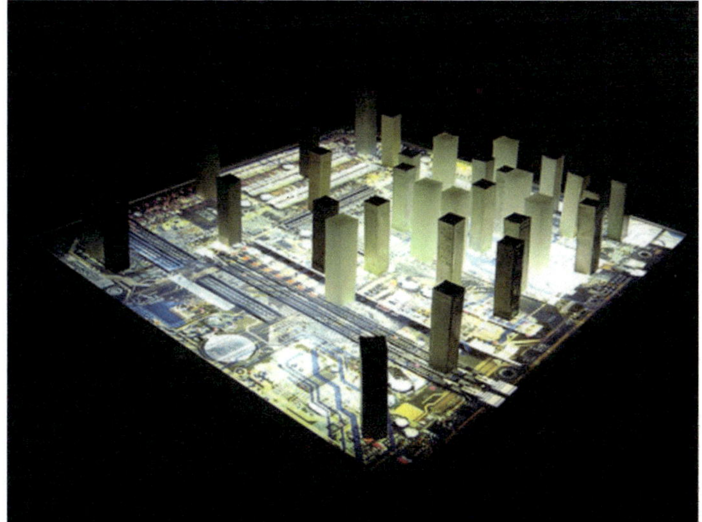

Dylan Beck, "If You Want to Have Cities, You Have to Build Roads", soda fired porcelain and mixed media[2]

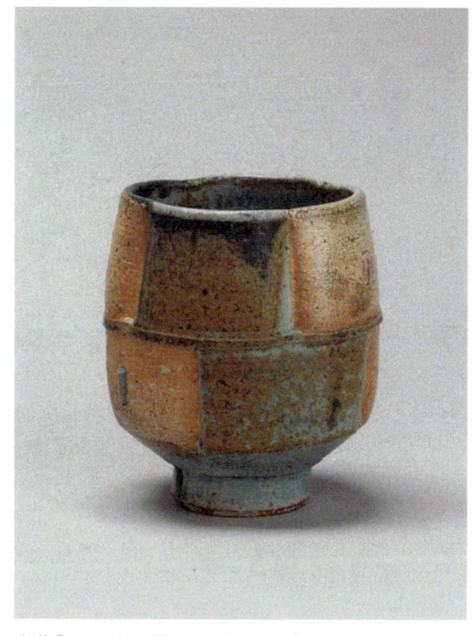

Jeff Oestreich, "Teabowl", soda fired stoneware[5]

Types of glaze / finish firing continued

Raku

This low-fire process was developed in Japan during the 16th century CE. Originally used in the production of tea bowls for the Japanese tea ceremony, the raku process has evolved into a very direct way of finished pieces. In this type of firing, glazes are applied to work and then a placed in a small kiln that is heated quickly to around 1600F. Once the glazes have melted, the pieces are removed from the hot kiln and placed into a metal container filled with combustable materials like sawdust, leaves, and/or newspaper. The container is closed with a lid and the work cools in a smokey atmosphere. In the end, the unglazed clay turns black from carbon and the glazes take on a unique character due to the cooling process. The raku process is a great way to finish work quickly but one drawback is that the pieces are still porous and non-functional.

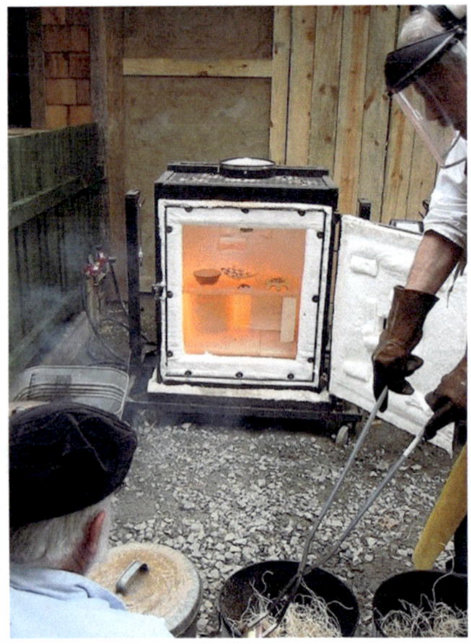

Raku kiln in action.[9]

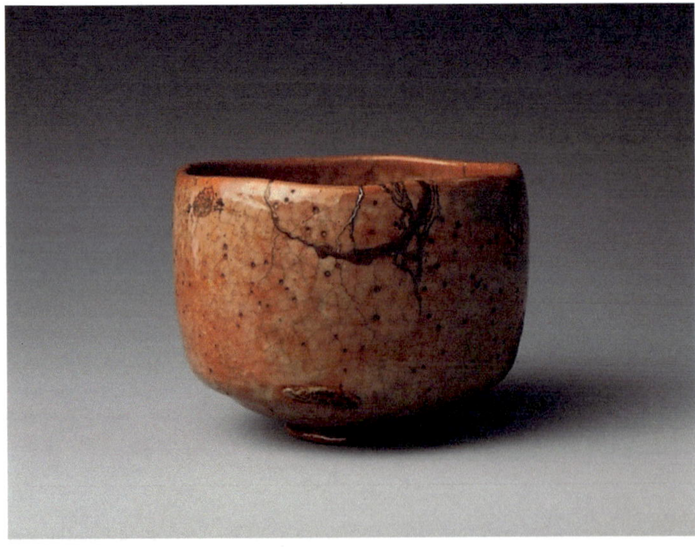

Japanese raku teabowl, 1750's CE[4]

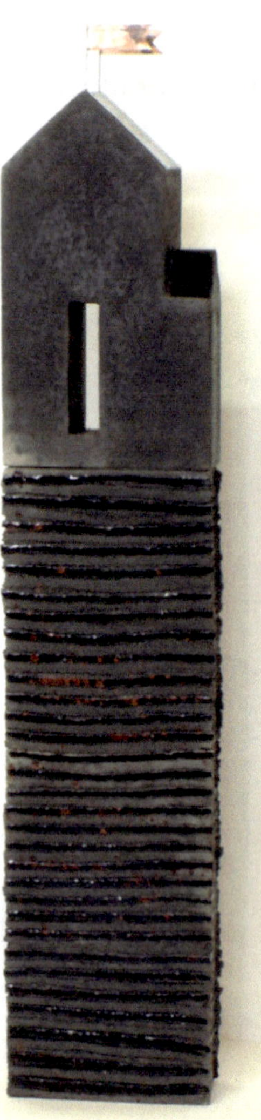

Margreet Zwetsloot, "2007-1", raku fired earthenware[3]

Pit, Saggar, and Smoke firing

Pit firing was the original firing technology that continues to be used today. A shallow pit is dug and filled with the ceramics. Wood and other materials are carefully placed on top and the pile is set on fire. This heats the ceramics to a low temperature and at the same time, creates organic "smokey" effects on the surface. Saggar firing is a variation of this idea in which a ceramic box (called a saggar) is placed inside another kiln. Then the ceramic work and combustible materials are placed inside the saggar and the kiln fired. Once again, the burning materials touching the pieces creates patterns on the surface. Objects fired this way will still be porous and nonfunctional.

Types of glaze / finish firing continued

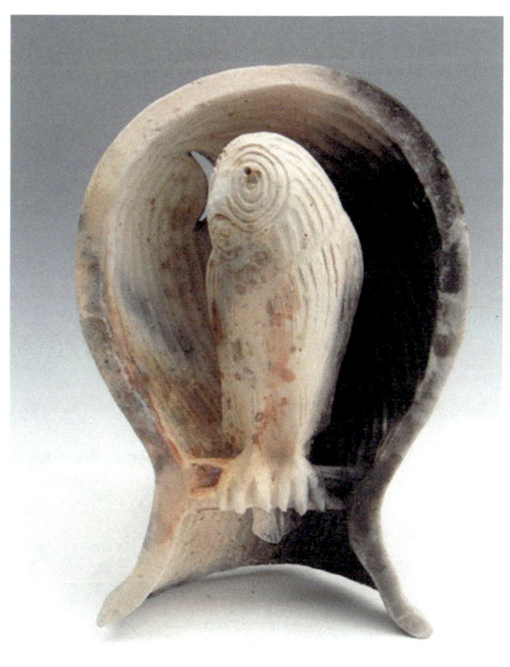

Rob Beishline, "Night Conference", pit fired earthenware[3]

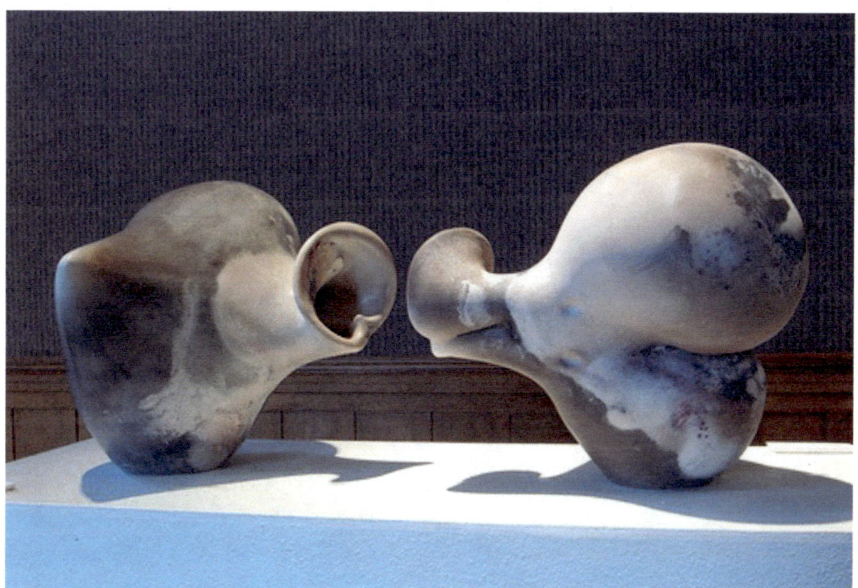

Mika Negishi Laidlaw, "Futari", smoke fired porcelain[2]

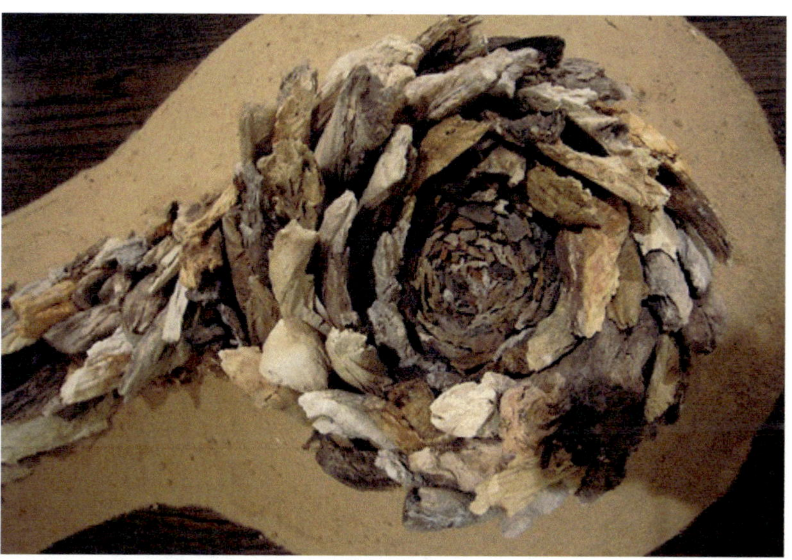

Steve Hilton, "46,738...46,739...46740" smoke fired stoneware, installation detail with sand[2]

Luster firing and Decals
The use of metallic lusters or decals is an example of multiple firings to finish a piece. In both techniques, the work must first be fired to a higher temperature and then cooled off. Luster, a liquid suspension of precious metal flakes) is then painted onto the glazed surface. With decals, the preprinted decal is soaked in water and then applied to the glazed surface. The pieces are then loaded into a kiln and fired to a much lower temperature, just enough to fuse or stick this material to the already fired glaze. Great care must be taken when using lusters because of the fumes produced by the liquid material during application and firing. Once fired the luster is food safe but not microwave safe since there is real metal now stuck to the glaze surface!

Types of glaze / finish firing
continued

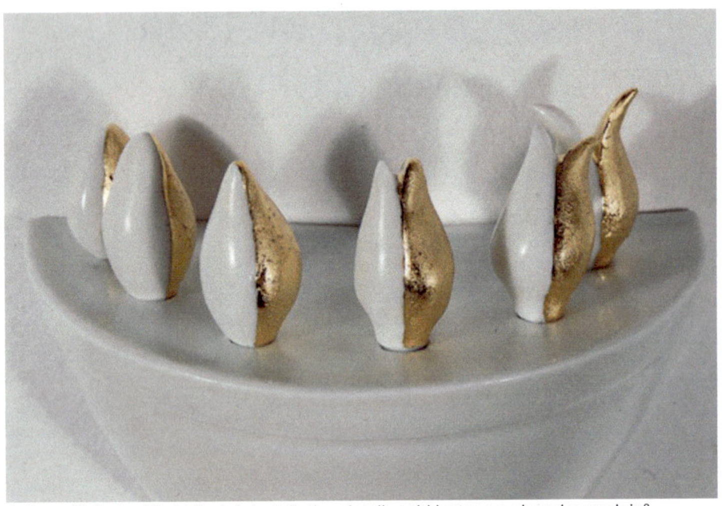

Juliane Shibata, "Gold Buds", installation detail, gold luster on glazed porcelain[3]

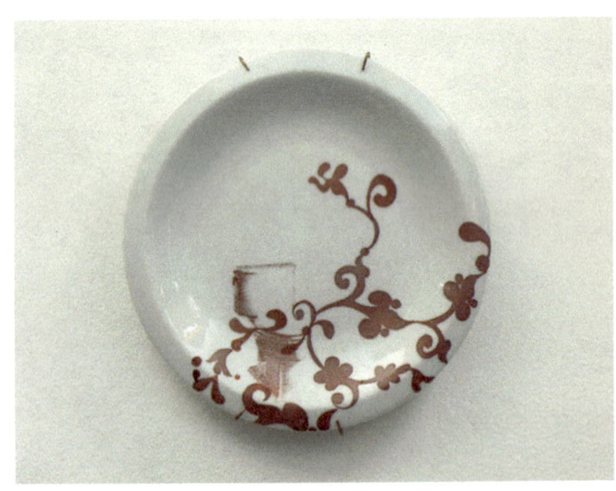

Tsehai Johnson, "Reclaimed Plate 36", decals on reclaimed dinnerware[2]

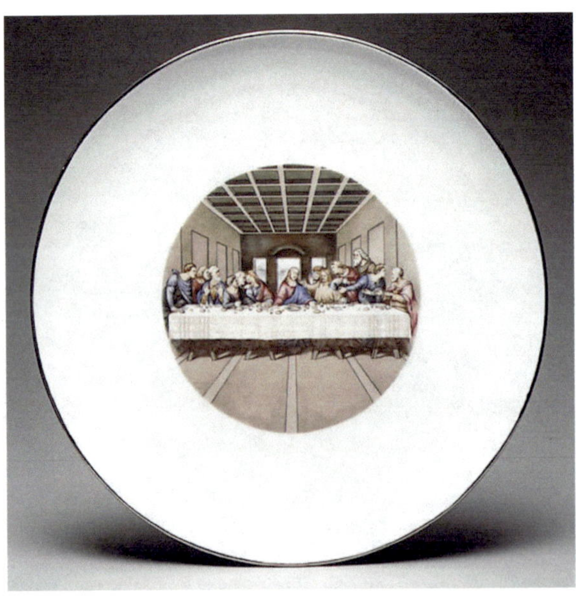

Howard Kottler, "Last Supperware", decal on glazed porcelain[4]

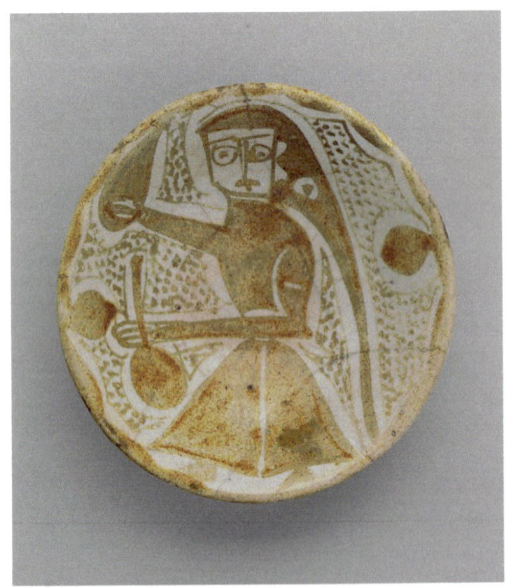

Islamic bowl from 10th century CE Iran, luster painted over white glaze[4]

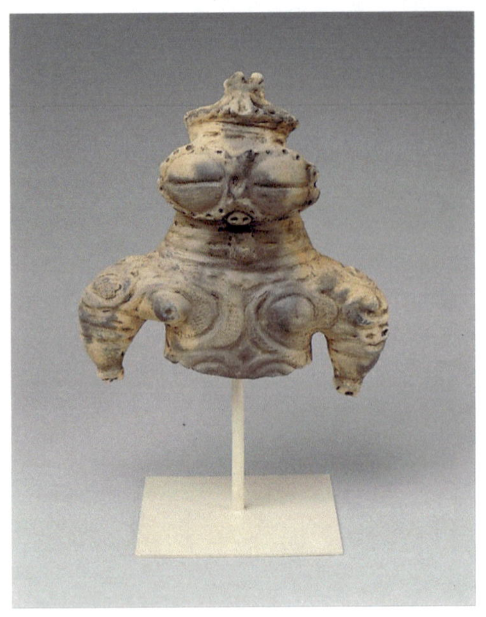
Japanese Jomon figure[4]

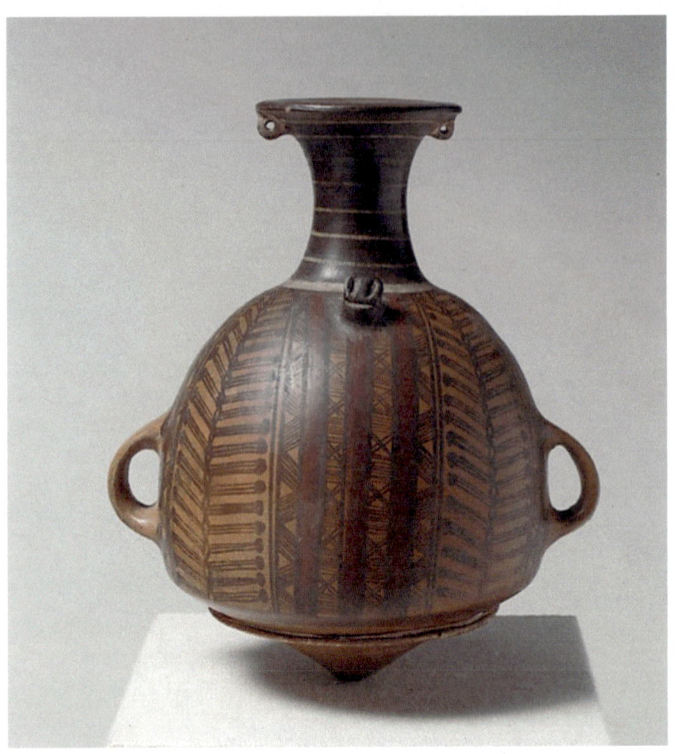
Inca vessel[4]

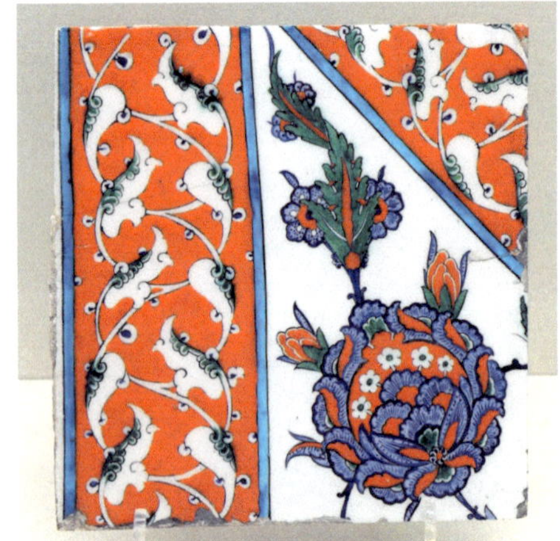
Iznik tile from Turkey[4]

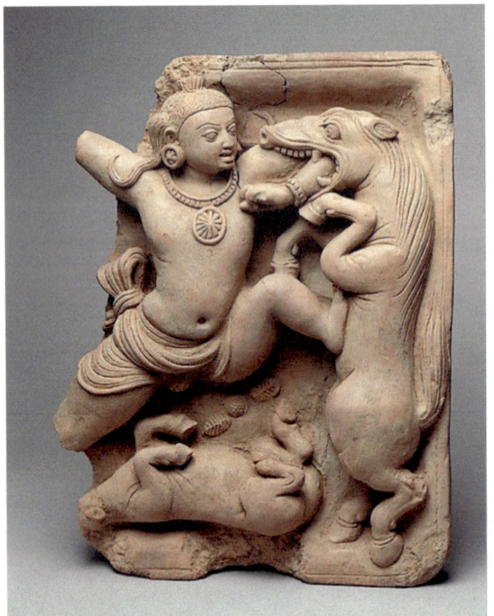
Tile of Vishnu from India[4]

11

CERAMICS HISTORY

The history of ceramics mirrors and helps reveal the history of our species. Because clay can be shaped and when fired becomes so durable, it has proven to be one of the most important materials used by humans. Changes in styles of ceramics can help us understand ancient cultural evolution and interaction between peoples. Many of the ancient masterworks of ceramics survive because they were buried in tombs sometimes hundreds or thousands of miles from where they were made.

The influence of older traditional forms of ceramics remains an important part of contemporary ceramics. In the scope of this studio handbook, we can only scratch the surface of the vast amount of ceramics made by humans. Each section has a summary of important information and a list of terms that should help lead you to more information. A basic understanding of the high points of historical ceramics will help you get started on making your own work a part of history!

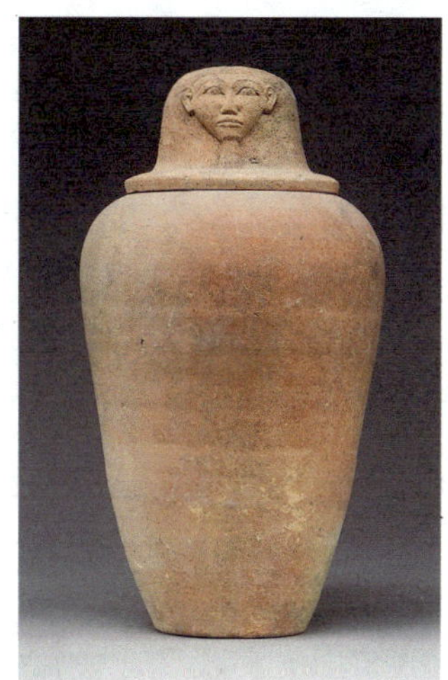
Egyptian canopic jar[4]

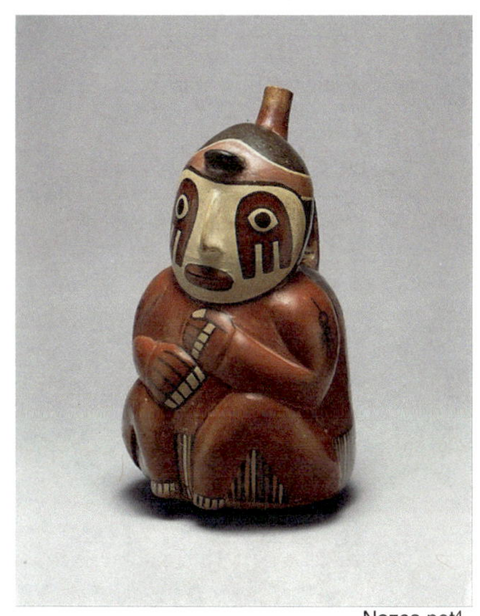
Nazca pot[4]

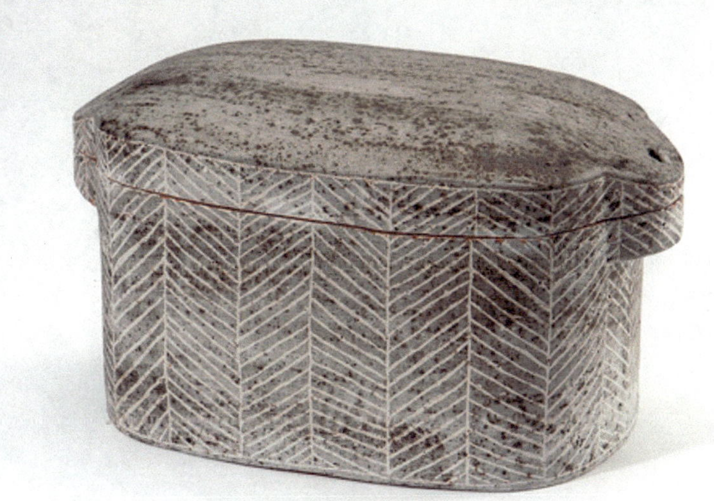
Joe Pintz, "Herringbone Box"[14]

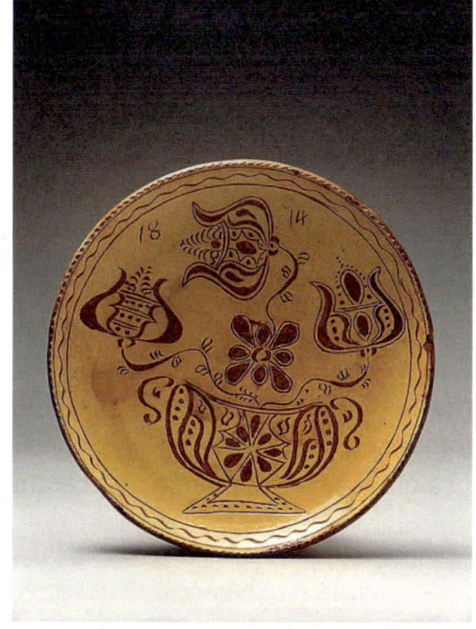
Early American slipware bowl[4]

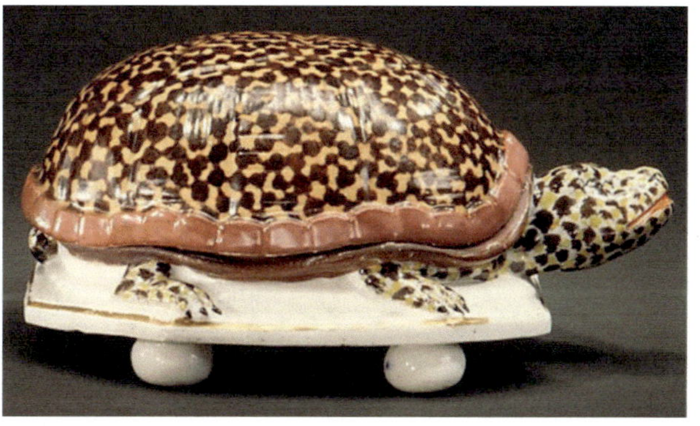
German Meissen turtle[4]

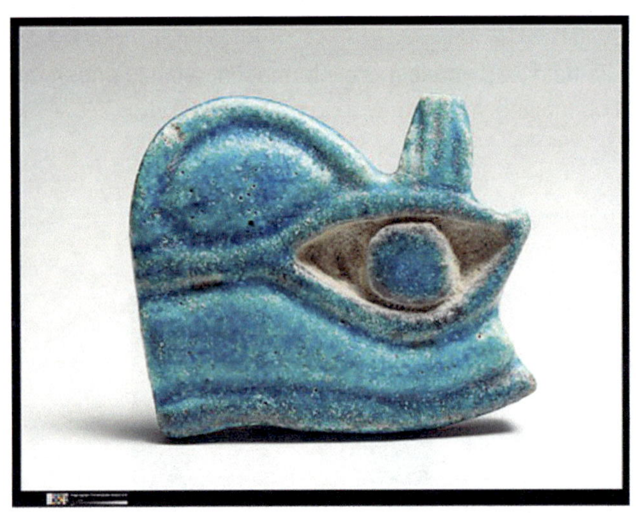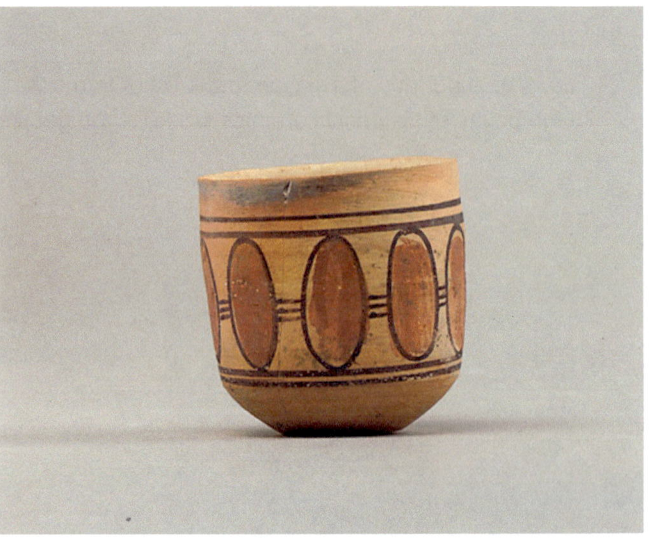

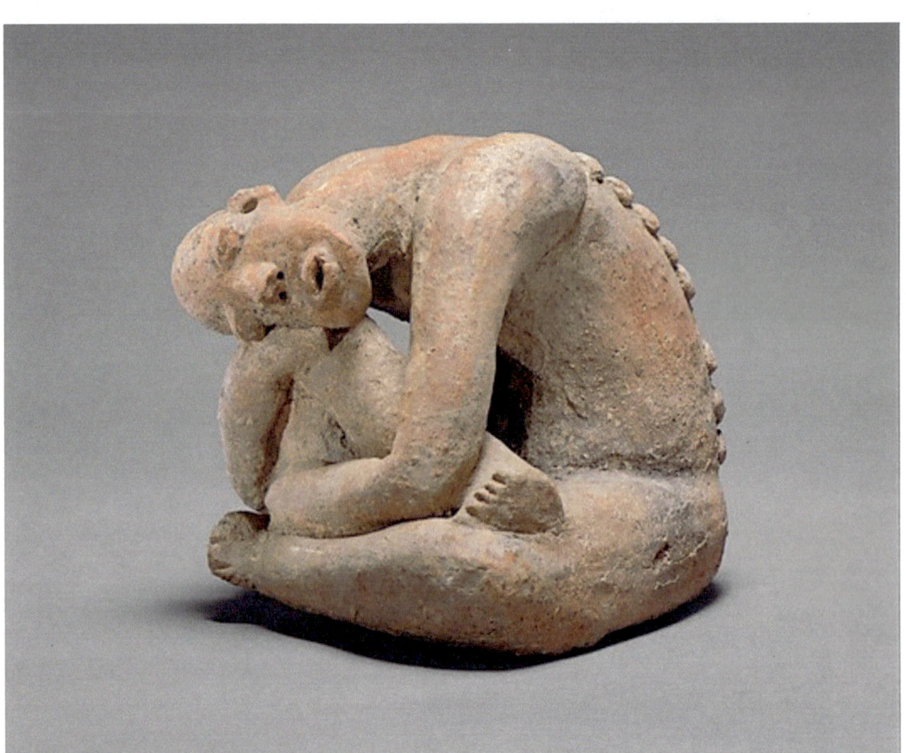

AFRICAN

Archaeological and DNA evidence has revealed that Africa was the birthplace of the human species. Various climate shifts and population patterns drove early humans to spread across the planet taking new ideas and technology with them.

The Egyptians, one of the most important early civilizations, formed in North Africa around the Nile River and the Mediterranean. Other African cultures continued to evolve across the continent and produce great works of pottery and ceramic sculpture.

Important terms / places:
Egyptian, Benin, Nok, Ashanti, Ife, Mali, Egyptian paste, Ushabti

all images this section[4]

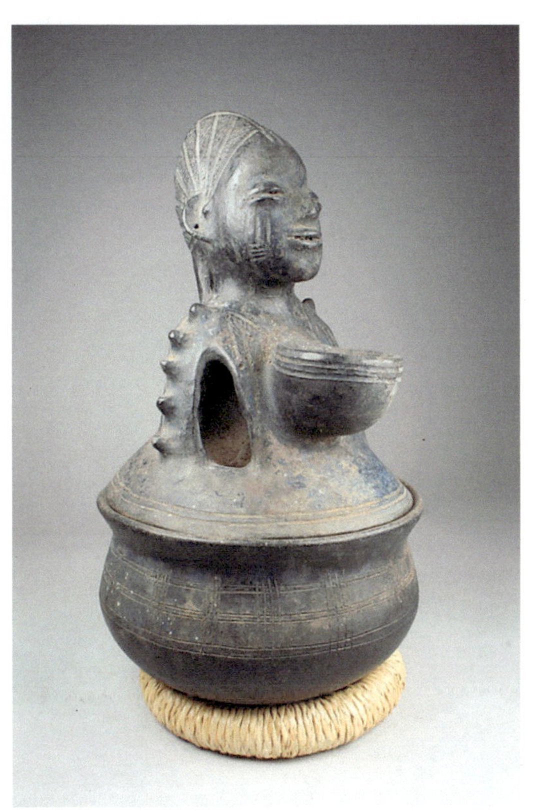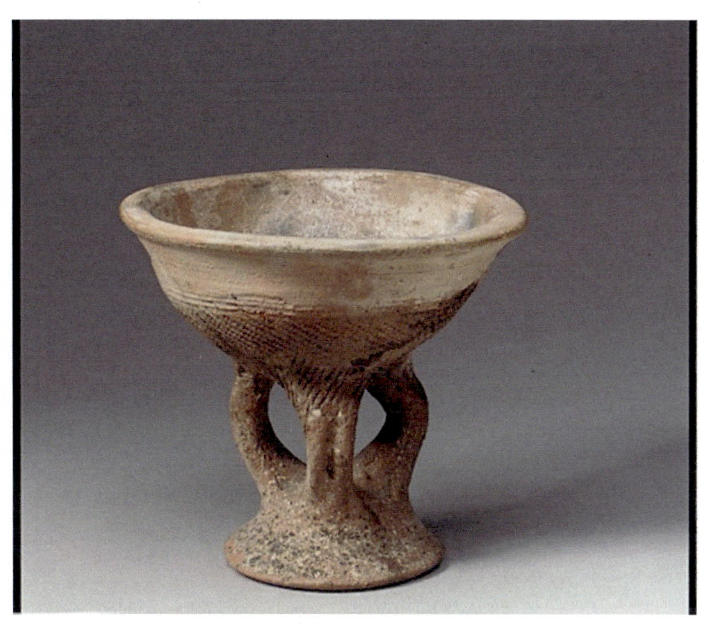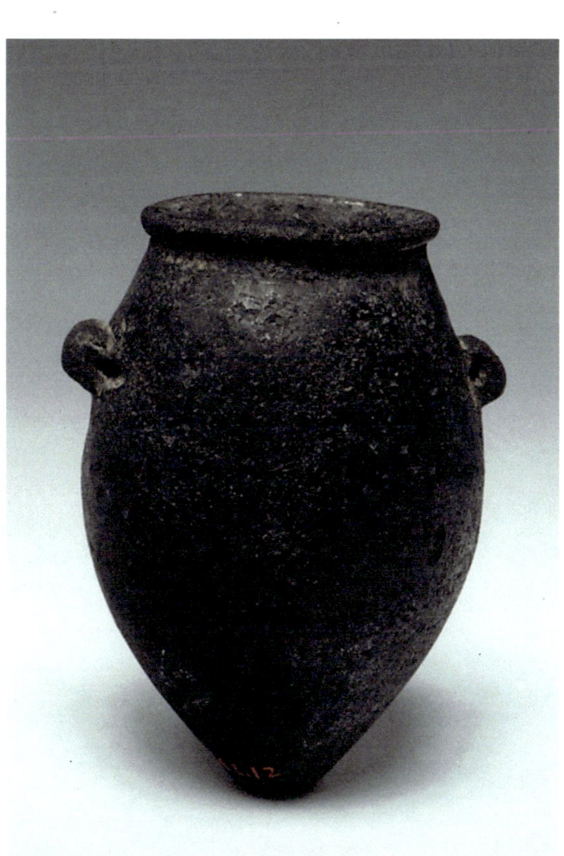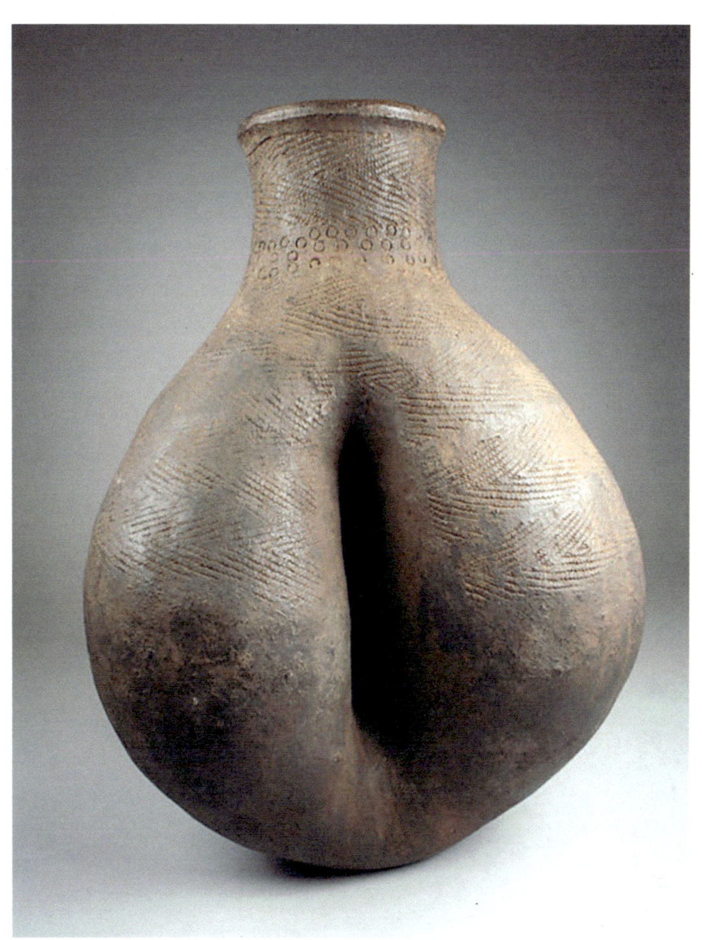

Notes / Images:

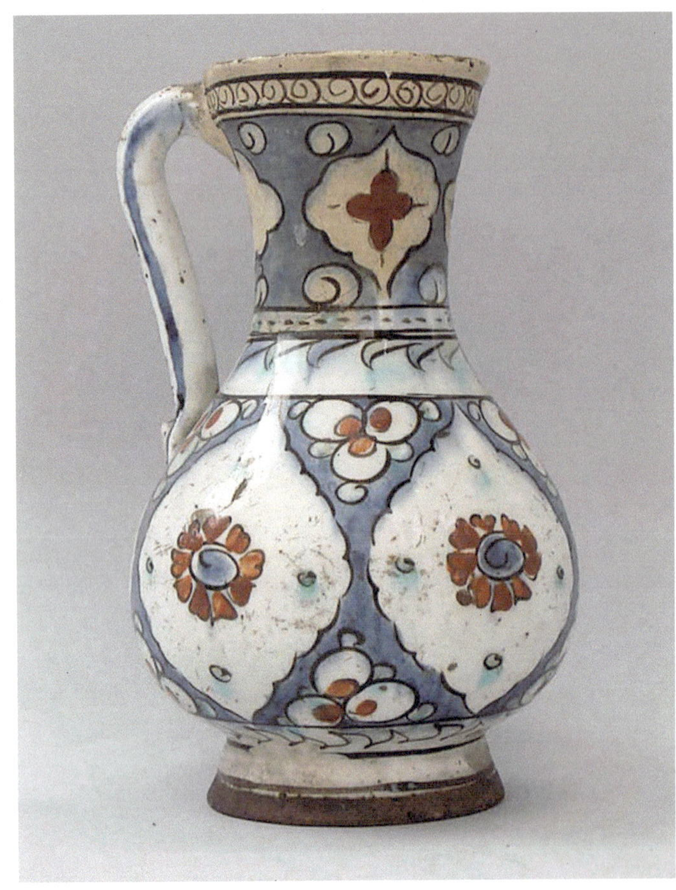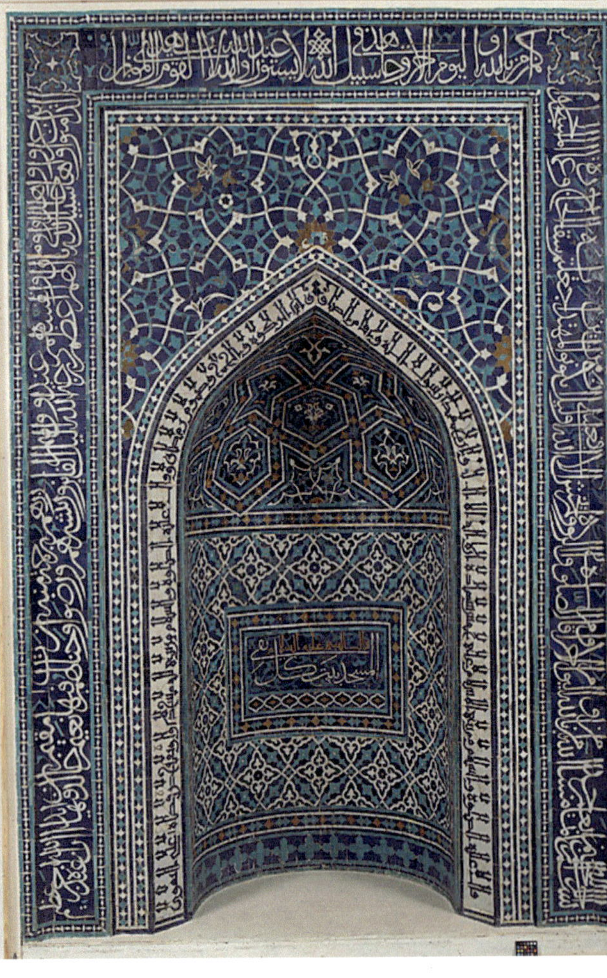

MIDDLE EASTERN
ISLAMIC

The Fertile Crescent, the area of modern Iraq, Iran, and Syria, was another location that saw the rise of important early civilizations. The Sumerians created the world's first writing system using unfired clay tablets. The Babylonians created imposing glazed brick architecture like the Ishtar Gate. Later Islamic cultures created beautiful colorful glazed pottery and tiled religious or palace architecture.

Important terms:
Mesopotamian, Babylonian, Persian, Iznik, Seljuk, luster ware, frit ware, minai, albarelli, Hispano-Moresque

all images this section[4]

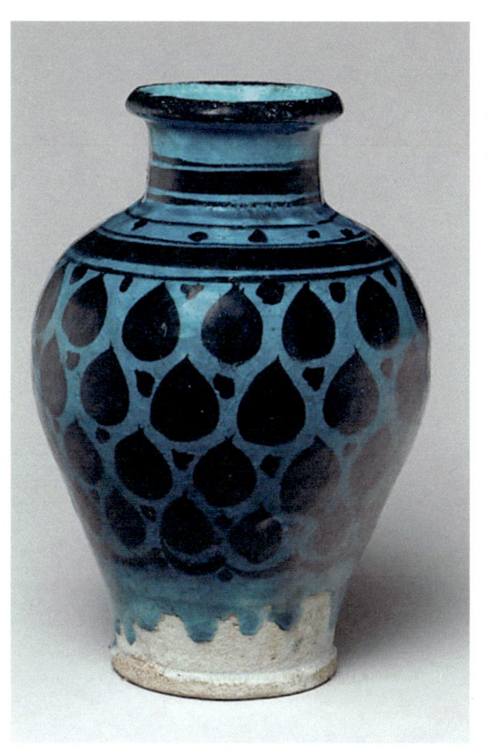
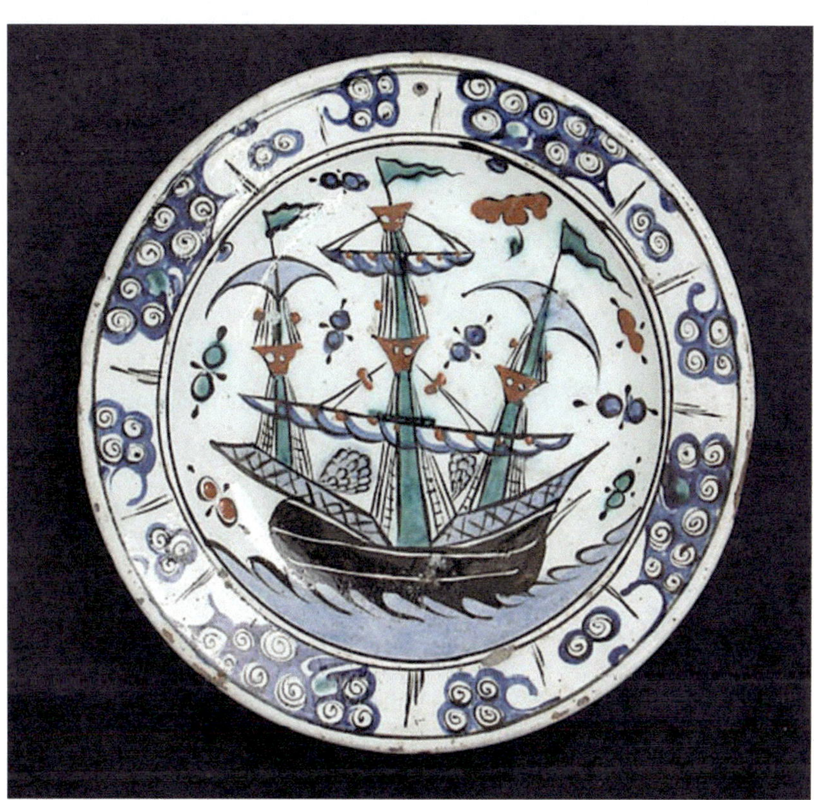
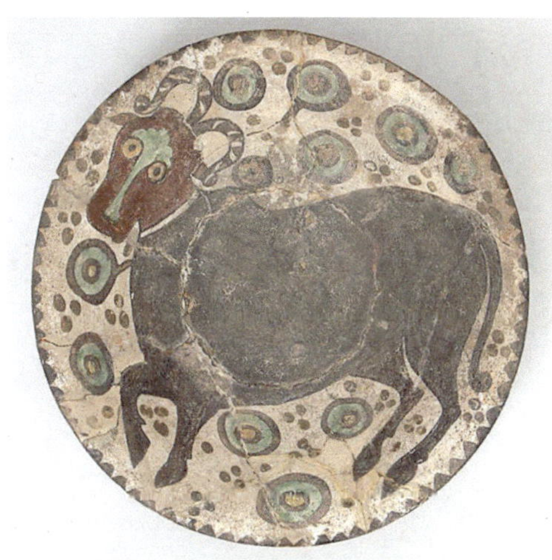
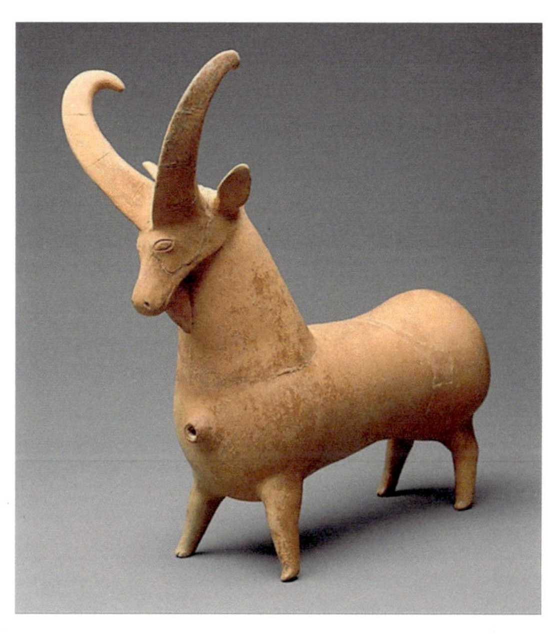
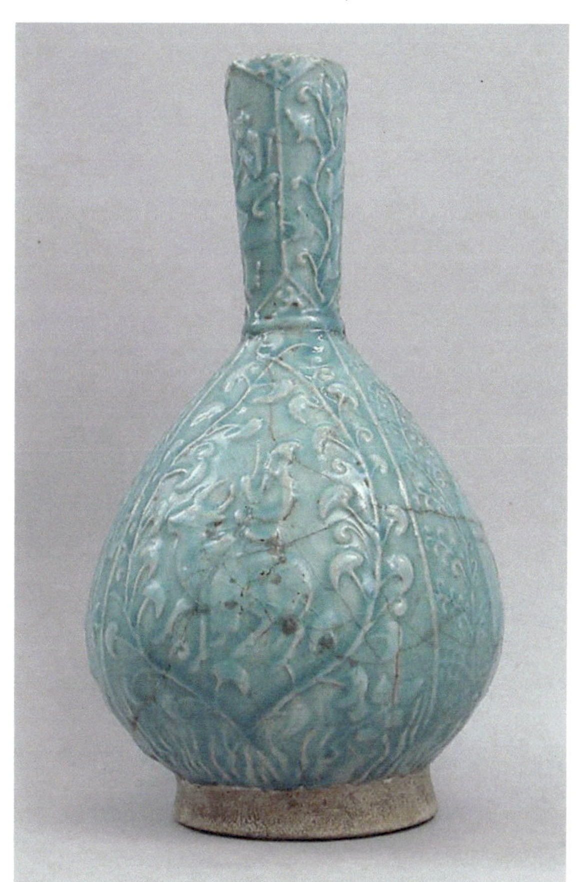

Notes / Images:

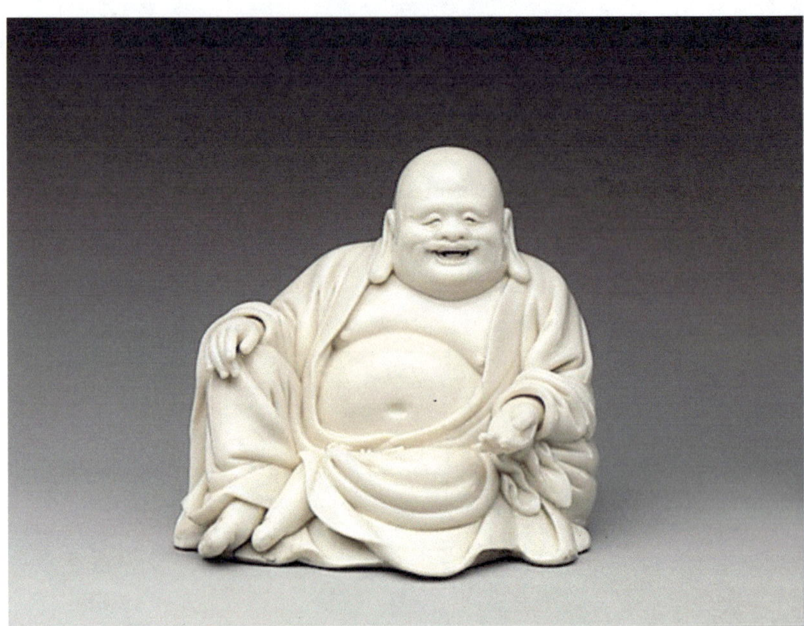

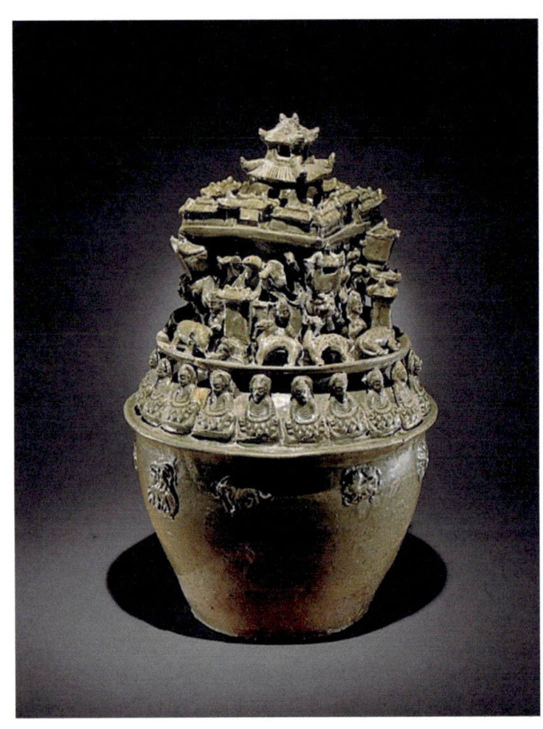

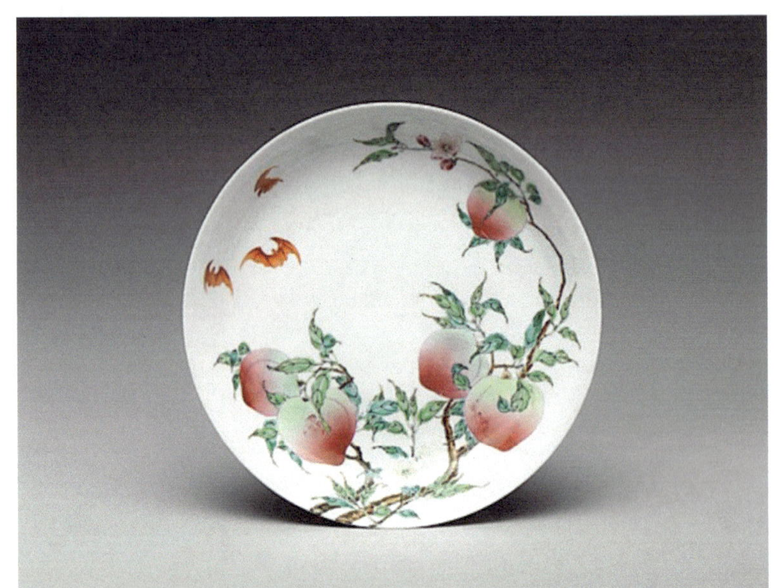

CHINESE

China has had a long, very important, and varied history of ceramics. The earliest known earthenware pots from China are dated to around 4,500 BCE. Chinese ceramic artists started making stoneware work around 1,600 BCE and they were the first to develop true porcelain around the year 650 CE. Eventually, porcelain was exported to the Europe and at one time was more valuable than gold as a trade item. This is also why porcelain is sometimes called "China" because of its origin.

There are numerous styles of Chinese ceramics that continue to influence world ceramics today. Here are some important terms/styles to know:

Ancient: Yang-Shao, Shang, Han, Tang sancai three color ware
Song dynasty: Kuan, Chun, Ding, Guan, Chien, Cizhou
Others: Ming, Dehua porcelain, famille rose

all images this section[4]

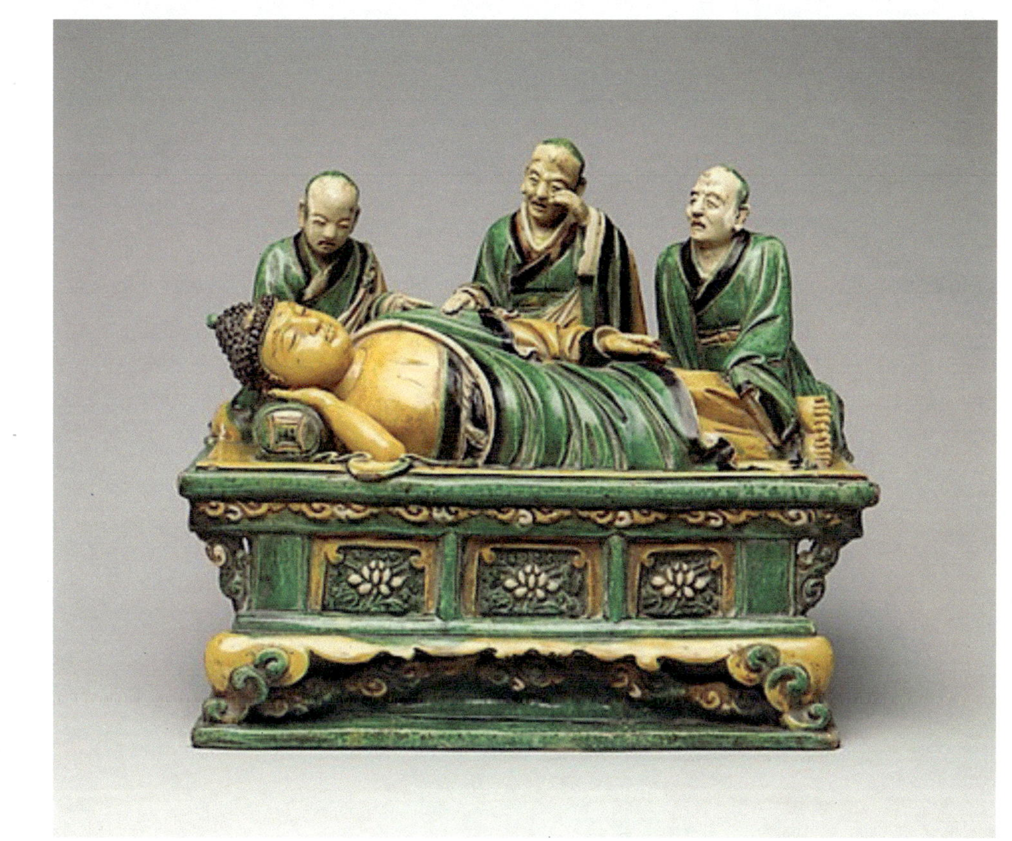

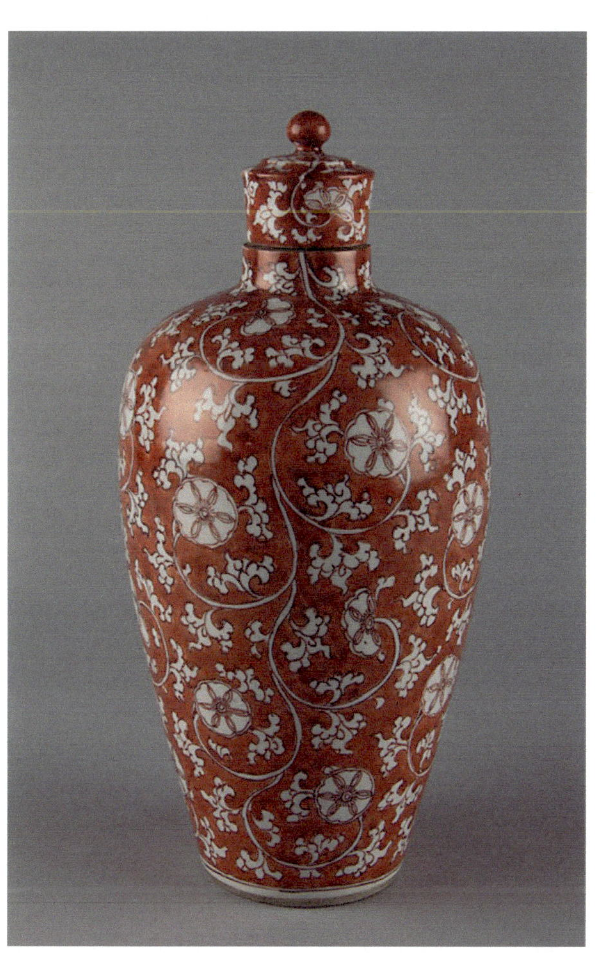

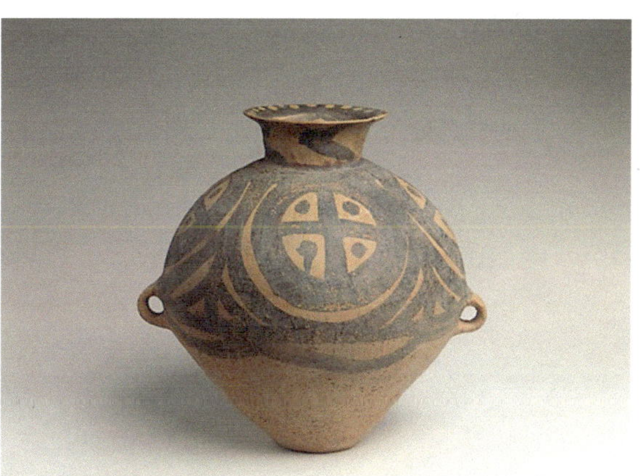

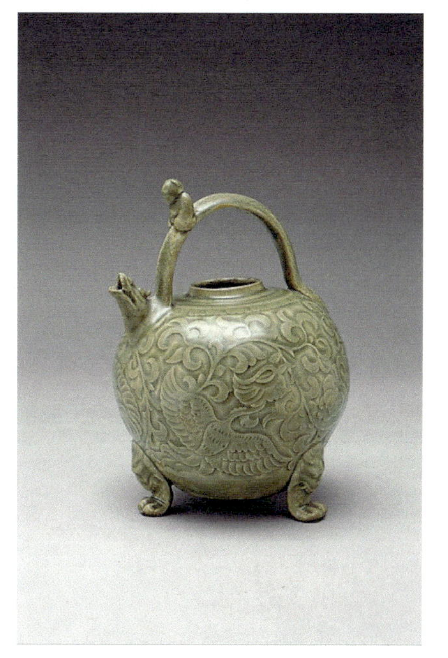

Notes / Images:

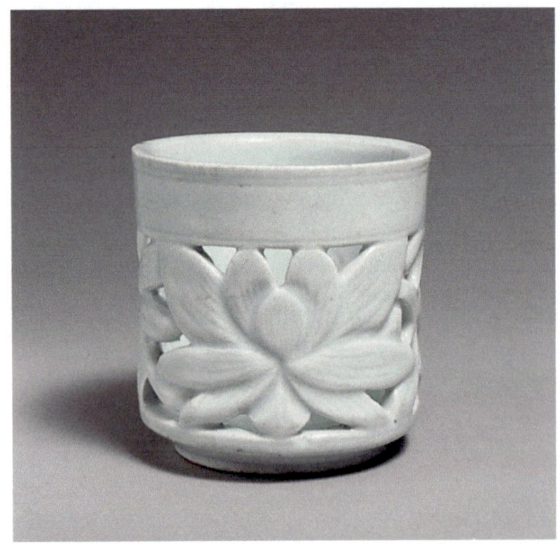

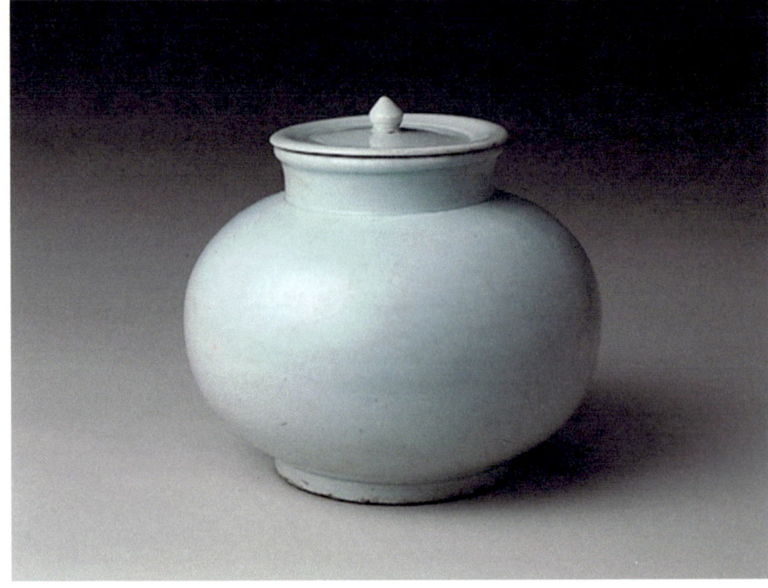

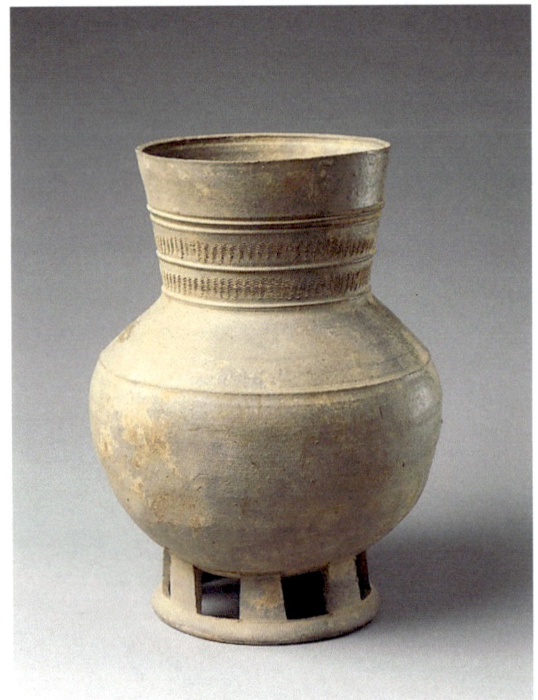

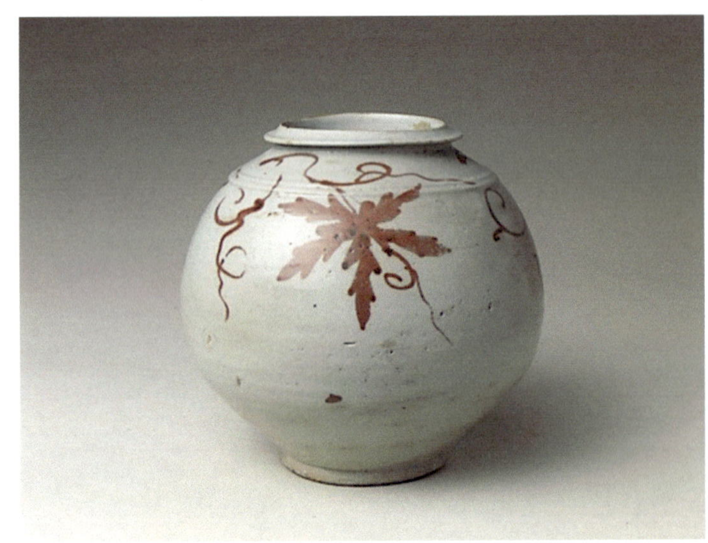

KOREAN

Korea has long been influenced by its neighbor, China. Early Korean pots were made from a reddish earthenware clay and used for storage and cooking. Later during the Three Kingdoms era (Kokuryo, Paekche, Silla), a variety of earthenware and stoneware forms were made. The highpoint of Korean ceramics came during the Koryo Period (918-1392 CE) when potters took influence from Chinese potters and surpassed them with a stunning blue-green celadon colored glaze.

Another important Korean development was the use of slip inlaid into carved or stamped decoration with a technique called "mishima". This kind of pottery and other Korean ceramics were in great demand in Japan for the tea ceremony and led to the forced "relocation" of Korean potters during Japanese invasions of 1592-98 CE.

Important terms: Silla, Koryo celadon, Onggi, Joseon, Buncheong

all images this section[4]

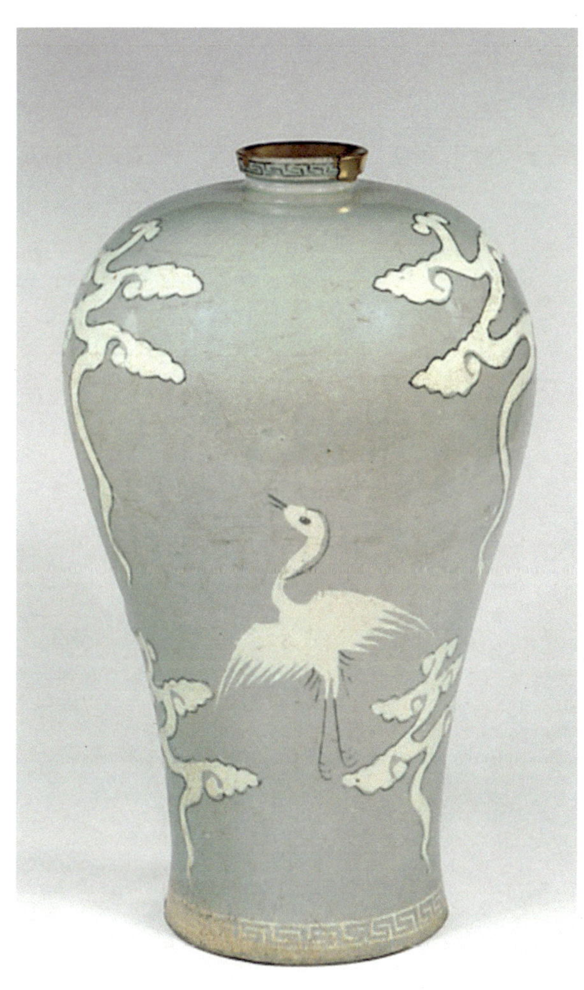

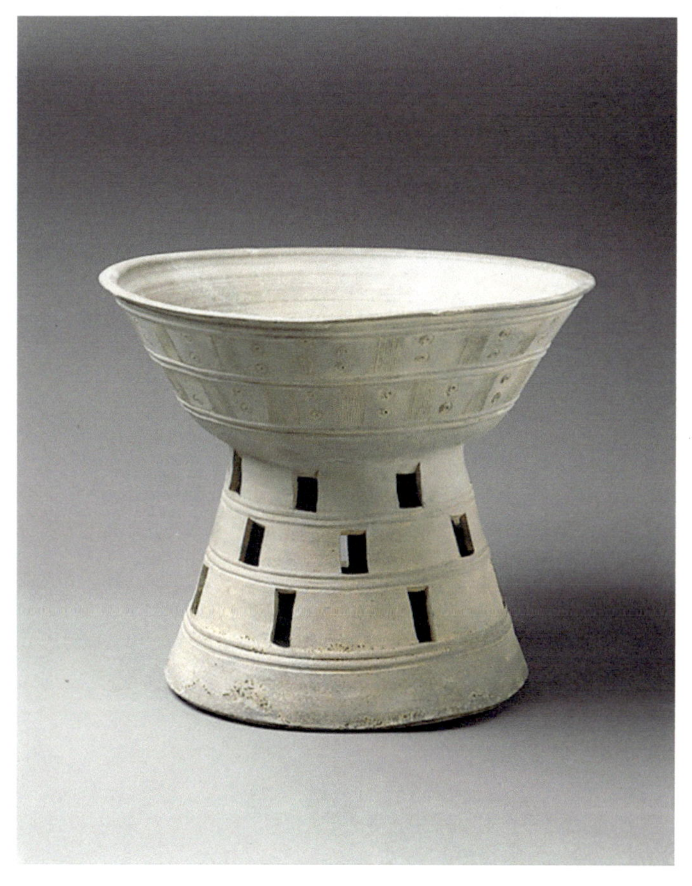

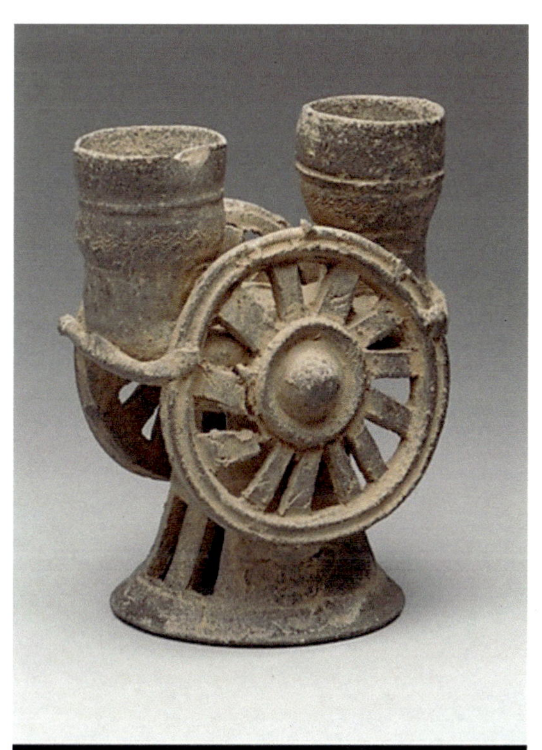

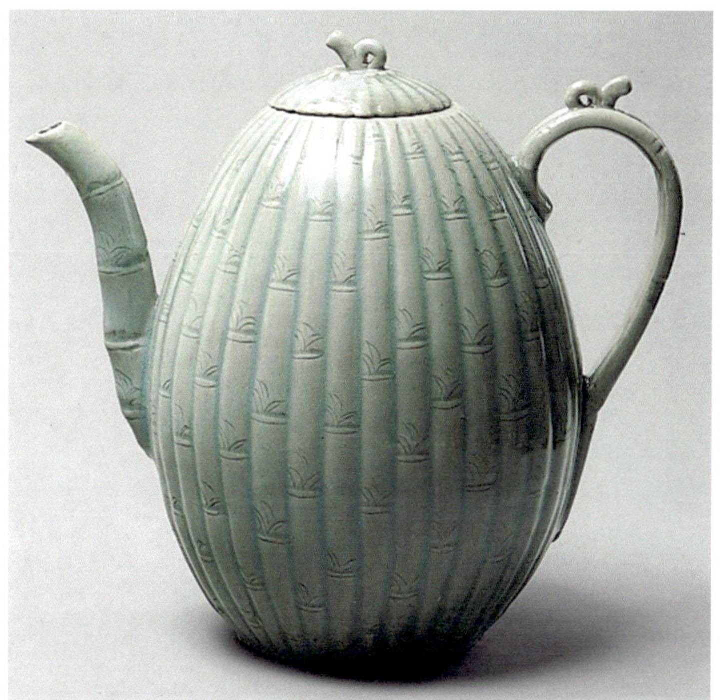

Notes / Images:

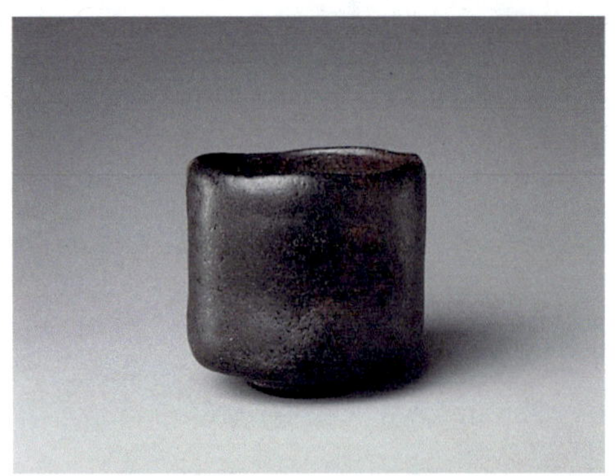

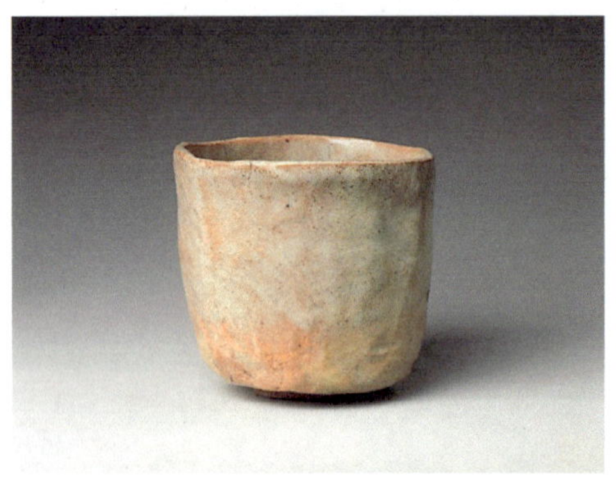

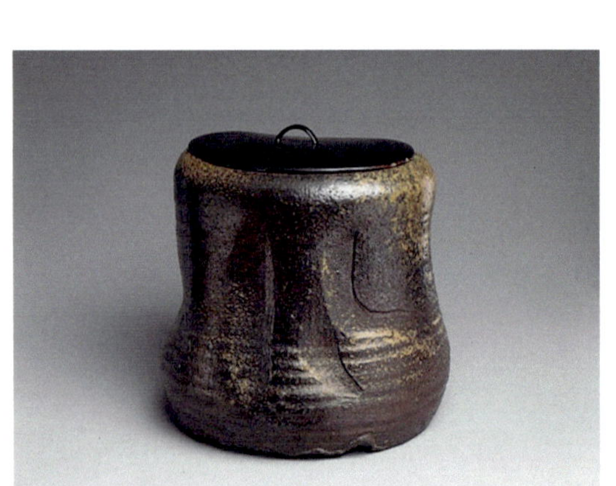

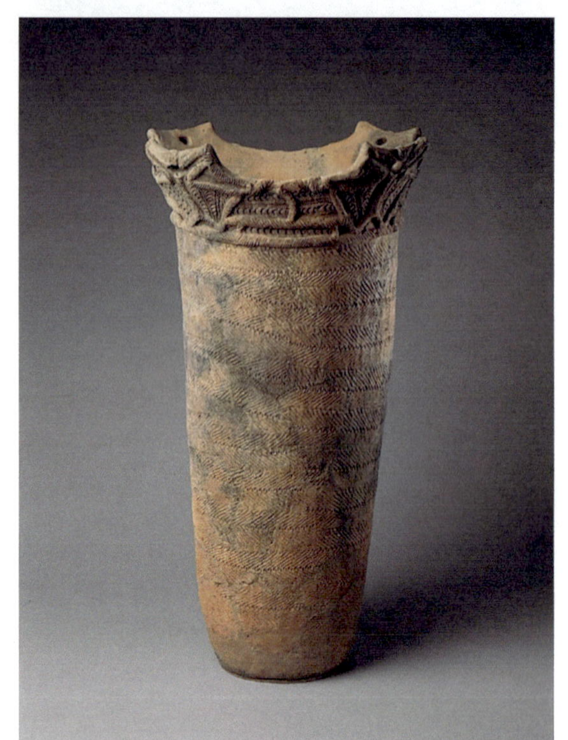

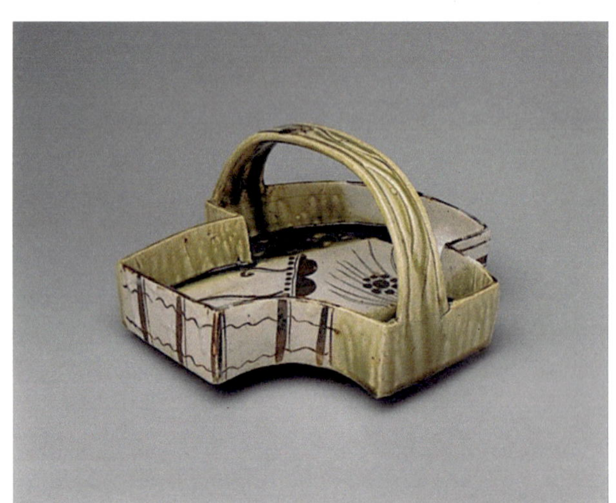

JAPANESE

The oldest known type of pottery, called Jomon, was made in Japan by a culture of fishing and gathering people. From around 10,000 BCE, these people produced the earliest clay pots used for cooking.

The Japanese culture has long been a "ceramics culture" producing a wide variety of types of ceramic sculpture and pottery. Stylistic and technological interactions with China and Korea helped the Japanese to develop these types of earthenware, stoneware, and porcelain ceramics.

Early styles to know: Jomon, Yayoi, Haniwa
Earthenware: Raku
Stoneware: Bizen, Shigaraki, Karatsu, Oribe, Hagi, Mino, Seto
Porcelain: Arita, Imari, Nabeshima, Kakiemon, Kutani
Other important terms: Tea ceremony, Kenzan

all images this section[4]

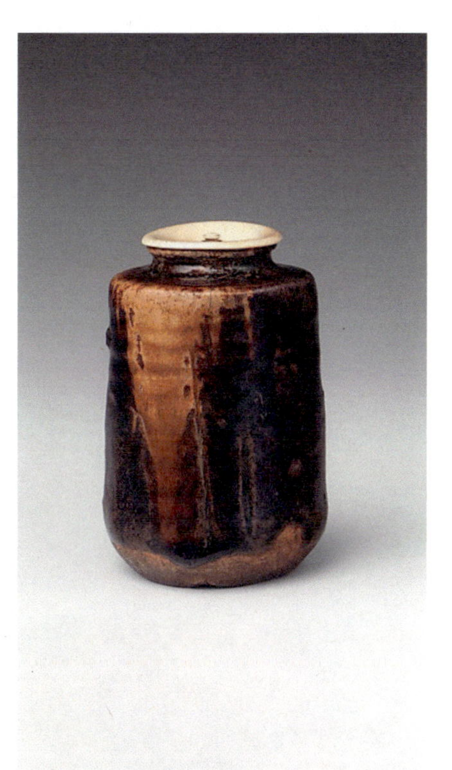

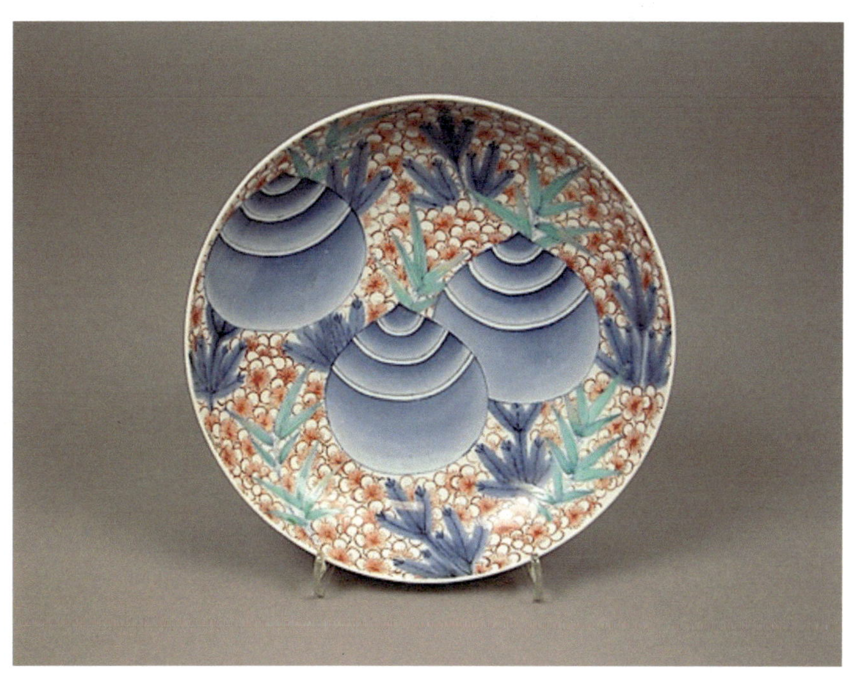

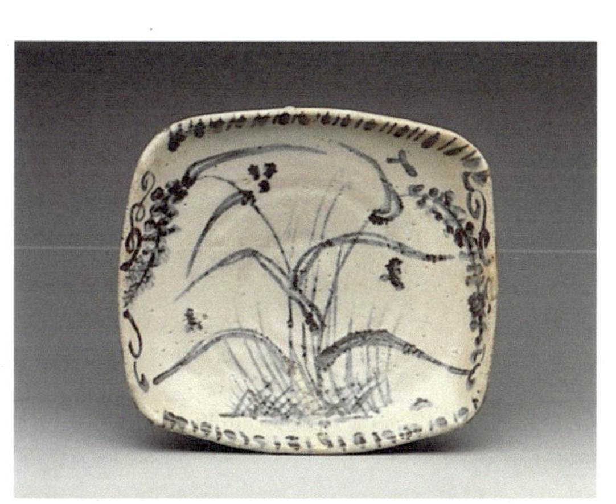

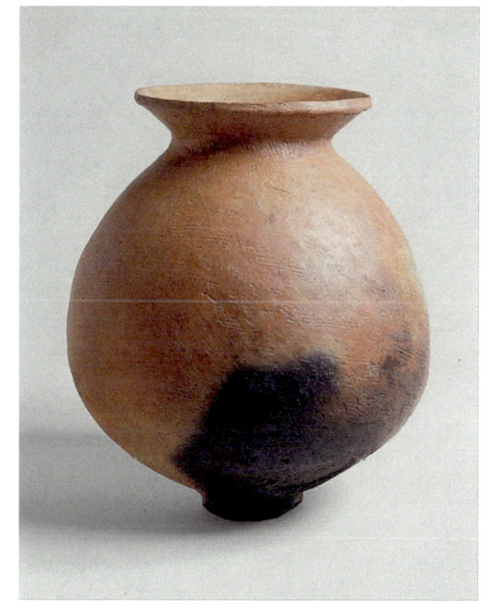

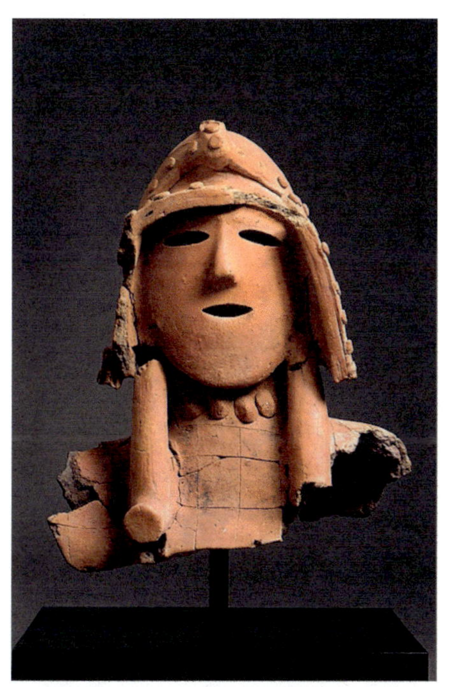

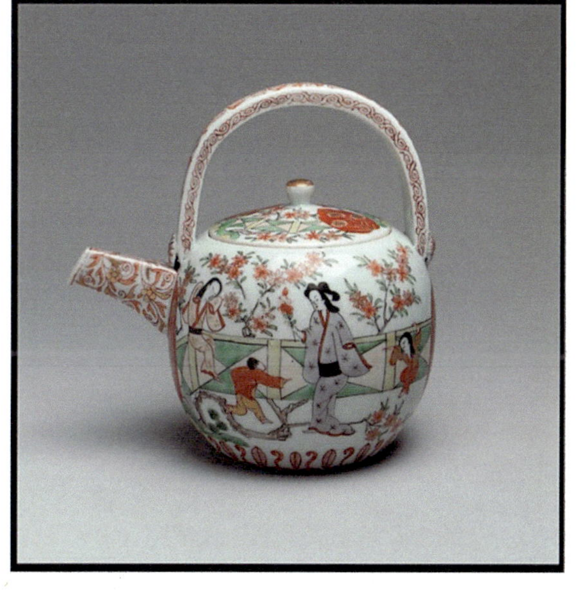

Notes / Images:

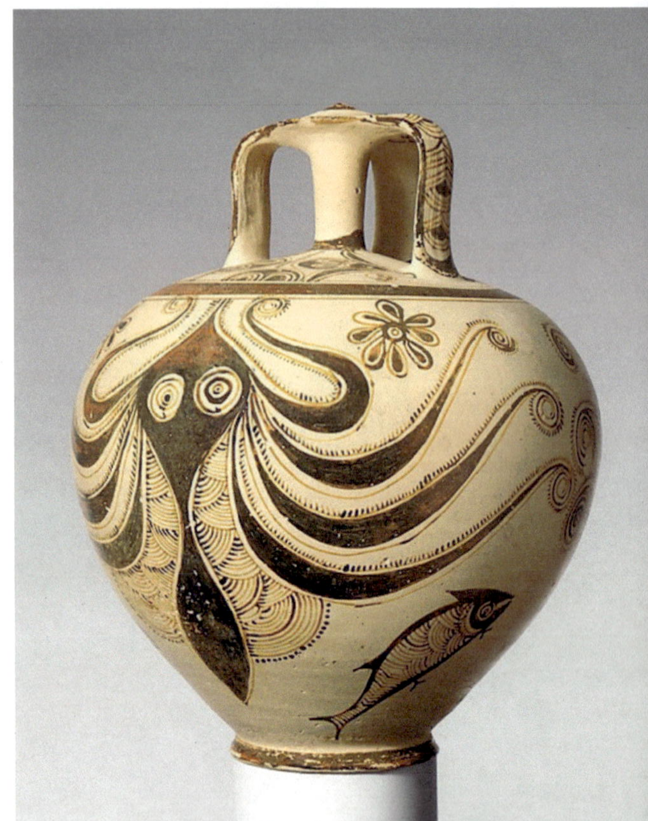

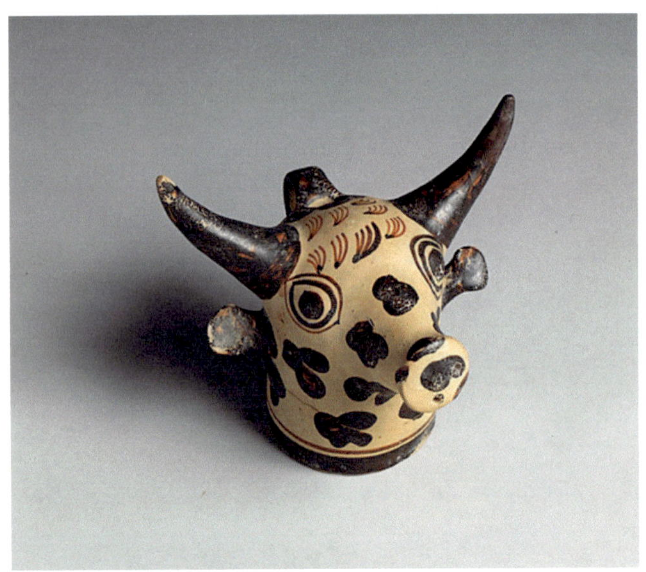

MINOAN

The Minoan people (named after mythical King Minos) created a highly developed culture on the island of Crete between 3,000 and 2,500 BCE. This Mediterranean culture traded widely with other people in southern Europe, Egypt, and Mesopotamia. Some scholars believe the Minoans may be the source for the story of the Atlantis and evidence of volcanic eruptions in the area may have caused widespread destruction and the decline of this culture.

Minoan ceramic artists created highly refined pottery often with imaginative decorative surface patterns. These patterns often reflected their sea faring and fishing culture.

Important terms:
Marine style
Kameres ware

all images this section[4]

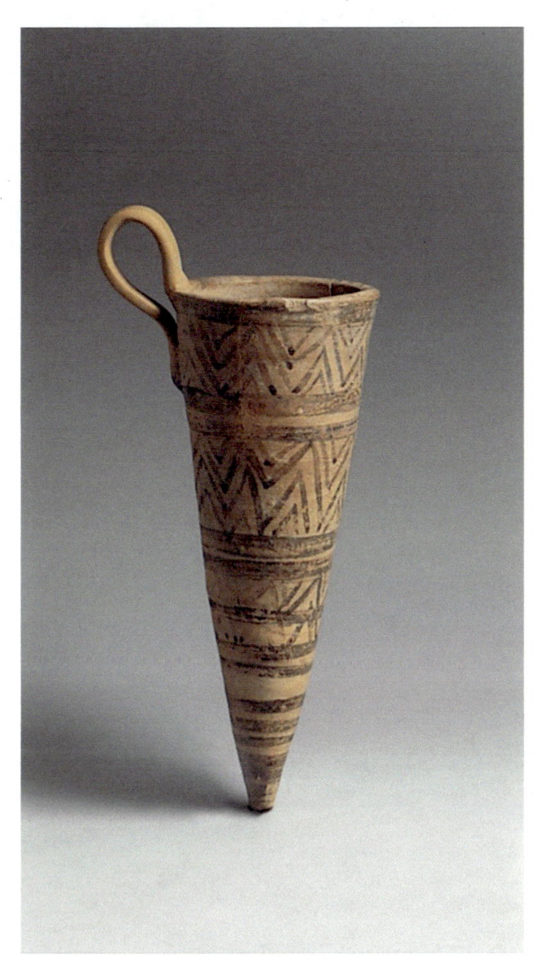

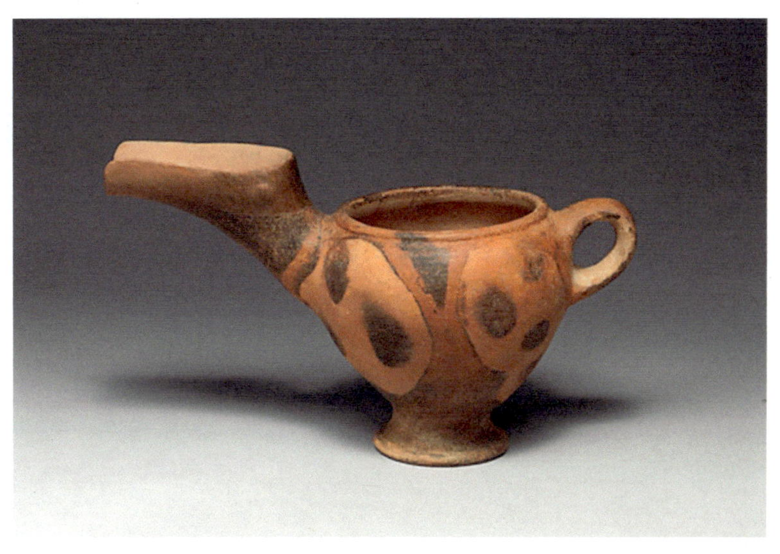

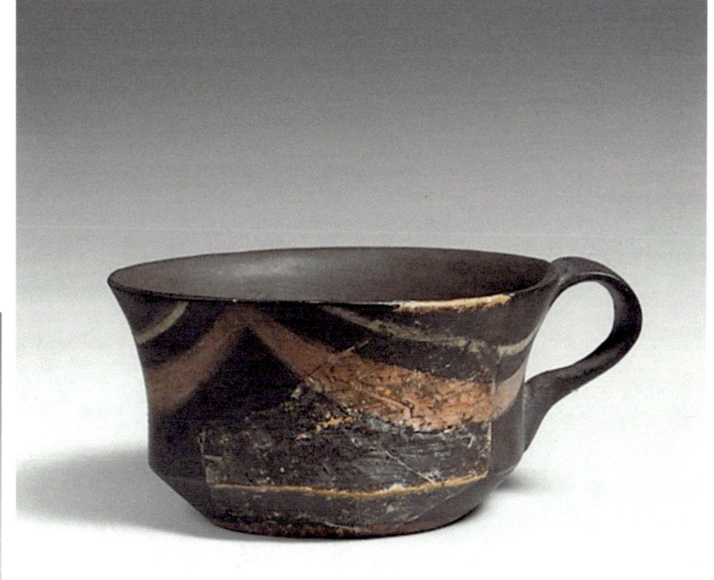

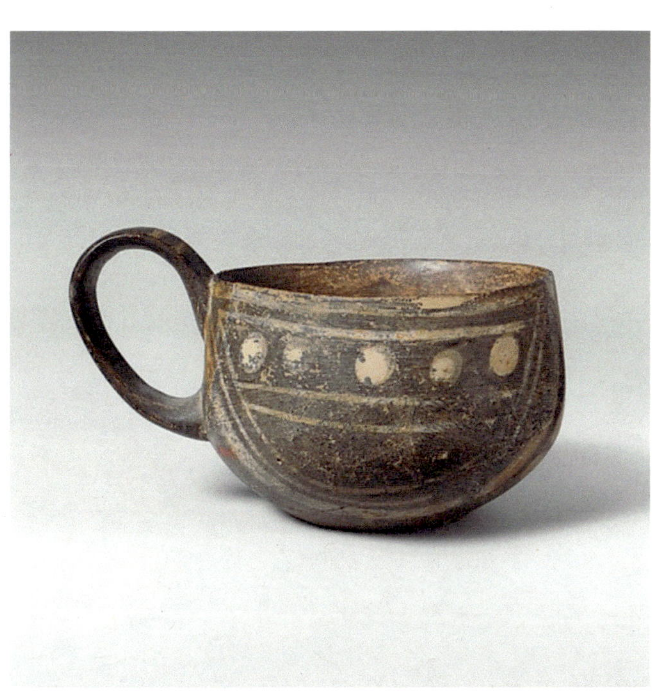

Notes / Images:

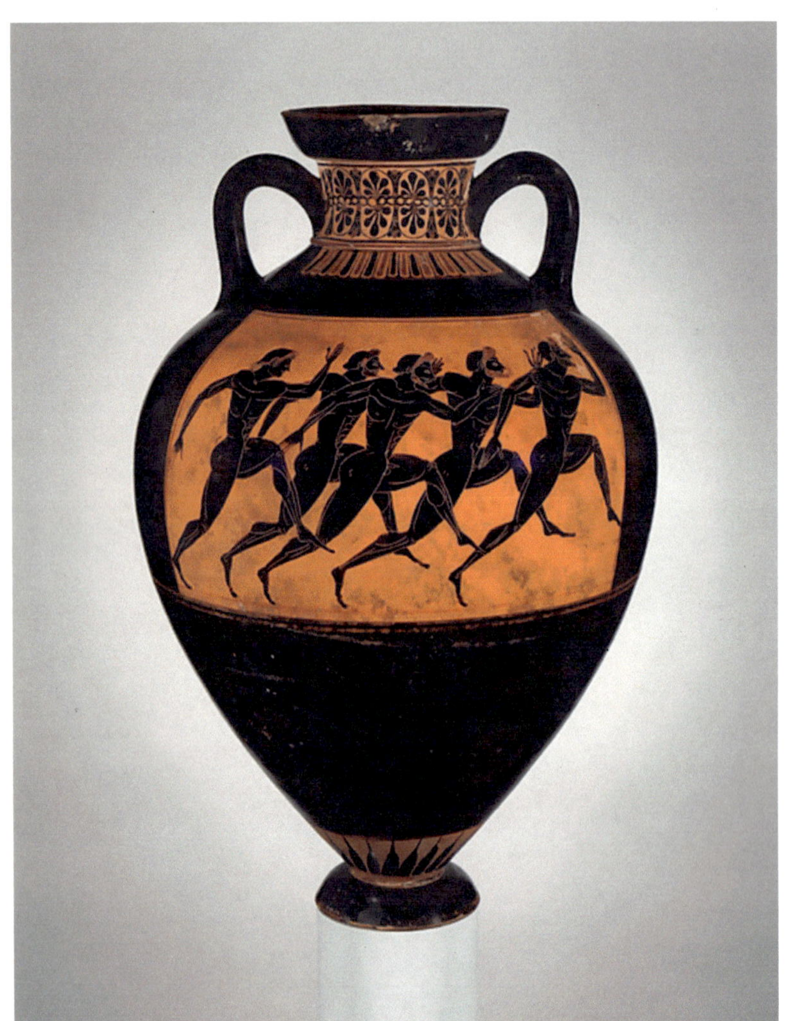

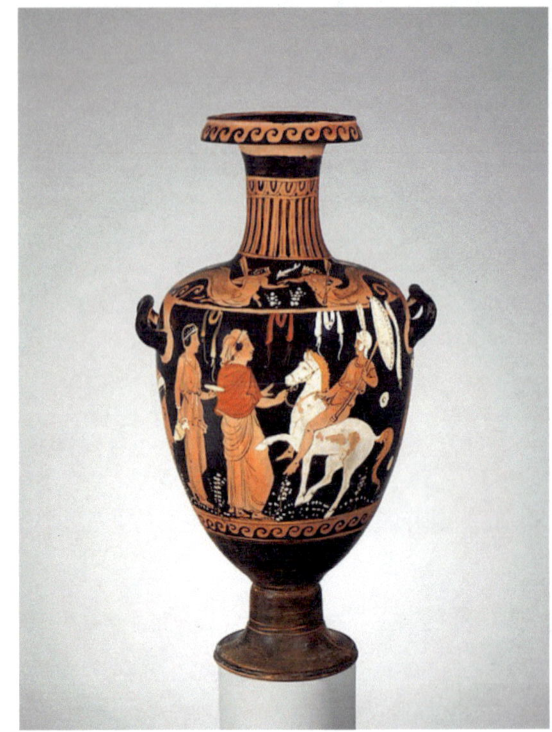

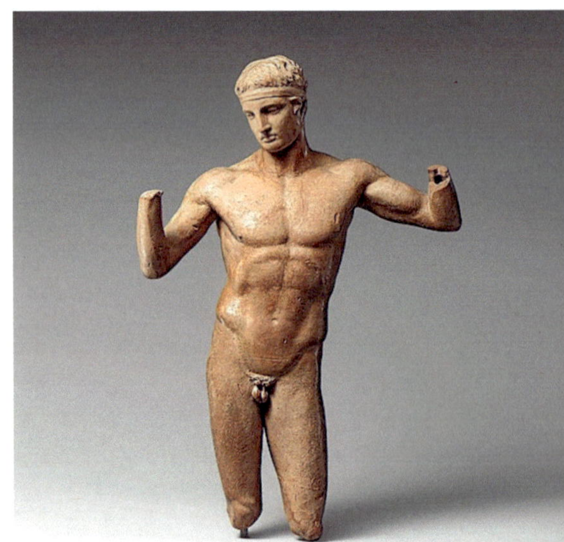

GREEK

The peoples of ancient Greece lived in city states and many of their ideas (philosophy, government, science) helped to form the foundation of Western culture. Greek artists pursued the goal of sculpting the "perfect" human figure and potters worked to create beautiful geometric shapes often covered in complex imagery and decoration. Some of the earliest signed art was created by the Greek potter and vase painter, Exekias, from around 550 to 525 BCE. These artists developed and used a special refined slip called terra sigilata to decorate their work.

Important terms:
Geometric style, Black figure style, Red figure style, amphora, kylix, krater

Artists:
Exekias, Andokides Painter, Euthymides, Achilles Painter

all images this section[4]

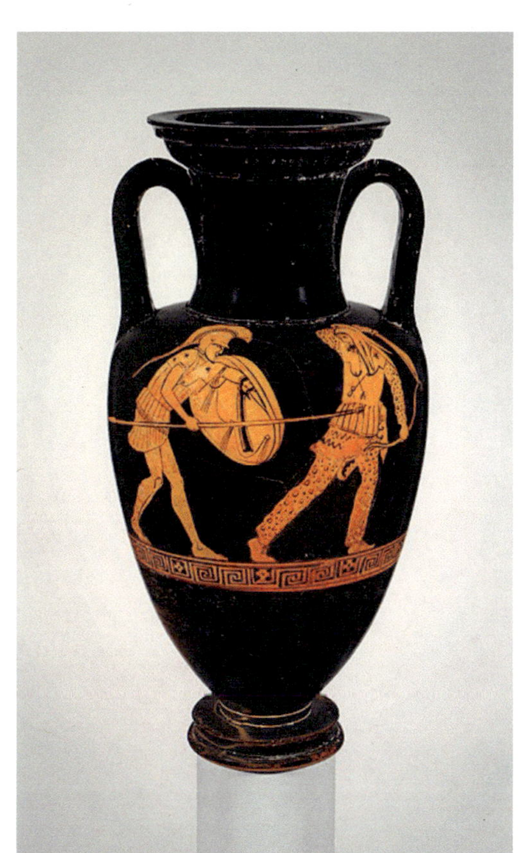

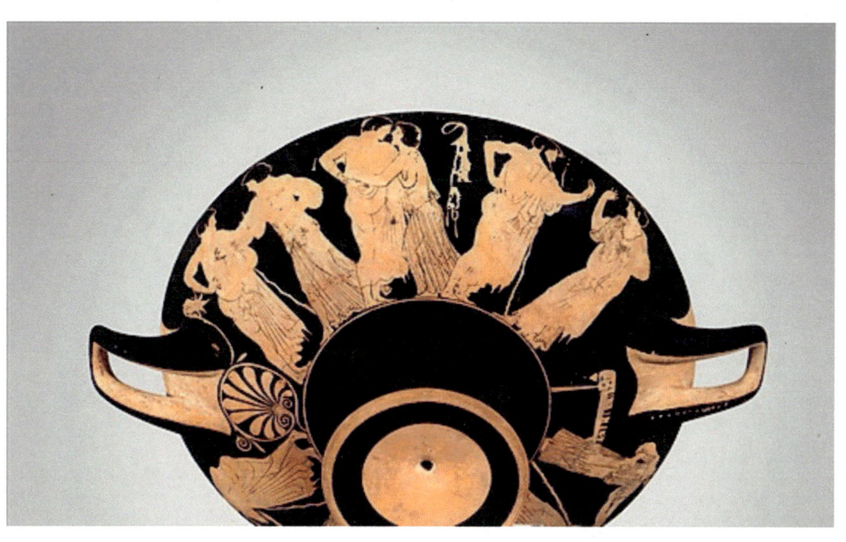

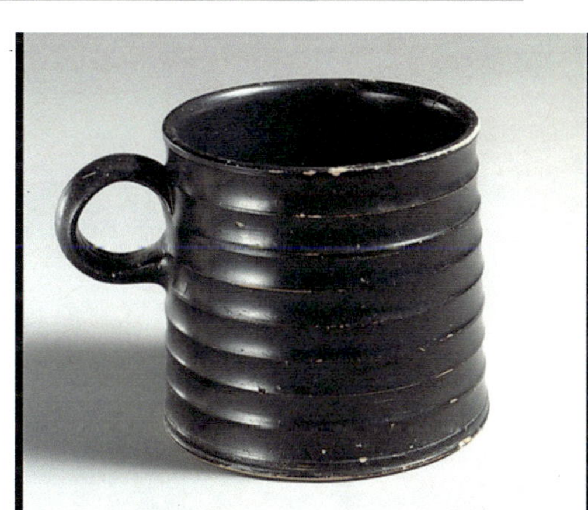

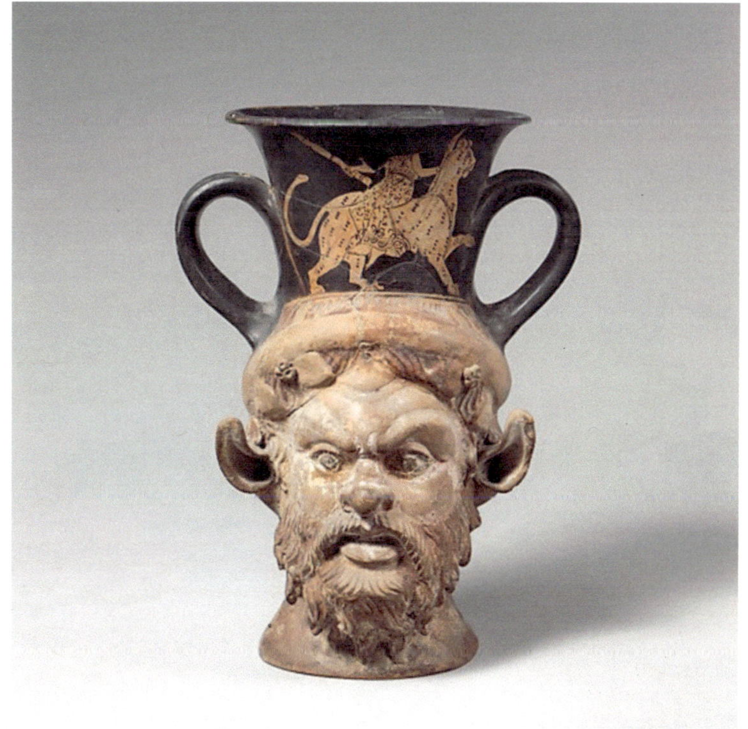

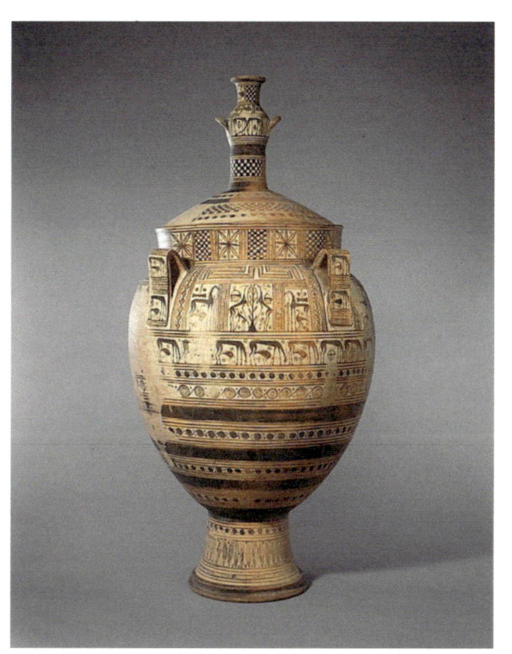

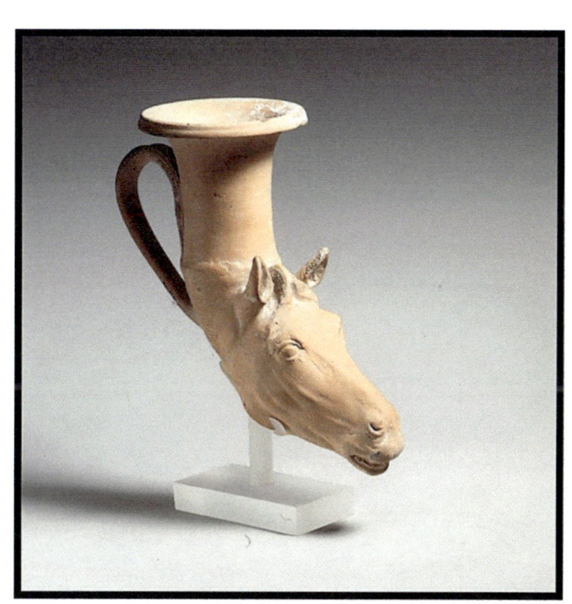

Notes / Images:

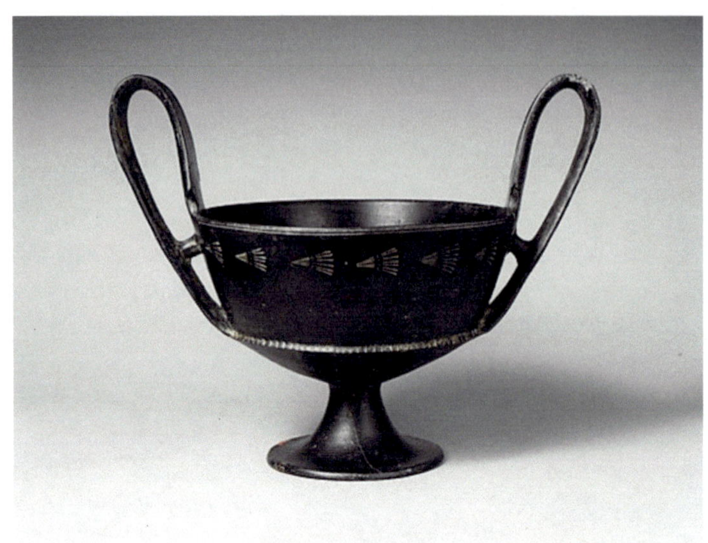

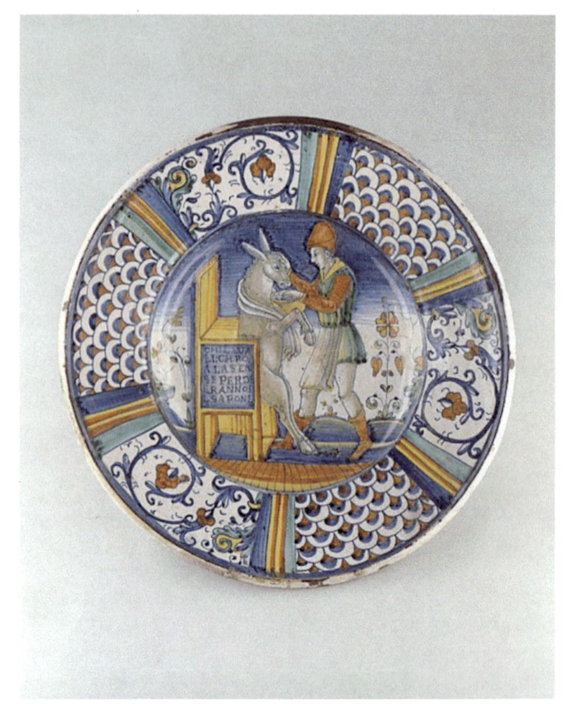

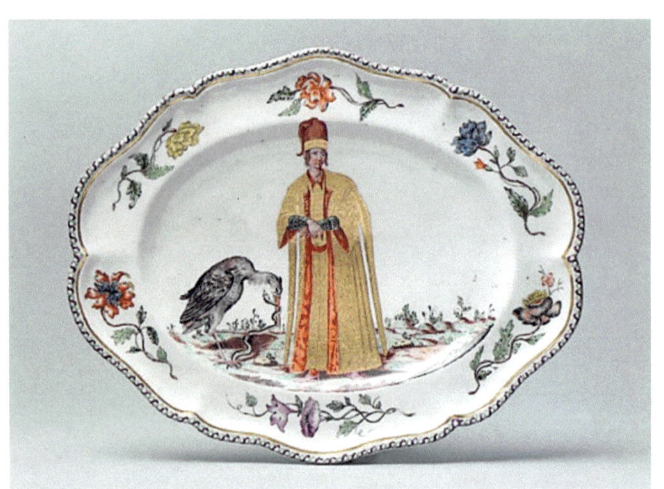

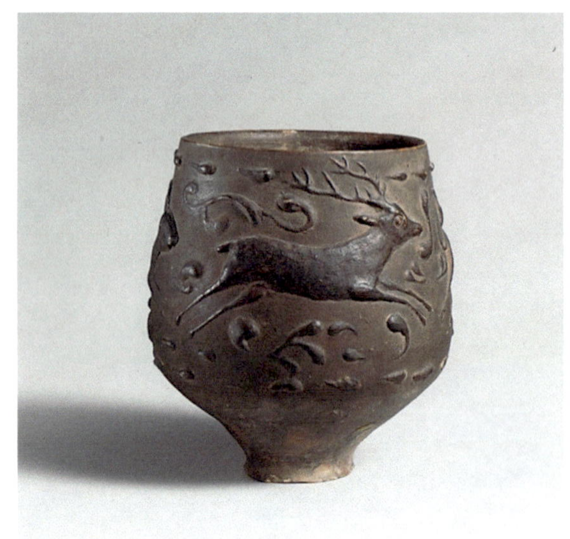

ETRUSCAN
ROMAN
ITALIAN

The importance of the Roman Empire in Western civilization cannot be overstated although they did not produce major ceramic works. The other cultures that existed before and after in Italy did have a great impact on ceramics history. The Etruscans were a group of people settled in western Italy by the 9th century BCE. They had strong trade ties with the Greeks and were masters of terra cotta sculpture and black pottery. Starting in the Italian Renaissance, artists were making masterworks of painting on ceramics using the majolica (maiolica) techniques originally imported from Spain.

Important terms:
majolica, Etruscan, Arretine ware, Deruta

Artists:
Luca Della Robbia, Piccolpasso

all images this section[4]

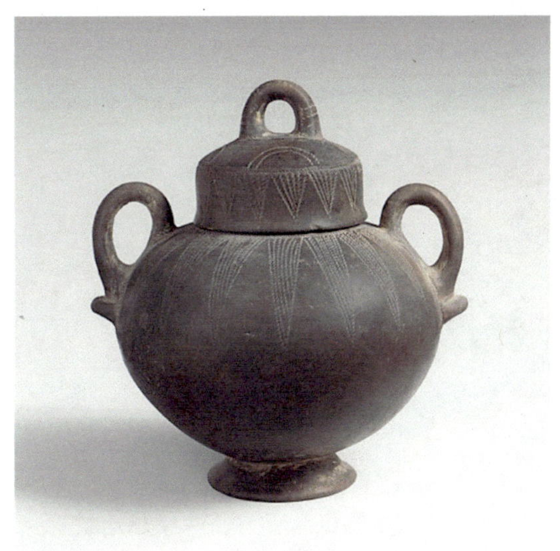

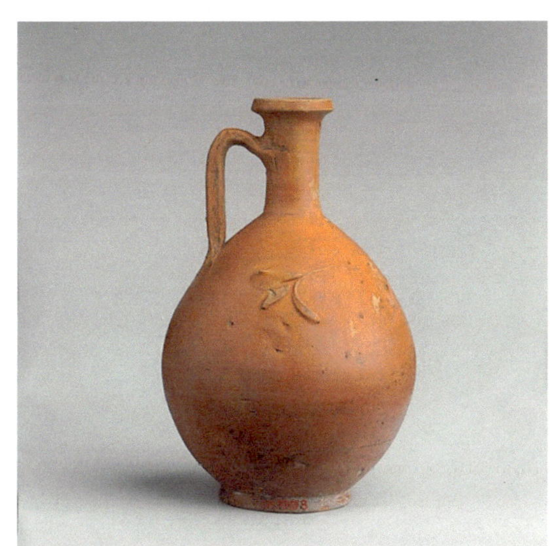

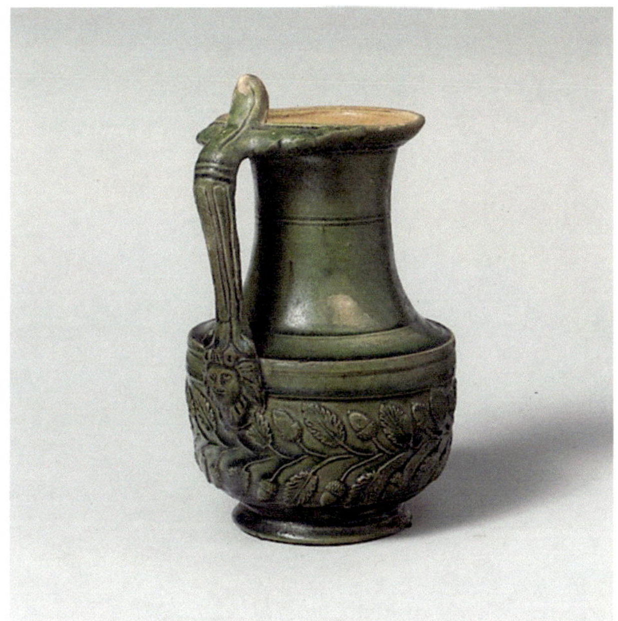

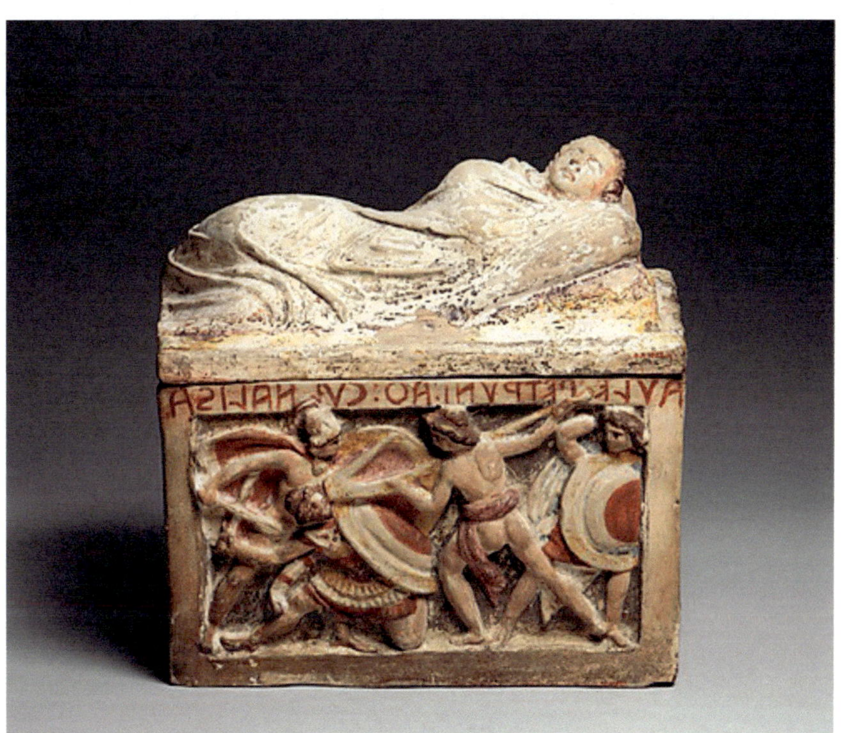
AVL·PETRVNI·AO·CVI·NAVISA

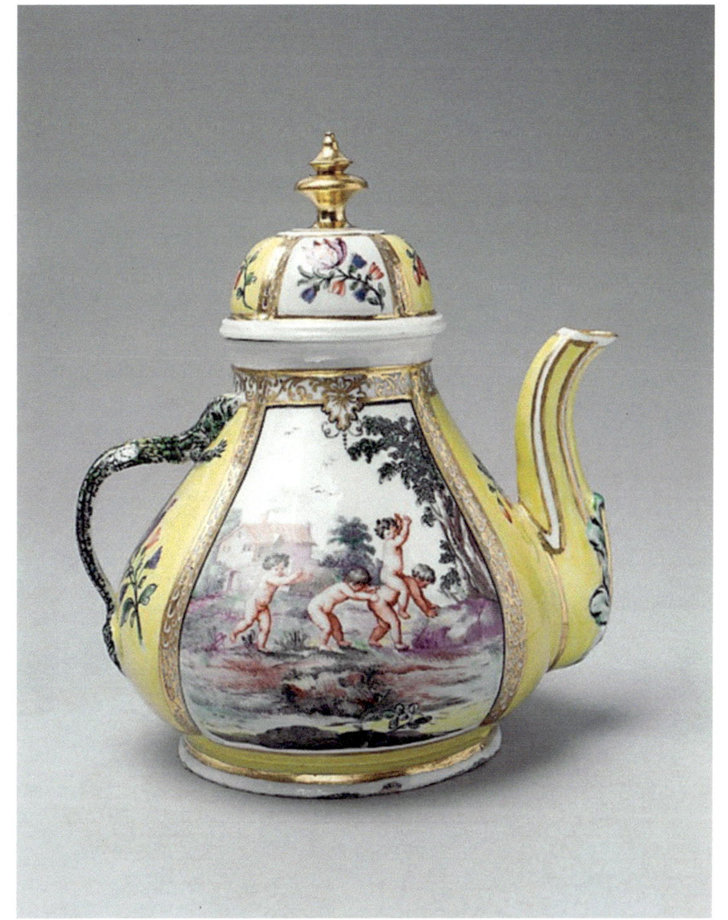

Notes / Images:

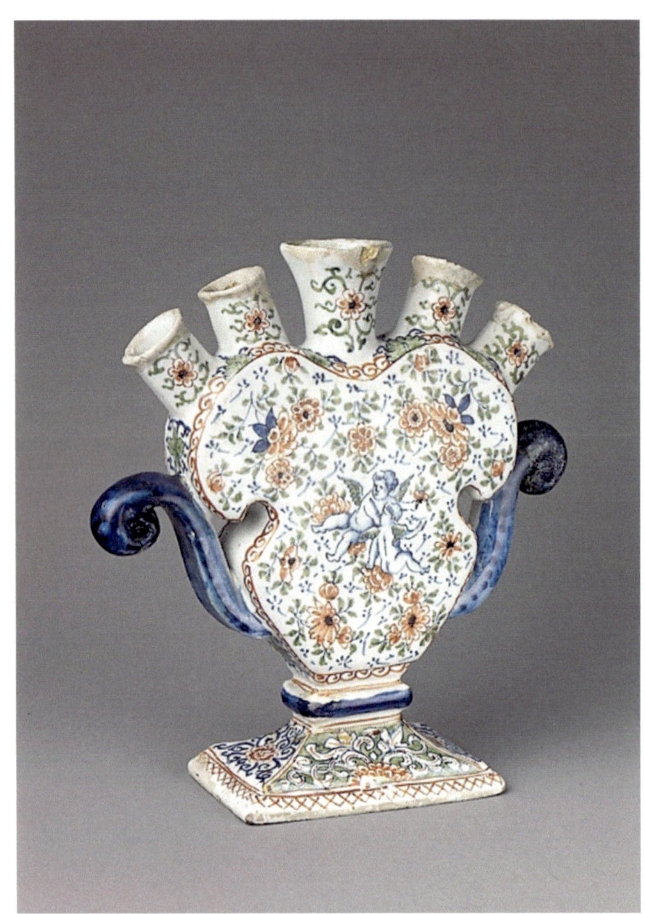

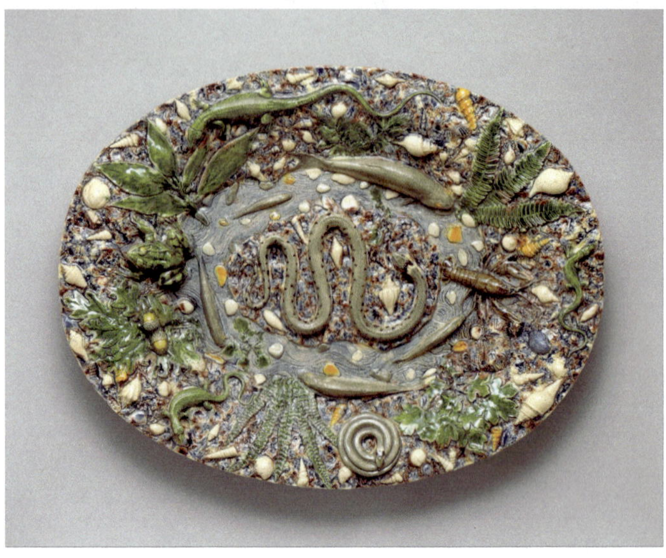

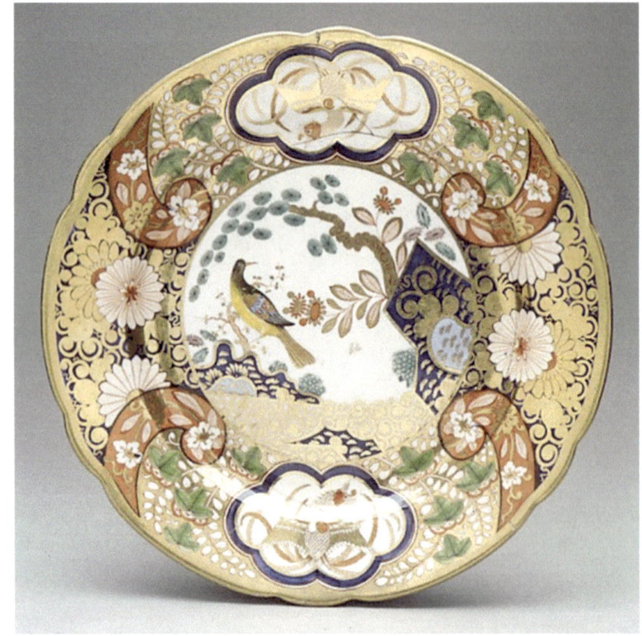

NORTHERN
EUROPEAN

Major centers of ceramics production existed across Northern Europe in England, Germany, France, and Holland from the Medieval Ages onward. A variety of styles evolved and new ways of working with materials were developed especially during the Industrial Revolution. Many of these styles and techniques were transferred to America when immigrant groups came here and many ceramic artists were looking for new opportunities.

Important terms and artists:
Bellarmine, Jasperware, Spode, Wedgewood, Bernard Palissy, bone china, soft paste porcelain, Böttger, Staffordshire, Ernest Chaplet, William Morris

Locations:
Delft, La Borne, Meissen, Sèvres, Limoges

all images this section[4]

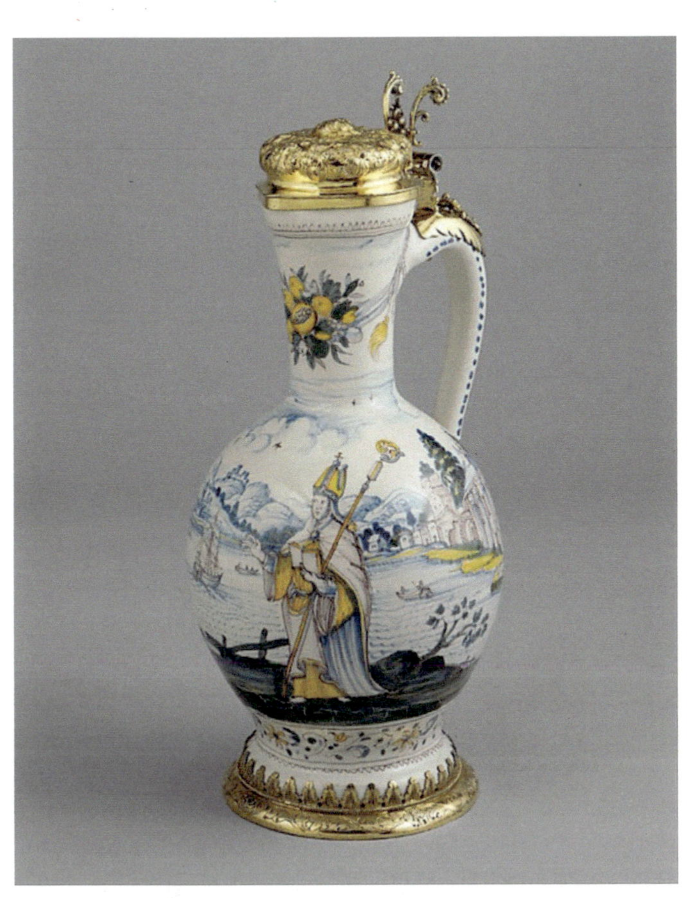

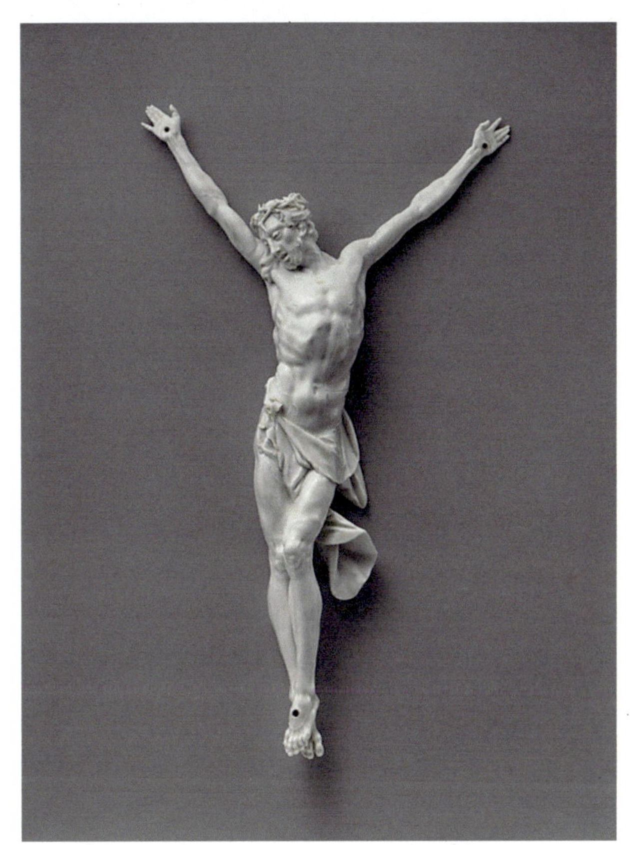

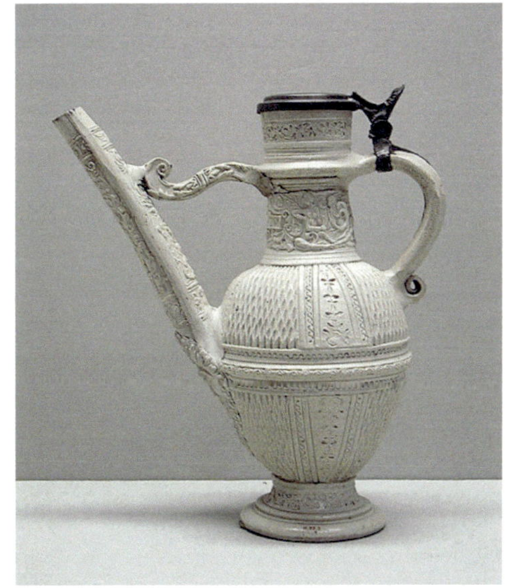

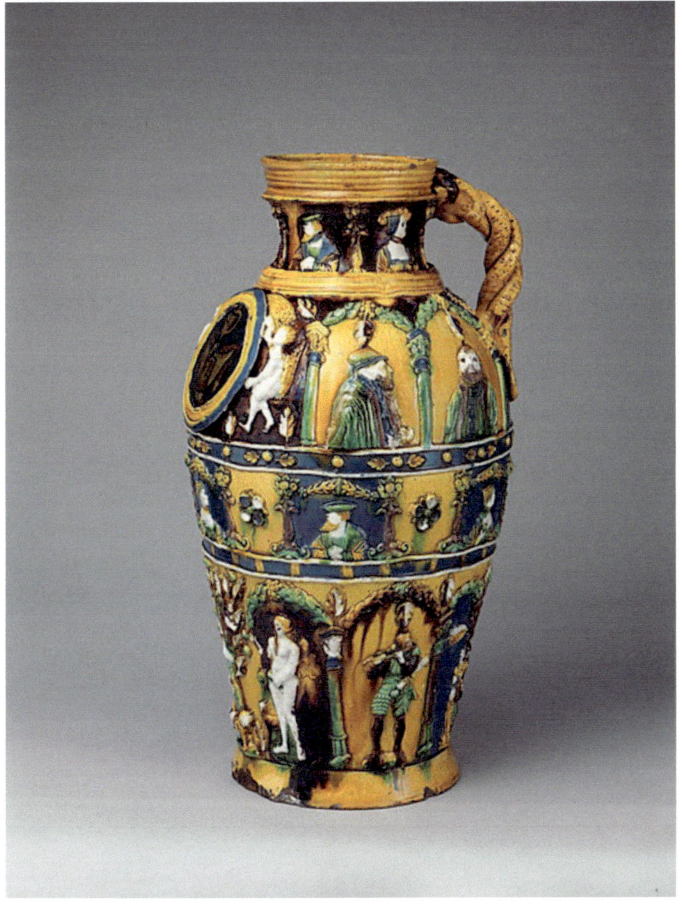

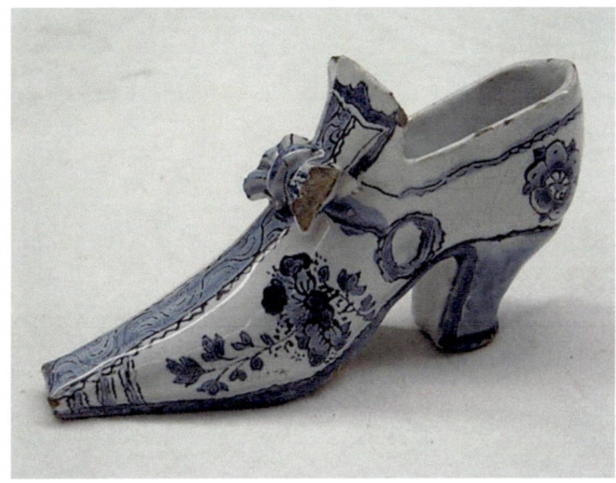

Notes / Images:

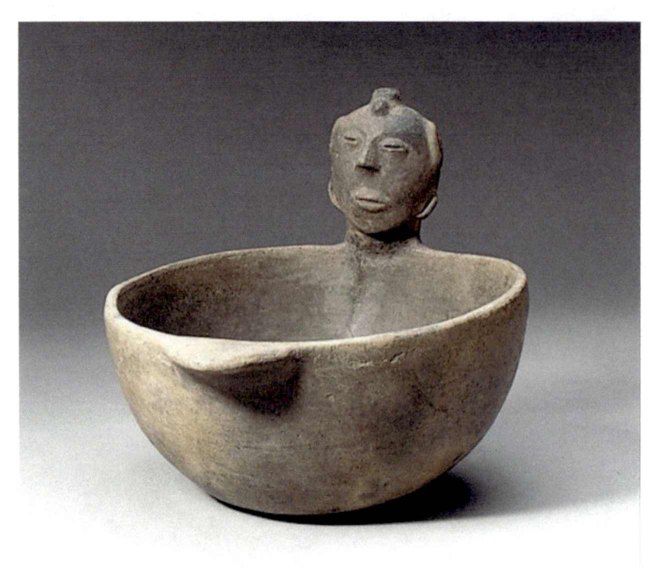

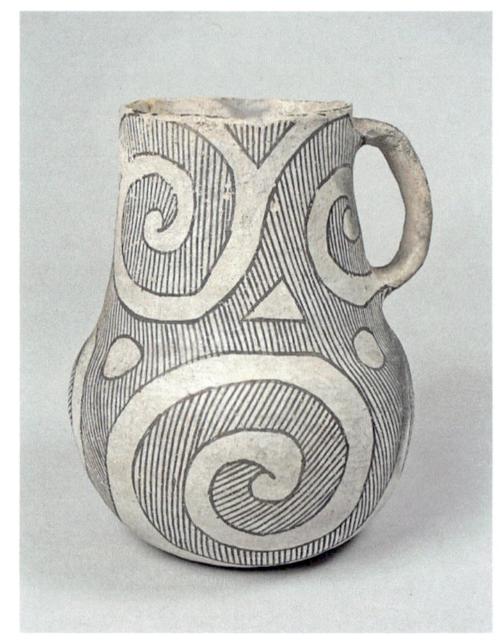

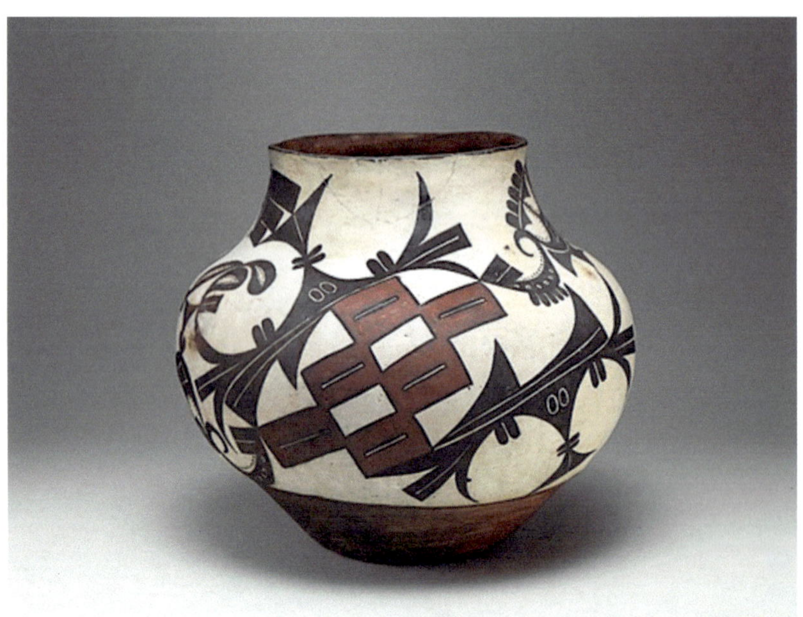

NATIVE AMERICAN

It is currently thought that the first people to come to the Americas arrived here between 30,000 to 28,000 years ago. As groups migrated and settled across North America, some began to make ceramics for cooking, storage, and other purposes. These works were made from local earthenware clays and the forms constructed by hand. Some of the most significant Native American pottery was and continues to be made in the Southwest (New Mexico, Arizona, and parts of Colorado). The Rockwell Museum of Western Art in Corning has a great collection of Native American pottery on display.

Important terms:
Mimbres, Hopi, Zuni, Santa Clara, San Ildefonso, Acoma, Mississippian

Artists:
Maria Martinez, Diego Romero, Lucy Lewis, Virgil Ortiz

all images this section[4]

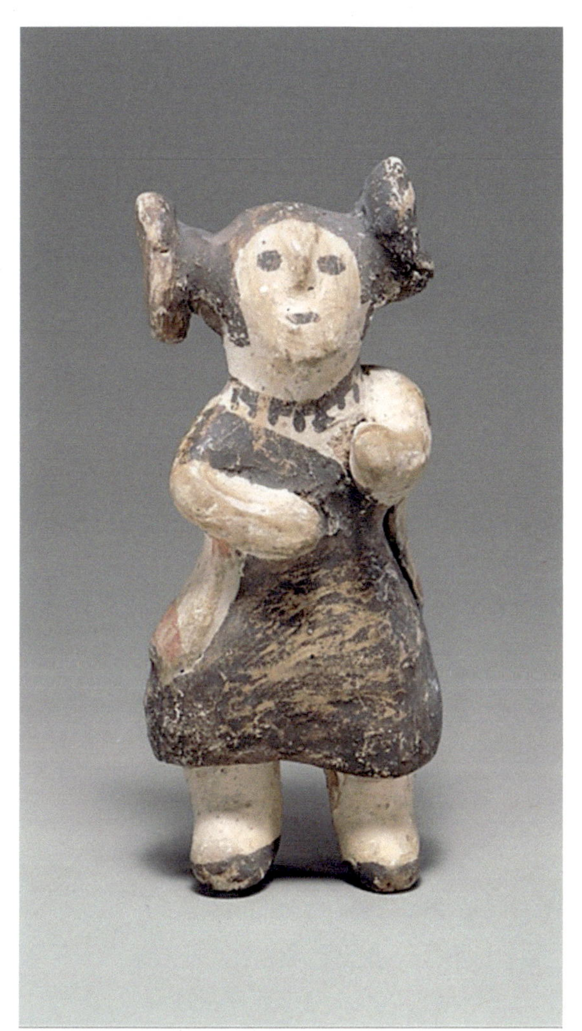

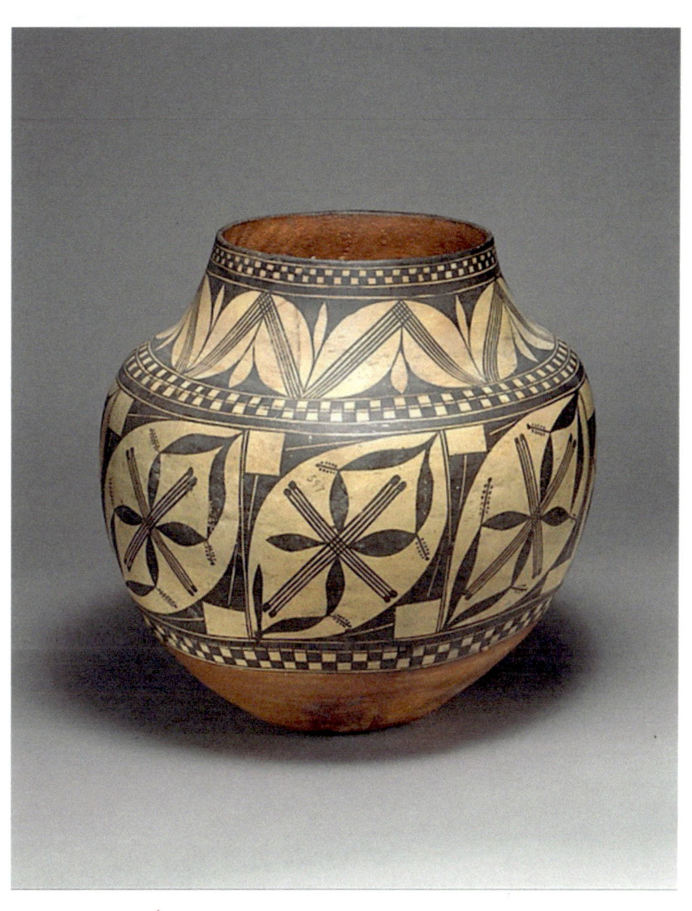

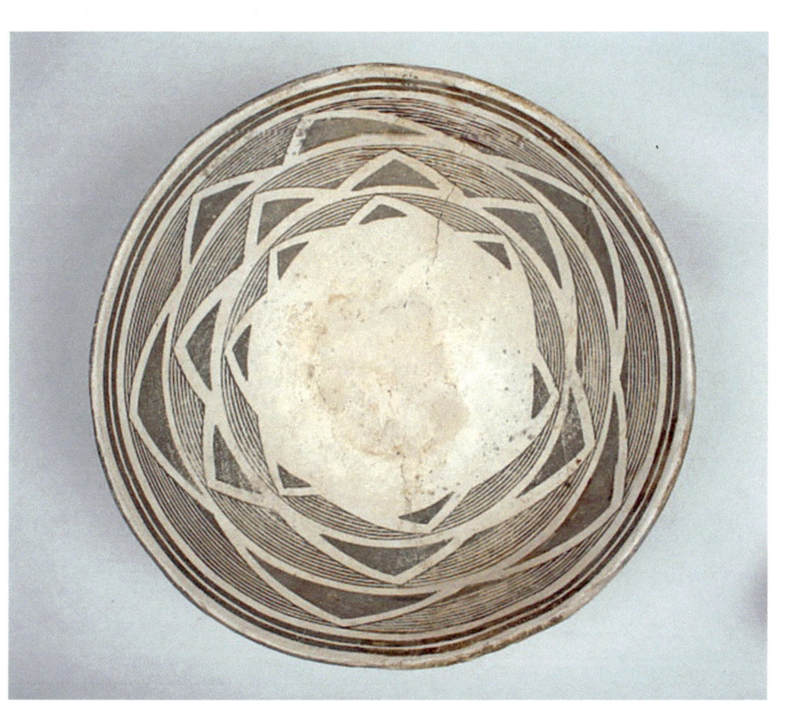

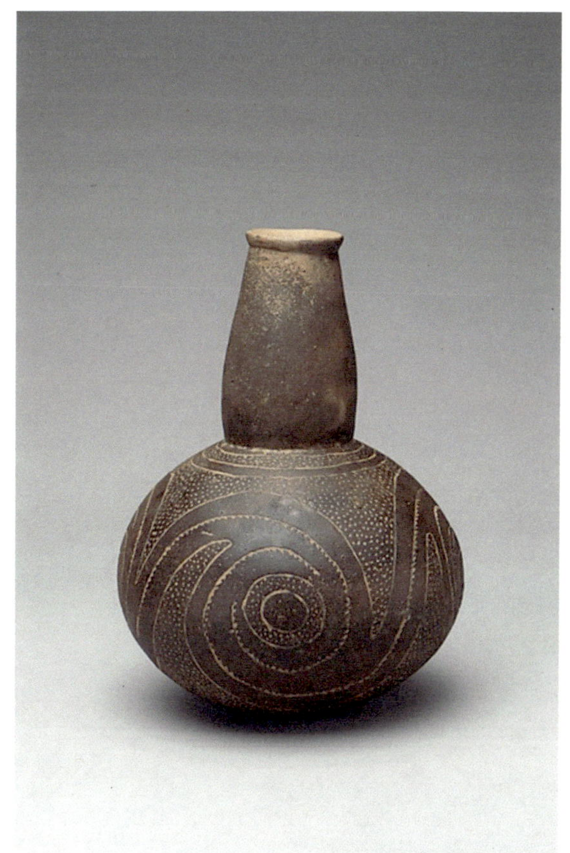

Notes / Images:

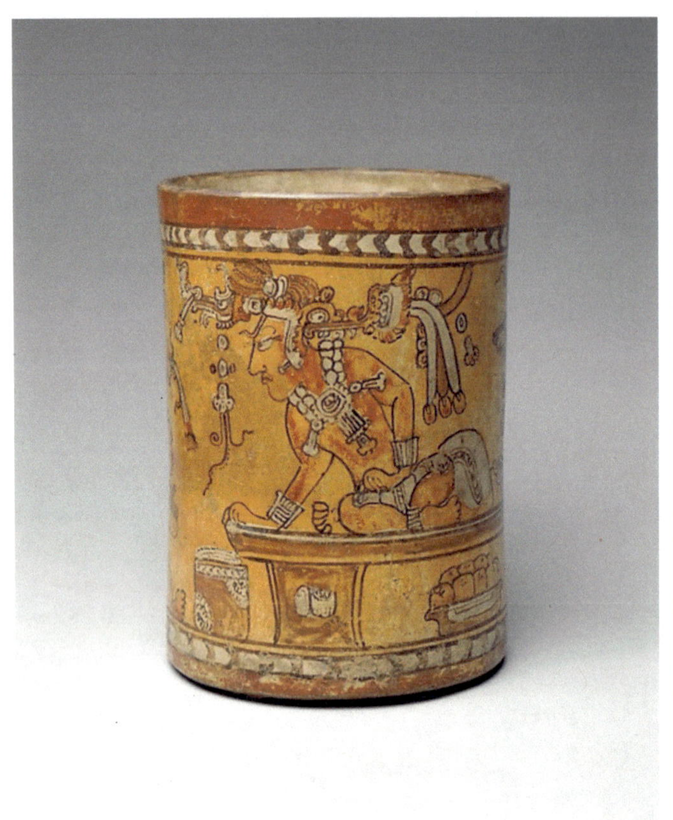

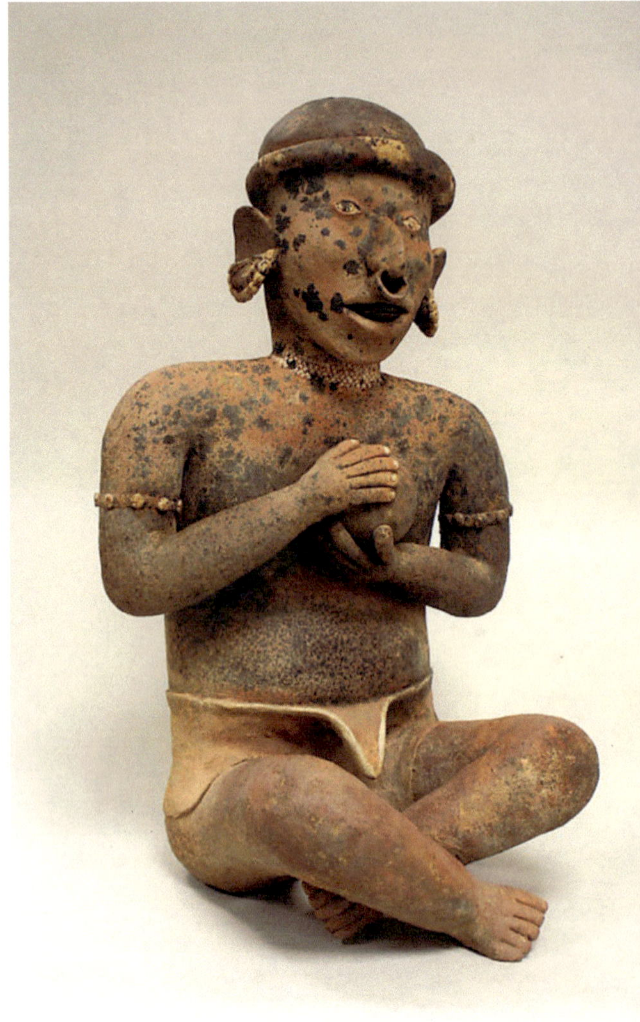

CENTRAL AND
SOUTH AMERICA

The earliest known ceramics being made in the Americas was being made 6,000 to 7,000 years ago near the mouth of the Amazon River. From the start, the people of the Americas were using relatively simple forming and firing techniques to create sophisticated functional and sculptural pieces. Many of these cultures overlapped in time and space and may have influenced each other. Much of what remains of their ceramics survives because it was made to be buried in tombs. When the Europeans arrived in the Americas, the lives of these groups changed forever and much of their knowledge and history was lost.

Important cultures:
Moche, Nazca, Inca, Olmec, Mayan, Aztec

all images this section[4]

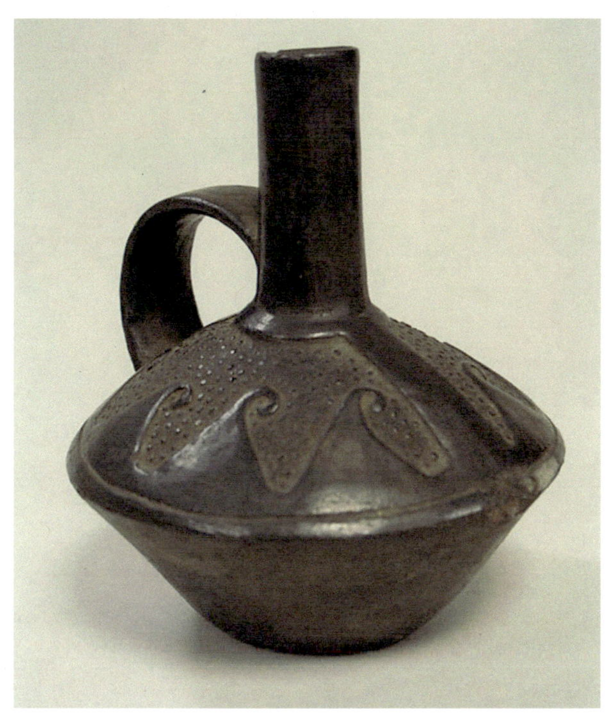

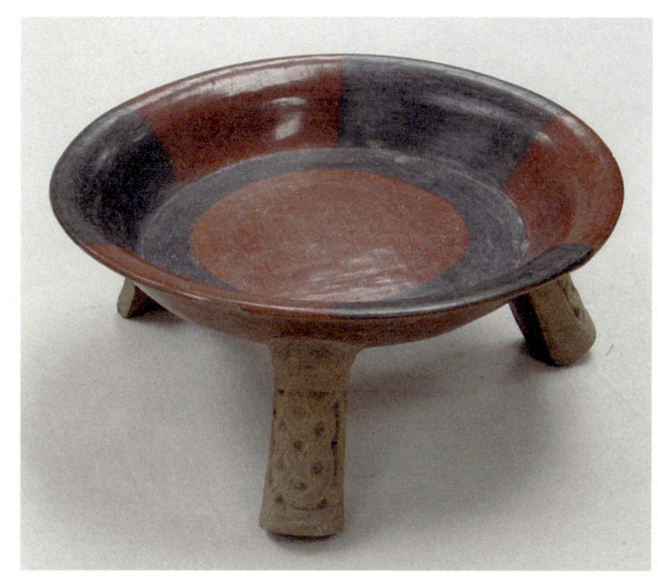

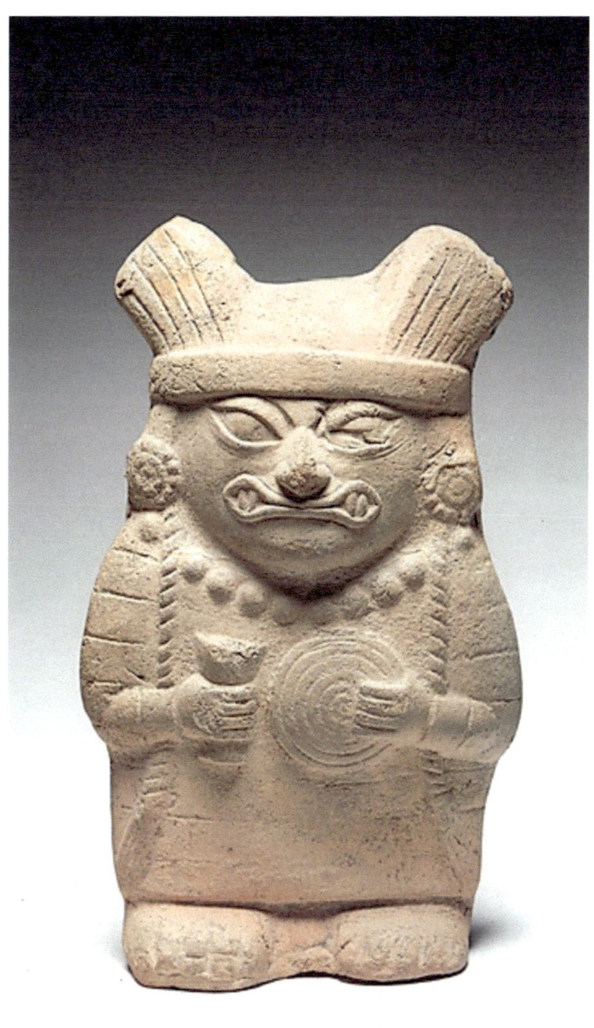

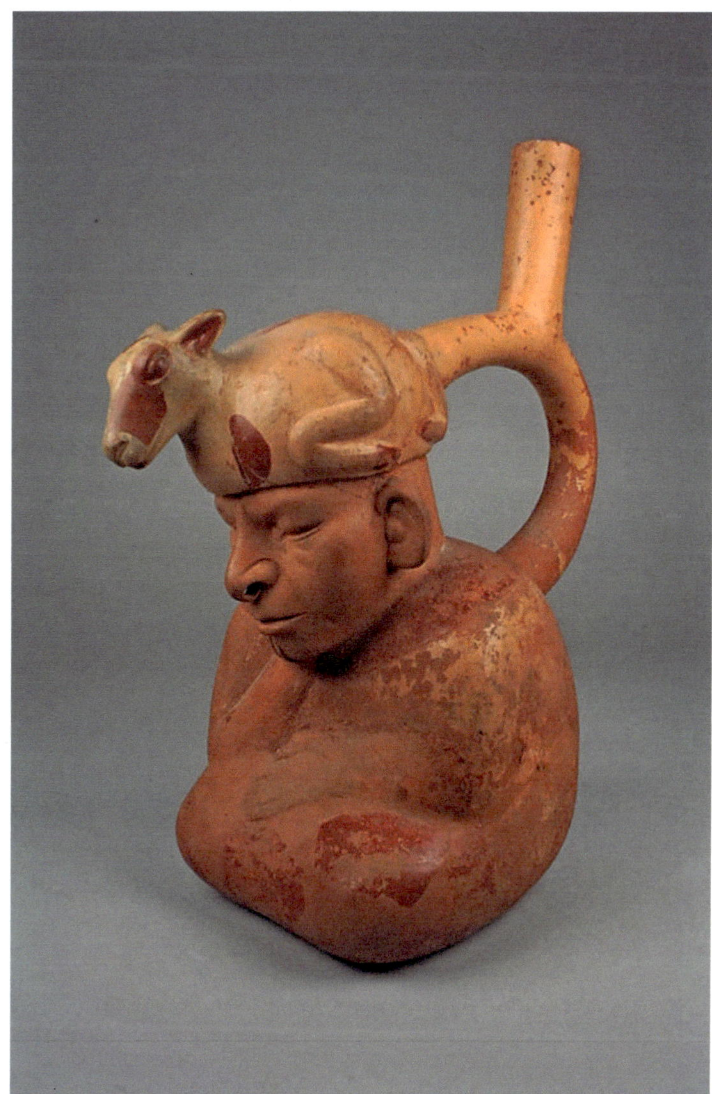

Notes / Images:

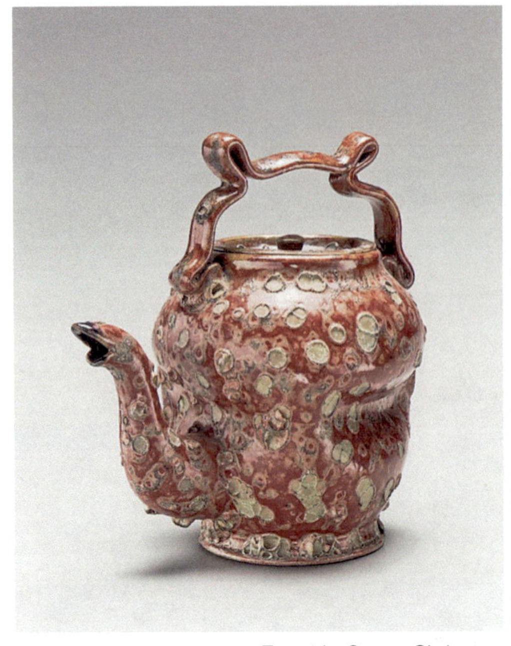

Teapot by George Ohr[4]

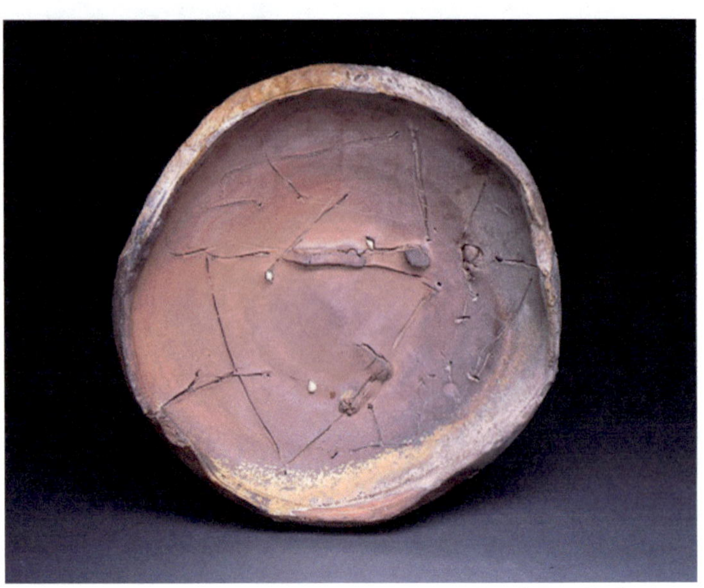

"Plate", Peter Voulkos[5]

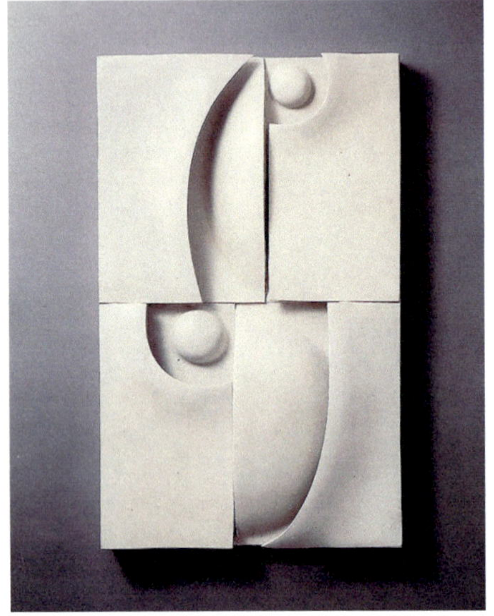

"Untittled", Ruth Duckworth[4]

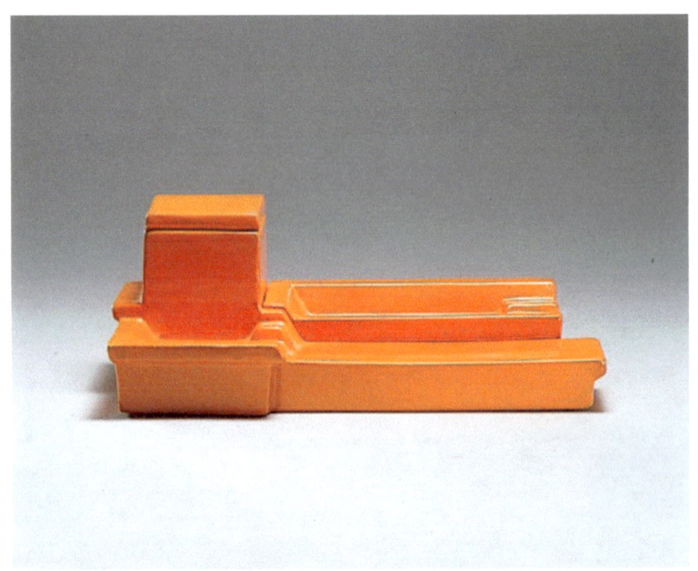

Inkwell designed by Eva Zeisel[4]

PRE 21ST CENTURY ARTISTS

The list of important artists working mostly before the 2000's is vast. Here are a few names to get started looking at people who helped set the stage for what's happening in ceramics today.

Bernard Leach
Michael Cardew
Richard Devore
Ruth Duckworth
Rudy Autio
Lucie Rie
Ken Ferguson
Toshiko Takaezu
David Shaner

George Ohr
Shoji Hamada
Robert Turner
Peter Voulkos
Hans Coper
Eva Zeisel
Robert Arneson
Isamu Noguchi

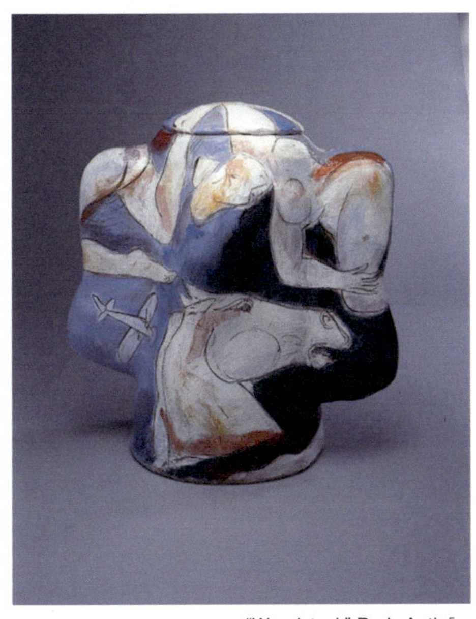

"Woodstack", Rudy Autio[5]

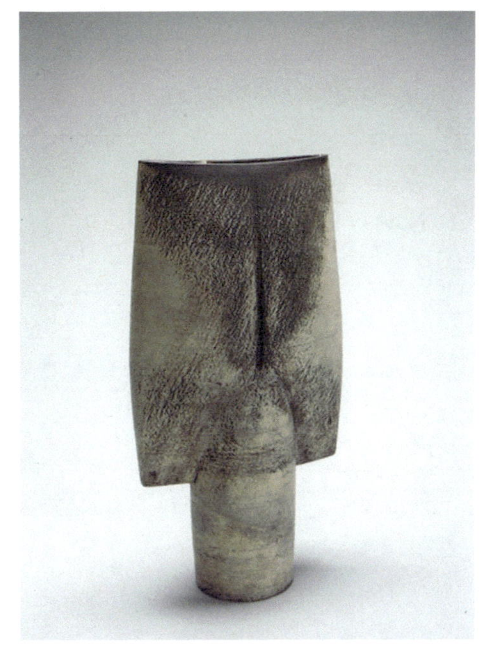

Untitled, Hans Coper[4]

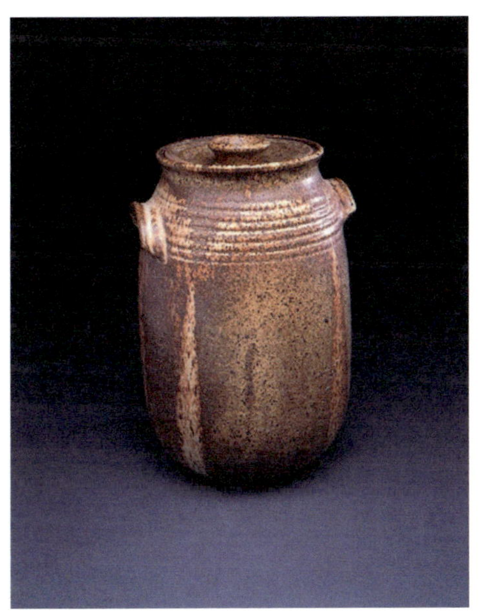

"Covered Jar", Ken Ferguson[4]

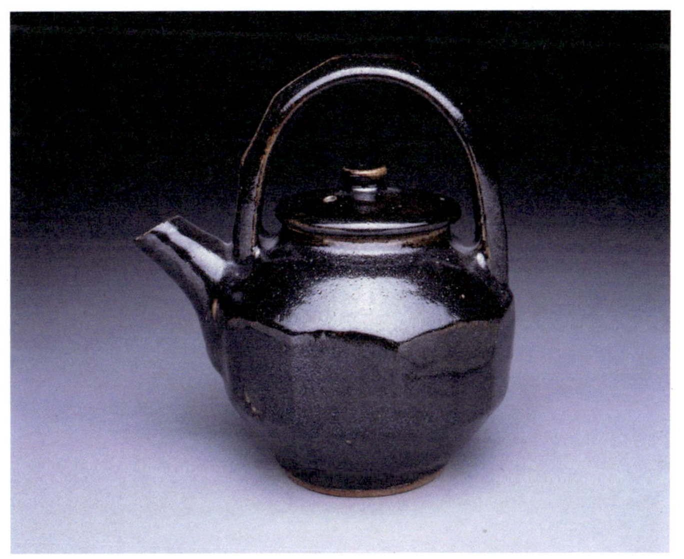

"Teapot", Shoji Hamada[5]

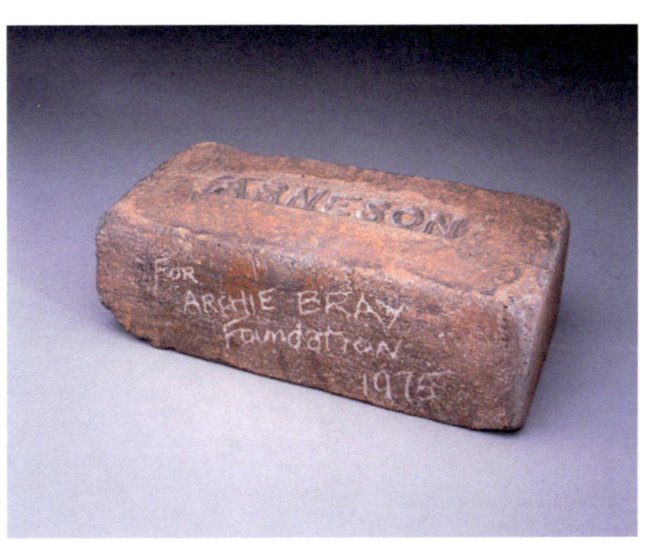

"Brick", Robert Arneson[5]

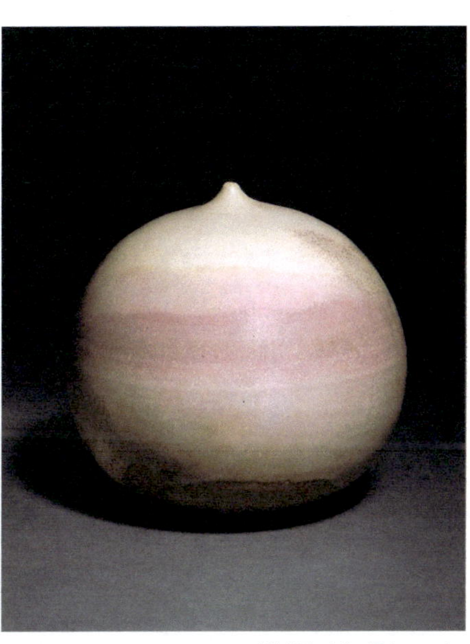

"Air" Toshiko Takaezu[4]

Notes / Images:

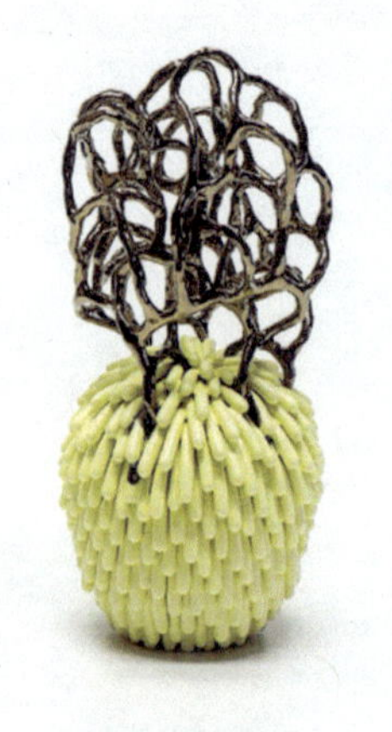

"Untitled (Pineapple)", Linda Lopez[3]

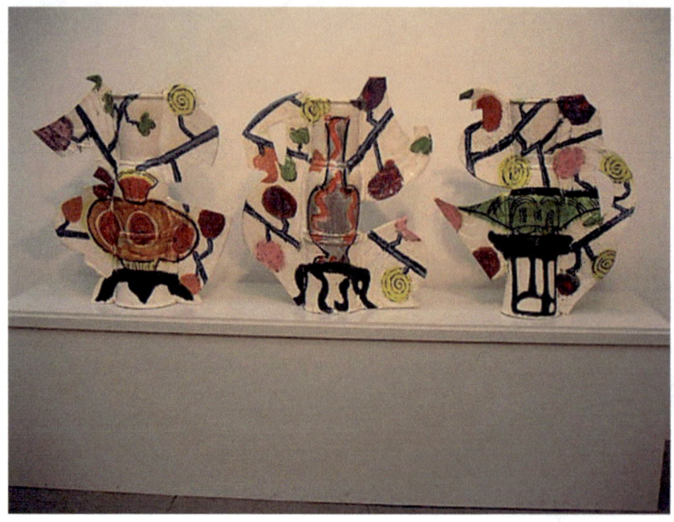

"The Ming Sisters", Betty Woodman[4]

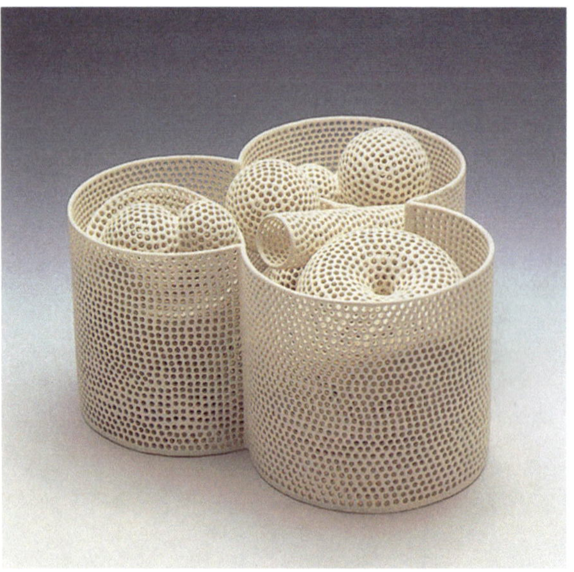

"Tri-lobed Vessel and Contents", Tony Marsh[4]

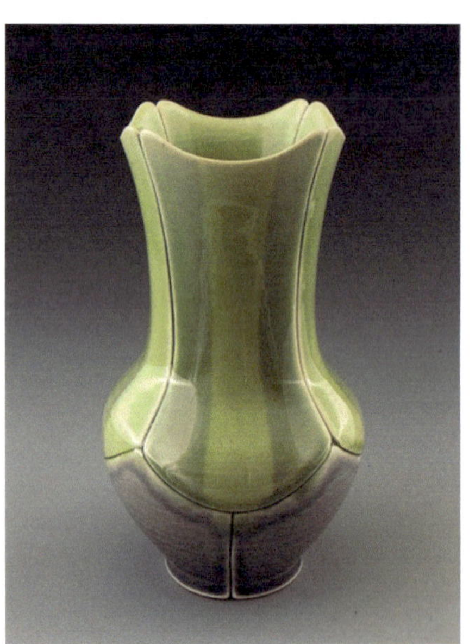

"Green Stripe Vase", Jeff Campana[2]

CONTEMPORARY ARTISTS

The world of contemporary ceramics is a varied and divergent field. Some artists are working and building on traditional ideas, others are pushing the boundaries of what can be done with clay, and a larger group works in between both approaches. A partial list of artists to investigate follows:

Artists making Vessels:
Warren Mackenzie, Ron Meyers, Richard Notkin, John Neely, Kirk Mangus, Chris Staley, Julia Galloway, Peter Beasecker, Sam Chung, Roberto Lugo, Simon Levin, Linda Arbuckle, Jeff Campana, Bede Clark, Ayumi Horie, Bryan Hopkins, Matt Metz, Linda Sikora, Steven Lee

Artists making Sculpture:
William Daley, Jun Kaneko, Ron Nagle, Tony Marsh, Betty Woodman, Wouter Dam, Clare Twomey, Grayson Perry, Akio Takamori, Ted Adler, Andrea Gill, Tom Bartel, Brendan Tang, Del Harrow, Peter Christian Johnson, Shalene Valenzuela, Beth Cavener, Linda Lopez

An outstanding online resource is the Art Axis database:
http://artaxis.org/artist.html

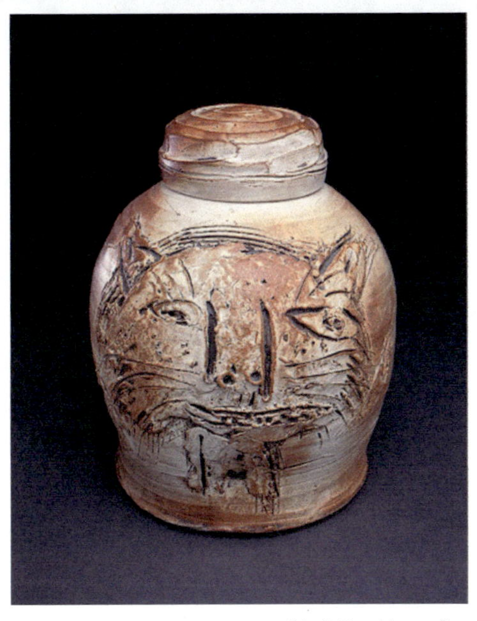

"Jar", Ron Meyers[5]

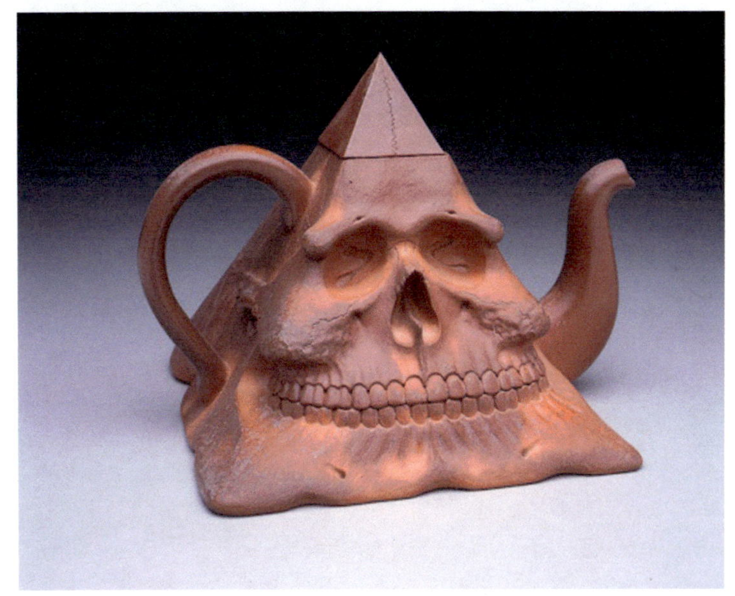

"Pyramid Skull Teapot", Richard Notkin[5]

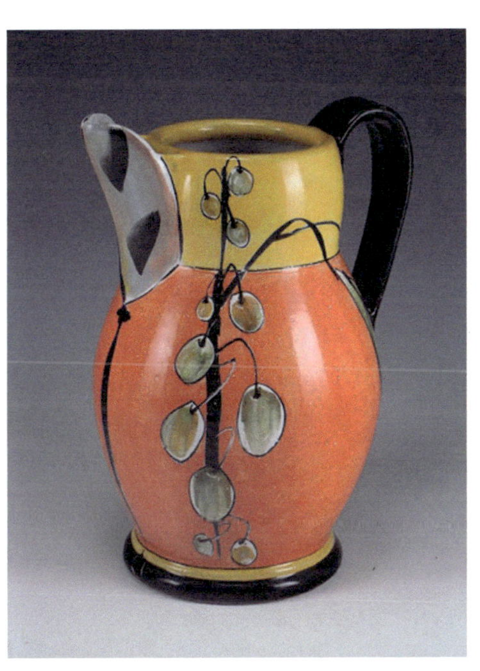

"Pitcher", Linda Arbuckle[2]

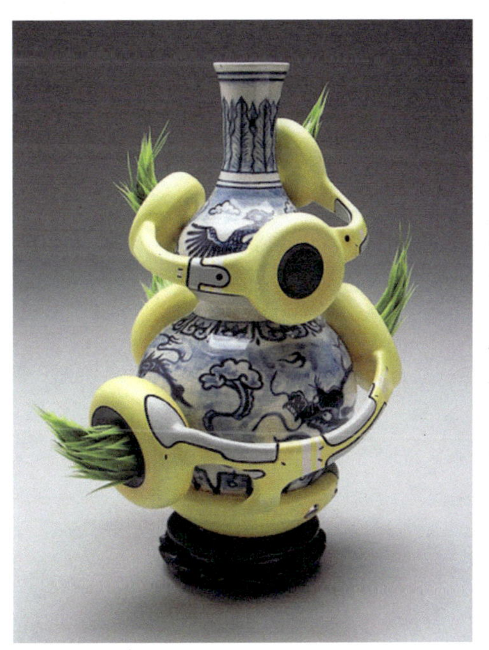

"Manga Ormolu ver. 4.0-k", Brendan Tang[2]

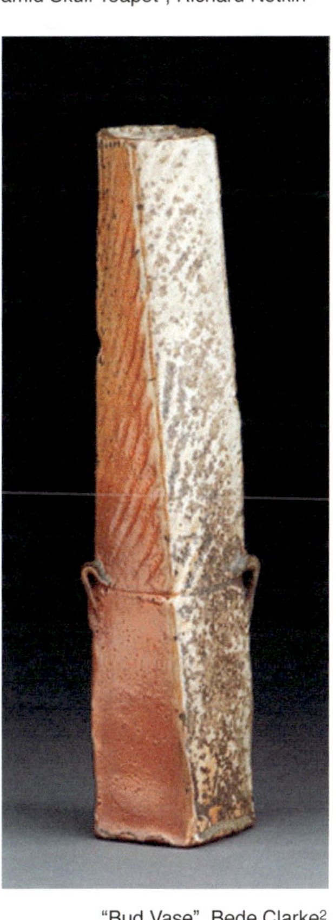

"Bud Vase", Bede Clarke[2]

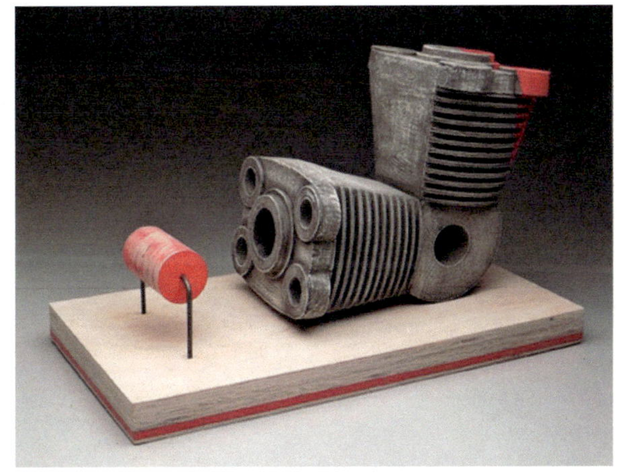

"Pink", Peter Christian Johnson[14]

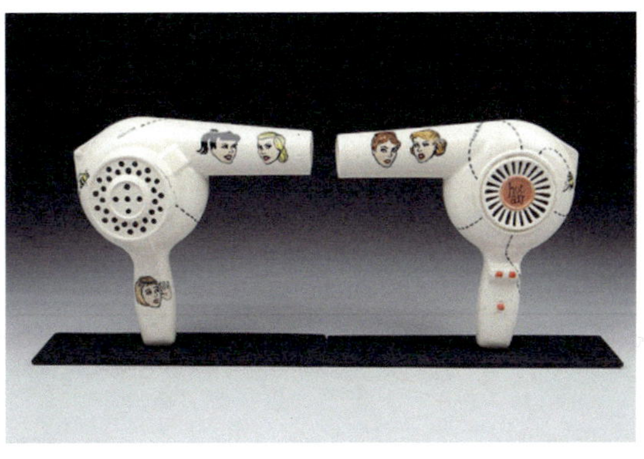

"Hot Air", Shalene Valenzuela[5]

Notes / Images:

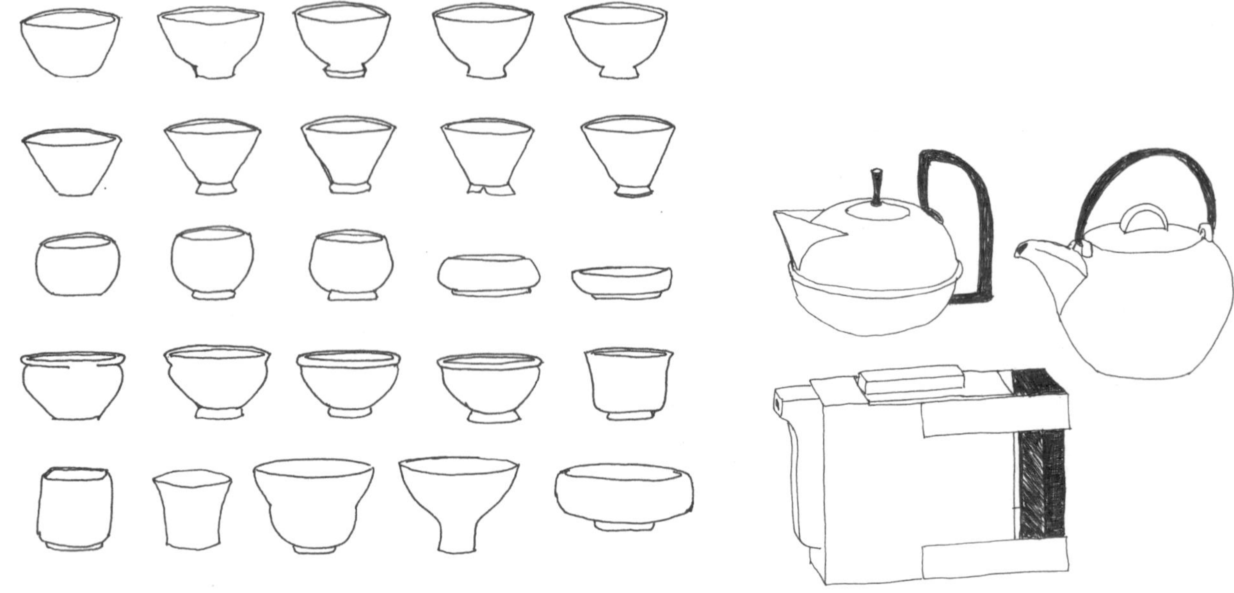

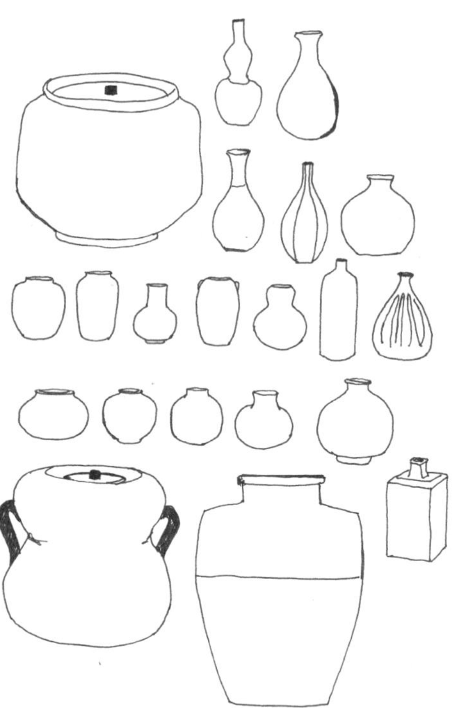

12

SKETCHBOOK / PICTURES

The artist's sketchbook is a critical tool in the development of their work. It is the location to sketch ideas, take notes, and plan the next steps in the production of work. Most artists carry a sketchbook (or something that functions like it) in their daily life in order to capture ideas before they are forgotten. In studio classes, professors will often ask you to make sketches of your ideas for projects before you begin. This will allow both you and the professor a chance to look at the idea and discuss any issues that may come up with design or construction. Having something on paper to share makes this process possible and the most effective. In addition, this section of the handbook can be used to paste required pictures for critiques.

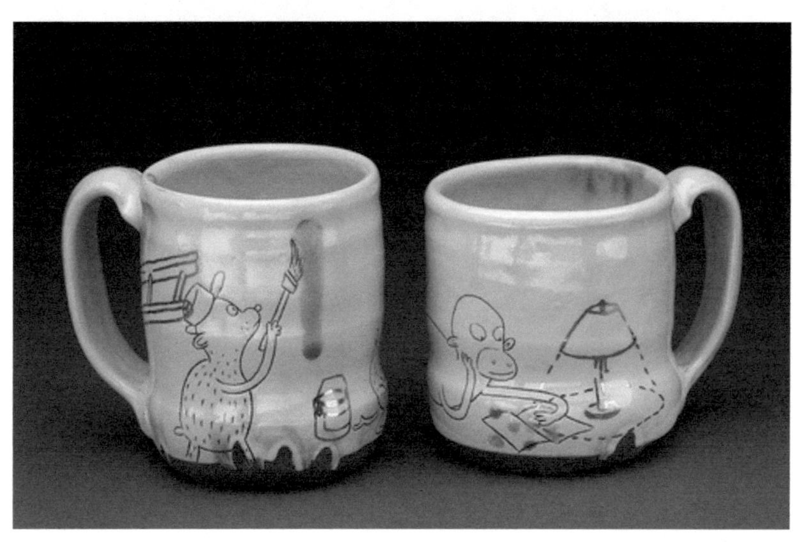

"House Painter and Reader Cup", Ayumi Horie[3]

CUPS / MUGS

BOWLS

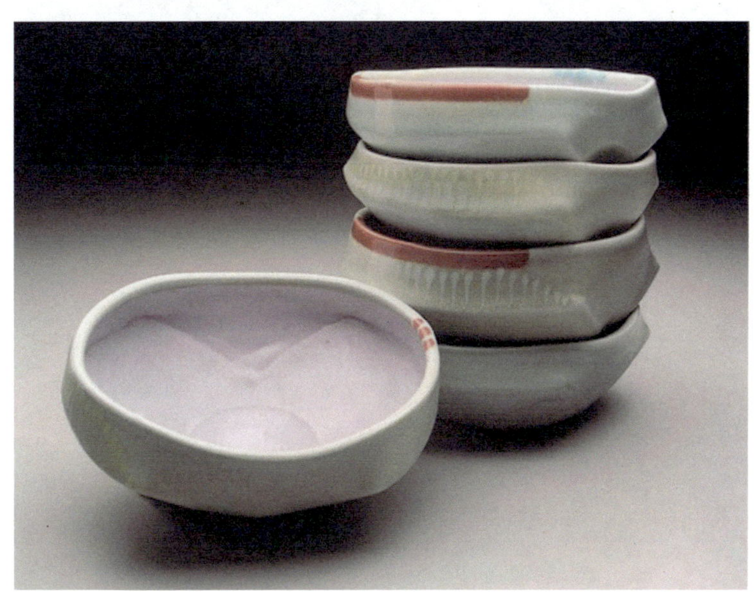

"Bowls", Deborah Schwartzkopf[2]

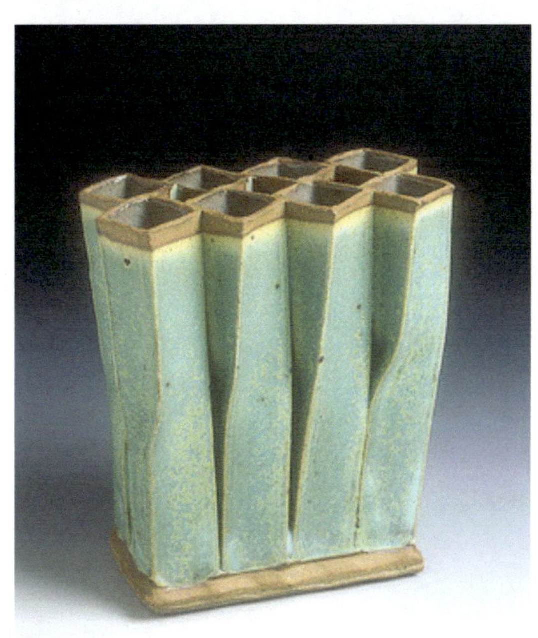
"Multivase", Hayne Bayless[3]

VASES

SERVING PIECES

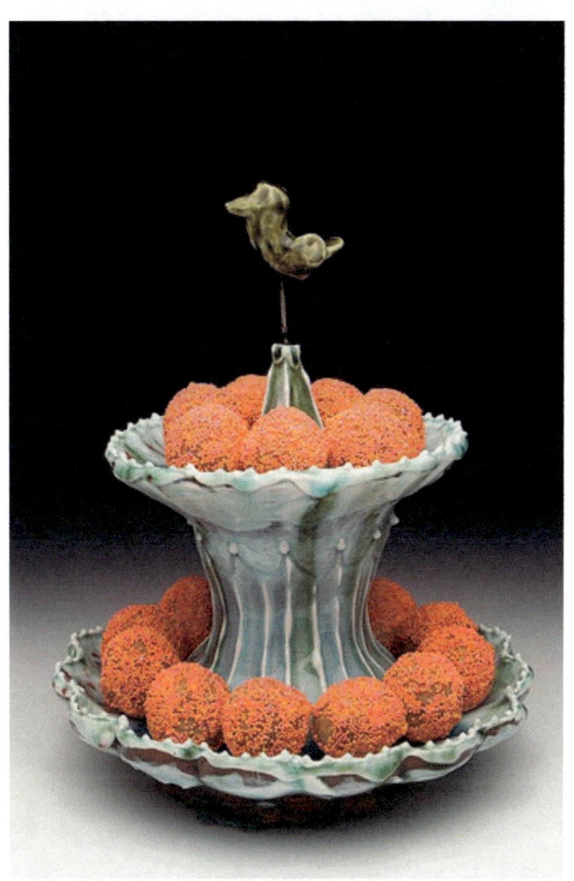

"Dessert Server", Arthur Halvorsen[2]

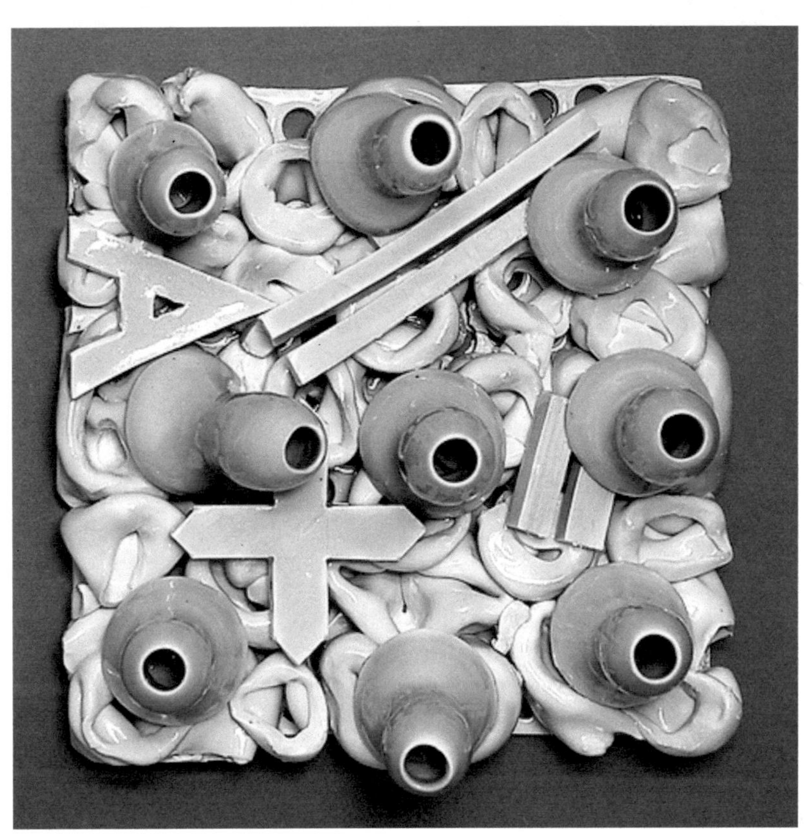
"Game Board #2", Yiu-Keung Lee[2]

COMBINED
FORMS

JARS

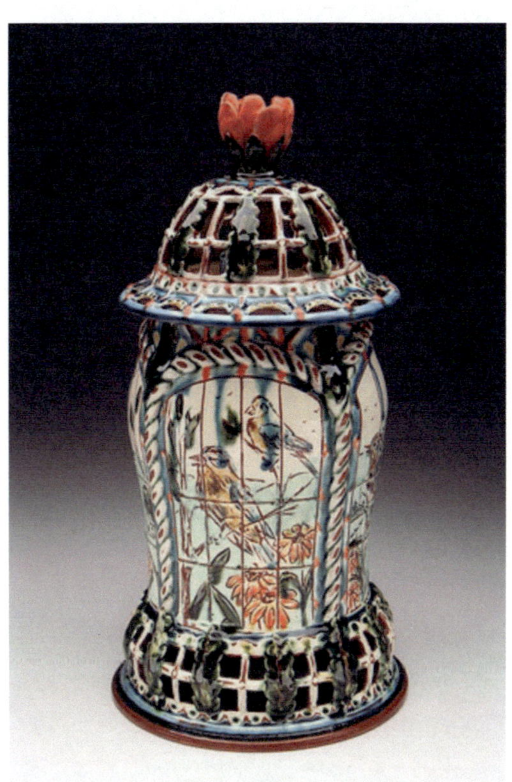

"Jar with Tulip Top & Birds", Kathryn Finnerty[3]

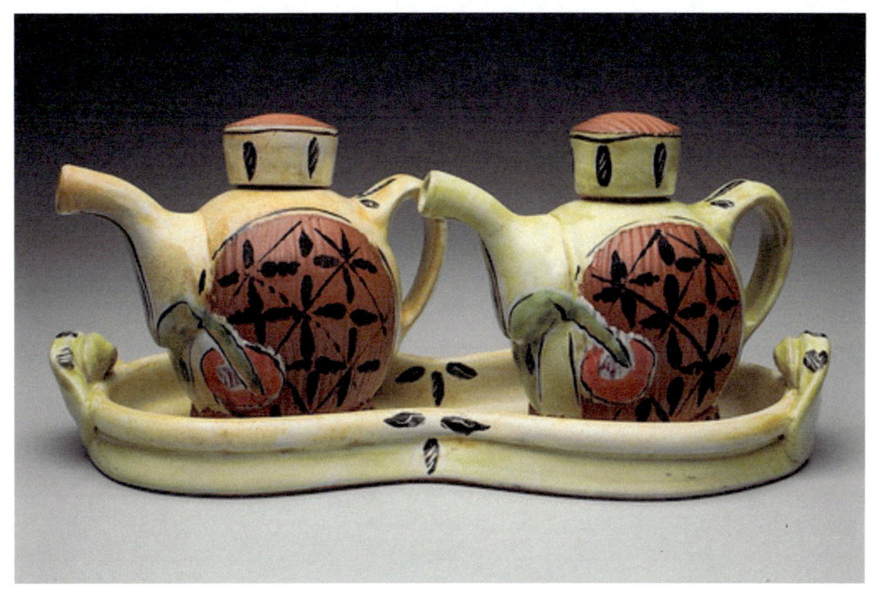

"Oil and Vinegar Set", Posey Bacopoulos[2]

SETS

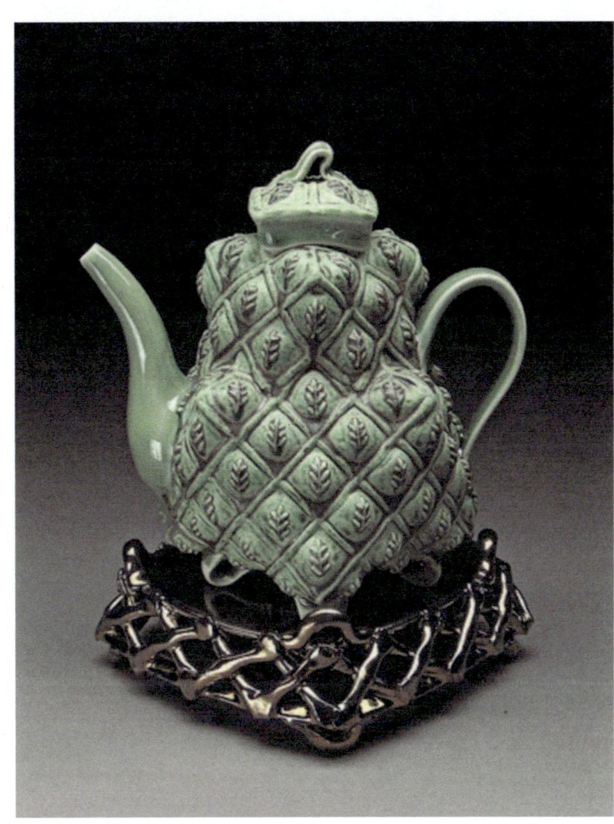

"Green Leaf Teapot with Trivet", Margaret Bohls[2]

TEAPOTS

POURING POTS

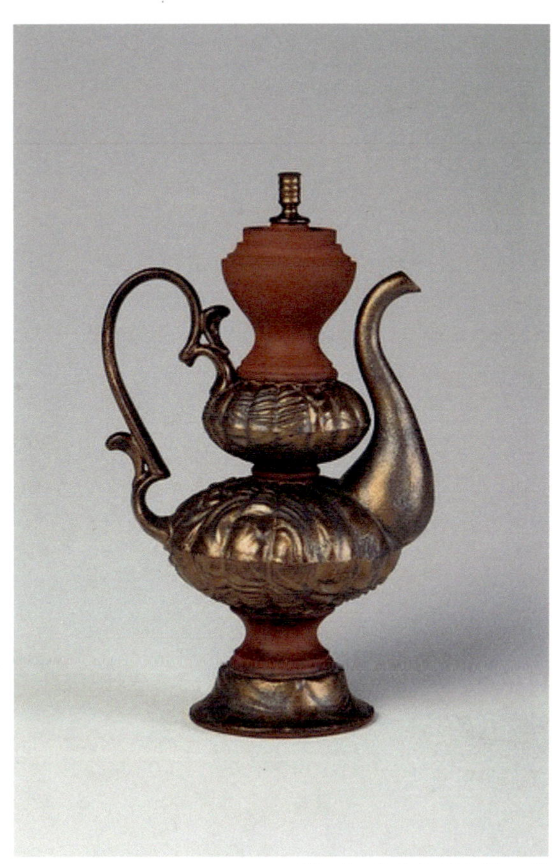

"Pouring Pot", A. Blair Clemo[14]

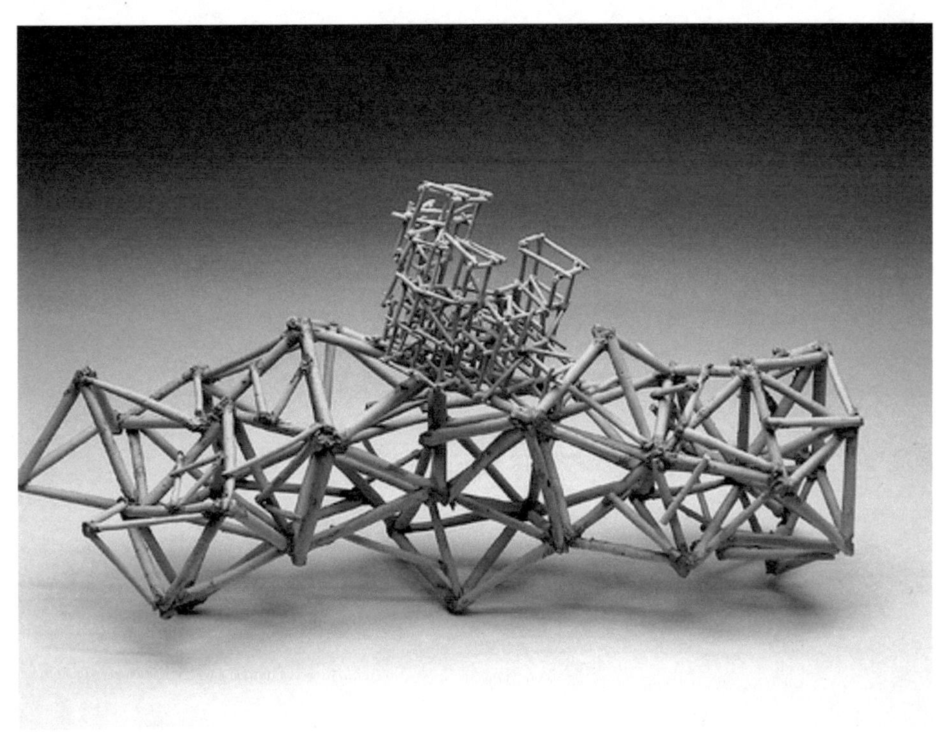

"Migration Grid #1", Stanton Hunter[5]

SCULPTURE

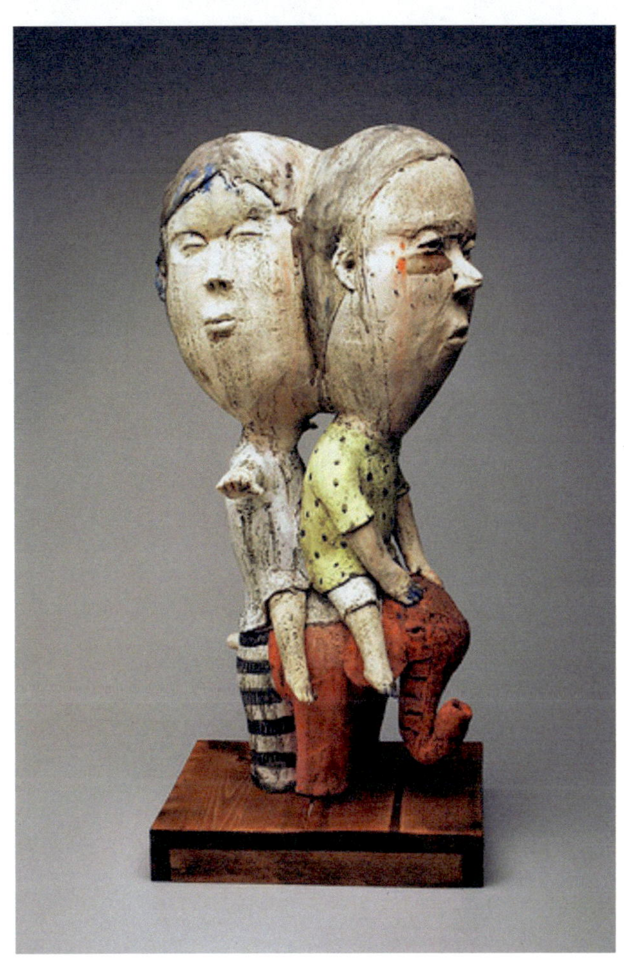

SCULPTURE:
THE FIGURE

"Elephant Rider", Kensuke Yamada[3]

SCULPTURE: THE ANIMAL

"Against the Tide, Souvenirs", Tim Berg and Rebekah Myers[3]

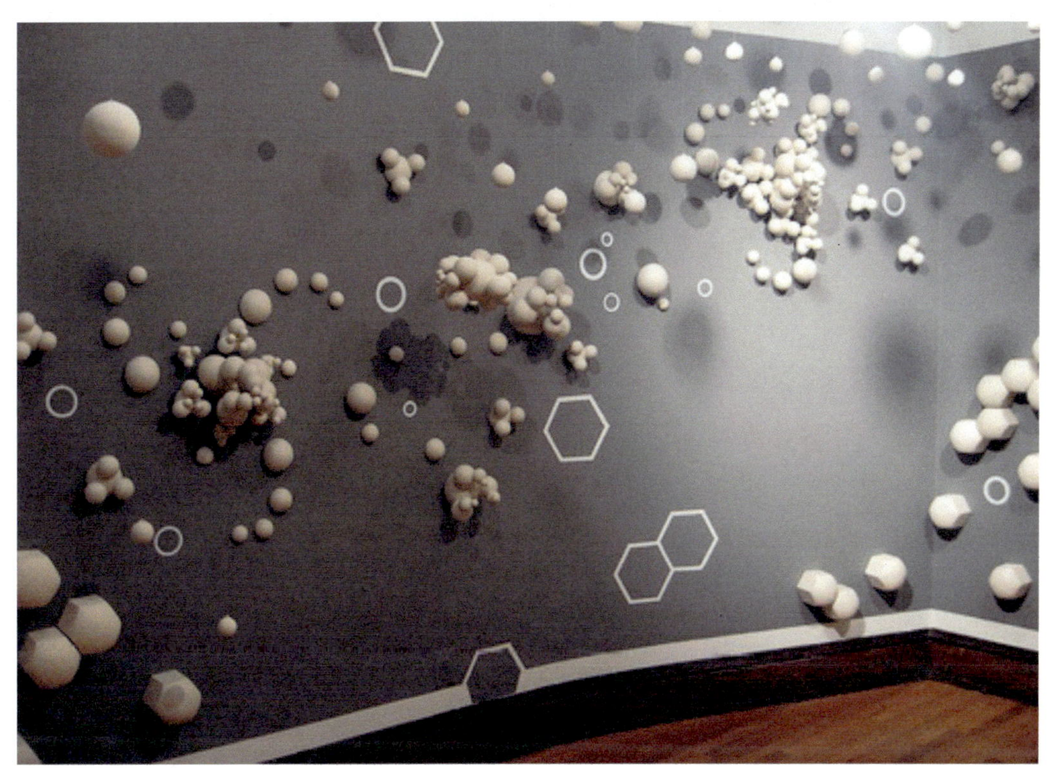

"A Stochastic System", Sarah House[3]

SCULPTURE: INSTALLATION

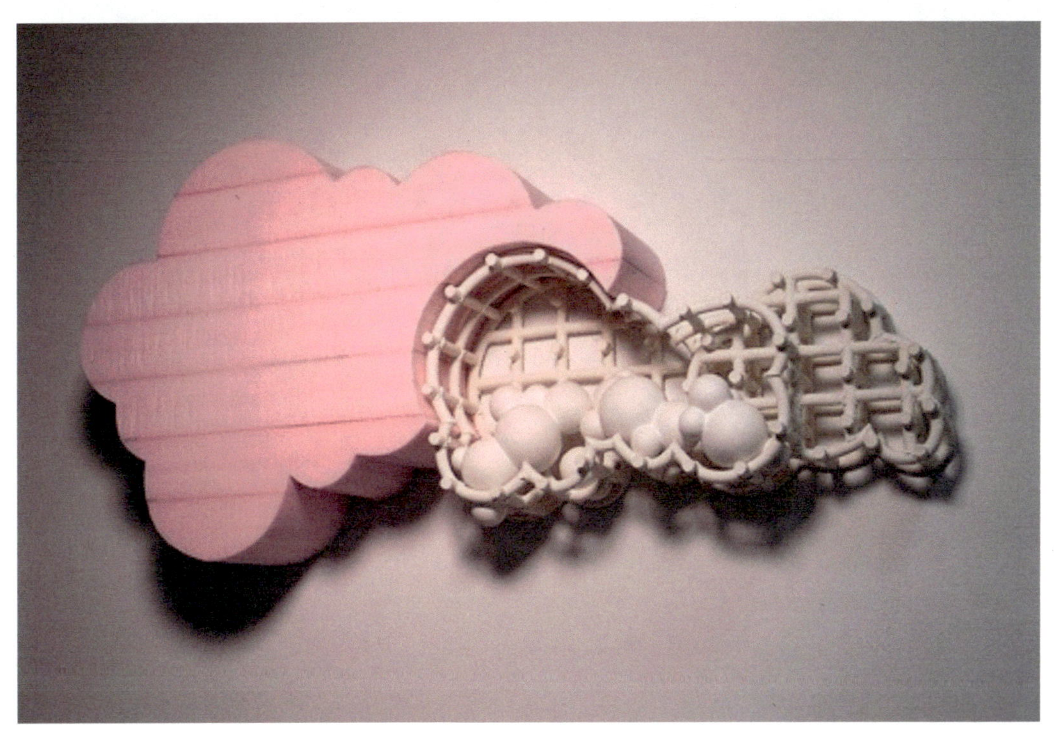

"Containment Cloud II", Joe Page[5]

SCULPTURE: THE WALL

RESOURCES

Recommended transfer schools in our region for Ceramics:

SUNY / Public

New York State College of Ceramics at Alfred University
SUNY - New Paltz
Penn State
Tyler School of Art at Temple University

Private

Syracuse University
RIT

Ceramics Suppliers

Bailey Ceramic Supply - Kingston, NY
Clayscapes Pottery, Inc. - Syracuse, NY
Studio Sales Pottery Supply Co. - Avon, NY

Books and Magazines

Ceramics books in the NK, TP, and TT sections in the CCC library
Ceramics related magazines at the CCC Library: *Ceramics Monthly, Ceramics; Art and Perception, Clay Times, American Craft, Pottery Making Illustrated*

Web Resources

Art Axis- artaxis.org
CFile Online- cfileonline.org
NCECA - nceca.net
Access Ceramics- accessceramics.org/
Ceramic Arts Network - ceramicartsnetwork.org
Julia Galloway's Field Guide for Ceramic Artisans- ceramicsfieldguide.org/

IMAGE ATTRIBUTIONS

Images in the Studio Handbook were used under a variety of Creative Commons licenses. The main sources were from the Access Ceramics database, the Metropolitan Museum of Art, and images taken by Fred Herbst. Number notations below correspond to the Supersript Number in each caption and also indicate the source and type of Creative Commons license of each image.

Any image not noted with a caption was taken by Fred Herbst and may be used under the Creative Commons license: Attribution-ShareAlike 3.0 Unported (CC BY-SA 3.0)

1- image by Fred Herbst, Attribution-ShareAlike 3.0 Unported (CC BY-SA 3.0)

Images from Access Ceramics Database - http://accessceramics.org

2- Attribution- 2.0 Generic (CC BY 2.0)
3- Attribution-NonCommercial-NoDerivs 2.0 Generic (CC BY-NC-ND 2.0)
5- Attribution-NoDerivs 2.0 Generic (CC BY-ND 2.0)
9- Attribution-ShareAlike 3.0 (CC BY-SA 3.0)
13- Attribution-NonCommercial-ShareAlike 2.0 Generic (CC BY-NC-SA 2.0)
14- Attribution-NonCommercial 2.0 Generic (CC BY-NC 2.0)

Online Collection of the Metropolitan Museum of Art
https://www.metmuseum.org/

4- Attribution- CC0 1.0 Universal (CC0 1.0) Public Domain Dedication

Other Images
6- Wikimedia Commons - This work is in the public domain in its country of origin and other countries and areas where the copyright term is the author's life plus 100 years or less. This work is in the public domain in the United States because it was published (or registered with the U.S. Copyright Office) before January 1, 1923.

7- Drawn by Dick Lyon and posted to Wikimedia Commons. I, the copyright holder of this work, release this work into the public domain. This applies worldwide.

8- By unknown -
http://libraryphoto.cr.usgs.gov/cgi-bin/show_picture.cgi?ID=ID.%20Bartsch-Winkler,%20S,%20%20%20%20%20%20%20%208, Public Domain,
https://commons.wikimedia.org/w/index.php?curid=26512534

10- www.blaauwproducts.com/kilns-for-arts-crafts/automatic-ceramic-ovens/

11- skutt.com/about-us/why-buy-a-skutt/innovation-and-quality/kiln-cutaway/

12- Coyau / Wikimedia Commons / CC BY-SA 3.0